ADOBE® ILLUSTRATOR® CS5
CLASSROOM IN A BOOK®

The official training workbook from Adobe Systems

**This book
contains a disc(s)**

**Do not put through the
machine**

www.adobepress.com

Adobe

Adobe® Illustrator® CS5 Classroom in a Book®

WHAT'S ON THE DISC

Here is an overview of the contents of the Classroom in a Book disc

The *Adobe Illustrator CS5 Classroom in a Book* disc includes the lesson files that you'll need to complete the exercises in this book, as well as other content to help you learn more about Adobe Illustrator CS5 and use it with greater efficiency and ease. The diagram below represents the contents of the disc, which should help you locate the files you need.

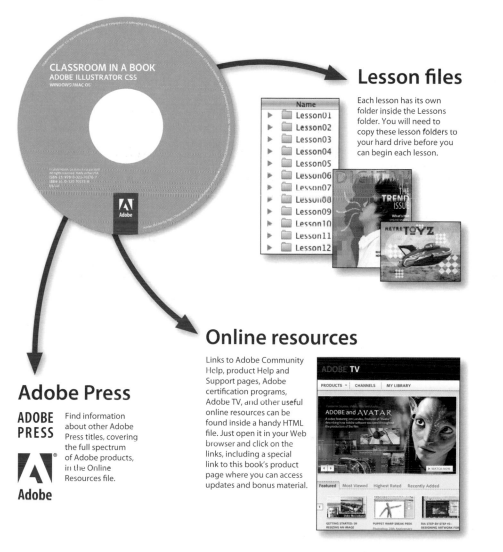

Lesson files

Each lesson has its own folder inside the Lessons folder. You will need to copy these lesson folders to your hard drive before you can begin each lesson.

Name
▶ 📁 Lesson01
▶ 📁 Lesson02
▶ 📁 Lesson03
▶ 📁 Lesson04
▶ 📁 Lesson05
▶ 📁 Lesson06
▶ 📁 Lesson07
▶ 📁 Lesson08
▶ 📁 Lesson09
▶ 📁 Lesson10
▶ 📁 Lesson11
▶ 📁 Lesson12

Online resources

Links to Adobe Community Help, product Help and Support pages, Adobe certification programs, Adobe TV, and other useful online resources can be found inside a handy HTML file. Just open it in your Web browser and click on the links, including a special link to this book's product page where you can access updates and bonus material.

Adobe Press

ADOBE PRESS

Find information about other Adobe Press titles, covering the full spectrum of Adobe products, in the Online Resources file.

CONTENTS

4   TRANSFORMING OBJECTS

10 BLENDING COLORS AND SHAPES

11 WORKING WITH BRUSHES

12 APPLYING EFFECTS

13   APPLYING APPEARANCE ATTRIBUTES AND GRAPHIC STYLES

14   WORKING WITH SYMBOLS

15 COMBINING ILLUSTRATOR CS5 GRAPHICS WITH OTHER ADOBE APPLICATIONS

GETTING STARTED

Adobe® Illustrator® CS5 is the industry-standard illustration application for print, multimedia, and online graphics. Whether you are a designer or a technical illustrator producing artwork for print publishing, an artist producing multimedia graphics, or a creator of web pages or online content, Adobe Illustrator offers you the tools you need to get professional-quality results.

About Classroom in a Book

Adobe Illustrator CS5 Classroom in a Book® is part of the official training series for Adobe graphics and publishing software developed with the support of Adobe product experts.

The lessons are designed so that you can learn at your own pace. If you're new to Adobe Illustrator, you'll learn the fundamentals you need to master to put the application to work. If you are an experienced user, you'll find that *Classroom in a Book* teaches many advanced features, including tips and techniques for using the latest version of Adobe Illustrator.

Although each lesson provides step-by-step instructions for creating a specific project, there's room for exploration and experimentation. You can follow the book from start to finish, or do only the lessons that correspond to your interests and needs. Each lesson concludes with a review section summarizing what you've covered.

Prerequisites

Before beginning to use *Adobe Illustrator CS5 Classroom in a Book*, you should have working knowledge of your computer and its operating system. Make sure that you know how to use the mouse and standard menus and commands, and also how to open, save, and close files. If you need to review these techniques, see the printed or online documentation for your Windows or Mac OS.

● **Note:** When instructions differ by platform, Windows commands appear first, and then the Mac OS commands, with the platform noted in parentheses. For example, "press Alt (Windows) or Option (Mac OS) and click away from the artwork." In some instances, common commands may be abbreviated with the Windows commands first, followed by a slash and the Mac OS commands, without any parenthetical reference. For example, "press Alt/Option" or "press Ctrl/Command+click."

Installing the program

Before you begin using *Adobe Illustrator CS5 Classroom in a Book*, make sure that your system is set up correctly and that you've installed the required software and hardware.

The Adobe Illustrator CS5 software is not included on the Classroom in a Book CD; you must purchase the software separately. For complete instructions on installing the software, see the Adobe Illustrator Read Me file on the application DVD or on the web at www.adobe.com/support.

Fonts used in this book

The Classroom in a Book lesson files use the fonts that come with Adobe Illustrator CS5 and install with the product for your convenience. These fonts are installed in the following locations:

- Windows: [startup drive]\Windows\Fonts\
- Mac OS X: [startup drive]/Library/Fonts/

For more information about fonts and installation, see the Adobe Illustrator CS5 Read Me file on the application DVD or on the web at www.adobe.com/support.

Copying the Classroom in a Book files

The Classroom in a Book CD includes folders containing all the electronic files for the lessons. Each lesson has its own folder. You must install these folders on your hard disk to use the files for the lessons. To save room on your hard disk, you can install the folder for each lesson as you need it.

To install the Classroom in a Book files

1   Insert the Classroom in a Book CD into your CD-ROM drive.

2   Do one of the following:

- Copy the entire Lessons folder onto your hard disk.
- Copy only the specific lesson folder that you need onto your hard disk.

Restoring default preferences

The preferences file controls how command settings appear on your screen when you open the Adobe Illustrator program. Each time you quit Adobe Illustrator, the position of the panels and certain command settings are recorded in different preference files. If you want to restore the tools and settings to their original default settings, you can delete the current Adobe Illustrator CS5 preferences file. Adobe Illustrator creates a new preferences file, if one doesn't already exist, the next time you start the program and save a file.

You must restore the default preferences for Illustrator before you begin each lesson. This ensures that the tools and panels function as described in this book. When you have finished the book, you can restore your saved settings.

To save current Illustrator preferences

1 Exit Adobe Illustrator CS5.

2 Locate the AIPrefs (Windows) or Adobe Illustrator Prefs (Mac OS) file, as follows.

- (Windows XP) The AIPrefs file is located in the folder [startup drive]\Documents and Settings\[username]\Application Data\Adobe\Adobe Illustrator CS5 Settings\en_US*.

- (Windows Vista or Windows 7) The AIPrefs file is located in the folder [startup drive]\Users\[username]\AppData\Roaming\Adobe\Adobe Illustrator CS5 Settings\en_US*.

- (Mac OS X) The Adobe Illustrator Prefs file is located in the folder [startup drive]/Users/[username]/Library/Preferences/Adobe Illustrator CS5 Settings/en_US*.

*Folder name may be different depending on the language version you have installed.

● **Note:** If you cannot locate the preferences file, use your operating system's Find command, and search for AIPrefs (Windows) or Adobe Illustrator Prefs (Mac OS).

> If you can't find the file, you either haven't started Adobe Illustrator CS5 yet or you have moved the preferences file. The preferences file is created after you quit the program the first time and is updated thereafter.

3 Copy the file and save it to another folder on your hard disk.

4 Start Adobe Illustrator CS5.

▶ **Tip:** To quickly locate and delete the Adobe Illustrator preferences file each time you begin a new lesson, create a shortcut (Windows) or an alias (Mac OS) to the Illustrator CS5 Settings folder.

● **Note:** In Windows XP, the Application Data folder is hidden by default. The same is true for the AppData folder in Windows Vista and Window 7. To make either one visible, open Folder Options in Control Panel and click the View tab. In the Advanced Settings pane, find Hidden Files and folders and select Show Hidden Files and Folders or Show hidden files, folders, or drives.

To delete current Illustrator preferences

1 Exit Adobe Illustrator CS5.

2 Locate the AIPrefs (Windows) or Adobe Illustrator Prefs (Mac OS) file, as follows.

- (Windows XP) The AIPrefs file is located in the folder [startup drive]\ Documents and Settings\[username]\Application Data\Adobe\Adobe Illustrator CS5 Settings\en_US*.

- (Windows Vista or Windows 7) The AIPrefs file is located in the folder [startup drive]\Users\[username]\AppData\Roaming\Adobe\Adobe Illustrator CS5 Settings\en_US*.

- (Mac OS X) The Adobe Illustrator Prefs file is located in the folder [startup drive]/Users/[username]/Library/Preferences/Adobe Illustrator CS5 Settings/en_US*.

*Folder name may be different depending on the language version you have installed.

3 Delete the preferences file.

4 Start Adobe Illustrator CS5.

To restore saved preferences after completing the lessons

1 Exit Adobe Illustrator CS5.

2 Delete the current preferences file. Find the original preferences file that you saved and move it to the Adobe Illustrator CS5 Settings folder.

Additional resources

Adobe Illustrator CS5 Classroom in a Book is not meant to replace documentation that comes with the program or to be a comprehensive reference for every feature. Only the commands and options used in the lessons are explained in this book. For comprehensive information about program features and tutorials refer to these resources:

Adobe Community Help: Community Help brings together active Adobe product users, Adobe product team members, authors, and experts to give you the most useful, relevant, and up-to-date information about Adobe products. Whether you're looking for a code sample or an answer to a problem, have a question about the software, or want to share a useful tip or recipe, you'll benefit from Community Help. Search results will show you not only content from Adobe, but also from the community.

● **Note:** In Windows XP, the Application Data folder is hidden by default. The same is true for the AppData folder in Windows Vista and Window 7. To make either one visible, open Folder Options in Control Panel and click the View tab. In the Advanced Settings pane, find Hidden Files and folders and select Show Hidden Files and Folders or Show hidden files, folders, or drives.

● **Note:** You can move the original preferences file rather than renaming it.

With Adobe Community Help you can:

- Access up-to-date definitive reference content online and offline

- Find the most relevant content contributed by experts from the Adobe community, on and off Adobe.com

- Comment on, rate, and contribute to content in the Adobe community

- Download Help content directly to your desktop for offline use

- Find related content with dynamic search and navigation tools

To access Community Help: If you have any Adobe CS5 product, then you already have the Community Help application. To invoke Help, choose Help > Illustrator Help. This companion application lets you search and browse Adobe and community content, plus you can comment on and rate any article just like you would in the browser. However, you can also download Adobe Help and language reference content for use offline. You can also subscribe to new content updates (which can be automatically downloaded) so that you'll always have the most up-to-date content for your Adobe product at all times. You can download the application from www.adobe.com/support/chc/index.html

Adobe content is updated based on community feedback and contributions. You can contribute in several ways: add comments to content or forums, including links to web content; publish your own content using Community Publishing; or contribute Cookbook Recipes. Find out how to contribute: www.adobe.com/community/publishing/download.html

See http://community.adobe.com/help/profile/faq.html for answers to frequently asked questions about Community Help.

Adobe Illustrator Help and Support: www.adobe.com/support/Illustrator where you can find and browse Help and Support content on adobe.com.

Adobe TV: http://tv.adobe.com is an online video resource for expert instruction and inspiration about Adobe products, including a How To channel to get you started with your product.

Adobe Design Center: www.adobe.com/designcenter offers thoughtful articles on design and design issues, a gallery showcasing the work of top-notch designers, tutorials, and more.

Adobe Developer Connection: www.adobe.com/devnet is your source for technical articles, code samples, and how-to videos that cover Adobe developer products and technologies.

Resources for educators: www.adobe.com/education includes three free curriculums that use an integrated approach to teaching Adobe software and can be used to prepare for the Adobe Certified Associate exams.

Also check out these useful links:

Adobe Forums: http://forums.adobe.com lets you tap into peer-to-peer discussions, questions and answers on Adobe products.

Adobe Marketplace & Exchange: www.adobe.com/cfusion/exchange is a central resource for finding tools, services, extensions, code samples and more to supplement and extend your Adobe products.

Adobe Illustrator CS5 product home page: www.adobe.com/products/Illustrator

Adobe Labs: http://labs.adobe.com gives you access to early builds of cutting-edge technology, as well as forums where you can interact with both the Adobe development teams building that technology and other like-minded members of the community.

Adobe certification

The Adobe training and certification programs are designed to help Adobe customers improve and promote their product-proficiency skills. There are four levels of certification:

- Adobe Certified Associate (ACA)

- Adobe Certified Expert (ACE)

- Adobe Certified Instructor (ACI)

- Adobe Authorized Training Center (AATC)

The Adobe Certified Associate (ACA) credential certifies that individuals have the entry-level skills to plan, design, build, and maintain effective communications using different forms of digital media.

The Adobe Certified Expert program is a way for expert users to upgrade their credentials. You can use Adobe certification as a catalyst for getting a raise, finding a job, or promoting your expertise.

If you are an ACE-level instructor, the Adobe Certified Instructor program takes your skills to the next level and gives you access to a wide range of Adobe resources.

Adobe Authorized Training Centers offer instructor-led courses and training on Adobe products, employing only Adobe Certified Instructors. A directory of AATCs is available at http://partners.adobe.com.

For information on the Adobe Certified programs, visit www.adobe.com/support/certification/main.html.

Accelerate your workflow with Adobe CS Live

Adobe CS Live is a set of online services that harness the connectivity of the web and integrate with Adobe Creative Suite 5 to simplify the creative review process, speed up website compatibility testing, deliver important web user intelligence and more, allowing you to focus on creating your most impactful work. CS Live services are complimentary for a limited time* and can be accessed online or from within Creative Suite 5 applications.

Adobe BrowserLab is for web designers and developers who need to preview and test their web pages on multiple browsers and operating systems. Unlike other browser compatibility solutions, BrowserLab renders screenshots virtually on demand with multiple viewing and diagnostic tools, and can be used with Dreamweaver CS5 to preview local content and different states of interactive pages. Being an online service, BrowserLab has fast development cycles, with greater flexibility for expanded browser support and updated functionality.

Adobe CS Review is for creative professionals who want a new level of efficiency in the creative review process. Unlike other services that offer online review of creative content, only CS Review lets you publish a review to the web directly from within InDesign, Photoshop, Photoshop Extended, and Illustrator and view reviewer comments back in the originating Creative Suite application.

Acrobat.com is for creative professionals who need to work with a cast of colleagues and clients in order to get a creative project from creative brief to final product. Acrobat.com is a set of online services that includes web conferencing, online file sharing and workspaces. Unlike collaborating via email and attending time-consuming in-person meetings, Acrobat.com brings people to your work instead of sending files to people, so you can get the business side of the creative process done faster, together, from any location.

Adobe Story is for creative professionals, producers, and writers working on or with scripts. Story is a collaborative script development tool that turns scripts into metadata that can be used with the Adobe CS5 Production Premium tools to streamline workflows and create video assets.

SiteCatalyst NetAverages is for web and mobile professionals who want to optimize their projects for wider audiences. NetAverages provides intelligence on how users are accessing the web, which helps reduce guesswork early in the creative process. You can access aggregate user data such as browser type, operating system, mobile device profile, screen resolution and more, which can be shown over time. The data is derived from visitor activity to participating Omniture SiteCatalyst customer sites. Unlike other web intelligence solutions, NetAverages innovatively displays data using Flash, creating an engaging experience that is robust yet easy to follow.

You can access CS Live three different ways:

1   Set up access when you register your Creative Suite 5 products and get complimentary access that includes all of the features and workflow benefits of using CS Live with CS5.

2   Set up access by signing up online and get complimentary access to CS Live services for a limited time. Note, this option does not give you access to the services from within your products.

3   Desktop product trials include a 30-day trial of CS Live services.

CS Live services are complimentary for a limited time. See www.adobe.com/go/cslive for details.

WHAT'S NEW IN ADOBE ILLUSTRATOR CS5

Adobe Illustrator CS5 is packed with new and innovative features to help you produce artwork more efficiently for print, web, and digital video publication. In this chapter, you'll learn about many of these new features—how they function and how you can use them in your work.

Perspective Drawing

Use perspective grids to draw shapes and scenes in accurate 1-, 2-, and 3-point linear perspectives. The new Perspective Grid tool allows you to turn on a grid that supports drawing directly on planes of true perspective. The new Perspective Selection tool allows objects to be moved, scaled, duplicated, and transformed dynamically in perspective. Easily move and duplicate objects from one plane to another.

Beautiful Strokes

In Illustrator CS5, a number of new features have been introduced that make designing with strokes even more powerful and flexible. The core drawing tools within Illustrator merit attention every software release, and with Illustrator CS5 there are five significant updates that new and long-time users will appreciate. You can finely control stroke width, dashes, arrowheads, and how brushes stretch along a path. And improvements in corner handling mean that stroke shapes behave predictably in tight angles or around sharp points.

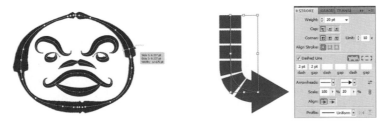

Bristle Brush

Paint with vectors that resemble real-world brush strokes. The new Bristle Brush provides breakthrough control of painting. You can set bristle characteristics such as size, length, thickness, and stiffness. Set brush shape and bristle density. And set paint opacity, which uses transparency variations to simulate lifelike blending. When you have chosen the perfect characteristics for your Bristle Brush, you can save it for later use.

Multiple artboard enhancements

Work on up to 100 artboards of varying sizes all in one document, organized and viewed the way you want. New and greatly expanded artboard options in Illustrator CS5 include a full Artboards panel, in which you can name and reorder artboards. Quickly add, delete, and duplicate them using panel controls or keyboard shortcuts.

Shape Builder tool

Intuitively combine, edit, and fill shapes on your artboard. Drag the cursor across overlapping shapes and paths to create new objects and add color without accessing multiple tools and panels. Quickly unite, exclude, trim, and more.

Drawing enhancements

Work faster with everyday tools. Improvements to familiar drawing tools make using Illustrator CS5 efficient and productive. Instant masking using Draw Inside mode and joining paths with a keystroke are just two of the enhancements that speed up your routine tasks.

Round-trip editing with Adobe Flash Catalyst CS5

Use Illustrator CS5 for interaction design, now enabled by new Adobe Flash Catalyst CS5, available in Adobe Creative Suite 5 Design Premium, Web Premium, Production Premium, and Master Collection. Develop your ideas and design your interface in Illustrator, creating screen layouts and individual elements such as logos and button graphics. Then open your artwork in Flash Catalyst and add actions and interactive components there—without writing code.

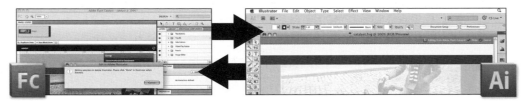

Resolution-independent Effects

See raster effects such as drop shadows, blurs, and textures maintain a consistent appearance across media. Have you ever found that your artwork mysteriously loses its smooth, high-quality look when you publish? You can now create work for different types of output and know that popular raster effects maintain an ideal appearance no matter how your resolution settings change—from print to web to video. You can even go up to a higher resolution. Work quickly and efficiently with low-resolution artwork and then scale up when you're ready to go to a finished output such as high-quality print.

Clean, sharp graphics for web and mobile devices

Create vector objects precisely on the file's pixel grid for delivering pixel-aligned artwork. When you're designing artwork for Flash Catalyst, Adobe Flash Professional software, and Adobe Dreamweaver® software, it's critical that raster images look sharp, especially standard web graphics at 72ppi resolution. Pixel alignment is also useful for video resolution rasterization control. And in Illustrator CS5, new web graphics tools include type enhancements. Choose one of four text anti-aliasing options for each of your Illustrator text frames.

 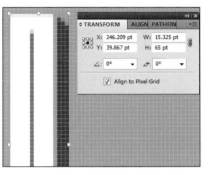

Integration with Adobe CS Review

Illustrator CS5 integrates with Adobe CS Review, one of several new CS Live online services*. With Adobe CS Review, you can create and share online reviews for clients and colleagues down the hall or around the world. From within Illustrator CS5, publish a review of your work to the web. Multiple reviewers can then access your review from a browser without any additional software and make comments right in their browser window with easy-to-use annotation tools.

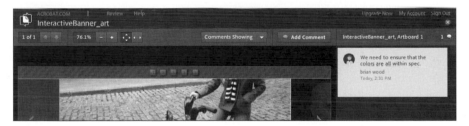

Although this list just touches on just a few of the new features of Illustrator CS5, it exemplifies Adobe's commitment to providing the best tools possible for your publishing needs. We hope you enjoy working with Illustrator CS5 as much as we do.

—The Adobe Illustrator CS5 Classroom in a Book Team

A QUICK TOUR OF
ADOBE ILLUSTRATOR CS5

Lesson overview

In this interactive demonstration of Adobe Illustrator CS5, you'll get an overview of the application while using some of the exciting new features.

 This lesson takes approximately an hour to complete. You'll need to first copy the Lesson00 folder onto your hard disk.

In this interactive demonstration of Adobe Illustrator CS5, you use new and exciting application features, like the Shape Builder tool and perspective drawing, as well as learn some key fundamentals for working in the application.

Getting started

You work with one file during this tour. All art files are on the Adobe Classroom in a Book CD that is included on the inside back cover of this book. Make sure that you copy the Lessons folder from the CD to your hard disk before starting this exercise. Before you begin, you need to restore the default preferences for Adobe Illustrator CS5. This lesson includes a finished art file so that you can see what you will be creating on your own.

● **Note:** If you have not already done so, copy the resource files for this lesson onto your hard disk from the Lesson00 folder on the Adobe Illustrator CS5 Classroom in a Book CD. See "Copying the Classroom in a Book files" on page 2.

1   To ensure that the tools and panels function as described in this lesson, delete or deactivate (by renaming) the Adobe Illustrator CS5 preferences file. See "Restoring default preferences" on page 3.

2   Start Adobe Illustrator CS5.

3   Choose File > Open and open the L00end_1.ai file and the L00end_2.ai file in the Lesson00 folder in the Lessons folder on your hard disk. These are the final artwork files. You can leave them open for reference, or choose File > Close to close them. For this lesson, you will start with a blank document.

Working with multiple artboards

An Illustrator document can contain up to one hundred artboards (pages). Next, you will create a document with multiple artboards, and then edit them. Read more about creating and editing artboards in Lesson 4, "Transforming Objects."

1   Choose File > New.

● **Note:** New document profiles in Illustrator are tailored to different kinds of projects—mobile, print, web, and video, for example.

2   In the New Document dialog box, name the file **teabook** and leave the New Document Profile setting to Print. Change Number Of Artboards to **2**, the Columns to **2**, Units to Inches, Width to **6.85** in, and Height to **9.75** in. Click OK. A new blank document appears.

New Document		
Name: teabook		OK
New Document Profile: [Custom]		Cancel
Number of Artboards: 2		Templates...
Spacing: 0.28 in	Columns: 2	
Size: [Custom]		
Width: 6.85 in	Units: Inches	Color Mode:CMYK
Height: 9.75	Orientation:	PPI:300 Align to Pixel Grid:No
	Top Bottom Left Right	
Bleed: 0 in 0 in 0 in 0 in		
▼ Advanced		

3 Choose File > Save As. In the Save As dialog box, leave the name as teabook.ai and navigate to the Lesson00 folder. Leave the Save As Type option set to Adobe Illustrator (*.AI) (Windows) or the Format option set to Adobe Illustrator (ai) (Mac OS), and click Save. In the Illustrator Options dialog box, leave the Illustrator options at their default settings, and then click OK.

4 Choose View > Rulers > Show Rulers to show rulers on the artboard.

5 Select the Artboard tool (▭) in the Tools panel. Click the artboard labeled 01 - Artboard 1 in the upper-left corner. In the Control panel, above the document, click the right, middle reference point (▦), and then change the Width to **3.5** in.

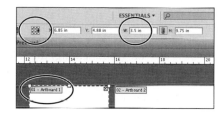

● **Note:** If you don't see the Width and Height fields in the Control panel, click the Artboard Options button (▣) in the Control panel and enter the value in the dialog box that appears.

Notice that the options for editing the artboard dimensions, orientation, and more appear in the Control panel, below the menus.

6 Select the Selection tool (▶) to stop editing the artboards. Click the right artboard to make it the active artboard. Choose View > Fit Artboard In Window.

Creating shapes

Shapes are the cornerstone of Illustrator and you will create many of them throughout these lessons. Next, you will create and copy several shapes. Read more about creating and editing shapes in Lesson 3, "Creating and Editing Shapes."

1 Select the Rectangle tool (▭) in the Tools panel and position the pointer over the upper-left corner of the artboard. Notice the word "intersect" next to the pointer, indicating that the rectangle you draw will snap to that corner of the artboard. Drag to the lower-right corner of the artboard.

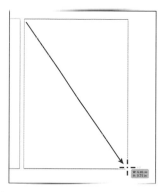

With the rectangle still selected, notice that there are controls for the fill and stroke at the bottom of the Tools panel. The stroke is essentially a border, and the fill is the interior of a shape. When the Fill box is in front, the selected color is assigned to the interior of the selected object.

2 Activate the fill by clicking the solid (white) Fill box, even if it's already selected.

Fill selected   Stroke selected

Note: If the color panel is not showing, click the Color panel icon (🎨) on the right side of the workspace to expand the panel.

3   With the rectangle still selected, in the Color panel that appears on the right side of the workspace, change the values in the panel to C=**0**, M=**2**, Y=**7**, K=**0**. After entering the last value, press Enter or Return to change the color. The rectangle now has a light yellow fill.

4   Select the Selection tool (▶) in the Tools panel and then choose Edit > Copy, Edit > Paste In Front.

5   With the Selection tool, drag the top, middle bounding point of the selected shape down. In the gray measurement label that appears as you drag, you will see a width and height. When the height is approximately 2.2 in, release the mouse. The measurement label is a part of smart guides, which you will learn about later.

6   Click the Swatches panel icon (▦) on the right side of the workspace to expand the Swatches panel. Make sure that the Fill box is selected at the bottom of the Tools panel, and then click the Black swatch to fill the new shape with black.

7   Choose Select > All On Active Artboard. Choose Object > Lock > Selection.

8   Choose File > Save. Leave the file open.

Working with the Shape Builder tool

The Shape Builder tool is an interactive tool for creating complex shapes by merging and erasing simpler shapes. Next, you will create a tea pot from simple shapes using the Shape Builder tool. Read more about working with the Shape Builder tool in Lesson 3, "Creating and Editing Shapes."

1   Select the Zoom tool (🔍) in the Tools panel and click twice on the black rectangle at the bottom of the artboard to zoom in.

Tip: If you don't see in (inches) in the rounded rectangle dialog box, you can still enter "in" after the value to create the rectangle in inches.

2   Select the Rounded Rectangle tool (▢) by clicking and holding down the Rectangle tool (▭) in the Tools panel. Click once in the center of the black rectangle.

3   In the Rounded Rectangle dialog box, change the Width to **1.7 in**, the Height to **1.5 in**, and the Corner Radius to **.8 in**. Click OK.

4 Click the Fill color (◼▾) in the Control panel and click the white swatch.

5 With the Rounded Rectangle tool still selected, drag to the left of the new shape to create a similar shape that is about .7 inches in width and .3 inches in height. Use the measurement label for sizing guidance.

● **Note:** Your original rounded rectangle may not be in the same position as shown in the figure below. That is okay.

6 Double-click the Rotate tool (⟳) in the Tools panel. In the Rotate dialog box, change the Angle to **−45**, and then click OK.

7 Select the Selection tool (▸) in the Tools panel and drag the shape to position it as in the figure, make a pouring spout.

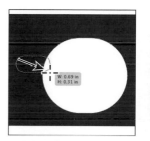  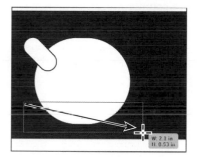

Create a rounded rectangle.   Rotate the rounded rectangle.   Drag it into position.

8 Select the Rectangle tool (▢) from the Rounded Rectangle group in the Tools panel. Drag to create a rectangle that covers the bottom quarter of the large rounded rectangle. See figure for position.

9 Select the Selection tool in the Tools panel. Holding down the Shift key, click the other two white shapes to select all three shapes.

10 Select the Shape Builder tool (◀▣) in the Tools panel. Position the pointer over the smaller rounded-rectangle shape, and drag through to the larger white rounded rectangle. This combines the shapes into one.

11 Holding down the Alt (Windows) or Options (Mac OS) key, drag through the bottom two shapes with the Shape Builder tool to remove them. Notice the minus sign in the pointer.

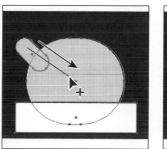 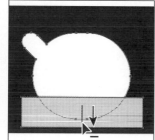

Working with drawing modes

Drawing modes allow you to draw inside shapes, draw behind existing shapes, or draw in normal mode, which typically layers shapes on top of each other. Next, you will draw a rectangle inside the tea pot shape. Read more about drawing modes in Lesson 3, "Creating and Editing Shapes."

Note: If the Tools panel you see is displayed as a single column, you can click the Drawing Modes button (◙) at the bottom of the Tools panel and choose a drawing mode from the menu that appears.

1 Select the Selection tool (▶) in the Tools panel. Click to select the tea pot shape.

2 Click the Draw Inside button (◙) at the bottom of the Tools panel. Notice that the teapot shape now has dotted lines around the corners, indicating that you can draw inside the shape.

3 Select the Rectangle tool (▭) in the Tools panel. Position the pointer over the center of the white teapot shape. Drag to draw a rectangle that is about .7 inches in width and .35 inches in height. It does not have to be exact.

4 Change the Fill color in the Control panel to a medium gray.

5 Select the Selection tool and drag the rectangle up into the pour spout.

▶**Tip:** If you don't like a shape you've drawn, you can always choose Edit > Undo to try again.

6 Select the Rotate tool (⟳) in the Tools panel. Position the pointer over the upper-right corner of the rectangle. Holding down the Shift key, drag in a counter-clockwise motion until you see 45°. Release the mouse button, and then the Shift key.

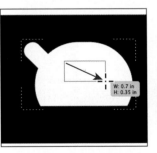
Create a rectangle.

Drag it into position.

Rotate the rectangle.

7 Click the Draw Normal button (◙) at the bottom of the Tools panel.

8 Choose Select > Deselect, then File > Save.

Working with strokes

The Width tool allows you to create a variable width stroke and save the width as a profile that can be applied to other strokes. Next, you will create a handle for the teapot.

1 Select the Selection tool (▶) in the Tools panel. Choose Select > All On Active Artboard. Drag the teapot close to the lower-right corner of the black rectangle.

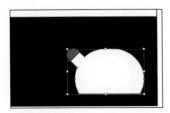

2 Select the Ellipse tool (⬭) from the Rectangle tool group in the Tools panel. Position the pointer above and to the right of the teapot spout. Drag to create an ellipse that is approximately 1.25 inches in width and 1.4 inches in height.

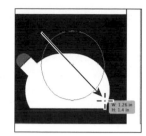

Tip: You can use the Selection tool (▶) in the Tools panel to reposition the ellipse after drawing it.

3 Click the Fill color in the Control panel and choose None (⬜) for the fill. Click the Stroke color in the Control panel and choose a light gray (C=0, M=0, Y=0, K=50).

4 Choose **2 pt** from the Stroke Weight to the right of the Stroke Color in the Control panel.

5 Choose Object > Arrange > Send Backward too send it behind the teapot.

6 Select the Zoom tool (🔍) in the Tools panel and click twice on the new ellipse to zoom in to it.

7 With the ellipse still selected, select the Width tool (🖊) in the Tools panel. Position the pointer over the top of the gray stroke, just to the left of center. Drag away from the line, as shown in the figure below.

Tip: Read more about the Width tool in Lesson 3, "Creating and Editing Shapes."

8 Position the pointer a little to the left of where you just dragged the stroke. Click and drag toward the center of the line. How far you drag doesn't have to exaclty match the figure below.

9 Choose Select > Deselect, then choose File > Save.

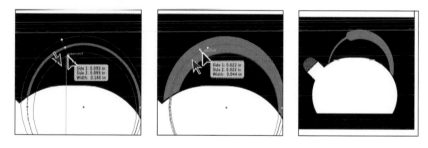

Working with color groups and recoloring artwork

A color group is an organization tool that lets you group related color swatches together in the Swatches panel. In addition, a color group can be a container for color harmonies, which you create using the Edit Color/Recolor Artwork dialog box or the Color Guide panel. Next, you will create more colors for the book cover.

Tip: Read more about color groups and recoloring artwork in Lesson 6, "Color and Painting."

1 Choose View > Fit Artboard In Window.

2 Select the Rounded Rectangle tool (⬜) in the Tools panel. Click in the middle of the artboard. In the Rounded Rectangle dialog box, change the Width to **4.5** in, the Height to **1.1** in, and the Corner Radius to **.2** in. Click OK.

Rounded Rectangle

Options
Width: 4.5 in
Height: 1.1 in
Corner Radius: 0.2 in

OK
Cancel

3 Click the Fill box in the Tools panel if it isn't already selected. Click the Swatches panel icon (▦) on the right side of the workspace to expand the Swatches panel.

4 In the Swatches panel, position the pointer over the brown swatches. Click the brown swatch that shows a tooltip with C=40, M=65, Y=90, K=35, to fill the rectangle.

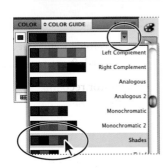

5 Select the Selection tool and click the Color Guide panel icon (◗) on the right side of the workspace. Click the Set Base Color To The Current Color icon (■). Choose Shades from the Harmony Rules menu (circled in the figure).

6 Click the Save Color Group To Swatch Panel button (▣⁺). This saves the four colors at the top of the panel as a group in the Swatches panel.

7 With the Selection tool (▶), drag a marquee across the tea pot and handle at the bottom-right of the artboard to select both objects.

8 Click the Swatches panel icon (▦) to expand the Swatches panel. Notice the new color group listed at the bottom of the panel (you may need to scroll down). Click the folder to the left of the four brown colors in the Swatches panel. Click the Edit Or Apply Colors button (◉) at the bottom of the Color Guide panel.

9 In the Recolor Artwork dialog box, click Color Group 1 in the Color Groups area. Click OK. Choose Select > Deselect.

The Recolor Artwork dialog box maps the colors in the artwork to the colors in the color group you select.

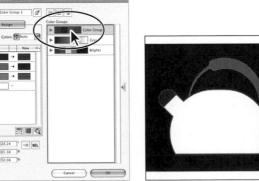

Placing Adobe Photoshop® images in Illustrator

In Illustrator, you can place Photoshop files and assign Layer Comps before you place images on the artboard. Next, you will place a hand drawn image. Read more about Layer Comps and placing Photoshop images in Lesson 15, "Combining Illustrator CS5 Graphics with Other Adobe Applications."

1 Choose View > Fit Artboard In Window to ensure that the Document window is centered.

2 Choose File > Place. In the Place dialog box, navigate to the Lesson00 in the Lessons folder, and select the floral.psd file. Make sure that the Link option in the lower-left corner is selected, and click Place.

> **Note:** By selecting Link in the Place dialog box, you are connecting the Photoshop image to the Illustrator file. If the image is later edited in Photoshop, it is updated in the Illustrator file.

Illustrator recognizes when a file has been saved with Layer Comps, and opens the Photoshop Import Options dialog box. The file in this example has been saved with two different Layer Comps.

3 In the Photoshop Import Options dialog box, select Show Preview. Make sure that No Background is chosen in the Layer Comp menu, and then click OK. The image of the floral pattern is placed on the artboard.

> **Note:** Your rounded rectangle may be in a different position than shown in the figure. That's okay.

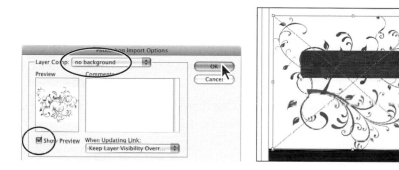

4 Choose File > Save.

Using Live Trace

You can use Live Trace to convert photographs (raster images) into vector artwork. Next, you will trace the Photoshop file to create a piece of black and white line art. Read more about Live Trace in Lesson 3, "Creating and Editing Shapes."

1 With the image still selected, click the Live Trace button in the Control panel. The image is converted to vector paths, but it is not yet editable.

> **Tip:** At this point, if the image were linked, and if you were to edit the floral.psd image in Photoshop, the Live Trace image would update in Illustrator.

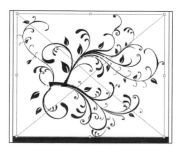

2 Choose One Color Logo from the Preset menu in the Control panel. This changes the trace settings and makes the white areas transparent.

3 Choose File > Save.

Using Live Paint

The Live Paint tool lets you color objects as you would on paper. Read more about Live Paint in Lesson 6, "Color and Painting."

1 With the traced image still selected, click the Live Paint button in the Control panel.

2 Select the Live Paint Bucket tool (🪣) from the Shape Builder tool (🔧) group in the Tools panel. Click the Fill color in the Control panel and select the first brown swatch in the color group you created earlier.

3 Press Ctrl++ (Windows) or Cmd++ (Mac OS) twice to zoom in.

> **Note:** If the area between the branches becomes painted, choose Edit > Undo Live Paint Bucket and try clicking again.

4 With the Live Paint Bucket tool (🪣) selected, position the pointer over one of the branches. Notice that much of the figure is highlighted in red, and colored squares appear above the pointer (🎨). Click to apply the brown fill color.

The color squares above the paint bucket represent the colors displayed before and after the selected color in the Swatches panel.

> **Note:** Even though this shape is created from many paths, Live Paint recognizes the visual shapes and highlights them in red as you move the pointer over them.

5 Press the right arrow key once to choose the darker brown color (■) from the three colored squares above the Live Paint Bucket tool. Using the Live Paint Bucket tool, click to apply the fill to one of the leaves.

Try painting the remaining leaves and branches, pressing the arrow keys to switch colors as you paint.

6 Select the Selection tool (▶) in the Tools panel. With the traced artwork selected, click the Expand button in the Control panel to convert the traced artwork to editable vector shapes. Choose Object > Arrange > Send Backward.

7 With the Selection tool click the rounded rectangle. In the Control panel, click the word Transform to open the Transform panel. Make sure that the center Reference Point (▦) is selected, then change the X value to **3.425** in and Y value to **4.1** in. Press Enter or Return to move the rounded rectangle.

● **Note:** You may need to type the "in" when entering the values in the Transform panel if it shows another type of unit.

8 Holding down the Shift key, with the Selection tool click the floral artwork. Release the Shift key, and then click the rounded rectangle once more to set it as the key object to align to.

9 Click the Vertical Align Center button (▮◻▮) in the Control panel. Notice that the floral artwork moves to align with the rectangle.

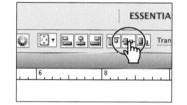

● **Note:** If you don't see the Align options, click the word Align in the Control panel to open the Align panel.

10 Choose Select > Deselect.

11 With the Selection tool, click the floral shape to select it. Choose Align to Artboard (▣) from the Align To button (▦) in the Control panel. This ensures that any selected objects are aligned to the artboard. Click the Horizontal Align left button (▮◻) to align the floral shape to the left edge of the artboard.

12 Choose Select > Deselect.

Working with the Blob Brush tool

The Blob Brush tool can be used to paint filled shapes that intersect and merge with other shapes of the same color. Next, you will use the Blob Brush tool to edit the floral artwork.

1 Choose View > Fit Artboard In Window. With the Selection tool (▶) selected, double-click the floral artwork. This enters isolation mode and allows you to edit the shapes in the floral artwork.

2 Select the Zoom tool (🔍) in the Tools panel. Drag a marquee across the top half of the floral artwork to zoom in.

3 With the Selection tool, click to select one of the main branches at the top (not a leaf). This selects most of the floral artwork.

● **Note:** Depending on the resolution of your screen, the Transform options may appear in the Control panel. If they do appear, you can set the options directly in the Control panel. You can also choose Window > Transform to open the Transform panel.

● **Note:** Read more about working with the Blob Brush tool in Lesson 11, "Working with Brushes."

4 Double-click the Blob Brush tool (🖋) in the Tools panel. In the Blob Brush Tool Options dialog box, select Keep Selected, change the Smoothness to **80**, and change the size to **5** pt. Click OK.

5 Position the pointer over the end of one of the top branches (see the figure below for position). Drag from the top branch up and to the left to create another small branch. As you release the mouse button, see how the shape changes and notice that the part you drew is now part of the branch.

6 Drag to create a larger, rounded end on the branch you drew. You can treat the Blob brush like a crayon; precision is not necessary.

7 Choose Select > Deselect. Press the Escape key to exit isolation mode.

8 Choose View > Fit Artboard In Window, then choose File > Save.

Working with type

▶ **Tip:** Read more about working with type in Lesson 7, "Working with Type."

Next, you will add some text to the book cover artwork.

1 Choose Window > Workspace > Essentials to reset the panels.

2 Select the Type tool (T), and click once on the artboard in an area where there are no objects. You will reposition the text later in the lesson.

3 Type **FeliciTea**. With the Type tool selected, choose Select > All, or press Ctrl+A (Windows) or Command+A (Mac OS) to select all the text that you typed. Choose Type > Change Case > UPPERCASE.

▶ **Tip:** If you don't see the Character options in the Control panel, then click the word Character to see the Character panel.

4 In the Control panel, drag to select the font name in the Font field in the Control panel (to the right of the word Character). Type "**tra**" with the font name selected to filter the font list to Trajan Pro. Type **45 pt** in the Font Size field and press Enter or Return.

5 With the Type tool, select the "Tea" part of the text. Change the font size to **64** pt in the Control panel.

6 Choose Select > All. Select the Eyedropper tool (🖋) in the Tools panel. Click the light yellow background shape to sample the color and apply it to the text.

7 With the text still selected, change the Stroke color in the Control panel to None (⬚).

8 With the Selection tool (▶), drag the text area down on top of the rounded rectangle toward the center of the artboard.

9 Choose Object > Hide > Selection to temporarily hide the text.

10 Choose File > Save.

The result before hiding the text.

Using the Appearance panel and effects

The Appearance panel allows you to control an object's attributes, such as stroke, fill, and effects.

1 With the Selection tool (▶), click to select the brown, rounded rectangle.

2 Click the Appearance panel icon (◉) on the right side of the workspace. Note that in the Appearance panel, the current selection, listed at the top of the panel, as Path.

3 Click the Stroke color in the Appearance panel and choose the light brown swatch (C=21, M=55, Y–83, K=5) from the color group you created. Change the Stroke Weight to the right of the color to **10** pt. Click the underlined word Stroke and in the Stroke panel that appears, click Align Stroke To Outside (⬚)

4 Click the Add New Stroke button (■) at the bottom of the Appearance panel to add a new stroke to the Appearance panel. Click the Stroke color, and select the first brown swatch (C=40, M=65, Y=90, K=35) in the swatch group you created. Click the Stroke color row in the Appearance panel to close the Swatches panel. Change the Stroke Weight to **4** pt.

5 Choose Effect > Path > Offset Path. In the Offset Path dialog box, change the offset to **11** pt, and then click OK.

6 Click the word Path at the top of the Appearance panel to apply the next effect to the entire path.

▶ **Tip:** Read more about working with the Appearance panel in Lesson 13, "Applying Appearance Attributes and Graphic Styles."

7 Click the Add New Effect button (*fx.*) at the bottom of the Appearance panel, and choose Stylize > Drop Shadow. In the Drop Shadow dialog box, change the Opacity to **40**, the X Offset and Y Offset to **.06** in, and the Blur to **.04** in. Click OK.

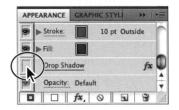

8 Scroll down in the Appearance panel. Click the eye icon (👁) to the left of the Drop Shadow effect to hide and disable it. Click the same box to reveal it again.

9 Choose Object > Show All to show the text.

10 Choose Select > Deselect and then choose File > Save.

Working with brushes

Brushes let you stylize the appearance of paths. You can apply brush strokes to existing paths, or you can use the Paintbrush tool to draw a path and apply a brush stroke simultaneously. Read more about working with brushes in Lesson 11, "Working with Brushes."

1 Choose Object > Unlock All. With the Selection tool (▶), click to select the black rectangle at the bottom of the artboard. Hold down the spacebar, and drag the artboard up to reposition it.

2 Click the Draw Inside button (◙) at the bottom of the Tools panel. Choose Select > Deselect.

3 Click the Brushes panel icon (🖌) on the right side of the workspace to expand the Brushes panel. Scroll down in the panel and click the Filbert brush. A tooltip appears when you position the pointer over a brush in the list.

4 Change the Fill color in the Control panel to None (⊘) and the Stroke color to White.

5 Select the Paintbrush tool (✎) in the Tools panel. Position the pointer of over the end of the teapot spout. Drag up and to the left, past the edge of the black rectangle, to create some steam. Draw a couple of lines to create the effect of steam.

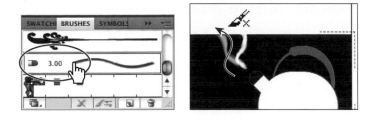

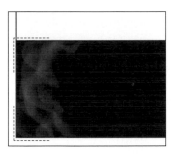

6   Double-click the Filbert brush in the Brushes panel to edit it. In the Bristle Brush Options dialog box, change the Shape to Flat Fan, the Size to **4**, the Bristle Length to **280**, the Paint Opacity to **15**, and the Stiffness to **20**. Select Preview to see the change in your painting. You may need to move the dialog box to see it. Click OK.

7   In the Brush Change Alert dialog box, click Apply To Strokes to change the strokes you already painted on the artboard.

8   With the Paintbrush tool, try painting some steam on the left side of the black rectangle so that it looks like the steam is wrapping around the inside of the box.

9   Click the Draw Normal button (◙) at the bottom of the Tools panel, and then choose File > Save.

Creating and editing a gradient

Gradients are color blends that use two or more colors. Next, you will apply a gradient to a shape in the background.

1   With the Selection tool (▶), click to select the light yellow rectangle in the background. Choose Edit > Copy.

2   Choose View > Fit All In Window. Click the first artboard on the left to make it the active artboard. Choose View > Fit Artboard In Window. Choose Edit > Paste In Place. Drag the right, middle bounding point to the left until it snaps to the right edge of the left artboard.

▶ **Tip:** Read more about working with gradients in Lesson 10, "Blending Colors and Shapes."

3   With the shape still selected, choose Edit > Copy, Edit > Paste In Front. Drag the top, middle point down to resize the copied rectangle. When the green alignment guide appears, indicating that it is aligned with the back rectangle on the artboard to the right, release the mouse button.

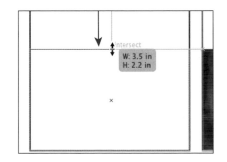

4 Click the Gradient panel icon (▦) on the right side of the workspace.

5 Click the Gradient menu button (▤) and choose Fade To Black from the menu. This applies a black-to-transparent gradient to the rectangle.

6 Select the Gradient tool (▦) in the Tools panel. Notice the gradient annotator (bar) that appears on the rectangle. Holding down the Shift key, drag across the rectangle from right to left above the gradient bar.

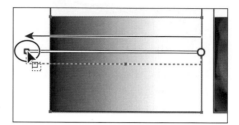

Dragging with the Gradient tool changes the direction of the gradient.

7 Position the pointer over the gradient annotator (the bar on the rectangle) so that it turns into a gradient slider. Notice the color stops beneath the gradient bar, which are similar to those in the Gradient panel. Double-click the black color stop (▦) on the right side of the gradient annotator. Click the Swatches button (▦) and click the first brown color in the color group you created, to change the color to brown. Press the Escape key to close the panel.

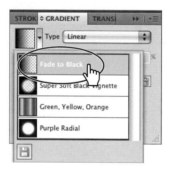
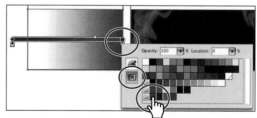

8 Position the pointer over the right end of the gradient annotator to reveal the brown color stop. Drag that stop a little to the left to change the appearance of the gradient.

9 Choose Select > Deselect, and then choose File > Save.

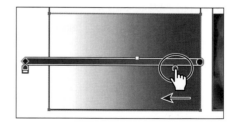

Working with symbols

A symbol is a reusable art object stored in the Symbols panel. You will now create a symbol from artwork. Read more about working with symbols in Lesson 14, "Working with Symbols."

1 Click the Artboards panel icon (⬚) on the right side of the workspace. Double-click Artboard 2 to fit the second artboard in the Document window.

2 Choose File > Open and open the symbol.ai file in the Lesson00 folder in the Lessons folder on your hard disk. Choose Select > All On Active Artboard. Choose Edit > Copy, then File > Close. Back in the teabook.ai file, choose Edit > Paste.

3 Click the Symbols panel icon (♣) on the right side of the workspace.

4 With the circle still selected on the artboard, click the New Symbol button (▣) at the bottom of the Symbols panel. In the Symbol Options dialog box, name the symbol **circle** and select Graphic as the Type. Click OK.

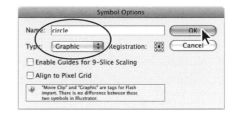

The circle now appears in the Symbols panel. This symbol is saved in the Symbols panel for use in this document only.

5 In the Symbols panel, drag the circle symbol onto the artboard. This creates an instance of the symbol. Drag out several more instances to create a loose pattern around the brown, rounded rectangle and text.

● **Note:** Your symbol instances may be in different locations than in the figure. That's okay. Use the figure as a guide.

6 Hold down the Shift+Alt (Windows) or Shift+Option (Mac OS) keys and, with the Selection tool (▶), drag a bounding point towards the center of one on the circles to make it smaller, while maintaining its proportions.

7 Try resizing each circle, making them smaller than the original in varying sizes.

8 Choose Select > Deselect, then File > Save.

Working with perspective

You will now render the book cover in perspective. The perspective feature in Illustrator allows you to easily draw or render artwork in perspective. Read more about this feature in Lesson 9, "Working with Perspective Drawing."

1 Choose File > New. In the New Document dialog box, name the file **teabook_persp** and choose Print from the New Document Profile menu. Change the Units to Inches and the Width to **15** in. Click OK.

2 Choose File > Save As. In the Save As dialog box, leave the name as teabook_ persp.ai and navigate to the Lesson00 folder. Leave the Save As Type option set to Adobe Illustrator (*.AI) (Windows) or the Format option set to Adobe Illustrator (ai) (Mac OS), and then click Save. In the Illustrator Options dialog box, leave the Illustrator options at their default settings, and then click OK.

3 Select the Perspective Grid tool (⊞) in the Tools panel. Notice the perspective grid that appears.

4 With the Perspective Grid tool selected, choose View > Perspective Grid > Lock Station Point. This allows you to edit the perspective grid planes together.

5 Drag the left vanishing point to the right to match the figure. This changes the perspective grid.

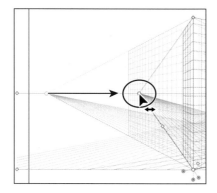

6 Click the teabook.ai tab at the top of the Document window.

7 Select the Selection tool (▶) in the Tools panel. Click the second (larger) artboard to make it active. Choose Select > All On Active Artboard.

8 Choose Edit > Copy.

9 Click the teabook_persp.ai tab to return to the perspective document.

10 Choose Edit > Paste, and then choose Object > Group.

11 With teabook_persp.ai showing in the Document window, select the Perspective Selection tool (▶⊡) in the same group as the Perspective Grid tool (⊞) in the Tools panel.

12 Click the Right Grid Plane in the Plane Switching Widget in the upper-left corner of the artboard. This allows you to bring the group that is selected into perspective on the right grid plane.

13 With the Perspective Selection tool, drag the group so that the left edge of the group approximately aligns to where the left and right planes meet in the center.

14 Click the teabook.ai tab at the top of the Document window.

15 Select the Selection tool (▶) in the Tools panel. Click the first (smaller) artboard to make it active. Choose Select > All On Active Artboard.

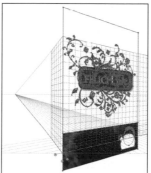

● **Note:** Dragging existing vector artwork with the Perspective Selection tool brings that content into perspective.

16 Choose Edit > Copy. Click the teabook_persp.ai tab to return to the perspective document. Choose Edit > Paste, and then choose Object > Group.

17 Select the Perspective Selection tool (▶•) in the Tools panel.

18 Click the left grid plane in the Plane Switching Widget in the upper-left corner of the artboard. This allows you to bring the group that is selected into perspective on the left grid plane.

19 With the Perspective Selection tool, drag the group so that the right edge of the group approximately aligns with the left edge of the group that you positioned previously. You can reposition the group once it's on the grid plane if it isn't quite fitting, as shown in the figure.

20 With the Perspective Selection tool, drag the left, middle bounding point on the spine of the book to the right, to make it narrower.

21 Choose Select > Deselect, then choose View > Perspective Grid > Hide Grid.

Position the spine artwork.   Resize the artwork.   The result

22 Choose File > Save, and then File > Close for each of the open files.

1 GETTING TO KNOW THE WORK AREA

Lesson overview

In this lesson, you learn how to do the following:

- Use the Welcome screen.

- Open an Adobe® Illustrator® CS5 file.

- Select tools in the Tools panel.

- Work with panels.

- Use viewing options to enlarge and reduce artwork.

- Navigate multiple artboards and documents.

- Understand rulers.

- Work with Document groups.

- Use Illustrator Help.

 This lesson will take approximately 45 minutes to complete. If needed, remove the Lesson00 folder from your hard disk and copy the Lesson01 folder onto it.

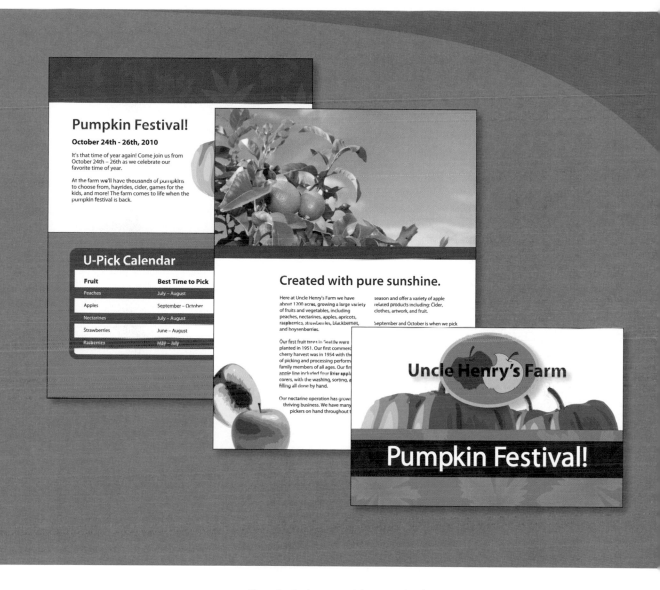

To make the best use of the extensive drawing, painting, and editing capabilities of Adobe Illustrator CS5, it's important to learn how to navigate the workspace. The workspace consists of the Application bar, the menu bar, Tools panel, Control panel, Document window, and the default set of panels.

Getting started

You'll be working in multiple art files during this lesson, but, first, before you begin, restore the default preferences for Adobe Illustrator CS5. Then, open the finished art file for this lesson to see an illustration.

1   To ensure that the tools and panels function exactly as described in this lesson, delete or deactivate (by renaming) the Adobe Illustrator CS5 preferences file. See "Restoring default preferences" on page 3.

   ● **Note:** If you have not already done so, copy the resource files for this lesson onto your hard disk from the Lesson01 folder on the Adobe Illustrator CS5 Classroom in a Book CD. See "Copying the Classroom in a Book files" on page 2.

2   Double-click the Adobe Illustrator CS5 icon to start Adobe Illustrator.

3   Choose Help > Welcome Screen to open the Welcome Screen. You'll see a Welcome screen with hyperlinked options.

▶ **Tip:** The Welcome screen does not appear at startup, by default. To show the Welcome Screen when you start Illustrator, deselect Don't Show Again in the lower-left corner of the Welcome Screen.

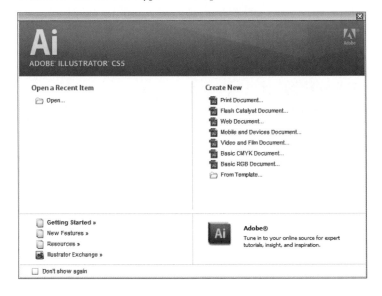

Use the Welcome screen to find out what's new in Illustrator and to gain access to resources such as videos, templates, and much more. The Welcome screen also lets you create a new document from scratch or from a template, or open an existing document. The Open A Recent Item area includes the Open link and a list of recently viewed files. This area will be blank when you first start to use Illustrator. For this lesson, you'll open an existing document.

4 Click Open on the left side of the Welcome screen, or choose File > Open to open the L1start_1.ai file. This file is located in the Lesson01 folder in the Lessons folder on your hard disk.

5 Choose View > Fit Artboard In Window.

6 Choose Window > Workspace > Essentials to ensure that the workspace is set to the default settings.

● **Note:** Due to the differences in Color Settings from one system to another, a Missing Profile dialog box may appear as you open various exercise files. Click OK if you see this dialog box.

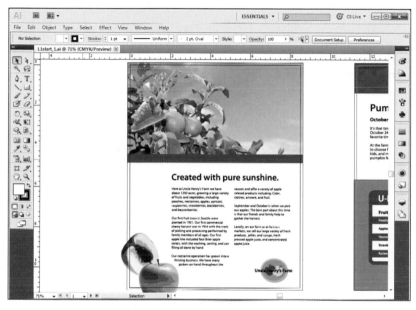

The artwork file contains the front and back of a brochure.

When the file is open and Illustrator is fully launched, the Application bar, menu bar, Tools panel, Control panel and panel groups appear on the screen. Notice that the panels are docked on the right side of the screen. This is where some of the panels are stored by default. Illustrator also consolidates many of your most frequently accessed panel options in the Control panel below the menu bar. This lets you work with fewer visible panels and gives you a larger workspace.

You will use the L1start_1.ai file to practice navigating, zooming, and investigating an Illustrator document and work area.

7 Choose File > Save As. In the Save As dialog box, name the file **brochure.ai** and save it in the Lesson01 folder. Leave the Save As Type option set to Adobe Illustrator (*.AI) (Windows) or leave the Format option set to Adobe Illustrator (ai) (Mac OS). Click Save. If a warning dialog box appears referencing spot colors and transparency, click Continue. In the Illustrator Options dialog box, leave the Illustrator options at their default settings, and click OK.

Artboard overview

Artboards represent the regions that can contain printable artwork. You can use artboards to crop areas for printing or placement purposes. Multiple artboards are useful for creating a variety of things such as multiple page PDFs, printed pages with different sizes or different elements, independent elements for websites, video storyboards, or individual items for animation in Adobe Flash or After Effects.

Note: You can have up to 100 artboards per document, depending on the size of the artboards. You can specify the number of artboards for a document when you create it, and you can add and remove artboards at any time while working in a document. You can create artboards of different sizes, resize them with the Artboard tool, and position them on the screen—they can even overlap each other.

A. Printable area
B. Nonprintable area
C. Edge of the page
D. Artboard
E. Bleed area
F. Canvas

A B C D E F

Note: If you are saving an Illustrator document to place it in a layout program such as InDesign, the printable and nonprintable areas are irrelevant; the artwork outside the bounds still appears.

A. **Printable area** is bounded by the innermost dotted lines and represents the portion of the page on which the selected printer can print. Many printers cannot print to the edge of the paper. Don't get confused by what is considered nonprintable.

B. **Nonprintable area** is between the two sets of dotted lines representing any nonprintable margin of the page. This example shows the nonprintable area of an 8.5" x 11" page for a standard laser printer. The printable and nonprintable area is determined by the printer selected in the Print Options dialog box.

C. **Edge of the page** is indicated by the outermost set of dotted lines.

D. **Artboard** is bounded by solid lines and represents the entire region that can contain printable artwork. By default, the artboard is the same size as the page, but it can be enlarged or reduced. The U.S. default artboard is 8.5" x 11", but it can be set as large as 227" x 227".

E. **Bleed Area** is the amount of artwork that falls outside of the printing bounding box, or outside the crop area and trim marks. You can include bleed in your artwork as a margin of error—to ensure that the ink is still printed to the edge of the page after the page is trimmed or that an image can be stripped into a keyline in a document.

F. **Canvas** is the area outside the artboard that extends to the edge of the 227" square window. Objects placed on the canvas are visible on-screen, but they do not print.

—From Illustrator Help

Understanding the workspace

You create and manipulate your documents and files using various elements such as panels, bars, and windows. Any arrangement of these elements is called a workspace. When you first start Illustrator, you see the default workspace, which you can customize for the tasks you perform. You can create and save multiple workspaces—one for editing and another for viewing, for example—and switch between them as you work.

Below the areas of the default workspace are described:

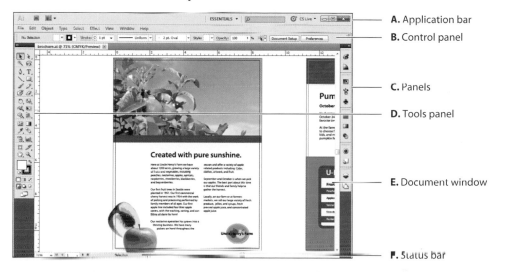

A. Application bar
B. Control panel
C. Panels
D. Tools panel
E. Document window
F. Status bar

A. The Application bar across the top contains a workspace switcher, a menu bar (Windows only, depending on screen resolution), and application controls.

● **Note:** For the Mac OS, the menu items appear above the Application bar.

B. The Control panel displays options for the currently selected object.

C. Panels help you monitor and modify your work. Certain panels are displayed by default, but you can add any panel by choosing it from the Window menu. Many panels have menus with panel-specific options. Panels can be grouped, stacked, docked, or free-floating.

D. The Tools panel contains tools for creating and editing images, artwork, page elements, and more. Related tools are grouped together.

E. The Document window displays the file you're working on.

F. The Status bar appears at the lower-left edge of the Document window. It displays information and navigation controls.

Working with the Tools panel

The Tools panel contains selection tools, drawing and painting tools, editing tools, viewing tools, the Fill and Stroke boxes, and Drawing Modes. As you work through the lessons, you'll learn about the specific function of each tool.

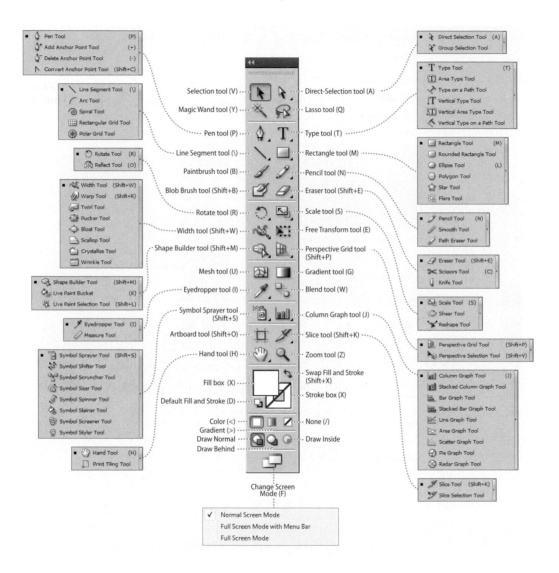

Pen Tool (P)
Add Anchor Point Tool (+)
Delete Anchor Point Tool (-)
Convert Anchor Point Tool (Shift+C)

Line Segment Tool (\)
Arc Tool
Spiral Tool
Rectangular Grid Tool
Polar Grid Tool

Rotate Tool (R)
Reflect Tool (O)

Width Tool (Shift+W)
Warp Tool (Shift+R)
Twirl Tool
Pucker Tool
Bloat Tool
Scallop Tool
Crystallize Tool
Wrinkle Tool

Shape Builder Tool (Shift+M)
Live Paint Bucket (K)
Live Paint Selection Tool (Shift+L)

Eyedropper Tool (I)
Measure Tool

Symbol Sprayer Tool (Shift+S)
Symbol Shifter Tool
Symbol Scruncher Tool
Symbol Sizer Tool
Symbol Spinner Tool
Symbol Stainer Tool
Symbol Screener Tool
Symbol Styler Tool

Hand Tool (H)
Print Tiling Tool

Direct Selection Tool (A)
Group Selection Tool

Type Tool (T)
Area Type Tool
Type on a Path Tool
Vertical Type Tool
Vertical Area Type Tool
Vertical Type on a Path Tool

Rectangle Tool (M)
Rounded Rectangle Tool
Ellipse Tool (L)
Polygon Tool
Star Tool
Flare Tool

Pencil Tool (N)
Smooth Tool
Path Eraser Tool

Eraser Tool (Shift+E)
Scissors Tool (C)
Knife Tool

Scale Tool (S)
Shear Tool
Reshape Tool

Perspective Grid Tool (Shift+P)
Perspective Selection Tool (Shift+V)

Column Graph Tool (J)
Stacked Column Graph Tool
Bar Graph Tool
Stacked Bar Graph Tool
Line Graph Tool
Area Graph Tool
Scatter Graph Tool
Pie Graph Tool
Radar Graph Tool

Slice Tool (Shift+K)
Slice Selection Tool

Selection tool (V)
Magic Wand tool (Y)
Pen tool (P)
Line Segment tool (\)
Paintbrush tool (B)
Blob Brush tool (Shift+B)
Rotate tool (R)
Width tool (Shift+W)
Shape Builder tool (Shift+M)
Mesh tool (U)
Eyedropper tool (I)
Symbol Sprayer tool (Shift+S)
Artboard tool (Shift+O)
Hand tool (H)

Direct-Selection tool (A)
Lasso tool (Q)
Type tool (T)
Rectangle tool (M)
Pencil tool (N)
Eraser tool (Shift+E)
Scale tool (S)
Free Transform tool (E)
Perspective Grid tool (Shift+P)
Gradient tool (G)
Blend tool (W)
Column Graph tool (J)
Slice tool (Shift+K)
Zoom tool (Z)

Fill box (X)
Default Fill and Stroke (D)

Swap Fill and Stroke (Shift+X)
Stroke box (X)

Color (<)
Gradient (>)
Draw Normal
Draw Behind

None (/)
Draw Inside

Change Screen Mode (F)

✓ Normal Screen Mode
Full Screen Mode with Menu Bar
Full Screen Mode

● **Note:** The Tools panel shown here has two columns. You may see a single-column Tools panel, depending on your screen resolution and workspace.

1 Position the pointer over the Selection tool (▶) in the Tools panel. Notice that the name and keyboard shortcut are displayed.

▶ **Tip:** You can turn the tool tips on or off by choosing Edit > Preferences > General (Windows) or Illustrator > Preferences > General (Mac OS), and deselecting Show Tool Tips.

▶ **Tip:** Because the default keyboard shortcuts work only when you do not have a text insertion point, you can also add other keyboard shortcuts to select tools, even when you are editing text. To do this, choose Edit > Keyboard Shortcuts. For more information, see "Keyboard Shortcuts" in Illustrator Help.

2 Position the pointer over the Direct Selection tool (▷) and click and hold down the mouse button. You'll see additional selection tools. Drag down and to the right. Release the mouse button over the additional tool to select it.

Any tool in the Tools panel that displays a small black triangle contains additional tools that can be selected in this way.

● **Note:** On Mac OS, the top of the free-floating Tools panel has a close button in the upper-left corner (to close the panel) and double arrows in the upper-right corner.

Next, you'll learn to resize and float the Tools panel.

3 Select hidden tools, using the following methods:

- Click and hold down the mouse button on a tool that has additional hidden tools. Then drag to the desired tool and release the mouse button.

- Hold down the Alt key (Windows) or the Option key (Mac OS), and click the tool in the Tools panel. Each click selects the next hidden tool in the hidden tool sequence.

- Click and hold down the mouse button on the Rectangle tool (□). Drag to the right of the hidden tools and release on the tearoff arrow. This separates the tools from the Tools panel so that you can access them at all times.

4 Click the double arrow in the upper-left corner of the Tools panel to collapse the two columns into one column, which conserves screen space. Click the double arrow again to expand to two columns.

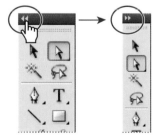

5 Click the dark gray title bar at the top of the Tools panel or the double line beneath the title bar, and drag the panel into the workspace. The Tools panel is now floating in the workspace.

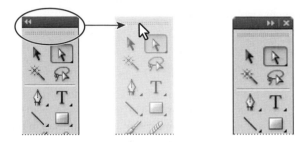

Drag the Tools panel so that it floats in the workspace.

6 With the Tools panel floating in the workspace, click the double arrow in the title bar to display the Tools panel in a single-column. Click again to display the Tools panel in two columns.

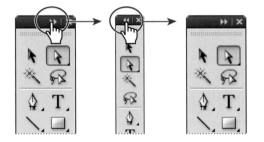

7 To dock the Tools panel again, drag its title bar or the double line below it to the left side of the application window (Windows) or screen (Mac OS). When the pointer reaches the left edge, a translucent blue border appears. This is called the drop zone. Release the mouse button to fit the Tools panel neatly into the side of the workspace.

Click and drag to dock the Tools panel at the edge of the workspace.

The Control panel

The Control panel is context-sensitive, meaning that it offers quick access to options, commands, and other panels relevant to the currently selected object(s). By default, the Control panel is docked at the top of the application window (Windows) or screen (Mac OS); however, you can dock it at the bottom, float it, or hide it altogether. You can click text that is blue and underlined to display a related panel. For example, click the underlined word Stroke to display the Stroke panel.

1   Take a look at the Control panel located below the menu bar. Select the Selection tool (▶) in the Tools panel and click the middle of reddish bar close to the center of the page. Notice that information for that object appears in the Control panel, including the "Path," Stroke, Style, and Opacity.

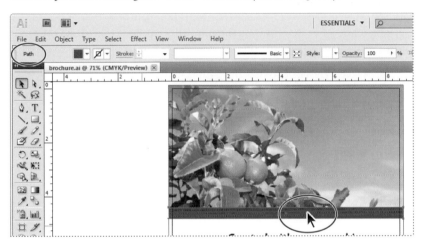

2   With any tool, drag the light gray double line along the left edge of the Control panel into the workspace. Once the Control panel is free-floating, you can drag the dark gray vertical bar that appears on the left edge of the Control panel, to move it to the top or bottom of the workspace.

3 Drag the Control panel to the bottom of the application window (Windows) or screen (Mac OS). When the pointer reaches the bottom, a blue line appears, indicating the drop zone in which it will be docked when you release the mouse button.

▶ Tip: You can also dock the Control panel by choosing Dock to Top or Dock to Bottom from the Control panel menu (▼☰).

4 If the Control panel is docked at the bottom, drag it to the top of the Document window. When the pointer reaches the top, above the brochure.ai document tab, a blue line appears indicating the drop zone. When you release the mouse button, the panel is docked.

5 Choose Select > Deselect so that the path is no longer selected.

▶ Tip: To move the Control panel back to the top of the workspace, you can also choose Window > Workspace > Essentials. This resets the workspace.

Working with panels

Panels, which are located in the Window menu, give you quick access to many tools that make modifying artwork easier. By default, some panels are docked and appear as icons on the right side of the workspace.

Next, you'll experiment with hiding, closing, and opening panels.

1 First, choose Essentials from the workspace switcher in the Application bar (to the left of the search field) to reset the panels to their original location.

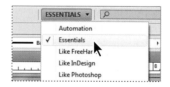

▶ Tip: You can also choose Window > Workspace > Essentials to reset the panels.

2 Click the Swatches panel icon (▦) on the right side of the workspace to expand the panel, or choose Window > Swatches. Notice that the Swatches panel appears with two other panels—the Brushes panel and Symbols panel. They are all part of the same panel group. Click the Symbols panel tab to view the Symbols panel.

3 Now click the Color panel icon (🎨). Notice that a new panel group appears, and the panel group that contained the Swatches panel closes.

4 Click the Color panel icon (🎨) to collapse the panel group.

▶ **Tip:** To find a hidden panel, choose the panel name from the Window menu. A check mark to the left of the panel name indicates that the panel is already open and in front of other panels in its panel group. If you choose a panel name that is already selected in the Window menu, the panel and its group collapses.

▶ **Tip:** To collapse a panel back to an icon, you can click its tab, its icon, or the double arrow in the panel title bar.

5 Click the double arrow at the top of the dock to expand the panels. Click the double arrow again to collapse the panels. Use this method to show more than one panel group at a time.

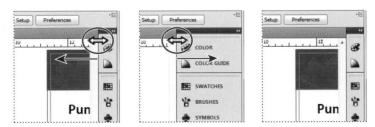

Click to expand.   Click to collapse.

6 To increase the width of all the panels in a dock, drag the left edge of the docked panels to the left until text appears. To decrease the width, click and drag the left edge of the docked panels to the right until the text disappears.

Next, you'll reorganize a panel group.

7 Choose Window > Workspace > Essentials to reset the workspace.

Tip: Press Tab to hide all open panels and the Tools panel. Press Tab again to show them all again. You can hide or show all panels except for the Tools and Control panels by pressing Shift+Tab to hide and Shift+Tab to show.

8 Drag the Swatches panel icon (▦) to remove the panel from the dock and make it a free-floating panel. Notice that the panel stays collapsed as an icon when it is free-floating. Click the double-arrow in the Swatches panel title bar to expand the panel so you can see its contents.

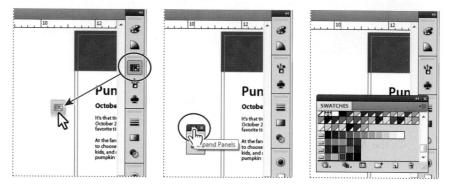

You can also move panels from one panel group to another. In this way you can create custom panel groups that contain the panels you use most often.

Tip: To close a panel, drag the panel away from the dock and click the close box (Windows) or the close button (Mac OS). You can also right-click or Ctrl-click a docked panel tab (not an icon) and choose Close from the menu.

9 Drag the Swatches panel by the panel tab, the panel title bar, or the area behind the panel tab onto the Brushes and Symbols panel icons. Release the mouse button when you see a blue outline around the Brushes panel group.

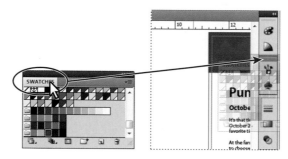

Next, you'll organize the panels to create more space in your work area.

10 Choose Essentials from the workspace switcher in the Application bar, to make sure that the panels are reset.

Note: Many panels only require that you double-click the panel tab twice to return to the full-size view of the panel.

11 Click the double arrow at the top of the dock to expand the panels. Click the Color panel tab to make sure it's selected. Double-click the panel tab to reduce the size of the panel. Double-click the tab again to minimize the panel. This can also be done when a panel is free-floating.

Tip: If you double-click one more time, the panel fully expands.

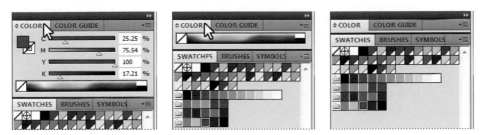

Double-click the panel tab.   Double-click again.

▶ **Tip:** To reduce and expand the panel size, instead of double-clicking you can click the small arrow icon to the left of the panel name in the panel tab.

12 Click the Appearance panel tab to expand that panel. Depending on your screen resolution, it may already be expanded.

Next, you will resize a panel group, which can make it easier to see more important panels.

13 Click the Symbols panel tab and drag up the dividing line between the Symbols panel group and the Stroke panel group, to resize the group.

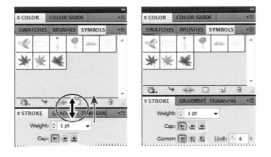

● **Note:** You may not be able to drag the divider very far, depending on your screen size, screen resolution, and number of panels expanded.

14 Choose Essentials from the workspace switcher in the Application bar.

Next, you'll arrange panel groups. Panel groups can be docked, undocked, and arranged in either collapsed or expanded modes.

15 Choose Window > Align to open the Align panel group. Drag the title bar of the Align panel group to the docked panels on the right side of the workspace. Position the pointer just below the Symbols panel icon (♣) so that a single blue line appears. Release the mouse button to add the group to the dock.

● **Note:** If you drag a group into the dock and drop it into an existing group, the two groups merge. Reset the workspace and open the panel group to reverse the merge.

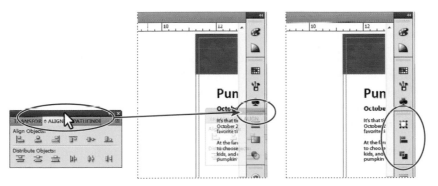

Next, you will drag a panel from one group to another in the docked panels.

▶ **Tip:** You can also reorder entire panel groups in the dock by dragging the double gray line at the top of each panel group up or down.

16 Drag the Transform panel icon (⊞) up so that the pointer is just below the Color panel icon (🎨). A blue line appears, outlining the Color panel group in blue. Release the mouse button.

Arranging the panels in groups can help you work faster.

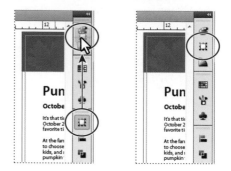

Resetting and saving your workspace

You can reset your panels and Tools panel to their default position, which you've been doing throughout this lesson. You can also save the position of panels so that you can easily access them at any time by creating a workspace. Next, you will create a workspace to access a group of commonly used panels.

▶ **Tip:** Docking panels next to each other on the right side of the workspace is a great way to conserve space. A docked panel can also be collapsed and resized to conserve even more space.

1 Choose Essentials from the workspace switcher in the Application bar.

2 Choose Window > Pathfinder. Click and drag the Pathfinder panel tab to the right side of the workspace. When the pointer approaches the left edge of the docked panels, a blue line appears. Release the mouse button to dock the panel. Click the close box (Windows) or close button (Mac OS) to close the remaining panel group, which contains the Align and Transform panels.

3 Choose Window > Workspace > Save Workspace. The Save Workspace dialog box opens. Enter the name **Navigation**, and then click OK. The workspace named Navigation is now saved with Illustrator until you remove it.

4 Return to the default panel layout by choosing Window > Workspace > Essentials. Notice that the panels return to their default positions. Choose Window > Workspace > Navigation. Toggle between the two workspaces using the Window > Workspace command and selecting the workspace you want to use. Return to the Essentials workspace before starting the next exercise.

● **Note:** To delete saved workspaces, choose Window > Workspace > Manage Workspaces. Select the workspace name and click the Delete Workspace button.

▶ **Tip:** To change a saved workspace, reset the panels as you'd like them to appear and then choose Window > Workspace > Save Workspace. In the Save Workspace dialog box, name the workspace with the original name, and click OK. A dialog box appears asking if you'd like to overwrite the existing workspace. Click Yes.

Using panel menus

Most panels have a panel menu in the upper-right corner of the panel. Clicking the panel menu button (▼≡) gives you access to additional options for the selected panel. You can also use the panel menu to change the panel display.

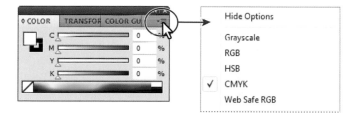

Next, you will change the display of the Symbols panel using its panel menu.

1   Click the Symbols panel icon (♣) on the right side of the workspace. You can also choose Window > Symbols to display this panel.

2   Click the panel menu (▼≡) in the upper-right corner of the Symbols panel.

3   Choose Small List View from the panel menu. This displays the symbol names, together with thumbnails. Because the options in the panel menu apply only to the active panel, only the Symbols panel view is affected.

4   Click the Symbols panel menu and choose Thumbnail View, to return the symbols to their original view. Click the Symbols panel icon (♣) to hide the panel again.

In addition to the panel menus, context-sensitive menus display commands relevant to the active tool, selection, or panel.

To display context-sensitive menus, position the pointer over the Document window or panel. Then right-click (Windows) or Ctrl-click (Mac OS) to show the menu. The context-sensitive menu shown here is displayed when you click the artboard with nothing selected.

A context-sensitive menu

Changing the view of artwork

When working in files, it's likely that you'll need to change the magnification level and navigate between artboards. The magnification level, which can range from 3.13% to 6400%, is displayed in the title bar (or document tab) next to the filename, and also in the lower-left corner of the Document window. Using any of the viewing tools and commands affects only the display of the artwork, not the actual size of the artwork.

Using the view commands

To enlarge or reduce the view of artwork using the View menu, do one of the following:

• Choose View > Zoom In to enlarge the display of the brochure.ai artwork.

▶ **Tip:** Zoom in using the keyboard shortcut Ctrl++ (Windows) or Cmd++ (Mac OS).

• Choose View > Zoom Out to reduce the view of the brochure.ai artwork.

▶ **Tip:** Zoom out using the keyboard shortcut Ctrl+– (Windows) or Cmd+–(Mac OS) .

Each time you choose a Zoom option, the view of the artwork is resized to the closest preset zoom level. The preset zoom levels appear in a menu in the lower-left corner of the Document window, identified by a down arrow next to the percentage.

You can also use the View menu to fit the artwork for the active artboard to your screen, to fit all artboards into the view area, or to view artwork at actual size.

1 Choose View > Fit Artboard In Window. A reduced view of the active artboard is displayed in the window.

● **Note:** Because the canvas (the area outside the artboards) extends to 227", you can easily lose sight of your illustration. By choosing View > Fit Artboard In Window, or using the keyboard shortcuts Ctrl+0 (Windows) or Command+0 (Mac OS), artwork is centered in the viewing area.

▶ **Tip:** You can also double-click the Hand tool in the Tools panel to fit the active artboard in the window.

2 To display artwork at actual size, choose View > Actual Size. The artwork is displayed at 100%. The actual size of your artwork determines how much of it can be viewed on-screen at 100%.

▶ **Tip:** You can also double-click the Zoom tool in the Tools panel to display artwork at 100%.

3 Choose View > Fit All In Window. You will see all artboards in the document displayed in the window. You can learn more about navigating artboards in the section "Navigating multiple artboards," later in this lesson.

4 Choose View > Fit Artboard In Window before continuing to the next section.

Using the Zoom tool

In addition to the View options, you can use the Zoom tool (🔍) to magnify and reduce the view of artwork. Use the View menu to select predefined magnification levels or to fit your artwork in the Document window.

1 Click the Zoom tool (🔍) in the Tools panel to select the tool, and then move the pointer into the Document window. Notice that a plus sign (+) appears at the center of the Zoom tool pointer.

2 Position the Zoom tool over the title text "Created with..." in the center of the artboard and click once. The artwork is displayed at a higher magnification.

3 Click two more times on the "Created with..." text. The view is increased again, and you'll notice that the area you clicked is magnified.

Next, you'll reduce the view of the artwork.

4 With the Zoom tool still selected, position the pointer over the text "Created with..." and hold down Alt (Windows) or Option (Mac OS). A minus sign (−) appears at the center of the Zoom tool pointer. Continue holding the key down for the next step.

5 With the Alt or Option key pressed, click the artwork twice to reduce the view of the artwork.

For a more controlled zoom, you can drag a marquee around a specific area of your artwork. This magnifies only the selected area.

6 Choose View > Fit Artboard In Window before proceeding.

7 With the Zoom tool still selected, drag a marquee around the Uncle Henry's Farm logo in the lower-right corner of the artboard. When you see the marquee around the area you are dragging, release the mouse button. The marqueed area is now enlarged to fit the size of the Document window.

● **Note:** The percent of the magnification is determined by the size of the marquee you draw with the Zoom tool—the smaller the marquee, the higher the level of magnification.

8 Double-click the Hand tool (✋) in the Tools panel to fit the artboard in the Document window.

The Zoom tool is used frequently during the editing process, to enlarge and reduce the view of artwork. Because of this, Illustrator allows you to select it using the keyboard at any time without first deselecting any other tool you may be using.

9 Before selecting the Zoom tool using the keyboard, select any other tool in the Tools panel and move the pointer into the Document window.

10 Now hold down Control+spacebar (Windows) or Command+spacebar (Mac OS) to use the Zoom tool. Click or drag to zoom in on any area of the artwork, and then release the keys.

● **Note:** In certain versions of Mac OS, the keyboard shortcuts for the Zoom tool open Spotlight or Finder. If you decide to use these shortcuts in Illustrator, you may want to turn off or change those keyboard shortcuts in the Mac OS System Preferences.

11 To zoom out using the keyboard, hold down Control+Alt+spacebar (Windows) or Command+Option+spacebar (Mac OS). Click the desired area to reduce the view of the artwork, and then release the keys.

12 Double-click the Hand tool in the Tools panel to fit the artboard in the Document window.

Scrolling through a document

Use the Hand tool to pan to different areas of a document. Using the Hand tool allows you to push the document around much like you would a piece of paper on your desk.

1 Select the Hand tool (✋) in the Tools panel.

2 Drag down in the Document window. As you drag, the artwork moves with the hand.

As with the Zoom tool (🔍), you can select the Hand tool with a keyboard shortcut without first deselecting the active tool.

3 Click any other tool except the Type tool (**T**) in the Tools panel and move the pointer into the Document window.

4 Hold down the spacebar to select the Hand tool from the keyboard, and then drag to bring the artwork back into the center of your view.

5 Double-click the Hand tool to fit the active artboard in the Document window.

● **Note:** The spacebar shortcut for the Hand tool does not work when the Type tool is active and your cursor is in text.

Viewing artwork

When you open a file, it is automatically displayed in preview mode, which shows how the artwork will print. When you're working with large or complex illustrations, you may want to view only the outlines, or wireframes, of objects in your artwork, so that the screen doesn't have to redraw the artwork each time you make a change. Outline mode can also be helpful when selecting objects, as you will see in Lesson 2, "Selecting and Aligning."

1 Choose View > Logo Zoom (at the bottom of the View menu) to zoom in to a preset area of the image. This custom view was saved with the document.

▶ **Tip:** To save time when working with large or complex documents, you can create your own custom views within a document so that you can quickly jump to specific areas and zoom levels. Set up the view that you want to save, and then choose View > New View. Name the view; it is saved with the document.

2 Choose View > Outline. Only the outlines of the objects are displayed. Use this view to find objects that might not be visible in preview mode.

3 Choose View > Preview to see all the attributes of the artwork.

If you prefer keyboard shortcuts, use Control+Y (Windows) or Command+Y (Mac OS) to toggle between preview and outline modes.

4 Choose View > Overprint Preview to view any lines or shapes that are set to overprint.

This view is helpful for those in the print industry who need to see how inks interact when set to overprint. You may not actually see much of a change in the logo when you change to this mode.

● **Note:** When switching between viewing modes, visual changes may not be readily apparent. Zooming in and out (View > Zoom In and View > Zoom Out) may help you see the differences more easily.

5 Choose View > Pixel Preview to see how the artwork will look when it is rasterized and viewed on-screen in a Web browser. Choose View > Pixel Preview to deselect pixel preview.

Preview view   Outline view   Overprint preview   Pixel preview

6 Choose View > Fit Artboard In Window to view the entire active artboard.

Navigating multiple artboards

Illustrator allows for multiple artboards within a single file. This is a great way to create a multi-page document so that you can have collateral pieces like a brochure, a postcard, and a business card in the same document. You can easily share content between pieces, create multi-page PDFs, and print multiple pages by creating multiple artboards.

Multiple artboards can be added when you initially create an Illustrator document by choosing File > New. You can add or remove artboards after the document is created using the Artboard tool in the Tools panel.

Next, you will learn how to efficiently navigate a document with multiple artboards.

1 Select the Selection tool (▶) in the Tools panel.

2 Choose View > Fit All In Window. Notice that there are two artboards in the document.

The artboards in a document can be arranged in any order, orientation, or artboard size–they can even overlap. Suppose that you want to create a four page brochure. You can create different artboards for every page of the brochure all with the same size and orientation. They can be arranged horizontally or vertically or in whatever way you like.

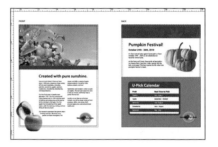

The brochure.ai document has two artboards, which are the front and back of a color brochure.

3 Press Ctrl+– (Windows) or Cmd+– (Mac OS) until you can see the logo in the upper-left corner of the canvas, which is outside the artboards.

4 Choose View > Fit Artboard In Window. This command fits the currently active artboard in the window. The active artboard is identified in the Artboard Navigation menu in the lower-left corner of the Document window.

● **Note:** Learn how to number artboards, and how to add and edit artboards in Lesson 3, "Creating and Editing Shapes," and in Lesson 4, "Transforming Objects."

5 Choose 2 from the Artboard Navigation menu. The back of the brochure appears in the Document window.

6 Choose View > Zoom Out. Notice that zooming occurs on the currently active artboard.

Notice the arrows to the right and left of the Artboard Navigation menu. You can use these to navigate to the first (⏮), previous (◀), next (▶), and last (⏭) artboards.

7 Click the Previous navigation button to view the previous artboard (artboard #1) in the Document window.

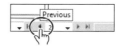

● **Note:** Since there are only 2 artboards in this document, you could have also clicked the First button (⏮) in this step.

8 Choose View > Fit Artboard In Window to make sure that the first artboard (artboard #1) is fit in the Document window.

Another method for navigating multiple artboards is to use the Artboards panel. Next you will open the Artboards panel and navigate the document.

9 Choose Essentials from the workspace switcher in the Application bar to reset the Essentials workspace.

10 Choose Window > Artboards to expand the Artboards panel on the right side of the workspace.

The Artboards panel lists all artboards in the document. This panel allows you to navigate between artboards, rename artboards, add or delete artboards, edit artboard settings, and more.

Next, you will focus on navigating the document using this panel.

11 Double-click the name "Artboard 2" in the Artboards panel. This fits artboard 2 in the Document window.

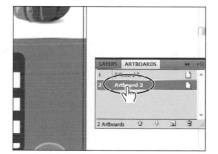

● **Note:** Double-clicking the number to the left of the artboard name in the Artboards panel does not allow you to navigate between artboards, it is there to indicate order. Double-clicking the page icon to the right of the artboard name in the panel allows you to edit artboard options.

12 Choose View > Zoom In to zoom in on the second artboard.

13 Double-click the name "Artboard 1" in the Artboards panel to show the first artboard in the Document window.

Notice that when you double-click an artboard name, that artboard is fit in the Document window.

14 Click the Artboards panel icon (▣) in the dock to collapse the Artboards panel.

Using the Navigator panel

The Navigator panel is another way to navigate a document with a single artboard or multiple artboards. This is useful when you need to see all artboards in the document in one window and edit content in any of those artboards in a zoomed in view.

1   Choose Window > Navigator to open the Navigator panel. It is free-floating in the workspace.

● **Note:** Dragging the slider in the Navigator panel tends to jump the magnification to set values. To zoom more precisely, type in a value in the lower-left corner of the Navigator panel.

2   In the Navigator panel, drag the slider to the left to approximately 50%, to decrease the level of magnification. As you drag the slider, the red box in the Navigator panel, called the proxy preview area, becomes larger, indicating the area of the document that is being shown.

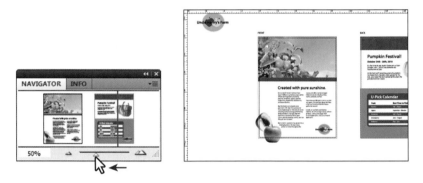

3   Click the larger mountain icon (⟁) in the lower-right corner of the Navigator panel several times to zoom into the brochure until the percentage in the Navigator panel shows approximately 150%.

4   Position the pointer inside the proxy preview area (the red box) of the Navigator panel. The pointer becomes a hand (🖐).

5   Drag the hand in the proxy preview area of the Navigator panel to pan to different parts of the artwork. Drag the proxy preview area over the logo in the lower-right corner of the brochure cover.

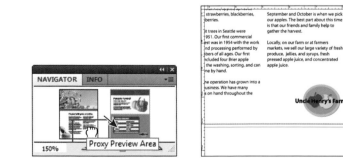

6 In the Navigator panel, move the pointer outside of the proxy preview area and click. This moves the box and displays a different area of the artwork in the Document window.

7 With the pointer (hand) still positioned in the Navigator panel, hold down the Control (Windows) or Command (Mac OS) key. When the hand changes to a magnifier, drag a marquee over an area of the artwork. The smaller the marquee you draw, the higher the magnification level in the Document window.

▶ **Tip:** Choosing Panel Options from the Navigator panel menu allows you to customize the Navigator panel. For example, you can change the color of the view box.

8 Choose View > Fit Artboard In Window.

9 Deselect View Artboard Contents Only in the Navigator panel menu (▼≡). So that you see any artwork that is in the canvas as well. Notice the logo on the canvas.

● **Note:** You may need to adjust the slider in the Navigator panel to see the logo in the proxy area.

● **Note:** The percentage and proxy preview area in your Navigator panel may appear differently. That's okay.

10 Close the Navigator panel group by clicking the close box (Windows) or close button (Mac OS) on the title bar.

Understanding rulers

Rulers can help you accurately place and measure objects in your document and are displayed in each document by default. Horizontal and vertical rulers appear at the top and left sides of each Document window. The place where 0 appears on each ruler is called the ruler origin.

Next, you will explore the rulers by turning them on and off and noticing where the ruler origin is located on each artboard.

1 Choose View > Rulers > Hide Rulers to hide the rulers.

2 Choose View > Rulers > Show Rulers to show them again.

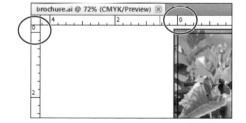

Notice that the 0 for the horizontal ruler is aligned with the left edge of the first artboard and the 0 for the vertical ruler (on the left side of the Document window) is aligned with the top edge of the artboard.

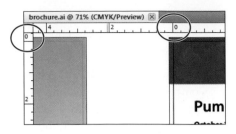

3 Navigate to the second artboard by choosing 2 from the Artboard Navigation menu.

Notice that the rulers start at 0 in the upper-left corner in this second artboard as well. Each artboard has it's own ruler system, with the zeros for horizontal and vertical rulers starting in the upper-left corner of each artboard. You will learn about changing the zero point and other ruler options in Chapter 4, "Transforming Objects."

4 Navigate back to the first artboard by choosing 1 from the Artboard Navigation menu.

Arranging multiple documents

When you open more than one Illustrator file, the Document windows are tabbed. You can arrange the open documents in other ways, such as side by side, so that you can easily compare or drag items from one document to another. You can also use the Arrange Documents window to quickly display your open documents in a variety of configurations.

Next, you will open several documents.

1 Choose File > Open and, in the Lesson01 folder, Shift-click to select the L1start_2.ai and L1start_3.ai files that are located in the Lessons folder on your hard disk. Click Open to open both files at once.

You should now have three Illustrator files open: brochure.ai, L1start_2.ai, and L1start_3.ai. Each file has its own tab at the top of the Document window. These documents are considered a group of Document windows. You can create document groups to loosely associate files while they are open.

2 Click the brochure.ai document tab to show the brochure.ai Document window.

3 Click and drag the brochure.ai document tab to the right, so that it is between the L1start_2.ai and L1start_3.ai document tabs.

● **Note:** Your tabs may be in a slightly different order. That's okay. Be careful to drag directly to the right. Otherwise, you could undock the Document window and create a new group. If that happens, choose Window > Arrange > Consolidate All Windows.

Dragging the document tabs allows you to change the order of the documents. This can be very useful if you use the document shortcuts to navigate to the next or previous document:

- Ctrl+F6 (next document), Ctrl+Shift+F6 (previous document) (Windows)
- Cmd+` (next document), Cmd+Shift+` (previous document) (Mac OS)

4 Drag the document tabs in the following order, from left to right: brochure.ai, L1start_2.ai, L1start_3.ai.

These three documents are versions of marketing pieces. To see all of them at one time, you can arrange the Document windows by cascading the windows or tiling them. Cascading allows you to cascade (stack) different document groups and is discussed further in the next section. Tiling shows multiple Document windows at one time, in various arrangements.

Next, you will tile the open documents so that you can see them all at one time.

5 On the Mac OS (Windows users can skip to the next step), choose Window > Application Frame.

Mac OS users can use the application frame to group all the workspace elements in a single, integrated window, similar to working in Windows. If you move or resize the application frame, the elements respond to each other so that they don't overlap.

6 Choose Window > Arrange > Tile.

This shows all three Document windows arranged in a pattern.

7 Click in each of the Document windows to activate the documents. Choose View > Fit Artboard In Window for each of the documents. Also, make sure that artboard 1 is showing for each document in the Document window.

Note: Your documents may be tiled in a different order. That's okay.

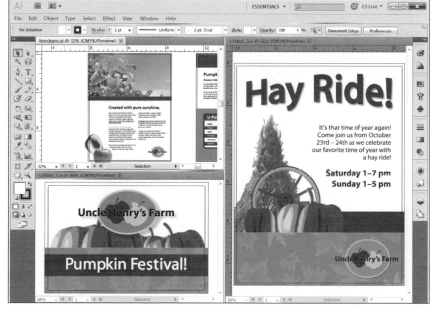

The documents tiled

With documents tiled, you can drag the dividing lines between each of the Document windows to reveal more or less of a particular document. You can also drag objects between documents to copy them from one document to another.

8 Click in the L1start_3.ai Document window. With the Selection tool, drag the wagon wheel image (behind the pumpkins on the artboard), to the L1start_2.ai Document window and release the mouse button. This copies the image from L1start_3.ai to L1start_2.ai.

● **Note:** After dragging the content in step 8, notice that the document tab for L1start_2.ai now has an asterisk to the right of the file name. This indicates that the file needs to be saved.

● **Note:** When you drag content between tiled documents, a plus sign appears next to the pointer (Windows only), as shown in the figure below.

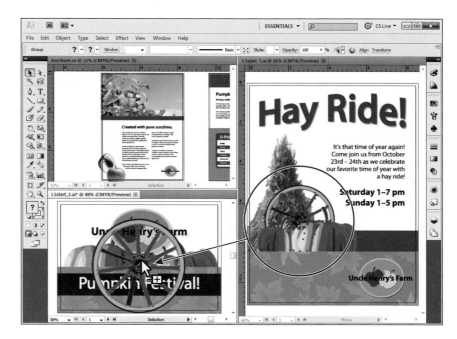

To change the arrangement of the tiled windows, it's possible to drag document tabs to new positions. However, it's easier to use the Arrange Documents window to quickly arrange open documents in a variety of configurations.

9 Click the Arrange Documents button (■ ▾) in the Application bar to display the Arrange Documents window. Click the Tile All Vertically button (▥) to tile the documents vertically.

● **Note:** On the Mac OS, the menu bar is above the Application bar. Also, depending on the resolution of your screen, the Windows menus may appear in the Application bar.

10 Click the 2-Up vertical button (▦) in the Arrange Documents window.

Notice that two of the documents appear as tabs in one of the tiled areas.

11 Click to select the L1start_2.ai tab if it is not already selected. Then click the "x" on the L1start_2.ai document tab to close the document. If a dialog box appears asking you to save the document, click No (Windows) or Don't Save (Mac OS).

12 Click the Arrange Documents button (▦ ▾) in the Application bar and click the Consolidate All button (▦) in the Arrange Documents window. This returns the two documents to tabs in the same group. Keep the brochure.ai and L1start_3.ai documents open.

Tip: You can also choose Window > Arrange > Consolidate All Windows to return the two documents to tabs in the same group.

Document groups

By default, open documents in Illustrator are arranged as tabs in a single group of windows. You can create multiple groups of files for easier navigation and temporarily associate files together. This can be helpful if you are working on a large project that requires you to create and edit multiple pieces. Grouping documents lets you float the groups so that they are separate from the application window (Windows) or screen (Mac OS).

Next, you will create and work with two groups of files.

1 Click to select the L1start_3.ai file tab, if not already selected.

2 Choose Window > Arrange > Float All In Windows. This creates separate groups for all open documents. By default, the groups are cascaded with one on top of the other.

Document windows floating in separate groups

3 Click the title bar for brochure.ai and notice that L1start_3.ai is not visible. L1start_3.ai is now behind brochure.ai.

● **Note:** If you cannot select the brochure.ai tab, choose Window > brochure.ai at the bottom of the Window menu.

4 Choose File > Open and, in the Lesson01 folder, select the L1start_2.ai file, which is located in the Lessons folder on your hard disk. Click Open. Notice that the newly opened document is added as a document tab to the group that contains brochure.ai.

● **Note:** When you open a document or create a new document, that document is added to the currently selected group.

5 Choose Window > Arrange > Cascade to reveal both groups.

6 Click the Minimize button in the upper-right corner (Windows) or the upper-left corner (Mac OS) of the L1start_3.ai group. Notice that in Windows, the group minimizes to the lower-left corner of the application window by default. In the Mac OS, the window minimizes to the operating system Dock.

7 Click the Restore button or the document tab to show the minimized group (Windows), or click the document thumbnail in the Mac OS Dock to show the minimized group (Mac OS).

8 Click the Close box (Windows) or Close button (Mac OS) to close the L1start_3.ai group.

9 Drag the document tab for L1start_2.ai down until the document appears to float freely. This is another way to create a floating group of documents.

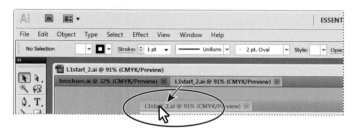

10 Close the L1start_2.ai file and leave brochure.ai open.

11 On Windows (Mac OS users can skip to the next step), choose Window > Arrange > Consolidate All Windows.

12 On the Mac OS, choose Window > Application Frame to deselect the Application frame. Then click the green button in the upper-left corner of the Document window so that the Document window fits as well as possible.

13 Choose View > Fit Artboard In Window to fit the first artboard of brochure.ai in the Document window.

Finding resources for using Illustrator

For complete and up-to-date information about using Illustrator panels, tools, and other application features, visit the Adobe website. By choosing Help > Illustrator Help, you'll be connected to the Adobe Community Help website, where you can search Illustrator Help and support documents, as well as other websites relevant to Illustrator users. You can also narrow your search results to view only Adobe help and support documents.

If you plan to work in Illustrator when you're not connected to the Internet, download the most current PDF version of Illustrator Help from www.adobe.com/support/documentation.

For additional resources, such as tips and techniques and the latest product information, check out the Adobe Community Help page at community.adobe.com/help/main.

● **Note:** If Illustrator detects that you are not connected to the Internet when you start the application, choosing Help > Illustrator Help opens the Help HTML pages installed with Illustrator. For more up-to-date information, view the Help files online or download the current PDF for reference.

Searching for a topic in the Search For Help box

You can use the Search For Help box on the right side of the Application bar to search for Help topics and other online content. If you are connected to the Internet, you can access all content on the Community Help website. If you search for Help without an active Internet connection, search results are limited to Help content that is included with your installed version of Illustrator.

1   Type **artboards** in the Search For Help box in the Application bar and press Enter or Return.

    If you are connected to the internet, the Adobe Community Help window is opened. From there, you can explore the different help topics available.

2   Close the window and return to Illustrator.

3   Choose File > Close to close the open file.

Checking for updates

Adobe periodically provides updates to software. You can easily obtain these updates through Adobe Updater, as long as you have an active Internet connection.

1 In Illustrator, choose Help > Updates. The Adobe Updater automatically checks for updates available for your Adobe software.

2 In the Adobe Application Manager dialog box, select the updates you want to install, and then click Download And Install Updates to install them.

3 When you are finished investigating updates, close the window and return to Illustrator.

● **Note:** To set your preferences for future updates, click Preferences. Select which applications to check for updates, and whether to notify you of those updates. Click Done to accept the new settings.

Exploring on your own

You will open a sample file from Adobe Illustrator CS5 to investigate and use some of the navigational and organization features learned in this lesson.

1 Open the file named L1start_2.ai in the Lesson01 folder.

● **Note:** A missing profile dialog box may appear. Click OK to continue.

2 Perform the following on this artwork:

- Practice zooming in and out. Notice that at the smaller zoom levels some text may be "greeked," appearing as though it is a solid gray bar. As you zoom in closer, the text can be viewed more accurately.

- Save zoomed-in views using View > New View for different areas such as; the front of the postcard (artboard 1), and the back of postcard (artboard 2).

- Create a zoomed-in view of the pumpkin on artboard 2 in Outline View.

- Enlarge the Navigator panel and use it to scroll around the artboards and to zoom in and out.

- Navigate between artboards using the Artboard Navigation menu and buttons in the lower-left corner of the Document window.

- Navigate between the artboards using the Artboards panel.

- Create a Saved workspace (Window > Workspace > Save Workspace) that shows only the Tools panel, Control panel and Layers panel.

3 Choose File > Close without saving.

Review questions

1 Describe two ways to change the view of a document.

2 How do you select tools in Illustrator?

3 Describe three ways to navigate between artboards in Illustrator.

4 How do you save panel locations and visibility preferences?

5 Describe how arranging Document windows can be helpful.

Review answers

1 You can choose commands from the View menu to zoom in or out of a document, or fit it to your screen; you can also use the Zoom tool in the Tools panel, and click or drag over a document to enlarge or reduce the view. In addition, you can use keyboard shortcuts to magnify or reduce the display of artwork. You can also use the Navigator panel to scroll artwork or change its magnification without using the Document window.

2 To select a tool, you can either click the tool in the Tools panel, or press the keyboard shortcut for that tool. For example, you can press V to select the Selection tool from the keyboard. Selected tools remain active until you click a different tool.

3 You can choose the artboard number from the Artboard Navigation menu at the lower-left of the Document window, you can use the Artboard Navigation arrows in the lower-left of the Document window to go to the first, previous, next, and last artboards, you can double-click the name of an artboard in the Artboards panel to navigate to an artboard, or you can use the Navigator panel to drag the proxy preview area to navigate between artboards.

4 Choose Window > Workspace > Save Workspace to create custom work areas and make it easier to find the controls that you need.

5 Arranging Document windows allows you to tile windows or cascade document groups. This can be useful if you are working on multiple Illustrator files and you need to compare or share content between them.

2 SELECTING AND ALIGNING

Lesson overview

In this lesson, you'll learn how to do the following:

- Differentiate between the various selection tools and employ different selection techniques.

- Recognize smart guides.

- Clone items with the Selection tool.

- Hide and lock items for organizational purposes.

- Save selections for future use.

- Group and ungroup items.

- Work in isolation mode.

- Use tools and commands to align shapes and points to each other and the artboard.

- Arrange content.

- Select behind content.

 This lesson takes approximately an hour to complete. If needed, remove the previous lesson folder from your hard disk and copy the Lesson02 folder onto it.

Selecting content in Adobe® Illustrator® CS5 is one of the more important things you'll do. In this lesson, you learn how to locate and select objects using the selection tools; protect other objects by grouping, hiding and locking them; and align objects to each other and the artboard.

Getting started

When changing colors or size and adding effects or attributes, you must first select the object to which you are applying the changes. In this lesson, you will learn the fundamentals of using the selection tools. More advanced selection techniques using layers are discussed in Lesson 8, "Working with Layers."

1 To ensure that the tools and panels function as described in this lesson, delete or deactivate (by renaming) the Adobe Illustrator CS5 preferences file. See "Restoring default preferences" on page 3.

2 Start Adobe Illustrator CS5.

● **Note:** If you have not already done so, copy the resource files for this lesson onto your hard disk, from the Lesson02 folder on the Adobe Illustrator CS5 Classroom in a Book CD. See "Copying the Classroom in a Book files" on page 2.

3 Choose File > Open, and open the L2start_1.ai file in the Lesson02 folder, located in the Lessons folder on your hard disk. Choose View > Fit Artboard In Window.

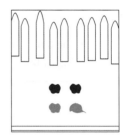

4 Choose Window > Workspace > Essentials.

Selecting objects

Whether you are starting artwork from scratch or editing existing artwork in Illustrator, you will need to become familiar with selecting objects. There are many methods for selecting objects in Illustrator. In this section, you will explore the main selection tools, including the Selection and Direct Selection tools.

Using the Selection tool

The Selection tool in the Tools panel lets you select entire objects.

1 Select the Selection tool ($\blacktriangleright$) in the Tools panel. Position the pointer over different shapes without clicking. The icon that appears as you pass over objects ($\blacktriangleright_\blacksquare$) indicates that there is an object that can be selected under the pointer. When you hover over an object, it is outlined in blue.

2 Select the Zoom tool ($\mathcal{Q}$) in the Tools panel and drag a marquee around the four colored shapes (the apples and hat) in the center of the page to zoom in.

3 Select the Selection tool, then hover the pointer over the edge of the red apple on the left. A word such as "path" or "anchor" may appear, because smart guides are turned on by default. Smart guides are snap-to guides that help you align, edit, and transform objects or artboards. Smart guides are discussed in more detail in Lesson 3, "Creating and Editing Shapes."

4 Click the left red apple on its edge or anywhere in its center to select it. A bounding box with eight handles appears.

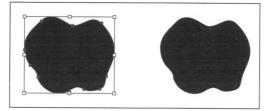

The bounding box is used when making changes to objects, such as resizing or rotating them. The bounding box also indicates that an item is selected and ready to be modified. The color of the bounding box indicates which layer the object is on. Layers are discussed more in Lesson 8, "Working with Layers."

5 Using the Selection tool, click the red apple on the right. Notice that the left red apple is now deselected and only the right apple is selected.

● **Note:** To select an item without a fill, you must click the stroke (border).

6 Add the left red apple to the selection by holding down the Shift key and clicking it. Both red apples are now selected.

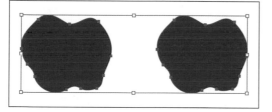

▶ **Tip:** To select all objects, choose Select > All. To select all objects in a single artboard, choose Select > All In Active Artboard. To learn more about artboards, see Lesson 3, "Creating and Editing Shapes."

7 Reposition the apples anywhere in the document by clicking the center of either selected apple and dragging. Because both apples are selected, they move together.

As you drag, you may notice the green lines that appear. These are called alignment guides and are visible because smart guides are turned on (View > Smart Guides). As you drag, the objects are aligned to other objects on the artboard. Also notice the gray box, or measurement label, that shows the object's distance from its original position. Measurement labels also appear because smart guides are turned on.

▶ **Tip:** Whenever you don't want to use smart guides deselect them by choosing View > Smart Guides.

8 Deselect the apples by clicking the artboard where there are no objects, or by choosing Select > Deselect.

9 Revert to the last saved version of the document by pressing the F12 key or choosing File > Revert. In the Revert dialog box, click Revert.

Using the Direct Selection tool

The Direct Selection tool selects points or path segments within an object, so that it can be reshaped. Next, you will select anchor points and path segments using the Direct Selection tool.

1 Choose View > Fit Artboard In Window.

2 Select the Direct Selection tool (🔖) in the Tools panel. Without clicking, position the pointer over the top of one of the fence pickets you see above the red apples.

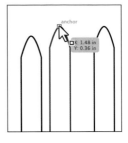

When the Direct Selection tool is over an anchor point of a path or object, a label, such as the word "anchor" or "path," appears. This label is showing because smart guides are selected.

3 Click the top point of the same picket. Note that only the point you selected is solid, indicating that it is selected, while the other points in the picket are hollow and not selected.

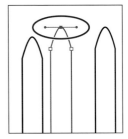

Notice the blue direction lines extending from the anchor point. At the end of the direction lines are direction points. The angle and length of the direction lines determine the shape and size of the curved segments. Moving the direction points reshapes the curves.

4 With the Direct Selection tool still selected, drag the individual point down, to edit the shape of the object. Try clicking another point, and notice that the previous point is deselected.

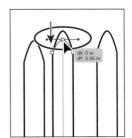

● **Note:** The gray measurement label that appears as you drag the anchor point has the values dX and dY. dX indicates the distance the pointer has moved along the x axis (horizontal), and dY indicates the distance the pointer has moved along the y axis (vertical).

▶ **Tip:** Using the Shift key, you can select multiple points to move them together.

5 Revert to the last saved version by choosing File > Revert. In the Revert dialog box, click Revert.

Selection and anchor point preferences

You can change selection preferences and how anchor points appear in the Illustrator Preferences dialog box.

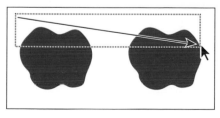

Choose Edit > Preferences > Selection & Anchor Display (Windows) or Illustrator > Preferences > Selection & Anchor Display (Mac OS). You can change the size of anchor points (called anchors in the dialog box) or the display of the direction lines (called handles in the dialog box).

You can also turn off the highlighting of anchor points as the pointer hovers over them. As you move the pointer over anchor points, they are highlighted. Highlighting anchor points makes it easier to determine which point you are about to select. You will learn more about anchor points and anchor point handles in Lesson 5, "Drawing with the Pen and Pencil Tools."

Creating selections with a marquee

Some selections may be easier to make by creating a marquee around the objects that you want to select.

1   Choose View > Fit Artboard In Window.

2   In the same file, switch to the Selection tool (▶). Instead of Shift-clicking to select multiple objects, position the pointer above and to the left of the upper left red apple and then drag downward and to the right to create a marquee that overlaps just the tops of the apples.

► **Tip:** When dragging with the Selection tool, you only need to encompass a small part of an object to include it in the selection

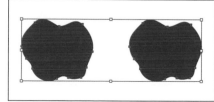

3   Choose Select > Deselect or click where there are no objects.

Now you will use the Direct Selection tool (⇱) to select multiple points in objects.

4 Click outside the top of one of the fence pickets above the red apples and drag across to select the tops of two pickets in the top row.

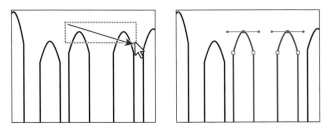

Dragging across the top points with the Direct Selection tool selects only those points.

Only the top points become selected. Click one of the selected anchor points and drag to see how the anchor points reposition together. Use this method when selecting points so that you don't have to click exactly on the anchor point that you want to edit.

● **Note:** Selecting points using this method might take some practice. You'll need to drag across only the points you want selected, otherwise, more will be selected. You can always click away from the objects to deselect them, and then try again.

5 Choose Select > Deselect.

6 With the Direct Selection tool, try dragging across the tops of the red apples. Notice how multiple points in each apple are selected.

7 Choose Select > Deselect.

Creating selections with the Magic Wand tool

You can use the Magic Wand tool to select all objects in a document that have the same or similar color or pattern fill attributes.

▶ **Tip:** You can customize the Magic Wand tool to select objects based on stroke weight, stroke color, opacity, or blending mode by double-clicking the Magic Wand tool in the Tools panel. You can also change the tolerances used to identify similar objects.

1 Select the Magic Wand tool (✴) in the Tools panel. Click the orange apple and notice that the orange hat is selected as well. No bounding box (a box surrounding the two shapes) appears because the Magic Wand tool is still selected.

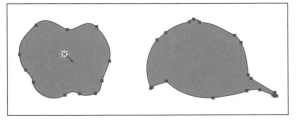

When selecting with the Magic Wand tool, objects with the same color fill are selected as well.

2 Click one of the red apples with the Magic Wand tool. Notice that both red apples are selected and that the orange apple and hat are deselected.

3 Holding down the Shift key, use the Magic Wand tool to click the orange hat. This adds the orange hat and orange apple to the selection, because they have the same fill color (orange). With the Magic Wand tool still selected, hold down the Alt (Windows) or Option (Mac OS) key, and then click the orange hat to deselect the orange objects. Release the key.

4 Choose Select > Deselect or click where there are no objects.

Selecting similar objects

You can also select objects based on fill color, stroke color, stroke weight, and more. The fill is a color applied to the interior area of an object, the stroke is its outline (border), and the stroke weight is the size of the stroke.

Next, you will select several objects with the same stroke applied.

1 With the Selection tool (▶), click to select one of the white fence picket objects at the top of the artboard.

2 Click the arrow to the right of the Select Similar Objects button (![icon]) in the Control panel to show a menu. Choose Fill Color to select all objects on any artboard with the same fill color (white).

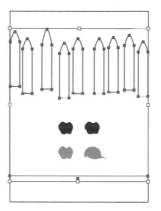

Notice that all of the pickets at the top are selected, in addition to the white rectangle at the bottom of the artboard.

● **Note:** The menu item Select > Same performs the same function as the Select Similar Objects button that appears in the Control panel.

3 Choose Select > Deselect.

4 Select one of the white picket shapes at the top of the artboard again, and then choose Select > Same > Stroke Weight.

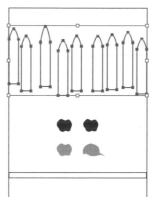

All of the fence picket shapes have a 1 pt stroke, so all strokes that are 1 pt are now selected.

5 With the previous selection still active, choose Select > Save Selection. Name the selection **Fence**, and click OK, so that you'll be able to choose this selection at a later time.

6 Choose Select > Deselect to deselect the objects.

▶ **Tip:** It is helpful to name selections according to use or function. In step 5, if you name the selection 1 pt stroke, for instance, the name may be misleading if you later change the stroke weight of the object.

Aligning objects

Multiple objects can be aligned or distributed relative to each other, the artboard, or a key object. In this section, you will explore the options for aligning objects and aligning points.

Align objects to each other

Note: The Align options may not appear in the Control panel. If you don't see the Align options, click the word Align in the Control panel to open the Align panel. The number of options displayed in the Control panel, depends on your screen resolution.

1 Choose Select > Fence to re-select the fence pickets.

2 Choose Align to Selection from the Align To button (⊡) in the Control panel. This ensures that the selected objects are aligned to each other.

3 Click the Vertical Align Bottom button (⬛) in the Control panel.

   Notice that the bottom edges of all the fence picket objects moves to align with the lowest picket.

● **Note:** If Align options do not appear in the Control panel, it may be because only one object is selected. You can also open the Align panel by choosing Window > Align.

4 Choose Edit > Undo Align to return the objects to their original positions. Leave the objects selected for the next section.

Aligning to a key object

A key object is an object that you want other objects to align to. You specify a key object by selecting all the objects you want to align, including the key object, and then clicking the key object again. When selected, the key object has a thick blue outline, and the Align To Key Object icon (⊡) appears in the Control panel and the Align panel.

▶ **Tip:** In the Align panel, you can also choose Align To Key Object from the Align To option. The object that is in front becomes the key object.

1 With the fence picket objects still selected, click the left-most picket with the Selection tool (▶).

   The thick blue outline indicates that it is the key object, which other objects will align to.

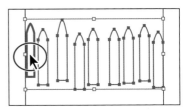

2 In the Align options in the Control panel or the Align panel, click the Vertical Align Bottom button (⬛). Notice that all of the pickets move to align to the bottom edge of the key object.

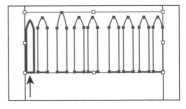

3 Choose Select > Deselect.

Aligning points

Next, you'll align two points to each other using the Align panel.

1   With the Direct Selection tool (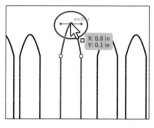), click the top-most point of the picket that is taller than the rest, and then Shift-click to select the top-most point of any other picket. In the figure, the picket to the right of the tallest picket is selected.

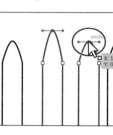 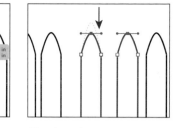

Select the first point.   Select the second point.   Align the points.

You select the points in a specific order because the last selected anchor point is the key anchor. Other points align to this point.

2   Click the Vertical Align Top button (▉) in the Control panel. The first point selected aligns to the second point selected.

● **Note:** If you don't see the Align options, click the word Align in the Control panel to show the Align panel.

3   Choose Select > Deselect.

Distributing objects

Distributing objects using the Align panel enables you to select multiple objects and distribute the spacing between those objects equally. Next, you will make the spacing between the fence pickets even, using a distribution method.

1   Select the Selection tool (▶) in the Tools panel. Choose Select > Fence to reselect all of the fence pickets.

2   Click the Horizontal Distribute Center button (▮▮) in the Control panel.

This moves all of the fence objects so that the spacing between the *center* of each of them is equal.

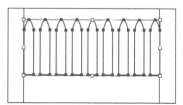

3   Choose Select > Deselect.

4   With the Selection tool (▶) selected, hold down the Shift key and drag the right-most fence picket slightly to the right, to keep the picket vertically aligned with the other pickets.

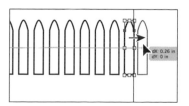

● **Note:** Using the Horizontal or Vertical Distribute Center buttons distributes the spacing equally between the *centers* of the objects. If the selected objects are not the same size, unexpected results may occur.

5 Choose Select > Fence to select all of the fence pickets again, and then click the Horizontal Distribute Center button (⬍⬍) again. Notice that, with the right-most picket repositioned, the objects move to redistribute the spacing between the centers of the objects.

● **Note:** When distributing objects horizontally using the Align panel, make sure that the left-most and right-most objects are where you want them, and then distribute the objects between them. For vertical distribution, position the top-most and bottom-most objects, and then distribute the objects between them.

6 Choose Select > Deselect.

Aligning to the artboard

You can also align content to the artboard rather than to other objects or a key object. With this method, each individual object is aligned separately to the artboard. Next you'll align the leaves shape to the center of the artboard.

1 Click the Next artboard button (▶) in the lower-left corner of the Document window to navigate to the next artboard in the document, which contains the tree.

2 With the Selection tool selected, click to select the green tree leaves shape.

● **Note:** The Align options may not appear in the Control panel, but are indicated by the word Align. The number of options displayed in the Control panel, depends on your screen resolution.

3 Click the Align To Selection button (▦) and choose Align To Artboard in the menu that appears. Setting this option ensures that all future alignments are aligned to the artboard. Click the Horizontal Align Center (⬓) button to align the group to the horizontal center of the artboard.

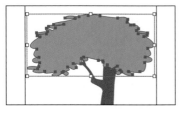

● **Note:** When you want to align all objects to the center of the artboard for a poster, for example, grouping the objects is an important step. Grouping moves the objects together as one object relative to the artboard. If this isn't done, centering everything horizontally moves all the objects to the center, independent of each other.

4 With the Selection tool, click to select the brown tree trunk shape.

5 Click the Horizontal Align Center (⬓) button and then click the Vertical Align Bottom (▮▮) button to align the bottom of the tree trunk to the bottom of the artboard.

Leave the tree trunk selected for the next step.

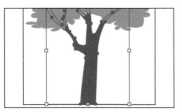

About align options

The Align panel has a lot of features that are very useful in Illustrator. Not only can you align objects, but you can also distribute objects as well. Select the objects to align or distribute, then, in the Align panel, do any of the following:

- To align or distribute relative to the bounding box of all selected objects, click the button for the type of alignment or distribution you want.

- To align or distribute relative to one of the selected objects (a key object), click that object again (you don't need to hold down Shift as you click this time). Then click the button for the type of alignment or distribution you want.

Note: *To stop aligning and distributing relative to an object, click again on the object to remove the blue outline, or choose Cancel Key Object from the Align panel menu.*

- To align relative to the active artboard, click the Align To Artboard button (▥) or click the Align menu (arrow to the right of the Align To Artboard button) and choose Align To Artboard. Then click the button for the type of alignment you want.

- To align relative to an anchor point, select the Direct-Selection tool, hold down Shift, and select the anchor points you want to align or distribute. The last anchor point you select becomes the key anchor point.

—From Illustrator Help

Working with groups

You can combine objects in a group so that the objects are treated as a single unit. This way, you can move or transform a number of objects without affecting their attributes or relative positions.

Group items

Next, you will select multiple objects and create a group from them.

1 With the Selection tool (▸), shift-click the green tree leaves to select them along with the tree trunk you had selected previously.

2 Choose Object > Group, and then choose Select > Deselect.

3 With the Selection tool, click the brown tree trunk. Because the trunk is grouped with the leaves, both are now selected. Notice that the word Group appears on the left side of the Control panel.

▶ **Tip:** To select the objects in a group separately, select the group, then choose Object > Ungroup. This ungroups them permanently.

4 Choose Select > Deselect.

Working in isolation mode

Isolation mode isolates groups or sublayers so that you can easily select and edit specific objects or parts of objects without having to ungroup the objects. When you use isolation mode, you don't need to pay attention to what layer an object is on, nor do you need to manually lock or hide the objects you don't want affected by your edits. All objects outside of the isolated group are locked so that they aren't affected by the edits you make. An isolated object appears in full color, while the rest of the artwork appears dimmed, letting you know which objects you can edit.

▶ **Tip:** To enter isolation mode, you can also select a group with the Selection tool and then click the Isolate Selected Object button (⊞) in the Control panel.

1 With the Selection tool (▶), click either the green tree leaves or the brown tree trunk to select the group.

2 Double-click the tree trunk to enter isolation mode.

3 Choose View > Fit All In Window and notice that the rest of the content in the document appears dimmed (you can't select it).

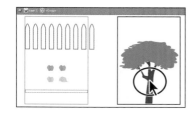

At the top of the Document window, a gray arrow appears with the words Layer 1 and <Group>. This indicates that you have isolated a group of objects that is on layer 1. You will learn more about layers in Lesson 8, "Working with Layers."

4 Hold down the Shift key and drag the brown tree trunk slightly to the right. The Shift key constrains its movement to the horizontal.

When you enter isolation mode, groups are temporarily ungrouped. This enables you to edit objects in the group without having to ungroup.

▶ **Tip:** To exit isolation mode, you can also click the gray arrow in the upper-left corner of the Document window until the document is no longer in isolation mode. Or, click the Exit Isolation Mode button (⊞) in the Control panel.

5 Double-click outside of the objects to exit isolation mode.

6 Click to select the green leaves shape. Notice that it is once again grouped with the tree trunk and you can now select other objects.

7 Choose Select > Deselect and then choose View > Fit Artboard In Window.

Adding to a group

Groups can also be nested—they can be grouped within other objects or grouped to form larger groups. In this section, you will explore how to add objects to an existing group.

1 Click the Previous Artboard button (◀) in the lower-left corner of the Document window to navigate to the previous artboard in the document, which contains the fence objects.

2 With the Selection tool (▶), drag a marquee across the pickets at the top of the artboard to select them all.

3 Choose Object > Group.

4 With Align To Artboard chosen from the Align To Selection button (▦) menu, click the Horizontal Align Center (≜) button to align the group to the horizontal center of the artboard. Choose Select > Deselect.

5 With the Selection tool, holding down the Shift key, drag the white rectangle at the bottom of the artboard on top of the group of pickets. You needn't pay attention to the alignment.

6 With the Selection tool, Shift-click a picket object to select the grouped objects as well.

7 Choose Object > Group.

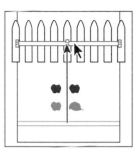

You have created a nested group—a group within a group. Nesting is a common technique used when designing artwork. It's a great way to keep associated content together.

8 Choose Select > Deselect.

9 With the Selection tool, click one of the grouped objects. All objects in the group become selected.

10 Click a blank area on the artboard to deselect the objects.

11 Hold down on the Direct Selection tool (▷) in the Tools panel, and drag to the right to access the Group Selection tool (▷⁺). The Group Selection tool adds the object's parent group(s) to the current selection.

12 Click the left-most fence picket once to select the object. Click again to select the object's parent group (the group of pickets). The Group Selection tool adds each group to the selection in the order in which it was grouped.

▶ **Tip:** If you were to click a third time, the white rectangle would also become selected.

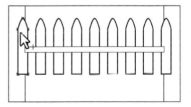

Click once to select a picket.

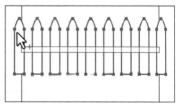

Click twice to select the parent group.

13 Choose Select > Deselect.

14 With the Selection tool, click any object to select the group of objects. Choose Object > Ungroup to ungroup the objects. Choose Select > Deselect.

15 Click to select the fence pickets; notice they are still grouped.

16 Choose Select > Deselect.

● **Note:** To ungroup all of the selected objects, even the fence pickets, choose Object > Ungroup twice.

Object arrangement

As you create objects, Illustrator stacks them in order on the artboards, beginning with the first object created. The order in which objects are stacked (called stack order) determines how they display when they overlap. You can change the stacking order of objects in your artwork at any time using either the Layers panel or Object > Arrange commands.

Arrange objects

Next, you will work with the Arrange commands to change how objects are stacked.

1   With the Selection tool (◄) selected, position the pointer over a red apple and click to select it.

2   Choose View > Fit All In Window to see both artboards in the document.

3   Drag the selected red apple on top of the leaves in the tree. Release the mouse and notice that the red apple goes behind the tree, but it is still selected.

It is behind the tree because it was probably created before the tree, which means it is lower in the stack of shapes.

4   With the apple still selected, choose Object > Arrange > Bring to Front. This brings the apple to the front of the stack, making it the top-most object.

About arranging objects

As you create more complex artwork, you may need to send content behind or bring it front of other content, by doing any of the following:

•   To move an object to the top or bottom position in its group or layer, select the object you want to move and choose Object > Arrange > Bring To Front or Object > Arrange > Send To Back.

•   To move an object by one object to the front or one object to the back of a stack, select the object you want to move, and choose Object > Arrange > Bring Forward or Object > Arrange > Send Backward.

—From Illustrator Help

Selecting objects behind

When you stack objects on top of each other, sometimes it becomes difficult to select objects that are underneath. Next, you will learn how to select an object through a stack of objects.

1   With the Selection tool (▶), select the other red apple on the left artboard and drag it on to the green leaves shape on the right artboard, and then release the mouse.

    Notice that the apple seems to disappear again. The apple went behind the leaves of the tree but is still selected. This time you will deselect the apple, then select it again by selecting through objects.

2   Click the red apple again. Notice that you have selected the object on top, which is the tree group, instead.

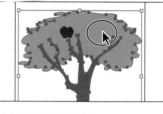

3   With the pointer still positioned over the location of the apple, behind the tree, hold down the Ctrl (Windows) or Cmd (Mac OS) key and click. Notice the angled bracket displayed with the pointer (▷). Click once more to select through the tree to the apple.

● **Note:** To select the hidden apple, make sure that you click where the apple and the tree overlap. Otherwise nothing will happen.

● **Note:** You may also see a plus next to the pointer when selecting behind. That's okay.

4   Choose Object > Arrange > Bring to Front to bring the apple on top of the tree.

5   Choose Select > Deselect.

Hiding objects

When working on complex artwork, selections may become more difficult to control. In this section, you'll combine some of the techniques you've already learned with additional features that make selecting objects easier.

1   With the Selection tool (▶), drag a marquee across the fence pickets and the white rectangle on top to select them. Drag them to the bottom of the right artboard with the tree on it.

2   Choose Object > Arrange > Bring to Front.

3   Choose View > Fit Artboard In Window.

4   Click somewhere to deselect the objects, and then click to select the white rectangle on top of the group of pickets. Choose Object > Arrange > Send Backward one or more times until the white rectangle is behind the picket group. Choose Select > Deselect.

5 Using the Selection tool (➤), select the picket group and choose Object > Hide > Selection or press Ctrl+3 (Windows) or Command+3 (Mac OS). The picket group is hidden so that you can more easily select other objects.

6 Click to select the white rectangle and, holding down the Alt (Windows) or Option (Mac OS) key, drag the rectangle down to create a copy.

7 Choose Object > Show All to show the picket group again.

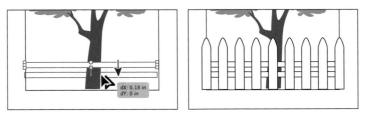

8 Choose File > Save to save the file and then choose File > Close.

Applying selection techniques

As stated earlier, selecting objects is an important part of working with Illustrator. In this part of the lesson, you will use most of the techniques discussed previously in this lesson to get more practice and learn a few new ones.

1 Choose File > Open, and open the L2start_2.ai file in the Lesson02 folder, located in the Lessons folder on your hard disk.

2 Choose View > Fit All In Window. Artboard #2 (the artboard on the right) shows the final artwork. Artboard #1 (the artboard on the left) shows the artwork in progress that you need to finish.

3 Choose View > Fit Artboard In Window to fit artboard #1 in the Document window. Choose View > Smart Guides to temporarily deselect the smart guides.

4 With the Selection tool (➤) selected, drag the steering wheel shape in the upper-right corner into place. Then drag the black rounded rectangle in the upper-left corner of the artboard on top of front of the bus, as shown in the figure.

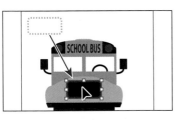

5 With the Selection tool, select the headlight shapes (the circles) in the lower-right corner of the artboard by dragging a marquee across them. Choose Object > Group.

Note: You drag from the center to avoid grabbing a bounding box handle and accidently resizing the shapes.

6 Drag the center of the headlight group to slide it to its new location to the right of the newly-aligned rounded rectangle.

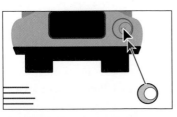

7 Double-click the center of the headlight group to enter isolation mode. Click to select the white shape and drag it so that it's visually centered on the other shapes. Choose Select > Deselect.

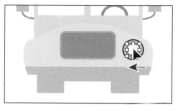

8 Press the Escape key to exit isolation mode.

9 With the Selection tool, press the Alt+Shift (Windows) or Option+Shift (Mac OS) keys and drag the headlight group to the left to duplicate it. Release the mouse button and then the modifier keys.

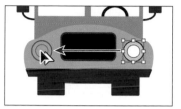

10 Shift-click the rounded rectangle and the headlight group to the right to select all three objects.

11 In the Control panel, choose Align to Selection from the Align To Selection button (⊡) menu, and then click the Horizontal Distribute Center (❚❙) button.

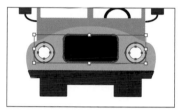

12 Choose Object > Group.

13 Shift-click the orange shape behind the selected group. Click the orange shape again to make it the key object. Click the Horizontal Align Center (⊥) button, and then the Vertical Align Center (❏➡) button to align the rounded rectangle to the orange shape. Choose Select > Deselect.

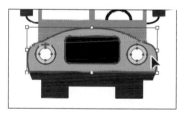

14 With the Selection tool, select the group of objects that contains the headlights. Choose Object > Lock > Selection to keep them in position. You cannot select the shapes until you choose Object > Unlock All. Leave them locked.

▶ **Tip:** Locking objects is a great way to keep from selecting or editing content and can be used in conjunction with hiding objects.

15 Select the Zoom tool (🔍) in the Tools panel and click three times on the dome at the top of the bus, above the text, SCHOOL BUS.

16 Select the Direct Selection tool (▷)and select the top anchor point in the dome, and then drag up to make the dome taller.

17 Double-click the Hand tool (✋) to fit the artboard in the Document window.

18 Select the Zoom tool (🔍) and click three times on the 4 lines in the lower left corner to zoom in.

Note: If you don't see the Align panel options in the Control panel, either click the word Align in the Control panel or choose Window > Align.

19 With the Selection tool (▸), drag a marquee across the 4 lines to select them.

20 In the Control panel, click the Horizontal Align Left (⊫) button.

21 Choose View > Smart Guides to turn them back on.

22 With the Direct Selection tool (▹), click the right end of the top, shorter line to select the anchor point, and then drag to the right until the anchor point aligns with the other lines.

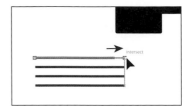

23 With the Selection tool, drag a marquee around the lines to select them. Choose Object > Group to group them.

24 Double-click the Hand tool (✋) to fit the artboard in the Document window.

Note: You may want to turn the smart guides off (View > Smart Guides) so that you can more easily drag the group of lines onto the bus. You can then align the group of lines with the other content if you want.

25 With the Selection tool, drag the line group to position it on the rounded rectangle between the headlights. Notice that you need to drag one of the lines, not between the lines, to move the group.

26 Choose Select > Deselect.

27 Choose File > Save and then File > Close.

Exploring on your own

1 Choose File > Open, and open the L2start_3.ai file in the Lesson02 folder, located in the Lessons folder on your hard disk.

2 Experiment by cloning a star several times, using the Alt (Windows) or Option (Mac OS) key.

3 Apply different colors and strokes to the shapes and reselect them by choosing Select > Same or the Select Similar Objects button (▨▾) in the Control panel.

4 Select three stars and arrange them, trying some of the distribute objects options in the Align panel options of the Control panel.

5 Select three stars and click one of them to set it as the key object. Align the other selected stars to the key object using the Align options in the Control panel.

6 With the stars still selected, choose Object > Group.

7 With the Selection tool, double-click one of the stars in the group to enter isolation mode. Resize several of the stars by dragging each star's bounding box. Then press the Escape key to exit isolation mode.

8 Close the file without saving.

Review questions

1 How can you select an object that has no fill?

2 Name two ways you can select an item in a group without choosing Object > Ungroup.

3 How do you edit the shape of an object?

4 What should you do after creating a selection that you are going to use repeatedly?

5 If something is preventing you from selecting an object, name two ways to select the blocked object.

6 To align objects to the artboard, what do you need to first select in the Align panel or Control panel before you choose an alignment option?

Review answers

1 You can select items that have no fill by clicking the stroke or dragging a marquee across the object.

2 Using the Group Selection tool, you can click once to select an individual item within a group. Click again to add the next grouped items to the selection. Read Lesson 8, "Working with Layers," to see how you can use layers to make complex selections. You can also double-click the group to enter isolation mode, edit the shapes as needed, and then exit isolation mode by pressing the Escape key or by double-clicking outside of the group.

3 Using the Direct Selection tool, you can select one or more individual anchor points and make changes to the shape of an object.

4 For any selection that you anticipate using again, choose Select > Save Selection. Name the selection so that you can reselect it at any time from the Select menu.

5 If something is blocking your access to an object, you can choose Object > Hide > Selection to hide the blocking object. The object is not deleted, just hidden in the same position until you choose Object > Show All. You can also use the Selection tool to select behind content by pressing the Ctrl (Windows) or Cmd (Mac OS) key, and then clicking on the overlapping objects.

6 To align objects to an artboard, first select the Align To Artboard option.

3 CREATING AND EDITING SHAPES

Lesson overview

In this lesson, you'll learn how to do the following:

- Create a document with multiple artboards.

- Use tools and commands to create basic shapes.

- Work with drawing modes.

- Use rulers and smart guides as drawing aids.

- Scale and duplicate objects.

- Join and outline objects.

- Edit strokes with the Width tool.

- Work with the Shape Builder tool.

- Work with Pathfinder commands to create shapes.

- Use Live Trace to create shapes.

 This lesson will take approximately an hour and a half to complete. If needed, remove the previous lesson folder from your hard disk and copy the Lesson03 folder onto it.

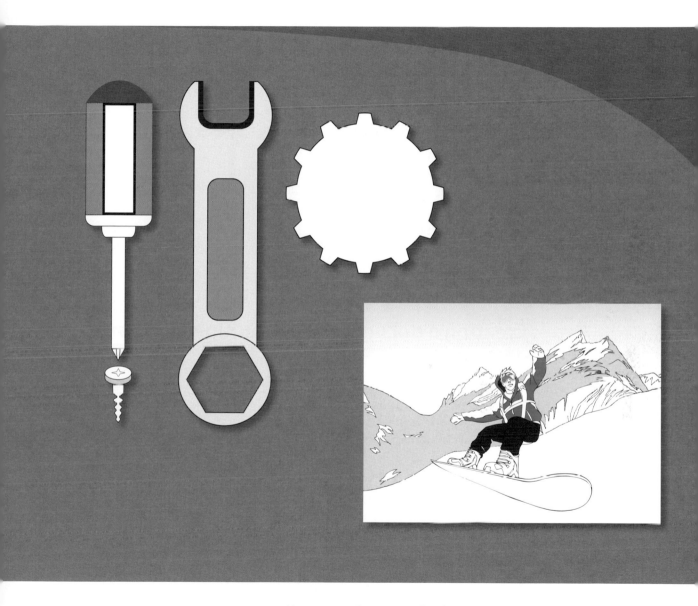

You can create documents with multiple artboards and many kinds of objects by starting with a basic shape and then editing it to create new shapes. In this lesson, you'll add and edit artboards, then create and edit some basic shapes for a technical manual.

Getting started

In this lesson, you'll create several illustrations for a technical manual.

1 To ensure that the tools and panels function as described in this lesson, delete or deactivate (by renaming) the Adobe® Illustrator® CS5 preferences file. See "Restoring default preferences" on page 3.

2 Start Adobe Illustrator CS5.

● **Note:** If you have not already done so, copy the resource files for this lesson onto your hard disk, from the Lesson03 folder on the Adobe Illustrator CS5 Classroom in a Book CD. See "Copying the Classroom in a Book files" on page 2.

3 Choose File > Open. Locate the file named L3end_1.ai, which is in the Lesson03 folder in the Lessons folder that you copied onto your hard disk. These are the finished illustrations that you will create throughout this lesson. Choose View > Fit All In Window and leave the file open for reference, or choose File > Close.

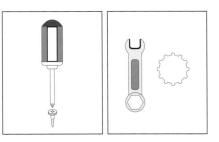

Creating a document with multiple artboards

You will now make two illustrations for a technical manual. The document that you create will have several artboards.

1 Choose File > New to open a new, untitled document. In the New Document dialog box, change the Name to **tools**, choose Print from the New Document Profile menu (if it isn't already selected) and change the Units to Inches. When you change the units, the New Document Profile automatically changes to [Custom]. Keep the dialog box open for the next step.

Using document profiles, you can set up a document for different kinds of output, such as print, web, video, and more. For example, if you are designing a web page mock-up, you can use a web document profile, which automatically displays the page size and units in pixels, changes the color mode to RGB, and changes the raster effects to Screen (72 ppi).

● **Note:** The spacing value is the distance between each artboard.

2 Change the Number Of Artboards option to **2** to create two artboards. Click the Arrange By Row button (⊶) and make sure that the Left To Right Layout arrow (→) is showing. In the Spacing field, type **1**. Click the word Width and type **7** in the Width field. Type **8** in the Height field. Click OK.

3   Choose File > Save As. In the Save As dialog box, ensure that the name of the file is **tools.ai**, and choose the Lesson03 folder. Leave the Save As Type option set to Adobe Illustrator (*.AI) (Windows) or the Format option set to Adobe Illustrator (ai) (Mac OS), and click Save. In the Illustrator Options dialog box, leave the Illustrator options at their default settings, and click OK.

Set up multiple artboards

Illustrator allows you to create multiple artboards. Setting up the artboards requires an understanding of the initial artboard settings in the New Document dialog box. After specifying the number of artboards for your document, you can set the order you'd like them laid out on screen. They are defined as follows:

* **Grid By Row:** Arranges multiple artboards in the specified number of rows. Choose the number of rows from the Rows menu. The default value creates the most square appearance possible with the specified number of artboards.

* **Grid By Column:** Arranges multiple artboards in the specified number of columns. Choose the number of columns from the Columns menu. The default value creates the most square appearance possible with the specified number of artboards.

* **Arrange By Row:** Arranges artboards in one straight row.

* **Arrange By Column:** Arranges artboards in one straight column.

* **Change To Right-To-Left Layout:** Arranges multiple artboards in the specified row or column format, but displays them from right to left.

—From Illustrator Help

4   Choose Select > Deselect (if it's not already dimmed) to make sure nothing is selected on either artboard. After deselecting, the Document Setup button appears in the Control panel. Click the Document Setup button.

Use this button to change the artboard size, units, bleeds, and more, after a document is created.

● **Note:** If the Document Setup button does not appear in the Control panel, you can choose File > Document Setup.

5 In the Bleed section of the Document Setup dialog box, change the value in the Top field to .125 in, either by clicking the up arrow to the left of the field once or by typing the value. Click in the Bottom field or press the Tab key to make all the Bleed settings the same. Click OK.

Notice the red line that appears around both artboards. The red line indicates the bleed area. Typical bleeds for printing are about 1/8 of an inch.

What is a bleed?

Bleed is the amount of artwork that falls outside of the printing bounding box, or outside the artboard. You can include bleed in your artwork as a margin of error—to ensure that the ink is still printed to the edge of the page after the page is trimmed or that an image can be stripped into a keyline in a document.

—From Illustrator Help

Working with basic shapes

In the first part of this lesson, you'll create a screwdriver using basic shapes like rectangles, ellipses, rounded rectangles, and polygons. You'll begin this exercise by setting up the workspace.

1 Choose Window > Workspace > Essentials.

2 Choose View > Rulers > Show Rulers, or press Ctrl+R (Windows) or Command+R (Mac OS), to display rulers along the top and left side of the window, if they are not already showing.

The ruler units are inches because you specified Units as inches in the New Document dialog box. You can change the ruler units for all documents or for the current document only. The ruler unit applies to measuring objects, moving and transforming objects, setting grid and guide spacing, and creating shapes. It does not affect the units used in the Character, Paragraph, and Stroke panels. The units used in these panels are specified in the Units category in the program preferences (Edit > Preferences (Windows) or Illustrator > Preferences (Mac OS)).

▶ **Tip:** You can change the units for the current document by right-clicking or Ctrl-clicking the horizontal or vertical ruler and choosing a new unit from the context menu.

Accessing the basic shape tools

The shape tools are organized under the Rectangle tool. You can tear this group off the Tools panel to display it as a separate free-floating panel.

1   Click and hold the Rectangle tool (▢) until a group of tools appears. Then drag to the small triangle at the right end and release the mouse button.

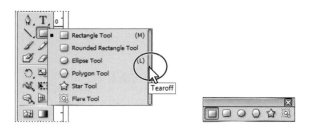

● **Note:** The Tools panel you see may appear as a single or double column, depending on the resolution of your screen. To switch between one and two columns, click the double arrow in the title bar of the Tools panel.

2   Move the Rectangle tool group away from the Tools panel.

Understanding drawing modes

Before starting to draw shapes in Illustrator, notice the three drawing modes found at the bottom of the Tools panel: Draw Normal, Draw Behind, and Draw Inside.

Each drawing mode allows you to draw shapes in a different way.

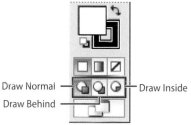

● **Note:** The Tools panel you see may be a single column. To select a drawing mode, click the Drawing Modes button (▣) at the bottom of the Tools panel and choose a drawing mode from the menu that appears.

*   **Draw Normal mode:** You start every document by drawing shapes in Normal mode, which stacks shapes on top of each other.

*   **Draw Behind mode:** This mode allows you to draw objects behind other objects without choosing layers or paying attention to the stacking order.

*   **Draw Inside mode:** This mode lets you draw objects or place images inside other objects, including live text, automatically creating a clipping mask of the selected object.

● **Note:** To learn more about clipping masks, see Lesson 15, "Combining Illustrator CS5 Graphics with Other Adobe Applications."

As you create shapes in the following sections, you will be using the different drawing modes and learning how they affect your shapes.

Creating rectangles

First, you'll draw a series of rectangles. You'll also use smart guides to align your drawing and work with two of the drawing modes.

1   Choose View > Fit Artboard In Window.

2   Make sure that 1 is showing in the Artboard Navigation area in the lower left of the Document window, which indicates that the first artboard is showing in the Document window.

3   Choose Window > Transform to display the Transform panel.

The Transform panel is useful for editing properties such as the width and height of an existing shape.

4   Select the Rectangle tool ( ) and start dragging from somewhere in the top center of the artboard, down and to the right. As you drag, notice the tooltip that appears as a gray box, indicating the width and height of the shape as you draw. This is called the measurement label and is a part of the smart guides, which will be discussed further in this lesson. Drag down and to the right until the rectangle is approximately 0.75 inches wide and 2.5 inches in height.

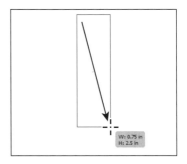

Note: You can make the center point visible or invisible using the Attributes panel, but you cannot delete it.

This will be the main body of the screwdriver. When you release the mouse button, the rectangle is automatically selected, and its center point appears. All objects created with the shape tools have a center point that you can drag to align the object with other elements in your artwork.

5   In the Transform panel, note the width and height of the rectangle. If necessary, change the measurements by typing **.75 in** for the height and typing **2.5 in** for the width.

6   Close the Transform panel group by clicking the x in the upper right corner of the group title bar (Windows) or the dot in the upper left corner (Mac OS).

Note: If the Tools panel you see is displayed as a single column, you can click the Drawing Modes button ( ) at the bottom of the Tools panel and choose a drawing mode from the menu that appears.

Next, you'll draw another rectangle behind the one you just drew, so that the first one is centered inside the second, to continue creating the body of the screwdriver.

7   Click the Draw Behind button at the bottom of the Tools panel. As long as this drawing mode is selected, every shape you create will be drawn behind the other shapes on the page.

8 With the Rectangle tool, position the pointer over the center point of the rectangle that you just drew. Notice that the word "center" appears next to the pointer. Press the Alt (Windows) or Option (Mac OS) key, and drag down and to the right, diagonally from the center, to draw a rectangle. When the measurement label tooltip shows a height of 2.5 in and a width of approximately 1.5 in and a green line appears indicating that you are snapping to the bottom of the existing rectangle, release the mouse button and then the Alt or Option key.

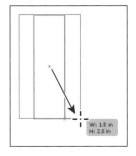

Holding down the Alt or Option key as you drag the Rectangle tool draws the rectangle from its center point rather than from its upper-left corner. As you drag the pointer, the smart guides snap the pointer to the edges of the existing rectangle and display the word "path." The new shape is behind the previous shape because of the selected drawing mode.

About smart guides

Smart Guides are temporary snap-to guides and pop-ups that appear when you create or manipulate objects or artboards. They help you align, edit, and transform objects or artboards relative to other objects, artboards, or both by snap-aligning and displaying location or delta values.

You can use Smart Guides in the following ways:

- When you create an object with the pen or shape tools, use the Smart Guides to position a new object's anchor points relative to an existing object. Or, when you create a new artboard, use Smart Guides to position it relative to another artboard or an object.

- When you create an object with the pen or shape tools, or when you transform an object, use the smart guides' construction guides to position anchor points to specific preset angles, such as 45 or 90 degrees. You set these angles in the Smart Guides preferences.

- When you move an object or artboard, use the Smart Guides to align the selected object or artboard to other objects or artboards. The alignment is based on the center point or edge of the objects or artboards. Guides appear as the object approaches the edge or center point of another object.

- When you rotate or move an item, use Smart Guides to snap to the last used angle or the nearest alignment option.

- When you transform an object, Smart Guides automatically appear to assist the transformation. You can change when and how Smart Guides appear by setting Smart Guide preferences.

—From Illustrator Help

9 With the new rectangle still selected, click the Fill color () in the Control panel and change the color to orange (hover over an orange swatch until the tooltip displays as C=0 M=50 Y=100 K=0) to fill the new shape, which is behind the smaller rectangle.

In addition to drawing a shape by dragging on the artboard with a tool, you can select a tool and then click the artboard to open a dialog box with options for that tool. Next, you will create a rectangle using this method.

● **Note:** Because the Swatches were showing in the Control panel in the previous step, you may need to click twice on the artboard to see the Rectangle dialog box.

10 With the Rectangle tool still selected, position the pointer to the left of the other rectangles on the artboard and click. The Rectangle dialog box appears.

11 In the Rectangle dialog box, change the Width to **.3** in, press the Tab key, and type **3** in the Height field. Click OK.

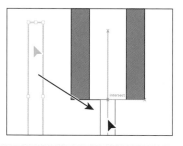

12 With the new rectangle still selected, click the Fill color (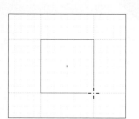) in the Control panel and change the fill color to white.

13 Select the Selection tool (▶) in the Tools panel. Drag the new rectangle from its center so that the top of the rectangle snaps to the bottom of the other rectangles and is center aligned horizontally with them. The word "intersect" appears.

14 Choose Select > Deselect, then File > Save.

Working with the document grid

The grid allows you to work more precisely by creating a grid behind your artwork in the Document window that objects can snap to, and it does not print. To turn the grid on and use it's features do the following:

- To use the grid, choose View > Show Grid.

- To hide the grid, choose View > Hide Grid.

- To snap objects to the gridlines, choose View > Snap To Grid, select the object you want to move, and drag it to the desired location. When the object's boundaries come within 2 pixels of a gridline, it snaps to the point.

- To specify the spacing between gridlines, grid style (lines or dots), grid color, or whether grids appear in the front or back of artwork, choose Edit > Preferences > Guides & Grid (Windows) or Illustrator > Preferences > Guides & Grid (Mac OS).

Note: When Snap To Grid is turned on, you cannot use Smart Guides (even if the menu command is selected).

—From Illustrator Help

Creating rounded rectangles

Next, you'll create a rounded rectangle for another part of the illustration by setting options in a dialog box. The Draw Behind drawing mode is still active from the previous steps, which means that the next shape you create will be behind the others on the artboard.

1   Select the Rounded Rectangle tool (▢), and click once in the artwork to open the Rounded Rectangle dialog box. Type **1.5** in the Width field, press the Tab key, and type **0.5** in the Height field. Press the Tab key again, and type **0.2** in the Corner Radius field. The radius determines the curvature of the corners. Click OK.

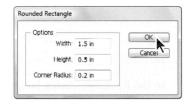

Note: When entering values, if the correct unit appears (such as in for inches), then you don't need to type the **in**. If the correct unit does NOT appear, then type the **in** and the units will be converted.

By default, shapes are filled with white and have a black stroke (border). A shape with a fill can be selected and moved by first positioning the pointer anywhere inside the shape. Next, you'll use smart guides to help you align the shape you created to the existing shapes.

2   Select the Selection tool (▶) in the Tools panel. Click anywhere inside the rounded rectangle and drag it so that it's centered horizontally and vertically with the bottom edge of the larger rectangle, as shown in the figure. When the word "intersect" and green line(s) appear, release the mouse button.

▶ **Tip:** The color of the smart guides can be changed from green to another color by choosing Edit > Preferences > Smart Guides (Windows) or Illustrator > Preferences > Smart Guides (Mac OS).

3   Choose Select > Deselect.

Notice that the rounded rectangle is behind all of the other rectangles you created. In Draw Behind mode, you draw an object behind all others. You will later put the rectangle for the shaft behind the rounded rectangle.

● **Note:** The gray box that appears as you drag the shape indicates the x and y distance that the pointer has moved.

You've been working in the default preview mode, which lets you see how objects are painted (in this case, with a black or white fill and black stroke). If paint attributes seem distracting, you can work in outline mode, which you'll do next.

4   Choose View > Outline to switch from preview to outline mode.

● **Note:** Outline mode removes all paint attributes, such as colored fills and strokes, to speed up selecting and redrawing artwork. You can't select or drag shapes by clicking in the middle of a shape, because the fill temporarily disappears.

Next, you'll create another shape by duplicating the rounded rectangle, using the Alt (Windows) or Option (Mac OS) key.

5   With the Selection tool (▶), press the Alt (Windows) or Option (Mac OS) key and drag the bottom edge (not a point) of the rounded rectangle straight down to duplicate it. Drag until the word "intersect" appears, indicating that the center of the shape is aligned with the bottom of the first rounded rectangle. Release the mouse button, and then the Alt or Option key.

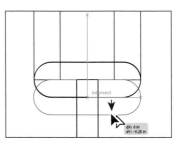

6   With the Selection tool, press the Alt (Windows) or Option (Mac OS) key, and drag the right bounding point of the bottom rounded rectangle to the left, toward the center of the shape, until the right edge is aligned with the right edge of the first rectangle you drew. The word "intersect" appears along with a green line, indicating that it's snapping to the rectangle shape.

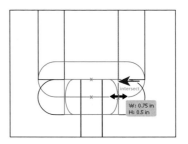

Drawing with the smart guides turned on can be very helpful, especially when precision is necessary. If you don't find them useful, you could turn the smart guides off by choosing View > Smart Guides.

Creating ellipses

You can control the shape of polygons, stars, and ellipses by pressing certain modifying keys as you draw. You'll draw an ellipse next, to represent the top of the screwdriver. Because the Draw Behind drawing mode is still selected, the ellipse you draw will be behind the other shapes.

1   Select the Ellipse tool (⬭) from the Rectangle tool group and position the pointer over the upper-left corner of the larger rectangle. Notice that the word "anchor" appears. Begin dragging down and to the right. Don't release the mouse button yet.

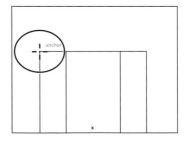

2 Drag the pointer down and to the right until it touches the right edge of the largest rectangle and the word "path" appears. Without releasing the mouse button, drag up or down slightly until measurement label shows a height of 1 in. Don't release the mouse button yet.

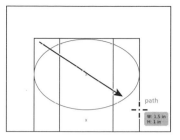

3 Hold down the spacebar and drag the ellipse up a little, making sure that as you drag up, you still see the word "path." This ensures that the ellipse is still aligned with the right edge of the larger rectangle. Release the mouse button when the ellipse is positioned and sized as in the figure at right, and then release the spacebar.

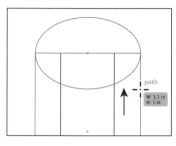

▶ **Tip:** When drawing shapes, holding down the Shift key constrains the proportions of the shape. In the case of the ellipse, it would create a perfect circle.

4 Choose Window > Transform to open the Transform panel. Select the Selection tool (▶), then click the edge of the ellipse to ensure it is selected. Note the width in the Transform panel. Next, click the larger rectangle to see if the widths are the same in the Transform panel. If not, correct the ellipse by typing the same width value as the larger rectangle, and pressing Enter or Return.

● **Note:** If you needed to correct the width in the Transform panel, the ellipse may no longer be aligned with the rectangles. With the Selection tool, drag the ellipse horizontally to align it again.

5 Choose Select > All On Active Artboard to select the shapes in this artboard only. Choose Object > Group to group them.

6 Choose Select > Deselect, then File > Save.

Creating polygons

Now you'll create two triangles for the screwdriver tip, using the Polygon tool. Polygons are drawn from the center by default, which is different than the other tools you've worked with so far.

1 Select the Zoom tool (🔍) and click three times on the bottom of the screwdriver shapes to zoom in.

2 Select the Polygon tool (⬡) from the Rectangle tool group and position the pointer over the center of the bottom of the rectangle (the word "intersect" appears as well as the green alignment guide).

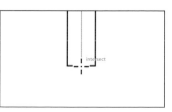

Tip: When drawing with the Polygon tool, pressing the Up Arrow and Down Arrow keys changes the number of sides. If you want to change the number of sides quickly while drawing a polygon, hold down one of the arrow keys as you drag out the shape.

3 Drag to begin drawing a polygon, but don't release the mouse button. Press the Down Arrow key three times to reduce the number of sides on the polygon to three (a triangle). Hold down the Shift key to straighten the triangle. Without releasing the Shift key, drag down and to the right until the smart guide measurement label displays a width of 0.3 in. Release the mouse, then the modifier key.

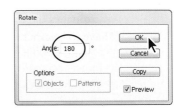

4 With the shape still selected, double-click the Rotate tool (⟳) in the Tools panel to open the Rotate dialog box. Change the angle value to **180**, and click OK. Leave the shape selected.

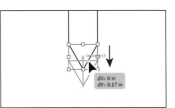

5 Select the Selection tool (▶) in the Tools panel and drag the top edge of the triangle, not a point, down until it snaps to the bottom of the rectangle. The word "intersect" appears when it is snapped.

6 With the Selection tool, hold down the Shift key and click the edge of the grouped objects to select the group as well as the triangle.

● **Note:** Because you are still in outline mode, you may need to either drag across to select objects or click on their strokes.

7 In the Control panel, click the Horizontal Align Center button (⬒) to ensure that the objects are aligned to each other.

● **Note:** If you don't see the align options, click the word Align in the Control panel. Otherwise, choose Window > Align to open the Align panel.

8 Choose Select > Deselect, and then choose View > Preview.

Draw Inside mode

Next, you will learn how to draw one shape inside of another using the Draw Inside drawing mode.

● **Note:** If the Tools panel is a single column, to access the drawing modes, click and hold down the Drawing Modes button at the bottom of the Tools panel and choose a drawing mode from the menu that appears.

1 With the Selection tool, click to select the triangle again. Click the Draw Inside button, located near the bottom of the Tools panel.

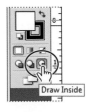

This button is active only when a shape is selected, and it allows you to draw within the selected shape only. Every shape you create will now be drawn inside of the selected shape.

2   Select the Ellipse tool (⬭). You will now draw a shape inside of the triangle.

3   Position the pointer over the bottom point of the triangle. Holding down the Alt (Windows) or Option (Mac OS) key, drag down and to the right to create an ellipse that has a width of about .18 in and the top of the ellipse touches the top of the triangle. It doesn't have to be exact. Release the mouse button and then the modifier key.

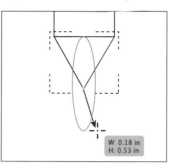

● **Note:** If you draw a shape outside of the triangle shape, it will seem to disappear. That is because the triangle is masking all shapes drawn inside of it. So only shapes positioned inside of the triangle bounds will appear.

4   Choose Select > Deselect.

Notice that after you deselect the shape, only part of the ellipse is showing, because it is being masked by the triangle. The triangle also has dotted lines around the corners, indicating that the Draw Inside mode is still active and the triangle is the focus.

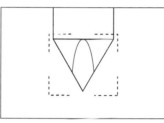

● **Note:** The triangle is masking part of the ellipse and is referred to as a clipping mask. You can learn more about clipping masks in Lesson 15, "Combining Illustrator CS5 Graphics with Other Adobe Applications."

Next, you will edit the ellipse that is inside of the triangle.

5   Select the Selection tool (▶) and click to select the ellipse. Notice that it selects the triangle instead.

To select shapes inside of another shape, you need to first perform the next step.

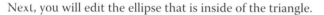

▶ **Tip:** You can remove the ellipse from inside the triangle by selecting the triangle with the Selection tool and choosing Object > Clipping Mask > Release. This makes two separate shapes, with one on top of the other.

6   With the triangle selected, click the Edit Contents button (⬤) on the left end of the Control panel.

This allows you to edit the ellipse shape drawn inside, which is now selected.

7   Choose View > Hide Bounding Box.

When you hide the bounding box, you can drag a shape from its edge without fear of dragging a bounding box handle and reshaping the shape.

8 With the Selection tool still selected, drag the bottom point of the ellipse up until it snaps to the bottom point of the triangle.

9 Choose View > Show Bounding Box.

10 Holding down the Alt (Windows) or Option (Mac OS) key, drag the right-middle bounding point of the ellipse to the left (into the center) to make it narrower. When the measurement label shows a width of approximately .1 in, release the mouse and then the modifier key.

▶ **Tip:** You can continue drawing inside of the triangle. You can also edit the triangle and ellipse by double-clicking the triangle with the Selection tool, to enter isolation mode. Then you can edit either shape independently. To learn more about isolation mode, visit Lesson 2, "Selecting and Aligning."

11 With the ellipse still selected, click the Edit Clipping Path button (⬚) on the left end of the Control panel. This selects the triangle shape so you can no longer select the ellipse.

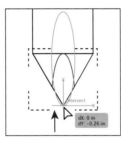 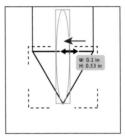 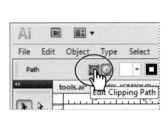

Drag the ellipse up.   Resize the ellipse.   Stop editing the ellipse.

12 Choose Select > Deselect.

13 Click the Draw Normal button, located in the bottom portion of the Tools panel.

▶ **Tip:** If an object is selected and the Draw Inside mode is active, you can place images or paste additional objects inside the selected object.

14 Choose View > Fit Artboard In Window.

15 With the Selection tool, select the rectangle between the handle group and the triangle at the bottom. Notice that it is part of a group.

16 Chose Object > Ungroup, and then choose Select > Deselect.

17 Click to select the rectangle between the handle group and the triangle at the bottom.

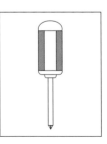

● **Note:** To learn more about arranging objects, see Lesson 2, "Selecting and Aligning."

18 Choose Object > Arrange > Send to Back.

19 Choose File > Save.

Tips for drawing polygons, spirals, and stars

You can control the shapes of polygons, spirals, and stars by pressing certain keys as you draw the shapes. Choose any of the following options to control the shape:

- To add or subtract sides on a polygon, points on a star, or number of segments on a spiral, hold down the Up Arrow or Down Arrow key while creating the shape. This only works if the mouse button is held down. When the mouse button is released, the tool remains set to the last specified value.
- To rotate the shape, move the mouse in an arc.
- To keep a side or point at the top, hold down the Shift key.
- To keep the inner radius constant, start creating a shape and then hold down Ctrl (Windows) or Command (Mac OS).

Changing stroke width and alignment

Every shape, by default, is created with a 1 pt. stroke. You can easily change the stroke weight of an object to make it thinner or thicker. Strokes are also aligned to the center of a path edge, by default, but you can easily change the alignment as well using the Stroke panel.

Next, you will change the stroke weight of the larger rectangle in the handle as well as its alignment.

1 With the Selection tool (▶), click to select the smaller white rectangle at the center of the handle.

2 Select the Zoom tool (🔍) in the Tools panel and click the top of the selected shape three times to zoom in.

3 Open the Stroke panel by clicking the Stroke icon (≣) on the right side of the workspace or by clicking the word Stroke in the Control panel.

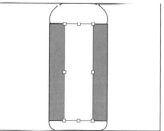

4 In the Stroke panel, choose **4 pt** from the Stroke Weight menu.

Notice that the stroke of the white rectangle causes the top and bottom of the two rectangles to no longer appear aligned. That is because a stroke is centered on the edge of the shape, by default.

5 In the Stroke panel, click the Align Stroke To Inside button (). This aligns the stroke to the inside edge of the rectangle.

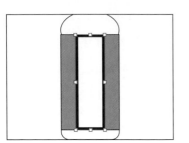

You set the stroke to the inside on the white rectangle so that the top and bottom edges of the orange and white rectangle are still visually aligned.

6 Choose View > Fit Artboard In Window.

7 Choose Select > All On Active Artboard, and then Object > Group.

8 Choose File > Save.

About aligning strokes

If an object is a closed path (such as a square), you can select an option in the Stroke panel to align the stroke along the path to the center (default), inside, or outside:

Note: *If you try to align paths that use different stroke alignments, the paths may not exactly align. Make sure the path alignment settings are the same if you need the edges to match up exactly.*

Working with line segments

Next, you'll work with straight lines and line segments, known as open paths, to create a screw for the screwdriver. Shapes can be created in many ways in Illustrator, and the simpler way is usually better.

1 Select the Zoom tool (🔍) in the Tools panel, and click four times below the screwdriver tip to zoom in.

● **Note:** You may need to drag the group of shapes up using the Selection tool to give yourself room to continue drawing.

2 Choose Essentials from the workspace switcher in the Application bar.

3 Select the Ellipse tool (⬭) in the Tools panel. Draw an ellipse roughly centered below the tip of the screwdriver that has a width of 0.6 in and a height of 0.3 in as shown in the measurement label that appears.

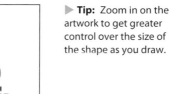

▶ **Tip:** Zoom in on the artwork to get greater control over the size of the shape as you draw.

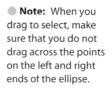

4 Click the Fill color (▢) in the Control panel and select None (⬚). Also, make sure that the stroke weight is **1 pt** in the Control panel. Leave the ellipse selected.

5 Select the Direct Selection tool (↘) in the Tools panel. Drag across the lower part of the ellipse to select the bottom half.

▶ **Tip:** To hide the Swatches menu in the Control panel, which you used to change the fill, press the Escape key.

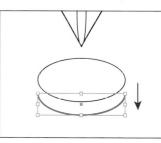

● **Note:** When you drag to select, make sure that you do not drag across the points on the left and right ends of the ellipse.

6 Choose Edit > Copy, and then Edit > Paste In Front to create a new path that is directly on top of the original.

This copies and pastes only the bottom half of the ellipse as a single path, because that is what you selected with the Direct Selection tool.

7 Select the Selection tool and press the Down Arrow key about eight times to move the new line down.

You could have dragged the line down instead, but this method is easier to control.

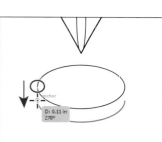

8 Select the Line Segment tool (╲) in the Tools panel. Hold down the Shift key while drawing a line from the left anchor point of the ellipse to the left anchor point of the new path. The anchor points are highlighted when the line snaps to them. Release the mouse button and then the modifier key. Repeat this on the right side of the ellipse.

9 Choose Select > Deselect.

10 Choose File > Save.

Next, you will take the three line segments that make up part of the screw head and join them together as one path.

Open path vs. closed path

As you draw, you create a line called a path. A path is made up of one or more straight or curved segments. The beginning and end of each segment are marked by anchor points, which work like pins holding a wire in place. A path can be closed (for example, a circle), or open, with distinct endpoints (for example, a wavy line).

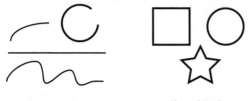

Open Paths   Closed Paths

Both open and closed paths can have fills applied to them.

—From Illustrator Help

Joining paths

When more than one open path is selected, you can join them together to create a closed path (like a circle). You can also join the end points of two separate paths.

Next, you will join the three paths to create a single open path.

1   Select the Selection tool (▶) in the Tools panel.

2   Holding down the Shift key, click each of the three paths that you just created to select them all.

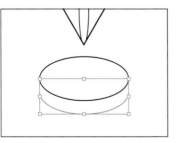

3   Choose Object > Path > Join.

The three paths are converted to a single path. Illustrator identifies the anchor points on the ends of each path and joins the closest points together. To test this, you can deselect the shape, then select it again, then drag it away from the bottom. If you do this, choose Edit > Undo Move.

▶ **Tip:** After the paths are selected, you can also join paths by pressing Ctrl+J (Windows) or Cmd+J (Mac OS).

4 With the path still selected, choose Object >
Path > Join, once more. This creates a closed
path, connecting the two endpoints of
the path.

If you select a single open path and choose
Object > Path > Join, Illustrator creates a
path segment between the endpoints of the
open path, creating a closed path.

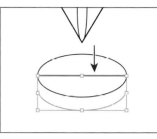

Note: If you only
want to fill the shape
with a color, it is not
necessary to join the
path to make a closed
path. An open path
can have a color fill. It
is, however, necessary
to do this if you want a
stroke to appear around
the entire fill area.

5 Change the Fill color in the Control panel to a light gray (we used K=20).

6 Choose Object > Arrange > Send To Back.

7 Click the stroke of the ellipse shape to select
it. In the Control panel, click Fill color (⬜▾)
and choose white. This covers the shape that
you just sent to the back.

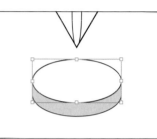

Note: To select a path without a fill, click the stroke or
drag across the path.

8 Hold down the Shift key, and click the gray
shape beneath the selected ellipse with the
Selection tool to select them both. Choose Object > Group.

9 With the group still selected, choose Object > Lock > Selection. This temporarily
locks the group so that it cannot be accidentally selected.

Creating Stars

Next, you'll create a star for the slots in the screw head, using the Star tool.

1 Select the Star tool (✩) from the same
group as the Ellipse tool (⬭) in the Tools
panel. Place the pointer in the center of the
ellipse shape. Notice that the word
"center" appears.

Drag slowly to the right to create a star
shape. Without releasing the mouse button,
press the Down Arrow key once to decrease
the number of points on the star to four.

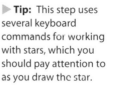

Tip: This step uses
several keyboard
commands for working
with stars, which you
should pay attention to
as you draw the star.

Hold down the Control (Windows) or Command (Mac OS) key and continue
dragging to the right. This keeps the inner radius constant. Without releasing
the mouse button, release the Control or Command key. Hold down the Shift
key and drag until the star has a width and height of about .3 in. Release the
mouse button and then the Shift key.

2 Select the Selection tool. Holding down the Alt (Windows) or Option (Mac OS) key, drag the top anchor point of the star down until the height is approximately .2 in. This resizes both sides of the star, giving it a more realistic appearance. Release the mouse button, and then the modifier key.

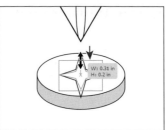

3 Change the Stroke Weight in the Control panel to **0.5 pt**. Click the Fill box in the Control panel and change the fill to white.

4 Choose Object > Unlock All.

5 Choose Select > Deselect, then File > Save.

Using the Eraser tool

The Eraser tool lets you erase any area of your artwork, regardless of the structure. You can use the Eraser tool on paths, compound paths, paths inside Live Paint groups, and clipping paths.

1 Select the Zoom tool (🔍) in the Tools panel, and click the star you just created twice to zoom in.

2 With the Selection tool (▶), click to select the star.

By selecting the star, you'll erase only the start shape and nothing else. If you leave all objects deselected, you can erase any object that the tool touches.

3 Select the Eraser tool (🗗) in the Tools panel. With the pointer on the artboard, press the Left Bracket key ([) several times to reduce the size of the eraser diameter.

4 Position the pointer just to the left of the bottom point of the star. Press the Shift key and drag across the bottom star point to cut off the tip. Repeat for the top star point. The path remains closed (the erased ends are joined).

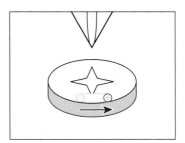

● **Note:** If you erase and nothing seems to happen, erase more of the star on the bottom and top. Zooming in can also be helpful.

5 Choose Select > Deselect.

6 Choose View > Fit Artboard In Window.

7 Choose File > Save.

Using the Width tool

Not only can you adjust the stroke weight and the alignment, but you can also alter regular stroke widths either by using the Width tool (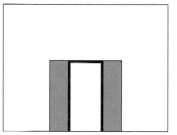) or by applying profiles to the stroke. This allows you to create variation along the stroke of a path.

Next, you will use the Width tool to finish the artwork.

1 Select the Zoom tool (🔍) in the Tools panel, and then click the ellipse at the top of the handle of the screwdriver three times to zoom in.

2 Select the Selection tool (▶) and then double-click the group at the top of the artboard with the orange rectangle in it to enter isolation mode. Click to select the ellipse at the top and press Delete.

   You are going to use the Width tool to simplify the drawing.

3 Select the smaller white rectangle on top and choose Object > Hide > Selection to temporarily hide it.

Next, you are going to use the Width tool to change the width of the top stroke of the orange rectangle. This will allow you to create the rounded top (where the ellipse used to be) by simply dragging the rectangle stroke.

4 Click to select the orange rectangle.

5 Select the Width tool (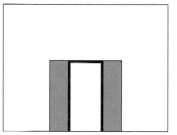) in the Tools panel.

6 Position the pointer to the right of the upper left corner of the orange rectangle (on the top edge), as shown in the figure. Notice the pointer has a plus next to it (▶₊).

7 Drag up, away from the orange rectangle. Notice that as you drag, you are stretching the stroke up and down equally. Release the mouse when the measurement label shows Side 1 and Side 2 at approximately .5 in.

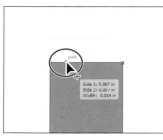
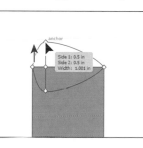
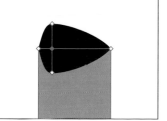

8 Choose Edit > Undo Width Point Change to set the stroke weight back to its previous setting.

9 Position the pointer over the same spot on the top edge of the orange rectangle, close to, but not on the upper left corner. This time, press the Alt (Windows) or Option (Mac OS) key and drag up, away from the top edge about .5 in. Release the mouse button and then the modifier key.

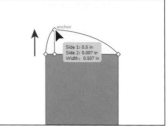

The modifier key allows you to drag one side of the stroke rather than both sides, as you did previously.

10 Position the pointer over the new point at the top of the orange rectangle, which is circled in the figure at right, and drag it to the right until the word "intersect" appears.

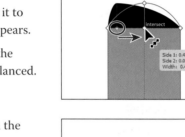

This aligns the point to the center of the shapes and makes the stroke width balanced.

11 Choose Select > Deselect.

12 Position the pointer half way between the point you just dragged and the upper right corner of the orange rectangle. Notice that the pointer has a plus next to it (▶₊), indicating that you can add another point. Drag up to add another point and reshape the stroke.

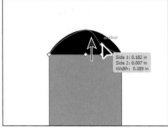

You can add lots of points to the stroke to reshape it. Every time you drag up or down from the stroke, you add a point that can then be edited. Notice that there is now a new blue point on the edge of the orange rectangle.

Next, you will delete that point.

13 The point on the stroke should still be selected. Press Delete to remove it.

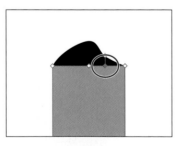

● **Note:** If you need to reselect the point before deleting it, click it with the Width tool to reselect it.

14 Select the Selection tool in the Tools panel, and, making sure that the orange rectangle is still selected, click the Stroke color (■▾) in the Control panel and choose a dark gray (C=0 M=0 Y=0 K=80). Notice how the stroke around the edge of the orange rectangle, including the stroke you just edited, is dark gray.

15 Choose Select > Deselect.

16 Press the Escape key to exit isolation mode.

17 Choose View > Fit Artboard In Window, and then choose Object > Show All.

Next, you will create the body for the screw at the bottom of the artboard by creating a line and using the Width tool.

1 Select the Zoom tool (🔍) in the Tools panel, and then click three times just below the screw head at the bottom of the artboard to zoom in.

2 Select the Line Segment tool (\\) in the Tools panel and position the pointer at the bottom-center of the screw head. Hold down the Shift key and drag straight down to create a line that is approximately .75 in in length. Release the mouse button and then the modifier key.

3 Change the Fill color of the line to black in the Control panel.

4 Select the Width tool (✎) in the Tools panel. Just below the screw head, position the pointer on the line and drag to the right to expand the stroke of the line. Drag until the measurement label shows a width of approximately .25 in.

5 Double-click the new point (on the line) to open the Width Point Edit dialog box. This allows you to adjust the sides together or separately, using more precision. Click the Adjust Widths Proportionately button (⬚) to link Side 1 with Side 2 (it should look like this: ⫯). Change the Total Width to **.2 in**. Click OK. Note that the Adjust Adjoining Width Points selection can be used to adjust other width points on the stroke as well.

▶ **Tip:** You can use the Width Point Edit dialog box to ensure that width points are the same.

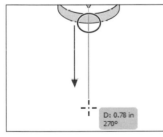
Draw the line.

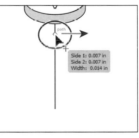
Drag to edit the stroke.

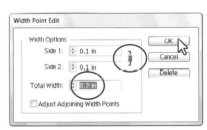
Edit the width point.

6 With the Width tool selected, position the pointer over the point on the line you just made. Holding down the Alt (Windows) or Option (Mac OS) key, drag the point up until it reaches the end of the line. Release the mouse button and then the key.

● **Note:** You may want to zoom in further for the next steps.

By dragging a width point with that modifier key, you create a copy and a straighter segment on the line.

7 Position the pointer below the first point you created, just to the right of the center of the line. The pointer will have a plus next to it (▶₊). Drag to the left or right to create a new point, until the width is approximately .06 in.

Tip: After creating a new point, you can drag to reposition it on the line using the Width tool or press Delete with the point selected to delete it.

Tip: You can drag one width point on top of another width point to create a discontinuous width point. If you double-click a discontinuous width point, the Width Point Edit dialog box allows you to edit both width points.

8 Below the .6 in width point you just made, drag a point to the right to make the stroke wider. Repeat this process down the length of the line, alternating between wider and narrower widths, but ultimately making sure the widths are getting narrower as you move down the line, as shown in the figure.

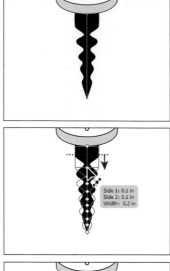

9 With the Width tool, hold down the Shift key and drag the second width point from the top down just a bit and notice that all the width points move together proportionately. Release the mouse button and then the modifier key.

10 Select the Selection tool in the Tools panel and leave the line selected.

This is one of the many ways to make a complex shape, working with a simple shape and the Width tool.

11 Choose File > Save.

Saving width profiles

After defining the stroke width, you can save the variable width profile from the Stroke panel or the Control panel.

Width profiles can be applied to selected paths by choosing them from the Width Profile drop-down list in the Control panel or Stroke panel. When there is no variable width profile, the list displays the Uniform option. You can also select the Uniform option to remove a variable width profile from an object. To restore the default width profile set, click the Reset Profiles button at the bottom of the Profile drop down list.

Note: *Restoring the default width profile set in the Stroke Options dialog box, removes any custom saved profiles.*

If you apply a variable width profile to a stroke, then it is indicated with an asterisk (*) in the Appearance panel.

—From Illustrator Help

Outlining strokes

Paths, such as a line, can show a stroke color but not a fill color, by default. If you create a line in Illustrator and you want to apply both a stroke and a fill, you can outline the stroke, which converts the line into a closed shape (or compound path).

Next, you will outline the stroke of the screw you just created.

▶ **Tip:** Outlining a stroke lets you add a gradient to a stroke or separate the stroke and fill into two separate objects.

1 With the line still selected, choose None from the Fill color (⬜▾) in the Control panel, if it is not already selected.

● **Note:** If the line initially has a color fill, a more complex group is created when you choose Outline Stroke.

2 Choose Object > Path > Outline Stroke. This creates a filled shape that is a closed path.

3 With the new shape selected, click the Fill color (◼▾) in the Control panel and change the color to white. Click the Stroke color (▨▾) and change the color to black.

4 Choose Object > Arrange > Send to Back.

5 Press the Up Arrow a few times to move the shape underneath the screw head shapes

6 Choose View > Fit Artboard In Window.

7 Choose Select > Deselect, then File > Save.

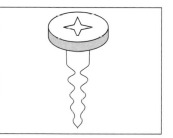

Combining and editing shapes

In Illustrator, you can combine vector objects to create shapes in a variety of ways. The resulting paths or shapes differ depending on the method you use to combine the paths. The first method you will learn for combining shapes involves working with the Shape Builder tool (🔖). This tool allows you to visually and intuitively merge, delete, fill and edit overlapping shapes and paths directly in the artwork.

Working with the Shape Builder tool

Next, you will finish the end of a wrench using shapes and the Shape Builder tool.

1 Click the Next button (▶) in the status bar in the lower-left corner of the Document window to navigate to the second artboard.

2 Choose File > Open and open the wrench.ai file in the Lesson03 folder in the Lessons folder.

3 Select the Selection tool (➤) in the Tools panel, and choose Select > All.

4 Choose Edit > Copy. Choose File > Close to close the wrench.ai file.

5 In the tools.ai file, choose Edit > Paste, and then choose Select > Deselect.

There are four gray shapes at the top end of the wrench, an ellipse, two rounded rectangles, and a rectangle on top of that. You are going to use them to create the end of the wrench.

6 Select the Zoom tool (🔍) in the Tools panel, and click three times on the gray shapes at the top of the wrench to zoom in.

7 Select the Selection tool. Drag a marquee across the top four gray shapes to select them.

8 With the shapes selected, select the Shape Builder tool (🔧) in the Tools panel.

Using the Shape Builder tool, you will now combine, delete, and paint these shapes.

▶ **Tip:** Zooming in helps you see what shapes you are going to combine.

9 Position the pointer over the left end of the large gray circle at the bottom of the selected shapes, indicated by the pink x in the figure. Drag up until the pointer touches part of the rectangle shape. See the figure at right. Release the mouse button to combine the shapes.

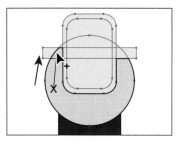

When shapes are selected and you select the Shape Builder tool, the overlapping shapes are divided into separate objects temporarily. As you drag from one part to another, a red outline appears showing you what the final shape outline will look like when it merges the shapes together.

10 With the Shape Builder tool selected, on the right side of the shapes, drag from the circle up until the pointer touches the right side of the rectangle, as shown in the figure.

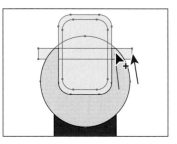

This combines the main parts of the end of the wrench. Next, you will delete some of the shapes that are not necessary.

11 With the shapes still selected, hold down the Alt (Windows) or Option (Mac OS) key and click the left end of the rectangle to delete it.

Notice that, with the modifier key held down, the pointer shows a minus sign (➤₋).

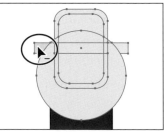

12 Repeat the same process to delete the end of the rectangle on the right side.

Next, you will delete a series of shapes using the Shape Builder tool.

13 With the Shape Builder tool still selected, position the pointer in the lower portion of the rounded rectangle. Hold down the Alt (Windows) or Option (Mac OS) key, and drag up to the top shape to delete them. Release the mouse button and then the modifier key.

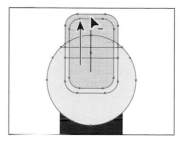

Notice that all of the shapes that will be deleted are highlighted as you drag.

14 With the Shape Builder tool, hold down the Shift+Alt (Windows) or Shift+Option (Mac OS) keys, and drag a marquee across the top four shapes that create the points of the wrench to delete them. Release the mouse first, then the modifier keys.

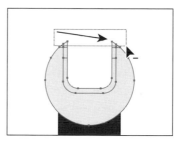

The Shift key allows you to drag a marquee around shapes, rather than dragging through them.

15 With the shapes still selected, change the Fill color ( ) in the Control panel to black. This won't change anything on the artboard.

The next shape you click with the Shape Builder tool will have a black fill.

Next, you will combine the remaining shapes.

16 With the Shape Builder tool, click the U shape and notice that the shape now has a black fill.

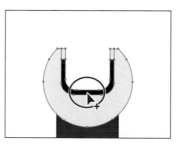

You can apply fills to any of the shapes by selecting the fill color first, and then clicking the shape.

17 Hold down the Shift key and drag a marquee across the inside shapes to merge them. Release the mouse first, then the key.

18 Double-click the Shape Builder tool in the Tools panel. This opens the Shape Builder Tool Options dialog box.

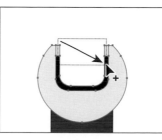

▶ **Tip:** This selection requires precision, so you may want to zoom in. If the results are unexpected, choose Edit > Undo Merge and try again.

Tip: For information on the Shape Builder tool and the options in the Shape Builder Tool Options dialog box, see "Shape Builder" in Illustrator Help.

19 In the Shape Builder Tool Options dialog box, choose Artwork from the Pick Color From menu. When merging shapes, this setting means that the first shape you drag from determines the color fill of the final merged shaped. Click OK.

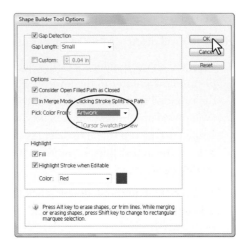

20 Choose Select > All On Active Artboard. Notice that the Fill color in the Control panel is set to black.

21 With the Shape Builder tool selected, drag from the top gray circular shape down to the dark gray rectangle (behind the orange shape). This merges the wrench end and the wrench body to make one shape.

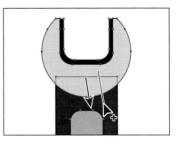

Notice that the resulting shape is the light gray of the wrench end. This is because you selected the Pick Color From Artwork setting in the Shape Builder Tools Options dialog box.

22 Choose Select > Deselect, then choose File > Save.

Working with Pathfinder effects

Pathfinder effects in the Pathfinder panel let you combine shapes in many different ways to create paths or groups of paths, by default. When a Pathfinder effect is applied (such as Merge), the original objects selected are permanently transformed. If the effect results in more than one shape, they are grouped automatically.

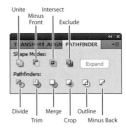

Next, you will create the other end of the wrench, using Pathfinder effects.

1 Choose View > Fit Artboard In Window.

2 Choose Window > Pathfinder to open the Pathfinder panel group.

3 Select the Polygon tool (⬡) in the Tools panel from the Star tool (☆) group. Click the artboard to open the Polygon dialog box. Change the radius to **0.4 in** and the sides to **6**. Click OK.

4 With the Selection tool (▶), hold down the Shift key and click the bottom circle of the wrench. Release the Shift key, then click the circle once more to set it as the key object. In the Control panel, click the Horizontal Align Center button (⬓) and the Vertical Align Center button (◫▸) to align the two objects to each other.

● **Note:** If the Align options do not appear in the Control panel, you can click the word Align to see the Align panel. You can also open the Align panel by choosing Window > Align.

5 With the shapes still selected, in the Pathfinder panel, click the Minus Front button (◻). With the new shape selected, notice the words Compound Path on the left side of the Control panel.

6 Select the Zoom tool (🔍) in the Tools panel and click twice on the selected content to zoom in.

7 With the Selection tool, double-click the newly created compound path to enter isolation mode. The compound path is temporarily ungrouped so that you can select its parts individually. Click the top edge of the polygon in the center of the circle to select it. Holding down the Alt+Shift (Windows) or Option+Shift (Mac OS) keys, drag the top bounding point up to resize that shape to a height of about 1 in. Release the mouse button and then the modifier keys.

▶ **Tip:** Another way to enter isolation mode is to select the object and click the Isolate Selected Object button (⬚) in the Control panel.

8 Press the Escape key to exit isolation mode, and then Select > All On Active Artboard.

9 Select the Shape Builder tool (🔩) and, holding down the Alt (Windows) or Option (Mac OS) key, click the dark gray shape showing behind the wrench end to delete it.

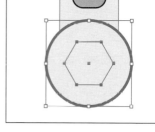
Align the shapes.

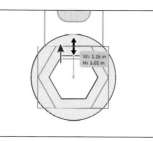
Resize the center shape.

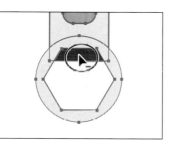
Delete the dark gray shape.

10 With the shapes still selected, choose Object > Group.

11 Select the Selection tool (▶) in the Tools panel and drag the group of objects to the left side of the artboard.

12 Choose Select > Deselect, then choose File > Save.

Working with shape modes

Shape modes create paths like Pathfinder effects, but they can also be used to create compound shapes. When several shapes are selected, clicking a shape mode while pressing the Alt (Windows) or Option (Mac OS) key creates a compound shape rather than a path. The original underlying objects of compound shapes are preserved. As a result, you can still select each object within a compound shape.

Next, you will use shape modes to create a gear.

1 Select the Star tool (⭐) in the Tools panel. Click the right side of the artboard and drag to create a star. Without releasing the mouse button, press the Up Arrow key until the star has 12 points. Hold down the Ctrl (Windows) or Command (Mac OS) key and drag toward the center of a star to decrease the radius to match the figure. Release the modifier key, but not the mouse button.

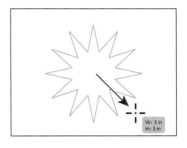

Hold down the Shift key and drag toward or away from the center of the star until the width and height are approximately 3 in, as shown in the measurement tooltip. Release the mouse button and then the modifier key.

2 Click the Fill color in the Control panel and select white in the Swatches panel that appears.

3 Select the Ellipse tool (◯) in the Tools panel. While holding down the Alt (Windows) or Option (Mac OS) key, click the center of the star you just created (the word "center" appears). In the Ellipse dialog box, change the width and height to **2 in** and click OK.

The modifier key in this step draws a circle from the center where you clicked.

4 With the Selection tool, hold down the Shift key and select the star to select both shapes.

5 With the objects selected, click the Merge button (⬜) in the Pathfinder panel (Window > Pathfinder).

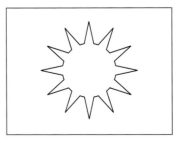

Notice that the shapes are combined but the stroke disappears. With the shape selected, click the Stroke color in the Control panel and select black.

6 Choose Select > Deselect.

7 Select the Ellipse tool (⬤) and click the center of the merged shape. In the Ellipse dialog box, change the width and height to **2.5 in** and click OK.

8 With the Selection tool, hold down the Shift key and select the star to select both shapes. In the Control panel, click the Horizontal Align Center button (⬚) and the Vertical Align Center button (⬚) to align the two shapes to each other.

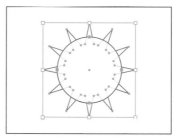

At this point, you have the two shapes selected that will combine to make a gear.

9 With the two shapes selected, hold down the Alt (Windows) or Option (Mac OS) key, and click the Intersect button (⬚) in the Pathfinder panel.

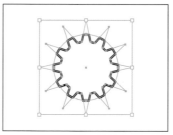

This creates a compound shape that traces the outline of the overlapping area of both objects. You can still edit the circle and the star shape separately.

⬤ **Note:** The stroke weight for the gear in the figure has been exaggerated so that it is easier to see.

10 With the Selection tool, double-click the gear to enter isolation mode.

11 Choose View > Outline so that you can see the two pieces (the circle and the star). Click the edge of the circle to select it, if it isn't already selected.

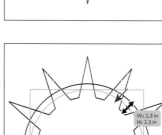

▶ **Tip:** To edit the original shapes in a compound shape like the gear, you can also select them individually with the Direct Selection tool (▷).

12 While pressing the Shift+Alt (Windows) or Shift+Option (Mac OS) keys, drag a corner of the circle bounding box toward its center to make it smaller. This resizes the circle from the center. Drag until the width and height show approximately 2.3 inches in the measurement tooltip. Release the mouse button, and then the modifier keys.

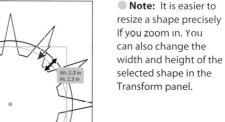

⬤ **Note:** It is easier to resize a shape precisely if you zoom in. You can also change the width and height of the selected shape in the Transform panel.

13 Choose View > Preview.

14 With the Selection tool, double-click outside the gear to exit isolation mode.

You will now expand the gear. Expanding a compound shape maintains the shape of the compound object, but you can no longer select or edit the original objects.

15 With the Selection tool, click to select the gear. Click the Expand button in the Pathfinder panel. Close the Pathfinder panel group.

16 Choose Select > Deselect.

17 With the Selection tool, drag the gear so that it is on the right side of the artboard.

18 Choose View > Fit Artboard In Window.

Position the wrench and gear so that they look something like the figure at right.

19 Choose File > Save, and then File > Close.

In the next lesson, you'll learn how to work with Live Trace.

Using Live Trace to create shapes

In this part of the lesson, you will learn how to work with the Live Trace command. Live Trace traces existing artwork, like a raster picture from Photoshop. You can then convert the drawing to vector paths or a Live Paint object.

1   Choose File > Open, and open the L3start_2.ai file in the Lesson03 folder.

2   Choose File > Save As, name the file **snowboarding.ai**, and select the Lesson03 folder in the Save As dialog box. Leave the Save As Type option set to Adobe Illustrator (*.AI) (Windows) or the Format option set to Adobe Illustrator (ai) (Mac OS), and click Save. In the Illustrator Options dialog box, leave the Illustrator options at their default settings, and click OK.

● **Note:** A Missing Profile dialog box may appear. Click OK to continue.

3   Choose View > Fit Artboard In Window.

4   With the Selection tool (▶), select the snowboarder sketch.

Note that the Control panel options change when the scanned image is activated. It says Image on the left side of the Control panel, and you can see the resolution (PPI: 150).

5 Click the Live Trace button in the Control panel. This converts the image from raster to vector.

With Live Trace, you can view your changes as you make them. You can change the settings, or even the original placed image, and then see the updates immediately.

6 Click the Tracing Options Dialog button (▦) in the Control panel, and choose Comic Art from the Preset menu. Select Preview to experiment with different presets and options. Leave the Tracing Options dialog box open.

▶ **Tip:** In the Tracing Options dialog box, notice the Ignore White option. Selecting this options allows the white areas become transparent, which is especially helpful when tracing an image with a white background.

▶ **Tip:** For information on Live Trace and the options in the Tracing Options dialog box, see "Tracing artwork" in Illustrator Help.

As shown by the options in the Tracing Options dialog box, the Live Trace feature can interpret black and white sketches as well as full-color images.

7 In the Tracing Options dialog box, change Threshold to **220**. After experimenting with other settings in the Tracing Options dialog box, make sure that Comic Art preset is selected, and click Trace.

The snowboarder is now a tracing object (vector). However, the anchor points and paths are not yet editable. To edit the content, you must expand the tracing object.

● **Note:** Threshold specifies a value for generating a black and white tracing result from the original image. All pixels lighter than the Threshold value are converted to white, and all pixels darker than the Threshold value are converted to black.

8 With the snowboarder still selected, click the Expand button in the Control panel.

9 Choose Object > Ungroup, and then Select > Deselect.

Note: If any unexpected white area is deleted, you can undo several steps by choosing Edit > Undo. Try tracing again by raising the Threshold value to more than 220 in the Tracing Options dialog box.

10 Select the Selection tool (➤) in the Tools panel, and then click the white background surrounding the snowboarder. Press Delete to remove the white shape.

11 With the Selection tool, try clicking to select other parts of the snowboarder. Notice that the figure is composed of many shapes and paths.

12 Choose File > Save, and close the file.

Exploring on your own

Now you'll experiment with a few of the tools you learned in this lesson.

1 Open the tools.ai file. Select the gear shapes and create an ellipse that is centered on the gear. Select the gear shape and the ellipse and click the Minus Front button (⬚) in the Pathfinder panel to create a compound path.

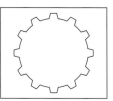 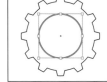 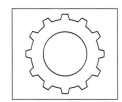

The original gear   Create the ellipse.   Create the compound path.

2 With the Selection tool, drag the gear shape on top of the wrench to see the hole in the middle of the gear.

3 In the tools.ai file, choose File > Place and place a raster image. Try selecting the raster image, and then clicking the Live Trace button in the Control panel. Choose a preset from the Tracing Preset menu in the Control panel.

4 Experiment with shapes by creating a shape such as a circle, star, or rectangle. Clone it several times using the Alt (Windows) or Option (Mac OS) key.

5 Choose File > Close without saving the file.

Review questions

1 What are the basic shape tools? Describe how to tear or separate a group of shape tools away from the Tools panel.

2 How do you select a shape with no fill?

3 How do you draw a square?

4 How do you change the number of sides on a polygon as you draw?

5 Name two ways you can combine several shapes into one.

6 How can you convert a raster image to editable vector shapes?

Review answers

1 There are six basic shape tools: Rectangle, Rounded Rectangle, Ellipse, Polygon, Star, and Flare. To tear off a group of tools from the Tools panel, position the pointer over the tool that appears in the Tools panel and hold down the mouse button until the group of tools appears. Without releasing the mouse button, drag to the triangle at the bottom of the group, and then release the mouse button to tear off the group.

2 Items that have no fill can be selected by clicking the stroke.

3 To draw a square, select the Rectangle tool in the Tools panel. Hold down the Shift key and drag to draw the square, or click the artboard to enter equal dimensions for the width and height in the Rectangle dialog box.

4 To change the number of sides on a polygon as you draw, select the Polygon tool in the Tools panel. Start dragging to draw the shape, and hold down the Down Arrow key to reduce the number of sides and the Up Arrow key to increase the number of sides.

5 Using the Shape Builder tool, you can visually and intuitively merge, delete, fill and edit overlapping shapes and paths directly in the artwork. You can also use the Pathfinder effects to create new shapes out of overlapping objects. You can apply Pathfinder effects by using the Effects menu or the Pathfinder panel.

6 If you want to base a new drawing on an existing piece of artwork, you can trace it. To convert the tracing to paths, click Expand in the Control panel or choose Object > Live Trace > Expand. Use this method if you want to work with the components of the traced artwork as individual objects. The resulting paths are grouped.

4 TRANSFORMING OBJECTS

Lesson overview

In this lesson, you'll learn how to do the following:

- Add, edit, rename, and reorder artboards in an existing document.
- Navigate artboards.
- Select individual objects, objects in a group, and parts of an object.
- Move, scale, and rotate objects using a variety of methods.
- Work with smart guides.
- Reflect, shear, and distort objects.
- Adjust the perspective of an object.
- Apply a distortion filter.
- Position objects precisely.
- Repeat transformations quickly and easily.
- Copy to multiple artboards.

 This lesson will take approximately an hour to complete. If needed, remove the previous lesson folder from your hard disk and copy the Lesson04 folder onto it.

You can modify objects in many ways as you create artwork, including quickly and precisely controlling their size, shape, and orientation. In this lesson, you'll explore creating and editing artboards, the various Transform commands, and specialized tools as you create several pieces of artwork.

Getting started

In this lesson, you'll create content and use it in three pieces of artwork to create a letterhead design, an envelope, and a business card. Before you begin, you'll restore the default preferences for Adobe® Illustrator®, and then open a file containing a composite of the finished artwork to see what you'll create.

1 To ensure that the tools and panels function as described in this lesson, delete or deactivate (by renaming) the Adobe Illustrator CS5 preferences file. See "Restoring default preferences" on page 3.

2 Start Adobe Illustrator CS5.

● **Note:** If you have not already done so, copy the resource files for this lesson onto your hard disk, from the Lesson04 folder on the Adobe Illustrator CS5 Classroom in a Book CD. See "Copying the Classroom in a Book files" on page 2.

3 Choose File > Open, and open the L4end_1.ai file in the Lesson04 folder, located in the Lessons folder on your hard disk.

This file contains the three pieces of finished artwork: a letterhead, a business card (front and back), and an envelope.

4 Choose View > Fit All In Window and leave the artwork on-screen as you work. Select the Hand tool ( ) to move the artwork where you want it in the window. If you don't want to leave the file open, choose File > Close.

To begin working, you'll open an existing art file set up for the letterhead artwork.

5 Choose File > Open to open the L4start_1.ai file in the Lesson04 folder, located in the Lessons folder on your hard disk. This file has been saved with the rulers showing and cyan colored guidelines for you to use when scaling objects as you create them.

6 Choose File > Save As. In the Save As dialog box, name the file **green_glow.ai**, and navigate to the Lesson04 folder. Leave the Save As Type option set to Adobe Illustrator (*.AI) (Windows) or the Format option set to Adobe Illustrator (ai) (Mac OS), and click Save. In the Illustrator Options dialog box, leave the Illustrator options at their default settings, and click OK.

7 Choose Window > Workspace > Essentials.

Working with artboards

Artboards represent the regions that can contain printable artwork, similar to pages in Adobe InDesign. You can use artboards to crop areas for printing or for placement purposes. Use multiple artboards for creating a variety of things, such as multiple page PDF files, printed pages with different sizes or different elements, independent elements for websites, video storyboards, or individual items for animation.

Adding artboards to the document

You can add and remove artboards at any time while working in a document. You can create artboards in different sizes, resize them with the Artboard tool or Artboards panel, and position them anywhere in the Document window. All artboards are numbered and can have a unique name assigned to them. The number and name appear in the upper-left corner of the artboard when the Artboard tool is selected.

To begin, this document has one artboard for the letterhead. You will add more artboards to create the business card (front and back) and envelope.

1 Choose View > Fit Artboard In Window. This is artboard number 1.

2 Press Ctrl++ (Windows) or Cmd++ (Mac OS) to zoom in twice.

3 Pressing the spacebar to temporarily access the Hand tool (✋). Drag the artboard to the left and down until you see the canvas off the upper-right corner of the artboard.

4 Select the Artboard tool (▱) in the Tools panel, and to the right of the existing artboard, bring the pointer in line with the top edge of the existing artboard until a green alignment guide appears. Drag down and to the right to create an artboard that is 3.5 inches (width) by 2 inches (height). A measurement label indicates when the artboard is the correct size.

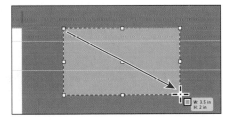

> **Tip:** If you zoom in on an artboard, the measurement labels have smaller increments.

5 Click the New Artboard button (▣) in the Control panel. This allows you to create a duplicate of the last selected artboard.

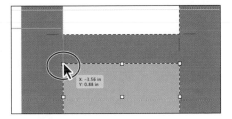

6 Position the pointer below the new artboard and line it up with the left edge of the artboard. When a vertical green alignment guide appears, click to create a copy of the artboard. This is artboard number 3.

7 Select the Selection tool (▶) in the Tools panel.

8 Click the Artboards panel icon (▣) on the right side of the workspace to expand the Artboards panel.

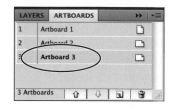

Notice that Artboard 3 is highlighted in the panel. The active artboard is always highlighted in this panel.

The Artboards panel allows you to see how many artboards the document currently contains. It also allows you to reorder, rename, add, and delete artboards and choose many other options related to artboards.

Next, you will create a copy of artboard 2 using this panel.

9 Click the New Artboard button (▣) at the bottom of the panel to create a copy of Artboard 3 (called Artboard 4).

Notice that a copy is placed to the right of artboard 2 in the Document window.

▶ **Tip:** With the Artboard tool, you can also copy artboards by holding down the Alt (Windows) or Option (Mac OS) key and dragging them until the copied artboard clears the original. When creating new artboards, you can place them anywhere; you can even overlap them.

10 Click the Artboards panel icon to collapse the panel.

11 Choose View > Fit All In Window.

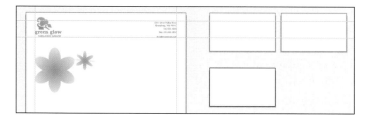

Editing artboards

You can edit or delete an artboard at any time by using the Artboard tool, the menu commands, or the Artboards panel. Next, you will reposition and change the sizes of several of the artboards using multiple methods.

1 Select the Artboard tool (▣) in the Tools panel and click the bottom artboard on the right to select it.

Next, you will resize an artboard by entering values in the Control panel.

2 Select the upper-left point in the reference point locator (▦) in the Control panel.

This allows you to resize an artboard from the upper-left corner of the artboard. By default, artboards are resized from the center.

3   With artboard named "03 - Artboard 3" selected, notice the bounding points around the artboard and the dotted box. In the Control panel, change the width to **9.5 in** and the height to **4 in**.

You will see the Constrain Width and Height Proportions button (⬚) in the Control panel between the Width and Height fields. This button, if selected, allows both fields to change in proportion to each other.

● **Note:** If you don't see the Width and Height fields in the Control panel, click the Artboard Options button (⊞) in the Control panel and enter the values in the dialog box that appears.

Another way to resize an artboard is to drag the active artboard handles using the Artboard tool, which is what you'll do next.

4   With the Artboard tool still selected and the bottom-right artboard selected, drag the bottom-center bounding point of the artboard down until the height is approximately 4.25 in as shown in the measurement label.

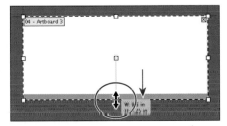

▶ **Tip:** To delete an artboard, select the artboard with the Artboard tool and either press Delete, click the Delete Artboard button (⬚) in the Control panel, or click the Delete icon (⊠) in upper-right corner of an artboard. You can delete all but the last artboard.

5   With the Artboard tool, click the top artboard on the right (artboard 04 - Artboard 4). Click the Show Center Mark button (⊡) in the Control panel to show a center mark for the active artboard only.

6   Select the Selection tool (▶) in the Tools panel to see the center mark. Also, notice the black outline around the artboard, which indicates the currently active artboard.

The center mark can be used for many purposes, including working with video content.

● **Note:** Clicking the Artboard Options button in the Control panel, with the Artboard tool selected, also displays the center mark for an artboard.

7   Click the Artboards panel icon (⬚) to expand the Artboards panel. Click the name "Artboard 1" in the Artboards panel to make it the active artboard. This is the original artboard. Notice that a dark border appears around Artboard 1 in the Document window. This indicates that it is active.

There can be only one active artboard at a time. Commands such as View > Fit Artboard In Window apply to the active artboard.

Next, you will edit the active artboard size by choosing a preset value.

8 Click the Artboard Options button (⬜) to the right of the name "Artboard 1" in the Artboards panel. This opens the Artboard Options dialog box.

▶ **Tip:** You also may have noticed that this button appears to the right of each artboard. It allows access to the artboard options for each artboard, but also shows the orientation of the artboard.

9 Locate the reference point locator (⬚) in the Position category and make sure that the upper-left dot still selected.

This ensures that the artboard will be resized from the upper-left corner.

10 Choose Letter from the Presets menu in the Artboard Options dialog box.

The Presets menu lets you change a selected artboard to a set size. Notice that the sizes in the Presets menu include web sizes (800x600, for instance) and video sizes (NTSC DV, for instance). You can also fit the artboard to the artwork bounds or the selected art, which is a great way to fit an artboard to a logo, for instance. Click OK.

11 Click the Document Setup button in the Control panel.

▶ **Tip:** You can also access the Document Setup dialog box by choosing File > Document Setup.

▶ **Tip:** To learn more about the Document Setup dialog box, search for "document setup" in Illustrator Help.

12 In the Document Setup dialog box, change the Top Bleed option to .125 in by clicking the up arrow to the left of the field. Notice that all the values change together, because Make All Settings The Same (⬚) is selected. Click OK.

The Document Setup dialog box contains many useful options for the current document, including units, type options, transparency settings and more.

● **Note:** All changes made in the Document Setup dialog box apply to all artboards in the document.

13 Select the Artboard tool (⬚) in the Tools panel.

14 Click the upper-right artboard and drag it to the right so that the two smaller artboards are a little farther apart and so that the bleed guides have some room between them.

You can drag artboards at any time and even overlap them if necessary.

15 Select the Selection tool (▶) in the Tools panel.

16 Choose Window > Workspace > Essentials.

17 Choose File > Save.

● **Note:** When you drag an artboard with content on it, the art moves with the artboard, by default. If you want to move an artboard, but not the art on it, select the Artboard tool, and then click to deselect Move/Copy Artwork With Artboard (⊞).

Renaming Artboards

By default, artboards are assigned a number and a name. When you navigate the artboards in a document, generic names make it difficult to keep the artboards straight.

Next, you are going to rename the artboards so that they are more useful.

1 Click the Artboards panel icon (🗐) to expand the Artboards panel.

2 Double-click the name Artboard 1 in the panel to make that artboard the active artboard and to fit it in the Document window.

3 Click the Artboard Options button (🗋) to the right of the name Artboard 1 in the panel, to open the Artboard Options dialog box.

▶ **Tip:** You can also access the Artboard Options dialog box by double-clicking the Artboard tool in the Tools panel. This opens the dialog box for the currently active artboard. You can make an artboard the currently active artboard by clicking the artboard with the Selection tool.

4 Change the Name field to **Letterhead** and click OK.

You will now rename the rest of the artboards.

5 Click the name Artboard 2 in the panel and then click the Artboard Options button (🗋) to the right of the name in the panel.

6 Change the Name field to **BC - Front** and click OK.

7 Do the same for the remaining two artboards, changing Artboard 3 to **Envelope**, and Artboard 4 to **BC - Back**.

8 Choose File > Save and keep the Artboards panel expanded for the next steps.

Reordering Artboards

When you navigate your document, the order in which the artboards appear can be important, especially if you are navigating the document using the Next artboard and Previous artboard commands. By default, artboards are ordered according to the order in which they are created, but you can change that order. Next, you will Reorder the artboards so that the two sides of the business card are in the correct order.

1 With the Artboards panel still open, click the name Envelope in the panel. This makes the envelope artboard the active artboard.

2 Choose View > Fit All In Window.

3 Click the Move Down button at the bottom of the panel.

   This moves the artboard down in order to become the last artboard, artboard 4. Notice that it does nothing to the artboards in the Document window.

4 Double-click BC - Front in the Artboards panel to fit that artboard in the Document Window.

5 Click the Next Artboard button (▶) in the lower-left corner of the Document window to navigate to the next artboard (BC - Back). This fits the BC - Back artboard in the Document window.

   If you had not changed the order, the next artboard would have been the envelope.

Now that the artboards are set up, you will concentrate on transforming artwork to create the content for the artboards.

Transforming content

Transforming content allows you to move, rotate, reflect, scale, and shear objects. Objects can be transformed using the Transform panel, selection tools, specialized tools, Transform commands, guides, and smart guides. In this part of the lesson, you will transform content using a variety of methods.

Working with rulers and guides

● **Note:** By default, the ruler origin appears in the upper-left corner of the active artboard, but you can change the location if necessary.

Rulers help you accurately place and measure objects. The point where 0 appears on each ruler is called the ruler origin. Some people refer to it as the zero, zero point. The ruler origin can be reset depending on which artboard is active. There are also two types of rulers available: document rulers and artboard rulers. Artboard rulers are the default, which means that when an artboard becomes active, the zero on each ruler is set to the upper-left corner of the active artboard.

Guides are non-printing lines that help you align objects. You can create horizontal and vertical ruler guides by dragging them from the rulers.

Next, you will make the rulers visible, reset the origin point, and create a guide.

1 In the Artboards panel, double-click the BC - Back artboard name to navigate to that artboard, if not already there.

2 Click the Layers panel icon (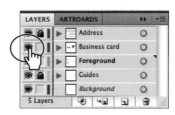) on the right side of the workspace. Click to select the Visibility column to the left of the Business card layer name. Click the Business card layer name to select it.

Any new content, including guides, is placed on the selected layer.

▶ **Tip:** To learn more about layers, see Lesson 8, "Working with Layers."

3 Shift-drag from the left vertical ruler toward the right, to create a vertical guide at 1/4 inch on the horizontal ruler. The Shift key snaps the guide to the ruler units as you drag. Release the mouse button and then the Shift key.

4 Choose View > Guides > Lock Guides to prevent them from being accidentally moved.

5 Click the Layers panel icon () to collapse the panel again. Choose File > Save.

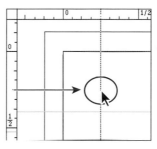

● **Note:** If the 0,0 point does not appear in the upper left corner of the artboard, choose View > Rulers > and make sure that you see Change To Global Rulers. If you see Change To Artboard Rulers, choose it.

▶ **Tip:** To change the units for a document, choose File > Document Setup or, with nothing selected, click the Document Setup button in the Control panel. You can also right-click (Windows) or Ctrl-click (Mac OS) either ruler to change the units.

Scaling objects

Objects are scaled by enlarging or reducing them horizontally (along the x axis) and vertically (along the y axis) relative to a fixed reference point that you designate. If you don't designate an origin, objects are scaled from their center point. You'll use three methods to scale the objects that make up parts of the business card.

First, you'll set the preference to scale strokes and effects. Then, you'll scale a logo background by dragging its bounding box and aligning it to the guides provided.

1 Choose Edit > Preferences > General (Windows) or Illustrator > Preferences > General (Mac OS), and select Scale Strokes & Effects. This scales the stroke width of any object scaled in this lesson. Click OK.

2 Select the Rectangle tool (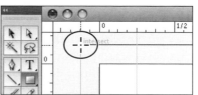) in the Tools panel. Position the pointer in the upper-left corner of the red bleed guides and click when the word "intersect" and the green alignment guides appear.

3 In the Rectangle dialog box, change the width to **3.75** in and the height to **2.25** in. Click OK.

4 Click the Fill color in the Control panel and select the business card gradient swatch. A tooltip appears when you hover over the colors in the panel.

5 With the rectangle still selected, choose Object > Hide > Selection. This makes it easier to edit other content.

6 Select the Rounded Rectangle tool (▢) from the Rectangle group, and then position the pointer at the vertical guide and in line with the center mark (green cross hairs) until a horizontal alignment guide appears. Drag down and to the right, so that the bottom of the shape is on the bottom horizontal guide and the right edge of the shape is aligned with the center mark. The width shown in the measurement label is 1.5 in.

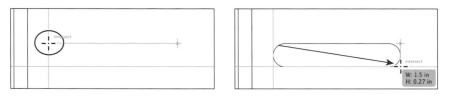

7 Select black for the fill color in the Control panel.

● **Note:** Pressing Shift as you drag constrains the object proportionally.

8 With the Selection tool (▶), Shift-drag the lower-right corner of the object's bounding box up and to the left until the width is about 1.4 in, as shown in the measurement label. Release the mouse button and then the Shift key.

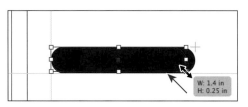

● **Note:** If you do not see the bounding box, choose View > Show Bounding Box.

9 With the object still selected, press the Alt (Windows) or Option (Mac OS) key and drag the bottom, middle bounding point down to just below the lower horizontal guide. This doesn't have to be exact. Release the mouse button and then the modifier key.

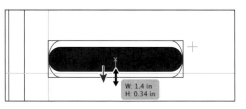

10 Choose 1 Letterhead from the Artboard Navigation menu in the status bar.

11 Choose View > Outline.

12 With the Selection tool, drag a marquee across the text below the large flower to select it all. Choose Edit > Cut.

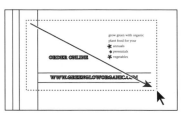

13 Choose 3 BC - Back from the Artboard Navigation menu in the status bar to return to the business card artboard.

14 Choose Edit > Paste. Choose Select > Deselect.

15 Holding down the Shift key, drag a vertical guide from the vertical ruler to 1½ in on the horizontal ruler.

16 With the Selection tool, select the text "Order Online" and drag it so that the right edge aligns with the new guide as closely as possible. Vertically align the text to the center of the rounded rectangle. Leave it selected and choose View > Preview.

17 In the Control panel, click the word Transform. In the Transform panel that appears, click the middle-right reference point of the Reference Point Locator (⊞) to set the reference point. Click to select the Constrain Width And Height Proportions icon (⊟) between the W and H fields in the Transform panel. Change the width to **1.1** in, and then press Enter or Return to decrease the size of the text.

● **Note:** Depending on the resolution of your screen, the Transform options may appear in the Control panel. If they do appear, you can set the options directly in the Control panel. You can also choose Window > Transform to open the Transform panel.

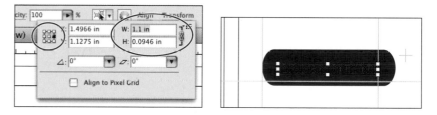

Next, you'll use the Scale tool to resize and copy the rounded rectangle.

18 With the Selection tool, click to select the rounded rectangle.

19 Double-click the Scale tool (⬚) in the Tools panel.

20 In the Scale dialog box, select the Preview option. Change Vertical to **80%** and click Copy to make a smaller copy on top of the other rounded rectangle.

21 Change the Fill color in the Control panel to white.

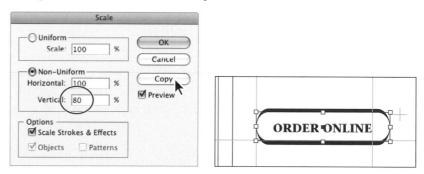

Reflecting objects

When you reflect an object, Illustrator creates a reflection of the object across an invisible vertical or horizontal axis. Copying objects while reflecting allows you to create a mirror image of the object based on a point. In a similar way to scaling and rotating, when you reflect an object, you either designate the reference point or use the object's center point by default. Next, you'll place a symbol on the artboard and use the Reflect tool to flip and copy it 90° across the vertical axis, and then scale and rotate the copy into position.

▶ **Tip:** To learn more about symbols, see Lesson 14, "Working with Symbols."

1 Click the Symbols panel icon (♣) on the right side of the workspace. Drag the Floral symbol onto the BC - Back artboard.

2 Click the Symbols panel icon (♣) to collapse the panel.

3 With the symbol selected, double-click the Scale tool (⬚) in the Tools panel.

4 In the Scale dialog box, change Uniform Scale to **30%,** and click OK.

5 Choose View > Smart Guides to turn them off temporarily.

6 Select the Selection tool (▶) and drag the symbol down below "Order Online," aligning the left edge of the symbol with the guide at 1/4". It doesn't have to be exact.

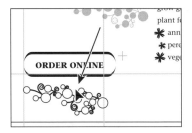

7 Choose View > Smart Guides to select them.

8 With the symbol still selected, choose Edit > Copy and Edit > Paste In Front to put a copy directly on top of the symbol.

▶ **Tip:** To reflect and copy in one step, you can Alt-click (Windows) or Option-click (Mac OS) with the Reflect tool while setting the reflect around point. Select Vertical in the Reflect dialog box, and then click Copy.

9 Select the Reflect tool (🔁) that's nested within the Rotate tool (⟳) in the Tools panel, and then click the right edge of the symbol (the word "edge" may appear).

This will set the reflect around point to the right edge rather than the center, which is the default.

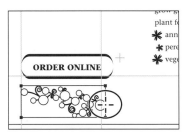

10 With the symbol copy selected, position the pointer off the right edge of the symbol and drag counter-clockwise. As you are dragging, hold down the Shift key. When the measurement label shows −90°, release the mouse, and then the modifier key.

The Shift key constrains the rotation to 45° as it is reflected.

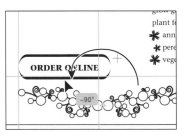

Rotating objects

Objects are rotated by turning them around a designated reference point. You can rotate objects by displaying their bounding boxes and moving the pointer to an outside corner. When the rotate pointer appears, click to rotate the object around its center point. You can also rotate objects using the Transform panel to set a reference point and a rotation angle.

You'll rotate both symbols using the Rotate tool.

1 With the Selection tool (▶), select the leftmost symbol. Select the Rotate tool (⟳) nested within the Reflect tool (⧗) in the Tools panel. Double-click the Rotate tool (⟳) in the Tools panel. Notice that the symbol's reference point (⊕) is its center.

2 In the Rotate dialog box, make sure that Preview is selected. Change the angle to **20**, and then click OK to rotate the symbol around the reference point.

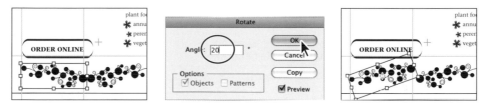

● **Note:** If you select an object and then select the Rotate tool, you can Alt-click (Windows)or Option-click (Mac OS) anywhere on the object (or artboard) to set a reference point and open the Rotate dialog box.

3 Select the Selection tool and click the symbol on the right. Repeat the steps above to rotate that symbol, this time entering **−20** in the Angle field.

4 With the Selection tool, Shift-click to add the symbol on the left to the current selection. Choose Object > Group.

5 Choose View > Zoom Out.

6 Select the Rotate tool. Click the bottom-right edge of the group to set the reference point (⊕). Drag from the left side of the group, up and to the right. Notice that the movement is constrained to a circle rotating around the reference point. While dragging, hold down the Shift key to constrain the rotation to 45°. When the group is vertical and the measurement label shows −90°, release the mouse button, and then the modifier key.

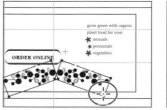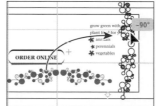

7 With the Selection tool, drag the group to the right edge of artboard, if it's not already there. Visually center it vertically on the artboard. The placement does not have to be exact.

8 Shift-drag the left-middle bounding point of the group to the right to resize it so that the group fits within the top and bottom bleed guides.

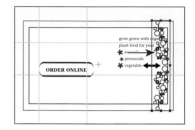

9 With the group still selected, click the word Opacity in the Control panel to reveal the Transparency panel. In the Transparency panel, click the word Normal and choose Overlay from the menu.

▶ **Tip:** To learn more about blending modes, see "about blending modes" in Illustrator Help.

10 Choose Object > Show All to see the business card background.

11 Choose View > Guides > Hide Guides.

12 Choose File > Save.

Distorting objects

You can distort the original shapes of objects in different ways, using various tools. Now, you'll create a flower, first using the Twist effect to twirl the shape of a star, and then applying the Pucker & Bloat distort filter to transform its center.

1 Click the First button (⏮) in the status bar to navigate to artboard 1.

2 Choose View > Guides > Show Guides.

3 With the Selection tool (▶), click to select the large flower shape below the Green Glow logo.

4 Choose Effect > Warp > Twist. Select Preview in the Warp Options dialog box. Change the Bend to **60** and click OK.

Twist distortion is applied as an effect, which maintains the original shape and lets you remove or edit the effect at any time in the Appearance panel. Learn more about using effects in Lesson 12, "Applying Effects."

Now, you'll draw the middle part of the flower which will be centered on top of the flower.

5   With the flower still selected, choose Window > Attributes to open the Attributes panel. Choose Show All from the panel menu (▼≡). Click the Show Center button (⊡) to display the center point of the flower.

6   Close the Attributes panel group.

7   Select the Zoom tool (🔍), and then click the flower shapes twice.

8   Select the Star tool (☆) nested within the Rounded Rectangle tool, and drag from the center point to draw a star over the center of the flower. Press the Up Arrow key once to add a point to the star, making a total of six points on the star. Press the Shift key and drag until the width is approximately .8 in, as shown in the measurement label. Release the mouse button and the Shift key, and keep the star selected.

9   Click Fill color in the Control panel and choose the light green swatch (12c 0m 47y 0k). Press the Escape key to close the Swatches panel that appears.

Now, you'll distort the frontmost star using the Pucker & Bloat effect. This effect distorts objects inward and outward from their anchor points.

10 With the center star selected, choose Effect > Distort & Transform > Pucker & Bloat.

11 In the Pucker & Bloat dialog box, select Preview, and drag the slider to the left to change the value to roughly −80% to distort the star. Click OK.

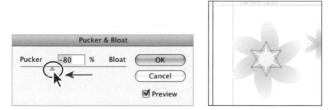

12 Choose View > Smart Guides to deselect smart guides.

13 With the Selection tool, position the pointer off the lower-right corner of the star bounding box until the rotate arrows (↩) appear. Drag down and to the left until the star points are approximately lined up with the flower shape behind it.

When you rotate or distort objects, the bounding box is also rotated or distorted. When necessary, you can reset the bounding box so that it is squared to the object again.

14 With the shape still selected, choose Object > Transform > Reset Bounding Box.

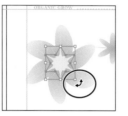 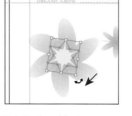 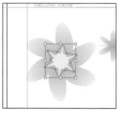

| Position the pointer. | Rotate the object. | Reset the bounding box. |

15 With the Selection tool, Shift-click the flower shape behind it and the smaller flower shape to the right to select all three shapes. Choose Object > Group.

16 In the Control panel, change Opacity value to **20**.

17 Choose Select > Deselect, and then File > Save.

Shearing objects

Shearing an object slants, or skews, the sides of the object along the axis you specify, keeping opposite sides parallel and making the object asymmetrical.

Next, you'll copy and shear the logo shape.

1 Choose View > Fit Artboard In Window.

2 Choose View > Smart Guides to select the smart guides.

3 Select the Zoom tool (🔍) in the Tools panel and drag a marquee around the green glow logo in the upper-left corner of the artboard.

4 Select the Selection tool (▶). Click to select the flower shape above the "green glow" text.

5 Choose Edit > Copy, and then choose Edit > Paste In Front to paste a copy directly on top of the original.

6 Select the Shear tool (⬚↗) nested within the Scale tool (⬚) in the Tools panel. Position the pointer at the bottom edge of the flower shape and click to set the reference point. Shift-drag from the center of the flower shape to the left and stop before it reaches the edge of the artboard. Release the mouse button, and then the Shift key.

7 Change the opacity in the Control panel to **20%**.

8 Choose Object > Arrange > Send Backward to put the copy behind the original flower shape.

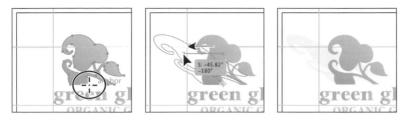

▶ **Tip:** In the Transform panel, you can also shear, rotate, and change the scale as well as the position on the x and y axes.

9 With the Selection tool, drag a marquee around the two flower shapes, the "green glow" text, and the "organic grow" text to select the logo pieces. Make sure not to select the dotted line to the right of the logo. Choose Object > Group.

10 Choose Edit > Copy, then Select > Deselect.

Positioning objects precisely

You can use the smart guides and the Transform panel to move objects to exact coordinates on the x and y axes of the page and to control the position of objects in relation to the edge of the artboard.

You'll add content to the envelope by pasting a copy of the logo into the envelope artwork, and then specifying its exact coordinates on the envelope.

1 Choose View > Fit All In Window to see all the artboards.

2 Choose 2 BC - Front from the Artboard Navigation menu in the lower-left corner of the Document window.

3 Choose Edit > Paste In Place. This positions the group in the same place on this artboard relative to the upper-left corner.

4 Using the Selection tool, hold down the Shift key and drag the logo group up. When the measurement label shows dX: 0 in and dY: −0.18, release the mouse button, and then the Shift key.

The dY indicates the distance moved along the Y axis (vertically).

● **Note:** The dY: −0.18 appears as a negative measurement in the measurement label for step 4 because the ruler origin (0,0) starts in the upper-left corner of the artboard. Dragging content up on an artboard gives you a negative value by default.

5 With the group still selected, choose Edit > Copy.

6 Choose Select > Deselect.

7 Choose 4 Envelope from the Artboard Navigation menu in the status bar to view the envelope. Choose Edit > Paste In Place.

8 Choose 3 BC - Back from the Artboard Navigation menu in the status bar to view the back of the business card.

9 With the Selection tool, Shift-click the text and all the small flowers in the upper-right corner of the business card.

10 Choose Object > Group, and then choose Edit > Copy.

11 Choose 4 Envelope from the Artboard Navigation menu in the status bar to return to the envelope artboard. Choose Edit > Paste.

● **Note:** Depending on your screen resolution, the word Transform may not appear in the Control panel. Instead, the Transform options may appear in the Control panel. You may also need to choose Window > Transform.

12 In the Control panel, click the word Transform, and then click the middle-left reference point (⊞) in the Transform panel. Change the X value to **0.45 in** and Y to **1.7 in**. Press Enter or Return to apply these settings. If the text is too close to the logo, press the down arrow key several times to better position it.

13 Click away from the artwork to deselect it, and then choose File > Save.

Changing the perspective

Now, you'll use the Free Transform tool to change the perspective of some text. The Free Transform tool is a multipurpose tool that, besides letting you change the perspective of an object, combines the functions of scaling, shearing, reflecting, and rotating.

1 With the Selection tool (▶), double-click the green glow logo in the upper-left corner. This puts the logo in isolation mode.

2 Select the text "organic grow" and choose Edit > Copy.

3 Double-click a blank area of the artboard to exit isolation mode.

4 Choose Edit > Paste. Drag the text to the bottom of the artboard, about 1 inch from the left edge of the artboard. Leave "organic grow" selected.

5 Select the Scale tool (⊞) nested within the Shear tool (⬚) in the Tools panel, and then Alt-click (Windows) or Option-click (Mac OS) the left side of the "organic grow" text to set the origin point. In the Scale dialog box select Preview, and then change Uniform Scale to **300**%. Click OK.

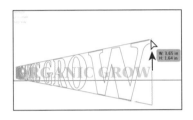

6 With the text selected, select the Free Transform tool (⬚) in the Tools panel.

7 Position the double-headed pointer (◄┃►) over the upper-right corner of the bounding box of the text shapes. Extra attention is required in the rest of this step, so follow directions closely. Slowly drag the upper-right corner handle upward. While dragging, press the Shift+Alt+Ctrl (Windows) or Shift+Option+Command (Mac OS) keys to change the perspective of the object. Release the mouse button, and then the modifier keys.

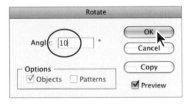

● **Note:** If you use the modifier keys while clicking to select, the perspective feature does not work.

Pressing Shift as you drag scales an object proportionally. Pressing Alt (Windows) or Option (Mac OS) scales an object from its center point. Pressing Ctrl (Windows) or Command (Mac OS) as you drag distorts an object from the anchor point or bounding box handle that you're dragging.

8 Double-click the Rotate tool (↻), select Preview in the Rotate dialog box, and then change the angle to **10**°. Click OK.

9 If necessary, with the Selection tool, drag the text up until the bottom is above the bottom of the artboard.

● **Note:** After rotating, the bottom of the text should be above the bottom of the artboard. If that isn't the case, try a different value in the Rotate dialog.

10 With the "organic grow" text still selected, change the Opacity to **30**% in the Control panel.

11 Choose Select > Deselect.

12 Choose File > Save.

Multiple transformations

Next, you will apply a transformation multiple times.

1 Choose 2 BC - Front from the Artboard Navigation menu in the status bar.

2 With the Selection tool, double-click the green glow logo. Click to select the green flower shape and choose Edit > Copy.

3 Press the Escape key to exit isolation mode, then choose Edit > Paste.

4 Drag the flower shape so that it snaps into the left and bottom of the artboard.

● **Note:** Depending on your screen resolution, the word Transform may not appear in the Control panel. Instead, the Transform options may appear in the Control panel. You may also need to choose Window > Transform.

5 Click the word Transform in the Control panel to see the Transform panel. Click the bottom-left point in the Reference Point locator (▦). Make sure that the Constrain Width and Height Proportions button (⌀) is selected and change the Height to **.3 in**. Press Enter or Return to apply.

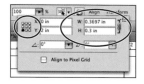

6 Choose Object > Transform > Transform Each. In the Transform Each dialog box, select Preview. Select Reflect X to reflect the shape along the X axis. Change the Move Horizontal field to **.4 in**. Leave the other settings as they are and click Copy (don't click OK).

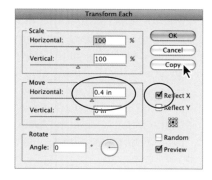

The options in the Transform Each dialog box let you apply multiple types of transformations in a random manner if you want.

▶ **Tip:** You can also apply multiple transformations as an effect, including scaling, moving, rotating, and reflecting an object. After selecting the objects, choose Effect > Distort & Transform > Transform. The dialog box looks the same as the Transform Each dialog box. Transforming as an effect has the advantage of letting you change or remove the transformation at any time.

7 Choose Object > Transform > Transform Again to create one more flower.

Now you'll use the keyboard shortcut to repeat the transformations.

8 Press Ctrl+D (Windows) or Command+D (Mac OS) to transform the flower shape, creating a total of nine flower shapes across the bottom.

9 With the Selection tool, drag a marquee across the flower shapes along the bottom.

10 Choose Object > Group.

11 Choose File > Save and leave the file open if you plan to do the tasks in the "Exploring on your own" section.

Using the Free Distort effect

Now, you'll explore a slightly different way of distorting objects. Free Distort is an effect that lets you distort a selection by moving any of its four corner points.

1 Choose File > Open, and open the L4start_2.ai file in the Lesson04 folder, located in the Lessons folder on your hard disk. This file has content that you will copy into another file that you create.

2 Choose File > New.

3 In the New Document dialog box, change the name to **business cards**, ensure that Print is chosen for New Document Profile, change Units to Inches, change the Number Of Artboards to **8**, make sure that the Grid By Row button (▦) is selected, change Spacing to **0** in, Columns to **2**, Width to **3.25** in, Height to **2** in, and Orientation to landscape (▦). Click the up arrow to the left of the Top Bleed field to make all the bleed values 0.125 in. Click OK.

4 With the Selection tool (▶), click the top-left artboard to make it the active artboard.

5 Choose File > Save As. In the Save As dialog box, leave the name as **business cards.ai** and navigate to the Lesson04 folder. Leave the Save As Type option set to Adobe Illustrator (*.AI) (Windows) or the Format option set to Adobe Illustrator (ai) (Mac OS), and click Save. In the Illustrator Options dialog box, leave the Illustrator options at their default settings, and then click OK.

6 Click the Arrange Documents button (▦ ▾) in the Application bar and choose 2-Up from the menu to arrange the documents side by side.

7 Click in the business cards.ai window, and choose View > Fit Artboard In Window. Click in the L4start_2.ai window and choose View > Fit Artboard In Window.

8 Choose Select > All to select the content on the L4start_2.ai artboard.

9 Choose Object > Group, then choose Edit > Copy.

10 Close the L4start2.ai document without saving.

11 Choose Consolidate All from the Arrange Documents button in the Application bar.

12 Choose View > Fit Artboard In Window to fit artboard 1 in the window.

13 Choose Edit > Paste.

14 With the Selection tool, double-click the group of objects you just pasted to enter isolation mode. Click to select the sandals.

15 Choose Effect > Distort & Transform > Free Distort.

16 In the Free Distort dialog box, drag one or more of the handles to distort the selection. In the figure, we dragged the upper anchor points to the outside and the bottom points in toward the center. Click OK.

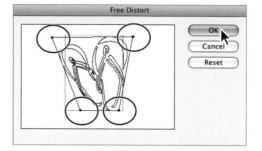

17 Double-click outside the artwork to exit isolation mode and to deselect it.

Now, you'll create multiple copies of the business card content.

18 Choose Select > All On Active Artboard.

19 Choose Edit > Cut.

20 Choose View > Fit All In Window, then choose Edit > Paste On All Artboards.

21 Choose Select > Deselect. Then choose View > Guides > Hide Guides to hide the red bleed guides.

22 Choose File > Save, and then File > Close.

▶ **Tip:** To print the business cards on a single page, choose File > Print, and select Ignore Artboards to fit all the artboards on a single page.

Exploring on your own

1 In the letterhead project, on artboard 2 BC - Front, transform the logo so that it's .5 in wide and resizes from the upper-left corner.

2 Copy other content, including the order online button on the 2 BC - Back artboard, onto the 2 BC - Front artboard.

3 Try flipping the flower in the green glow logo by double-clicking the logo to enter isolation mode.

● **Note:** Depending on your screen resolution, the word Transform may not appear in the Control panel. Instead, the Transform options may appear in the Control panel. You may also need to choose Window > Transform.

4 Select the flower and click the word Transform in the Control panel to reveal the Transform panel (or click X, Y, W, or H). Select the center reference point and choose Flip Horizontal from the Transform panel menu (▼≡).

5 Rename a few of the artboards and add another for the back of the envelope.

Review questions

1 Name two ways to change the size of an existing active artboard.

2 How can you rename an artboard?

3 How can you select and manipulate individual objects in a group (as described in this chapter)?

4 How do you resize an object? Explain how you determine the point from which the object resizes. How do you resize a group of objects proportionally?

5 What transformations can you make using the Transform panel?

6 What does the square diagram (▦) indicate in the Transform panel, and how does it affect transformations?

Review answers

1 Double-click the Artboard tool and edit the dimensions of the active artboard in the Artboard Options dialog box. Select the Artboard tool and position the pointer over an edge or corner of the artboard and drag to resize.

2 To rename an artboard, you can select the Artboard tool and click to select an artboard. Then change the name in the Name field in the Control panel. You can also click the Artboard Options button in the Artboards panel to enter the name in the Artboard Options dialog box.

3 You can double-click the group with the Selection tool to enter isolation mode. This temporarily ungroups objects so that you can edit objects within a group without ungrouping.

4 You can resize an object several ways: by selecting it and dragging handles on its bounding box, by using the Scale tool or the Transform panel, or by choosing Object > Transform > Scale to specify exact dimensions. You can also scale by choosing Effect > Distort & Transform > Transform.

5 You use the Transform panel for making the following transformations:: Moving or precisely placing objects in your artwork (by specifying the x and y coordinates and the reference point), scaling, rotating, shearing, and reflecting.

6 The square diagram in the Transform panel indicates the bounding box of the selected objects. Select a reference point in the square to indicate the reference point from which the objects as a group move, scale, rotate, shear, or reflect.

5 DRAWING WITH THE PEN AND PENCIL TOOLS

Lesson overview

In this lesson, you'll learn how to do the following:

- Draw curved lines.

- Draw straight lines.

- Use template layers.

- End path segments and split lines.

- Select and adjust curve segments.

- Create dashed lines and add arrowheads.

- Draw and edit with the Pencil tool.

 This lesson will take approximately an hour and a half to complete. If needed, remove the previous lesson folder from your hard disk and copy the Lesson05 folder onto it.

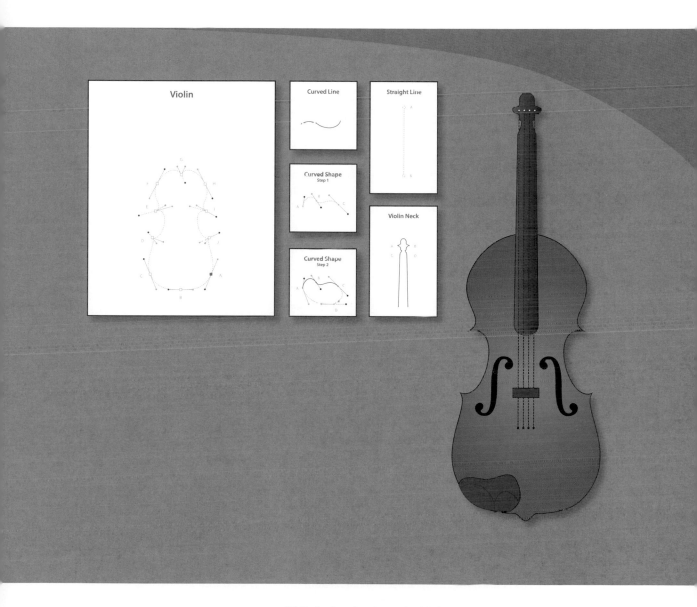

While the Pencil tool is preferable for drawing and editing free-form lines, the Pen tool is excellent for drawing precisely, including straight lines, Bezier curves, and complex shapes. You'll practice using the Pen tool on a blank artboard, and then use it to create an illustration of a violin.

Getting started

In the first part of this lesson, you learn how to manipulate the Pen tool on a blank artboard.

1 To ensure that the tools and panels function as described in this lesson, delete or deactivate (by renaming) the Adobe® Illustrator® CS5 preferences file. See "Restoring default preferences" on page 3.

2 Start Adobe Illustrator CS5.

● **Note:** If you have not already done so, copy the resource files for this lesson onto your hard disk from the Lesson05 folder on the Adobe Illustrator CS5 Classroom in a Book CD. See "Copying the Classroom in a Book files" on page 2.

3 Open the L5start_1.ai file in the Lesson05 folder, located in the Lessons folder on your hard disk. The top artboard shows the path that you will create. Use the bottom artboard for this exercise.

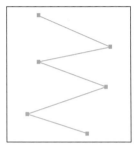

4 Choose File > Save As. In the Save As dialog box, navigate to the Lesson05 folder and open it. Type **path1.ai** in the File Name text field. Choose Adobe Illustrator (.AI) from the Save As Type menu (Windows) or choose Adobe Illustrator (ai) from the Format menu (Mac OS). In the Illustrator Options dialog box, leave the default settings and click OK.

5 Press Alt+Ctrl+0 (zero) (Windows) or Option+Command+0 (Mac OS) to fit both artboards in the window. Then hold down the Shift key and press the Tab key once to close all the panels, except for the Tools panel. You don't need the panels for the first part of this lesson.

6 Choose View > Smart Guides to deselect the smart guides.

7 In the Control panel, click the Fill color and choose the None swatch (▨). Then click the Stroke color and make sure that the black swatch is selected.

8 Make sure the stroke weight is 1 pt in the Control panel.

When you draw with the Pen tool, it is best to have no fill on the path you create. You can add a fill later if necessary.

● **Note:** If you see a crosshair instead of the pen icon, the Caps Lock key is active. Caps Lock turns tool icons into crosshairs for increased precision.

9 Select the Pen tool (✒) in the Tools panel. Notice the x next to the pen icon (✒ₓ), indicating that you are starting a path. Click in the bottom artboard to set the first point, then move the pointer to the right of the original anchor point. The x disappears.

10 Click down and to the right of the original point to create the next anchor point in the path.

> **Note:** The first segment you draw is not visible until you click a second anchor point. If direction handles appear, you have accidentally dragged with the Pen tool; choose Edit > Undo, and click again.

11 Click a third anchor point beneath the initial anchor point to create a zigzag pattern. Create a zigzag that has six anchor points, which means you will click the artboard a total of six times.

One of the many benefits of using the Pen tool is that you can create custom paths and continue to edit the anchor points that make up the path.

Next, you'll see how the Selection tools work with the Pen tool.

12 Select the Selection tool (▶) in the Tools panel and click directly on the zigzag path. Notice that all the anchor points become solid, signifying that all anchor points are selected. Drag the path to a new location anywhere on the artboard. All the anchor points travel together, maintaining the zigzag path.

13 Deselect the zigzag path in one of the following ways:

• With the Selection tool, click an empty area of the artboard.

• Choose Select > Deselect.

• With the Pen tool selected, Ctrl-click (Windows) or Command-click (Mac OS) in a blank area of the artboard to deselect the path. This temporarily selects the Selection tool. When you release the Ctrl or Command key, the Pen tool is again selected.

• Click the Pen tool once. Even though it looks like the path is still active, it will not connect to the next anchor point created.

14 Select the Direct Selection tool (▷) in the Tools panel and click on any point in the zigzag, or drag a marquee selection around an anchor point. The selected anchor point turns solid, and the deselected anchor points are hollow.

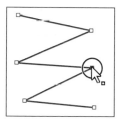

15 With the anchor point selected, drag to reposition it. The anchor point moves but the others remain stationary. Use this technique to edit a path.

16 Choose Select > Deselect.

● **Note:** If the entire zigzag path disappears, choose Edit > Undo Clear and try again.

17 With the Direct Selection tool, click any line segment that is between two anchor points, and then choose Edit > Cut.

This cuts only the selected segment from the zigzag.

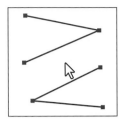

18 With the Pen tool, position the pointer over one of the anchor points that was connected to the line segment that was cut. Notice that the Pen tool shows a forward slash (/) indicating a continuation of an existing path. Click the point. Notice that it becomes solid. Only active points appear solid.

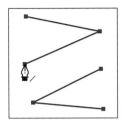

19 Position the pointer over the other point that was connected to the cut line segment. The pointer now shows a merge symbol next to it (●), indicating that you are connecting to another path. Click the point to reconnect the paths.

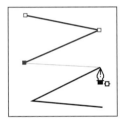

20 Choose File > Save, and then File > Close.

Creating straight lines

In Lesson 4, "Transforming Objects," you learned that using the Shift key and smart guides in combination with shape tools constrains the shape of objects. The Shift key and smart guides also constrain the Pen tool, to create paths of 45˚.

Next, you will learn how to draw straight lines and constrain angles.

1 Open the L5start_2.ai file in the Lesson05 folder, located in the Lessons folder on your hard disk. The top artboard shows the path that you will create. Use the bottom artboard for this exercise.

2 Choose File > Save As. In the Save As dialog box, navigate to the Lesson05 folder and open it. Name the file **path2.ai**. Choose Adobe Illustrator (.AI) from the Save As Type menu (Windows) or choose Adobe Illustrator (ai) from the Format menu (Mac OS). In the Illustrator Options dialog box, leave the default settings and click OK.

3 Choose View > Smart Guides to select the smart guides.

4 Select the Pen tool (●) in the Tools panel and click once in the work area of the artboard.

5 Move the pointer to the right of the original anchor point 1.5 inches, as indicated by the measurement label. It doesn't have to be exact. A green construction guide appears when the pointer is vertically aligned with the previous anchor point. Click to set the second anchor point.

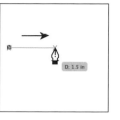

The measurement label and construction guide are part of the smart guides.

▶ **Tip:** If smart guides are deselected, the measurement label and construction guide won't appear. If you don't use smart guides, you can press the Shift key and click to create straight lines.

6 Click to set four more points, creating the same shape as shown in the top half of the artboard. Press the Shift key, move the pointer to the right and down, until it is aligned with the bottom two points. Click to set the anchor point, and then release the modifier key.

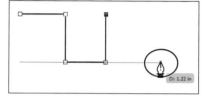

● **Note:** The points you set don't have to be in exactly the same position as the path at the top of the artboard.

Pressing the Shift key creates angled lines constrained to 45°. The smart guides will show a green construction guide when the pointer is aligned with the existing points, which can be very useful when you are drawing paths with straight lines.

7 Position the pointer below the last point and click to set the last anchor point for the shape.

8 Choose File > Save and close the file.

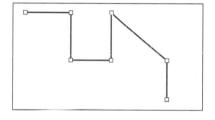

Creating curved paths

In this part of the lesson, you'll learn how to draw smooth, curved lines with the Pen tool. In vector drawing applications such as Illustrator, you draw a curve, called a Bezier curve, with control points. By setting anchor points and dragging direction handles, you can define the shape of the curve. Although drawing curves this way can take some time to learn, it gives you the greatest control and flexibility in creating paths.

1 Open the L5start_3.ai file in the Lesson05 folder. This file contains a template layer that you can trace to practice using the Pen tool (🖋). (See Lesson 8, "Working with Layers," for information about creating layers.) You will draw below the path in the bottom artboard for this exercise.

2 Choose File > Save As. In the Save As dialog box, navigate to the Lesson05 folder. Type **path3.ai** in the File Name text field. Choose Adobe Illustrator (.AI) from the Save As Type menu (Windows) or choose Adobe Illustrator (ai) from the Format menu (Mac OS). In the Illustrator Options dialog box, leave the default settings and click OK.

3 Choose View > Fit All In Window.

4 In the Control panel, click the Fill color and choose the None swatch (⊘). Then click the Stroke color and make sure that the black swatch is selected.

5 Make sure the stroke weight is 1 pt in the Control panel.

6 With the Pen tool (✎), click anywhere on the artboard to create the initial anchor point. Click another location, and drag away from the point to create a curved path.

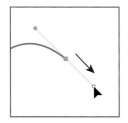

Continue clicking and dragging at different locations on the page. The goal for this exercise is not to create anything specific, but to get accustomed to the feel of the Bezier curve.

Notice that as you drag, direction handles appear. Direction handles consist of direction lines that end in round direction points. The angle and length of the direction handles determine the shape and size of the curve. Direction handles do not print and are not visible when the anchor is inactive.

7 Choose Select > Deselect.

8 Select the Direct Selection tool (⬏) in the Tools panel and click a curved segment to display the direction handles. If smart guides are selected, the word "path" appears when you click. Moving the direction handles reshapes the curve.

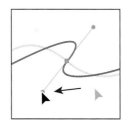

9 Leave the file open for the next section.

Components of a path

As you draw, you create a line called a path. A path is made up of one or more straight or curved segments. The beginning and end of each segment are marked by anchor points, which work like pins holding a wire in place. A path can be closed (for example, a circle) or open, with distinct end points (for example, a wavy line). You change the shape of a path by dragging its anchor points, the direction points at the end of direction lines that appear at anchor points, or the path segment itself.

Paths can have two kinds of anchor points: corner points and smooth points. At a corner point, a path abruptly changes direction. At a smooth point, path segments are connected as a continuous curve.

You can draw a path using any combination of corner and smooth points. If you draw the wrong kind of point, you can always change it.

—From Illustrator Help

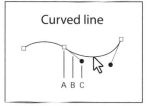

Curved line

A. Anchor point
B. Direction line
C. Direction handle (or point)

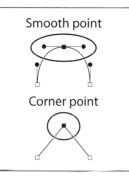

Smooth point

Corner point

Building a curve

In this part of the lesson, you will learn how to control the direction handles to control curves. You will use the top artboard to trace shapes.

1   Press Z to switch to the Zoom tool (🔍) and drag a marquee around the curve in the top artboard, labeled A.

2   Choose View > Smart Guides to deselect them.

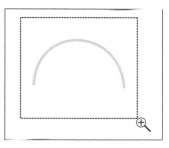

● **Note:** The artboard may scroll as you drag. If you lose visibility of the curve, choose View > Zoom Out until you see the curve and anchor point. Pressing the spacebar allows you to use the Hand tool to reposition the artwork.

3 Select the Pen tool (✒) in the Tools panel. Click at the base of the left side of the arch and drag up to create a direction line going the same direction as the arch. Remember to always follow the direction of the curve. Release the mouse button when the direction line is above the gray arch.

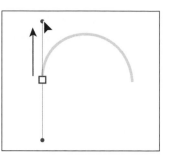

▶ **Tip:** If you make a mistake while drawing with the Pen tool, choose Edit > Undo Pen to undo the points you have set.

4 Click the lower-right base of the arch path and drag down. Release the mouse button when the path you are creating looks like the arch.

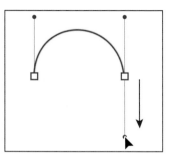

● **Note:** Pulling the direction handle longer makes a higher slope; when the direction handle is shorter the slope is flatter.

5 If the path you created is not aligned exactly with the template, use the Direct Selection tool (▷) to select the anchor points one at a time. Then adjust the direction handles until your path follows the template more accurately.

6 Use the Selection tool (▶) and click the artboard in an area with no objects, or choose Select > Deselect. If you click with the Pen tool while path A is still active, the path connects to the next point you draw. Deselecting the first path allows you to create a new path.

▶ **Tip:** To deselect objects, you can also press the Ctrl (Windows) or Command (Mac OS) key to temporarily switch to the Selection or Direct Selection tool, whichever was last used. Then click the artboard where there are no objects.

7 Choose File > Save.

8 Zoom out to see path B.

9 Using the Pen tool, drag up from the left base of path B in the direction of the arch. Click and drag down on the next square point, adjusting the arch with the direction handle before you release the mouse button.

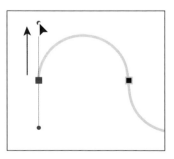

● **Note:** Don't worry if the path you draw is not exact. You can correct the line with the Direct Selection tool when the path is complete.

10 Continue along the path, alternating between dragging up and down. Put anchor points only where there are square boxes. If you make a mistake as you draw, you can undo your work by choosing Edit > Undo Pen.

11 When the path is complete, use the Direct Selection tool and select an anchor point. When the anchor is selected, the direction handles appear, and you can readjust the slope of the path.

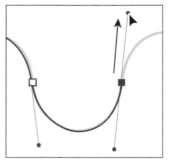

● **Note:** You can undo a series of actions—the number is limited only by your computer's memory—by choosing Edit > Undo, or by pressing Ctrl+Z (Windows) or Command+Z (Mac OS).

12 Practice repeating these paths in the work area.

13 Choose File > Save, and then File > Close.

Converting curved points to corner points

When creating curves, the directional handles help to determine the slope of the path. Returning to a corner point requires a little extra effort. In the next part of the lesson, you will practice converting curve points to corners.

1 Open the L5start_4.ai file in the Lesson05 folder. On the top artboard, you can see the paths that you will create. Use the top artboard as a template for the exercise. Create your paths directly on top of those that you see on the page. Use the bottom artboard for additional practice on your own.

2 Choose File > Save As. In the Save As dialog box, navigate to the Lesson05 folder. Type **path4.ai** in the File Name text field. Choose Adobe Illustrator (.AI) from the Save As Type menu (Windows) or choose Adobe Illustrator (ai) from the Format menu (Mac OS). In the Illustrator Options dialog box, leave the default settings and click OK.

3 Choose View > Fit All In Window.

4 In the top artboard, use the Zoom tool (Q) and drag a marquee around path A.

5 In the Control panel, click the Fill color and choose the None swatch (⬜). Then click the Stroke color and make sure that the black swatch is selected.

6 Make sure the stroke weight is 1 pt in the Control panel.

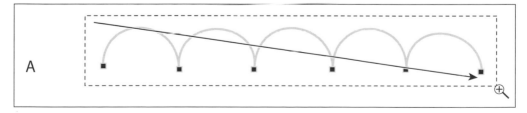

Note: Pressing the Shift key when dragging constrains the angle of the handle to a straight line.

7 Select the Pen tool (✒) and, pressing the Shift key, click the first anchor point and drag up. Release the mouse button and then the Shift key when the direction line is slightly above the arch. Click the second anchor point and drag down without releasing the mouse button. As you drag down, press the Shift key. When the curve looks correct, release the mouse button and then the Shift key.

Next, you will split the direction lines to convert a smooth point to a corner point.

▶ **Tip:** After you draw a path, you can also select single or multiple anchor points and click the Convert Selected Anchor Points To Corner button (⌐) or Convert Selected Anchor Points To Smooth button (⌐) in the Control panel.

8 Press the Alt (Windows) or Option (Mac OS) key and position the pointer over either the last anchor point created or the bottom direction point. When you see the caret (^) symbol, click and drag a direction line up. Release the mouse button and then the Alt or Option key. If you do not see the caret (^), you will create an additional loop.

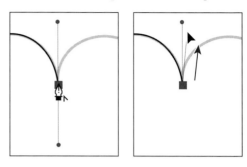

Note: If you don't click exactly on the anchor point or the direction point at the end of the direction line, a warning dialog box appears. Click OK and try again.

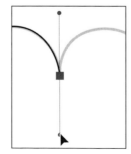

You can practice adjusting the direction handles with the Direct Selection tool when the path is completed.

9 Click the next square point and drag down. Release the mouse button when the path looks correct.

10 Press the Alt (Windows) or Option (Mac OS) key and, after the caret (^) appears, drag up the last anchor point or direction point for the next curve. Release the mouse button and then the modifier key.

▶ **Tip:** Steps 11 and 12 show how to split direction lines without releasing the mouse button.

11 For the third anchor point, click the next square point on the path and drag down until the path looks correct. Do not release the mouse button.

12 Press the Alt (Windows) or Option (Mac OS) key and drag up for the next curve. Release the mouse button, and then the modifier key.

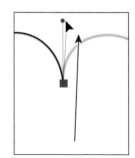

Step #11   Step #12

13 Continue this process using the Alt (Windows) or Option (Mac OS) key to create corner points, until the path is completed. Use the Direct Selection tool (🔧) to fine-tune the path, and then deselect the path.

14 Choose File > Save.

Next, you will switch from a curve to a straight line.

1 Choose View > Fit Artboard In Window. You can also press Ctrl+0 (zero) (Windows) or Command+0 (Mac OS). Use the Zoom tool to drag a marquee around path B to enlarge its view.

2 With the Pen tool, click the first anchor point on the left and drag up. Then drag down on the second anchor point and release the mouse button when the arch matches the template. This method of creating an arch should be familiar to you by now. You will now switch from the curve to a straight line. Pressing the Shift key and clicking does not produce a straight line, because this last point is a curved anchor point.

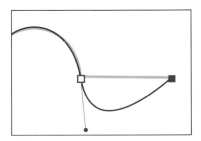

The figure in this step shows what the path would look like if you simply clicked with the Pen tool on the last point.

3 To create the next segment as a straight line, click the last point created to delete one direction line from the path, as shown in the figure. Shift-click to set the next point to the right, creating the straight segment.

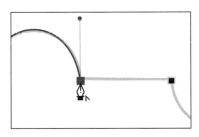

4 For the next arch, position the pointer over the last point created (notice that the carat appears ✒ₐ) and then drag down from that point. This creates a new direction line.

5 Click the next point and drag up to complete the downward arch. Click the last anchor point of the arch to remove the direction line.

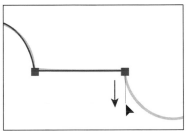

6 Shift-click the next point to create the second straight segment.

7 Click and drag up from the last point created, and then click and drag down the last point to create the final arch. Practice repeating these paths in the lower artboard. Use the Direct Selection tool to adjust your path if necessary.

8 Choose File > Save, and then File > Close.

Creating the violin illustration

In this next part of the lesson, you'll create an illustration of a violin. You'll use the new skills you learned in the previous exercises, and also learn some additional Pen tool techniques.

1 Choose File > Open, and open the L5end_5.ai file in the Lesson05 folder, located in the Lessons folder.

2 Choose View > Fit All In Window to see finished products. (Use the Hand tool (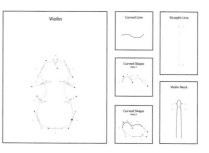) to move the artwork to where you want it.) If you don't want to leave the image open, choose File > Close.

3 Choose File > Open, and open the L5start_5.ai file in the Lesson05 folder.

4 Choose File > Save As, name the file **violin.ai**, and select the Lesson05 folder in the Save As dialog box. Choose Adobe Illustrator (.AI) from the Save As Type menu (Windows) or choose Adobe Illustrator (ai) from the Format menu (Mac OS) and click Save. In the Illustrator Options dialog box, leave the options set at the defaults and click OK.

5 In the Control panel, click the Fill color and choose the None swatch (⬚). Then click the Stroke color and make sure that the black swatch is selected.

6 Make sure the stroke weight is 1 pt in the Control panel.

Drawing curves

In this part of the lesson, you will review drawing curves by drawing the violin, its neck, the strings, and a curved path. You'll examine a single curve and then draw a series of curves together, using the template guidelines to help you.

Selecting a curve

1 Choose 2 Curved Line from the Artboard Navigation menu in the lower-left corner of the Document window.

2 Using the Direct Selection tool (▷), click one of the segments of the curved line to view its anchor points and direction handles, which extend from the points. The Direct Selection tool lets you select and edit individual segments in the curved line.

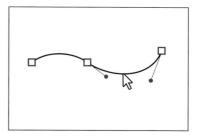

With a curve selected, you can also select the stroke and fill of the curve. When you do this, the next line you draw will have the same attributes. For more on these attributes, see Lesson 6, "Color and Painting."

Drawing a curved shape

Next, you'll draw the first curve of the curved shape.

1 Choose 3 Curved Shape step 1 from the Artboard Navigation menu in the lower-left corner of the Document window.

Instead of dragging the Pen tool (✒) to draw a curve, you will drag it to set the starting point and the direction of the line's curve.

2 Select the Pen tool and position it over point A on the template. Drag from point A to the red dot.

Next, you'll set the second anchor point and its direction handles.

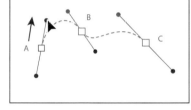

3 Drag with the Pen tool (✒) from point B to the next red dot. The two anchor points are connected with a curve that follows the direction handles you created. Notice that if you vary the angle of dragging, you change the degree of the curve.

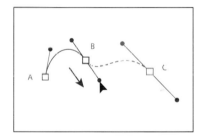

4 To complete the curved line, drag with the Pen tool from point C to the last red dot.

5 Control-click (Windows) or Command-click (Mac OS) away from the line to end the path.

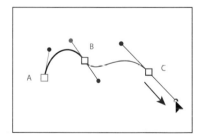

▶ **Tip:** You can also end a path by clicking the Pen tool, pressing P for the Pen tool shortcut, or choosing Select > Deselect.

Drawing different kinds of curves

Next, you'll finish drawing the curved shape by adding to an existing curved segment. Even after ending a path, you can return to the curve and add to it. Use the Alt (Windows) or Option (Mac OS) key to control the type of curve you draw.

1   Choose 4 Curved Shape step 2 from the Artboard Navigation menu in the lower-left corner of the Document window.

Next you'll add a corner point to the path. A corner point lets you change the direction of the curve. A smooth point lets you draw a continuous curve.

2   Position the Pen tool (✎) over point A. The slash (/) next to the pen icon indicates that you're aligned with an anchor and are continuing the path of the existing line, rather than starting a new line.

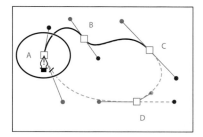

3   Press the Alt (Windows) or Option (Mac OS) key and notice that the status bar in the lower-left corner of the Document window displays Pen: Make Corner. Press the Alt (Windows) or Option (Mac OS) key and drag the Pen tool from anchor point A to the gray dot. Release the mouse button, and then the Alt or Option key.

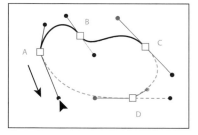

So far, you have drawn curves that are open paths. Now you'll draw a closed path in which the final anchor point is drawn on the first anchor point of the path. Examples of closed paths include ovals and rectangles.

Next, you'll close the path using a smooth point.

4   With the Pen tool, drag from point D to the red dot. Press the Alt (Windows) or Option (Mac OS) key and drag the direction handle from the red dot to the gold dot. Release the mouse button and then the key.

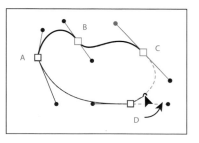

5   Position the pointer over anchor point C on the template. An open circle appears next to the Pen tool (✎₀), indicating that you can click to close the path. Drag from this point to the gray dot at point C. As you drag, pay attention to the line segments on either side of point C.

Notice that the direction handles that appear on both sides of a smooth point where you close the path are aligned along the same angle.

● **Note:** The dotted template lines are guides only. The shapes you create do not need to follow the lines exactly.

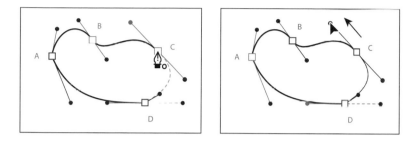

6 Control-click (Windows) or Command-click (Mac OS) away from the line, and choose File > Save.

Drawing the violin shape

Next, you'll draw a single, continuous path that consists of smooth points and corner points. Each time you want to change the direction of a curve at a specific point, you'll press the Alt (Windows) or Option (Mac OS) key to create a corner point.

1 Choose View > Violin to display a magnified view of the violin.

You'll start drawing the lower-right part of the violin by creating smooth points and corner points.

2 Select the Pen tool (✑) in the Tools panel. Starting at the blue square (point A), drag from point A to the red dot to set the starting anchor point and direction of the first curve.

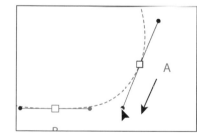

● **Note:** You do not have to start at the blue dot (point A) to draw this shape. You can set anchor points for a path with the Pen tool in a clockwise or counter-clockwise direction.

3 With the Pen tool, begin dragging from point B to the red dot on the left. As you drag, hold down the Shift key. Release the mouse button and then the Shift key when you reach the red dot.

4 Drag from point C to the red dot.

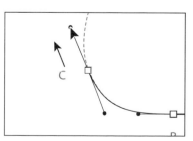

Tip: In step 5, you drag the pointer to the red dot first. This sets the preceding curve. Once the curve matches the template, pressing Alt or Option splits the direction lines and lets you drag the next direction line to control the shape of the next curve.

5   Drag from point D to the red dot, When the pointer reaches the red dot, hold down the Alt (Windows) or Option (Mac OS) key and drag from the red dot to the gold dot. Release the mouse button, and then the modifier key. This splits the direction handles.

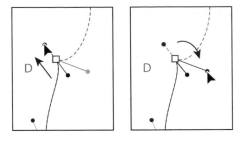

6   With the Pen tool, drag from point E to the red dot. Press the Alt (Windows) or Option (Mac OS) key and drag the direction handle from the red dot to the gold dot.

7   Drag from point F to the red dot.

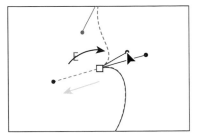

8   With the Pen tool, drag from point G to the red dot. Holding the mouse button down, press the Alt (Windows) or Option (Mac OS) key and drag the direction handle from the red dot to the gold dot.

9   Drag from point H to the red dot.

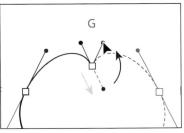

10 Continue drawing to points I and J by first dragging from the anchor point to the red dot, and then pressing the Alt (Windows) or Option (Mac OS) key and dragging the direction handle from the red dot to the gold dot.

Next, you'll complete the drawing of the violin by closing the path.

11 Position the Pen tool over point A. Notice that an open circle appears next to the pen pointer, indicating that the path will close when you click.

12 Drag down and to the left, to the red dot below point A. Notice that as you drag down, another direction line appears above the point. As you drag, you are reshaping the path.

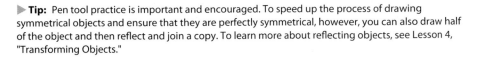

13 Ctrl-click (Windows) or Command-click (Mac OS) away from the path to deselect it, and then choose File > Save.

Tip: Pen tool practice is important and encouraged. To speed up the process of drawing symmetrical objects and ensure that they are perfectly symmetrical, however, you can also draw half of the object and then reflect and join a copy. To learn more about reflecting objects, see Lesson 4, "Transforming Objects."

Creating the strings

There are many ways to create straight paths including using the Pen tool. Next, you'll draw a straight line for the strings using the Pen tool. The artwork has a template layer that lets you draw directly over the artwork.

1   Choose 5 Strings from the Artboard Navigation menu in the lower-left corner of the Document window.

2   Choose Window > Workspace > Essentials.

3   In the Control panel, make sure that None (⊘) is the fill color and black is the stroke color in the Control panel. Also make sure that the stroke weight is 1 pt.

● Note: When drawing with the Pen tool, it can be easier to draw paths with no fill selected. You can also change the fill and other properties of the path after you begin drawing.

4   Choose View > Hide Bounding Box to hide the bounding boxes of selected objects. Select the Pen tool (✎) and place it in the middle of the circle (point A) in the artboard. Notice that the pointer has an x next to it, indicating that your next click begins a new path.

5   Click point A to create the starting anchor point, indicated by a small solid square.

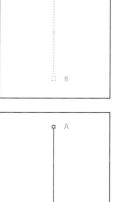

6   Pressing the Shift key, click point B to create the ending anchor point. The Shift key constrains the placement of the anchor point to a multiple of 45°.

After clicking to create point B, a caret (^) appears next to the Pen tool when the pointer is positioned over the new point, indicating that you can create a direction line for a curve by dragging the Pen tool from this anchor point. The caret disappears when you move the Pen tool away from the anchor point.

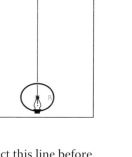

7   Press the letter V to switch to the Selection tool (▶). The straight line will still be selected. Click in a blank area to deselect this line before you can draw other lines that aren't connected to this path.

Next, you'll make the straight line thicker by changing its stroke weight.

8   With the Selection tool, click the line you just drew. In the Control panel, change the Stroke Weight to **3** pt. Leave the line segment selected.

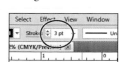

● Note: If you don't see the Stroke Weight option in the Control panel, click the line again, even though it may still be selected. This indicates to Illustrator that you are no longer drawing. You can also expand the Stroke panel by clicking its icon on the right side of the workspace.

Splitting a path

To continue creating the strings, you'll split the path of the straight line using the Scissors tool, and then adjust the segments.

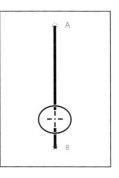

●**Note:** If you click the stroke of a closed shape (a circle, for example) with the Scissors tool, it simply cuts the path so that it becomes open (a path with two end points).

1   With the straight line selected, in the Tools panel, click and hold down the Eraser tool (🖉) to reveal the Scissors tool (✂). Select the Scissors tool and click about 2/3 the way down the line to make a cut.

Cuts made with the Scissors tool must be on a line or a curve rather than on an end point.

When you click with the Scissors tool, a new anchor point appears, and is selected. The Scissors tool actually creates two anchor points each time you click, but because they are on top of each other, you can see only one.

2   Select the Direct Selection tool (▷) and click the top portion of the path, which is now split, to select it and show the anchor points. Click to select the bottom anchor point of that selected path. Begin dragging that point up, and as you drag hold down the Shift key to widen the gap between the two split segments. Leave the top path selected.

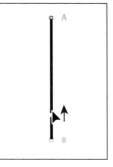

Adding arrowheads

You can add arrowheads and tails to open paths using the Stroke panel. There are many different arrowhead styles to choose from in Illustrator, as well as arrowhead editing options.

Next, you'll add different arrowheads to line segments.

1   With the top line segment still selected, open the Stroke panel by clicking the Stroke panel icon (▤) on the right side of the workspace.

2   In the Stroke panel, choose Arrow 24 from the menu directly to the right of Arrowheads. This adds an arrowhead to the start (top) of the line.

3   In the Stroke panel, change the Scale (beneath the start of the line arrowhead menu) to **30**% by clicking the word Scale and typing the value in the field, and then pressing Enter or Return.

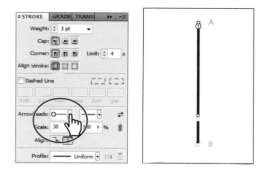

4 With the Selection tool (▶), click to select the lower, shorter line. In the Stroke panel, choose Arrow 22 from the arrowheads menu to the far right of the word Arrowheads, to add an arrowhead to the end of the line, as shown in the figure.

5 In the Stroke panel, change the Scale (beneath the end of the line arrowhead menu) to **40**% by typing the value in the field, and press Enter or Return.

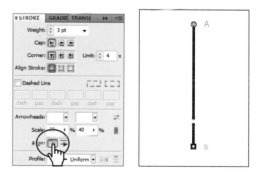

Notice that the arrowheads are positioned inside the endpoints of the line, by default. Next, you will extend the arrowheads beyond the ends of the paths.

▶ **Tip:** The Link Start And End Arrowhead Scales button (🔒) to the right of the Scale values in the Stroke panel allows you to link the scale values together so that if one changes, the other changes proportionately.

6 With the Selection tool, Shift-click to select the upper line segment. Click the Extend Arrow Tip Beyond End of Path button (➥) beneath the Scale value in the Stroke panel.

Notice that the arrowheads on both lines move slightly beyond the end of the lines. Leave both lines selected for the next steps.

▶ **Tip:** Click the Swap Start And End Arrowheads button (⇄) in the Stroke panel to swap the starting and ending arrowheads on selected lines.

Creating a dashed line

Dashed lines apply to the stroke of an object, and can be added to a closed path or an open path. Dashes are created by specifying a sequence of dash lengths and the gaps between them.

Next, you'll add a dash to the line segment.

▶ **Tip:** The Preserve Exact Dash And Gap Lengths button (┌─┐) allows you to retain the appearance of the dashes without aligning.

1 With both line segments still selected, make sure that the Butt Cap button (▣) is selected in the Stroke panel to the right of the word Cap. Select Dashed Line in the middle of the Stroke panel.

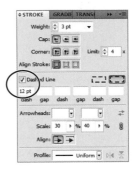

   By default, this creates a repeating dash pattern of 12 pt dash, 12 pt gap.

   ▶ **Tip:** To learn about the Cap and Corner options in the Stroke panel, search for "Change the caps or joins of a line" in Illustrator Help.

Next, you will change the size of the dash.

2 In the Stroke panel, select the 12 pt value in the first Dash field on the left below the Dashed Line check box. Change the value to **3** and press Enter or Return to set the value.

   This creates a 3 pt dash, 3 pt gap repeating line pattern. Next, you will adjust the gap between each dash, using the Stroke panel.

3 Insert the cursor in the Gap field to the right of the first Dash value. Type **1** and press Enter or Return to set the value. This creates a 3 pt dash, 1 pt gap line pattern.

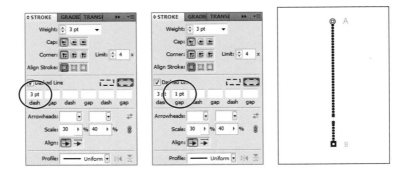

   ▶ **Tip:** If you want to create a custom dash pattern that has multiple dash and gap sizes, continue adding values in the next dash and gap fields in the Stroke panel. This pattern will be repeated in the line segment.

4 With both lines still selected, choose Object > Group.

5 Choose Select > Deselect, and then File > Save.

Editing curves

In this part of the lesson, you'll adjust the curves you've drawn by dragging either the curve's anchor points or direction handles. You can also edit a curve by moving the line. You will hide the template layer so that you can edit the actual path.

1 Choose 4 Curved Shape step 2 from the Artboard Navigation menu in the lower-left corner of the Document window.

2 Choose Window > Workspace > Essentials. Then click the Layers panel icon (🌑) on the right side of the workspace to expand the Layers panel. Click the Template Layer icon (🖾) in the Layers panel to make the template layer invisible.

▶ **Tip:** To learn more about layers, see Lesson 8, "Working with Layers."

3 Select the Direct Selection tool (▷) and click the outline of the curved shape. All of the points will appear.

Clicking with the Direct Selection tool displays the curve's direction handles and lets you adjust the shape of individual curved segments. Clicking with the Selection tool (▶) selects the entire path.

4 Click the anchor point that is at the top, just to the left of center on the curved shape, to select it. Press the Down Arrow key three times to nudge the point down.

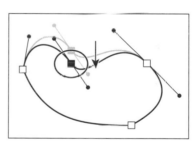

● **Note:** You can also drag the anchor point with the Direct Selection tool.

▶ **Tip:** Pressing and holding down the Shift key, then pressing an arrow key moves the point 5 times further.

5 With the Direct Selection tool, drag across the top half of the shape to select the top two anchor points.

Notice that when both points are selected, the handles disappear.

6 In the Control panel, click Show Handles For Multiple Selected Anchor Points (▣), to the right of Handles, to see the direction lines for both points. This lets you edit the direction handles for both selected anchor points.

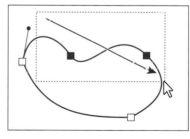

● **Note:** If you don't select both points the first time, try dragging across them again. If you have at least one of the anchor points selected, you can also Shift-click with the Direct Selection tool on the other anchor point to add it to the selection.

7 For the selected point on the right, drag the bottom control handle up and to the left to edit the curve.

As you drag, notice that both direction lines for the point are moving. Also notice that you can control the length of each direction line independently.

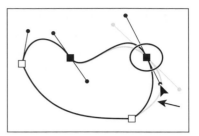

8 For the selected point on the left, drag the bottom control handle up and to the right to reshape the curve.

9 Choose Select > Deselect.

10 Choose File > Save.

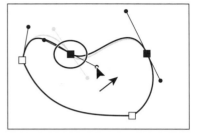

Deleting and adding anchor points

It is easier to work with paths if you don't add more anchor points than necessary. A path with fewer points is easier to edit, display, and print. You can reduce a path's complexity or change its overall shape by deleting unnecessary points. You can also reshape a path by adding points to it.

Next, you will delete an anchor point and then add points to the path.

1 Choose 1 Violin from the Artboard Navigation menu in the lower-left corner of the Document window.

2 Select the Zoom tool (🔍) in the Tools panel and click once in the center of the violin shape to zoom in. You need to see the whole violin shape for the next steps.

3 Select the Direct Selection tool (▷) in the Tools panel, then click the edge of the violin.

4 Position the pointer over the top corner point of the violin. Click to select the anchor point.

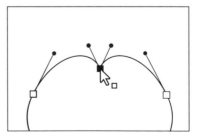

5 In the Control panel, click Remove Selected Anchor Points (🖊) to delete the anchor point.

6 With the Direct Selection tool, position the pointer over the top part of the path. Click and begin dragging the path up to reshape the top curve. As you drag, hold down the Shift key. Release the mouse button and then the modifier key when the path is reshaped. Leave the shape selected.

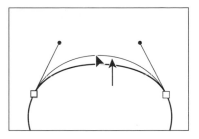

● **Note:** Don't use the Delete, Backspace, or Clear keys or the Edit > Cut or Edit > Clear command to delete anchor points; you will delete the point and the line segments that connect to that point.

▶ **Tip:** You can also delete a point by selecting the Pen tool and clicking an anchor point.

Next, you will add anchor points and reshape the bottom of the violin.

1 Select the Zoom tool (🔍) in the Tools panel, and click on the bottom part of the violin shape twice to zoom in.

▶ **Tip:** Another way to add anchor points is to select the Add Anchor Point tool (✒) in the Tools panel, position the pointer over a path, and click to add a point.

2 Select the Pen tool (✒) in the Tools panel and position the pointer over the violin path to the right of the bottom anchor point. A plus sign (+) appears to the right of the Pen tool pointer. Click to add another point to the path.

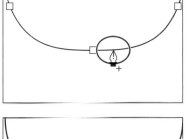

3 Position the pointer over the path to the left of the bottom anchor point until a plus sign (+) appears to the right of the pointer. Click to add another point, making three points in a row.

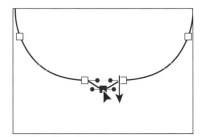

4 With the Direct Selection tool, click to select the bottom-center point. Begin dragging the point down and, as you drag, hold down the Shift key. Drag the point down just a bit. Release the mouse button and then the modifier key.

You may need to zoom in.

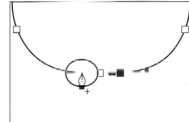

▶ **Tip:** When adding points to a shape that is symmetrical, it can be difficult to make sure that they are the same distance from the bottom-center point. You can select the points and distribute their spacing based on the bottom-center point. To learn more about distributing points, see Lesson 2, "Selecting and Aligning."

5 Choose Select > Deselect, and then File > Save.

Convert between smooth points and corner points

Next, you'll finish the violin neck by adjusting a path. You'll be converting a smooth point on the curve to a corner point, and a corner point to a smooth point.

● **Note:** When dragging a direction handle with Direct Selection tool, both handles remain parallel to each other, but can each be made longer or shorter independent of each other.

1 Choose 6 Violin Neck from the Artboard Navigation menu in the lower-left corner of the Document window.

2 In the Layers panel click the blank box to the left of the Template layer lock icon (🔒) to turn on the visibility for the template layer again.

3 With the Direct Selection tool (⬚), position the pointer over point A on the left side of the shape. When an open square appears next to the pointer, click the anchor point to select it and display any red direction handles.

4 With the point selected, click the Convert Selected Anchor Points To Smooth button (⌐) in the Control panel.

● **Note:** You may want to zoom in.

5 With the Direct Selection tool, hold down the Shift key, click and drag the bottom direction handle down to reshape the bottom half of the curve. Release the mouse button and then the key.

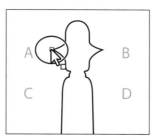
Select the point.

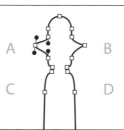
Convert the anchor point.

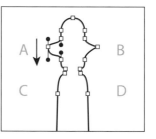
Drag the direction handle down.

6 Perform steps 3–5 on point B on the right side of the shape.

7 With the Direct Selection tool, click the point to the right of the letter C to select it. With the point selected, click the Convert Selected Anchor Points To Corner button (⌐) in the Control panel.

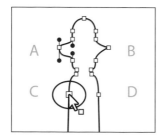

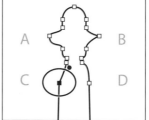

8 Repeat step 7 on point D.

9 With the Direct Selection tool (⊵), click to select the top point of the neck shape. In the Control panel, click the Cut Path At Selected Anchor Points button (⬚). Choose Select > Deselect.

10 With the Selection tool (▸), hold down the Shift key and drag the right side of the neck shape a little to the right. Release the mouse button and then the modifier key. This creates a gap between the two open paths.

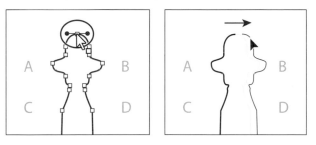

11 With the Direct Selection tool, drag a small marquee across the top two points of both paths. Then click the Connect Selected End Points button (⌒) in the Control panel to create a straight line across the top.

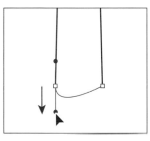

12 Select the Selection tool in the Tools panel, then click the path to select it (even though it looks selected). Choose Object > Path > Join to join the open endpoints at the bottom of the neck shape. Leave the shape selected.

Next, you will round the bottom of the shape using the Convert Anchor Point tool.

13 Select the Convert Anchor Point tool (⼊), nested in the Pen tool in the Tools panel.

14 Drag the bottom left-corner point of the neck shape down. As you drag, press the Shift key to constrain the movement. Release the mouse and then the Shift key.

The Convert Anchor Point tool also allows you to convert points from smooth to corner points and corner to smooth points, and much more.

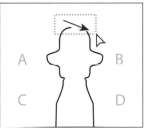

● **Note:** Make sure to press the Shift key AFTER you start dragging away from the point.

15 Drag from the bottom-right corner of the neck shape up, pressing the Shift key as you drag, to make a smooth point. This makes the bottom of the shape round. Release the mouse button and then the modifier key.

16 Choose Select > Deselect, and then choose File > Save.

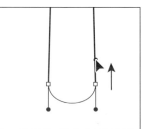

● **Note:** As mentioned earlier in the chapter, if you don't click on the point exactly, a warning dialog box may appear.

Drawing with the Pencil tool

The Pencil tool (🖉) lets you draw open and closed paths as if you were drawing with a pencil on paper. Anchor points are created by Illustrator, and are placed on the path as you draw. However, you can adjust the points when the path is complete. The number of anchor points set down is determined by the length and complexity of the path and by tolerance settings in the Pencil Tool Options dialog box. The Pencil tool is most useful for free-form drawing and creating more organic shapes.

Next, you will draw a few lines that will be a chin rest on the curved shape you drew earlier.

1   Choose 4 Curved Shape step 2 from the Artboard Navigation menu in the lower-left corner of the Document window.

2   In the Layers panel, click the Template Layer icon (🗒) to hide the template layer. Click the Layers panel icon to collapse the panel.

3   Double-click the Pencil tool (🖉) in the Tools panel. In the Pencil Tool Options dialog box, drag the Smoothness slider to the right until the value is 100%. This reduces the number of points on the paths drawn with the Pencil tool and makes them appear smoother. Click OK.

4   With the Pencil tool selected, click the Stroke color in the Control panel, and select black in the Swatches panel that appears. Then click the Fill color in the Control panel and choose None (⬛), if not already selected.

● **Note:** The colors may already be set for the stroke and fill.

5   Position the pointer inside the curved shape, on the left side of the shape. When you see an x to the right of the pointer, drag to create an arc inside the curved shape from the left side toward the right side. See figure for position and shape.

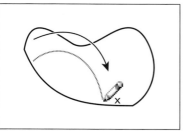

The x that appears to the right of the pointer before you begin drawing indicates that you are about to create a new path. If you don't see the x, it means that you are about to redraw a shape that the pointer is near. If necessary, move the pointer further from the edge of the curved shape.

▶ **Tip:** To create a closed path, like a circle, select the Pencil tool and press the Alt (Windows) or Option (Mac OS) key and drag. The Pencil tool displays a small circle to indicate that you're creating a closed path. When the path is the size and shape you want, release the mouse button, but don't release the Alt or Option key until the path closes. The beginning and ending anchor points are connected with the shortest line possible.

Notice that as you draw, the path may not look perfectly smooth. When you release the mouse button, the path is smoothed based on the Smoothness value that you set in the Pencil Tool Options dialog box.

6   Position the pointer over the right end of the newly created path. Notice that the x is no longer next to the Pencil tool pointer. This indicates that if you drag to start drawing, you will edit the path rather than draw a new path.

Next, you will set more options for the Pencil tool, then draw another curve to the right of the curved line you just drew.

7   Double-click the Pencil tool (✐) in the Tools panel.

8   In the Pencil Tool Options dialog box, deselect Edit Selected Paths. Change the Fidelity value to **10** pixels. Click OK.

9   With the Pencil tool, click the end of the previous curved path and drag to the right draw another arc shape.

10 Choose Select > Deselect.

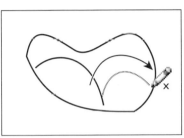

▶ **Tip:** The higher the Fidelity value, the greater the distance between anchor points and the fewer the anchor points created. Fewer anchor points can make the path smoother and less complex.

Editing with the Pencil tool

You can also edit any path using the Pencil tool and add free-form lines and shapes to any shape.

Next, you will edit the curved shape using the Pencil tool.

1   With the Selection tool (▶), select the closed curved path (not the arcs).

2   Double-click the Pencil tool. In the Pencil Tool Options dialog box, click Reset. Notice that the Edit Selected Paths option is selected (this is important for the next steps). Change the Fidelity to **10** and the Smoothness to **30%**. Click OK.

▶ **Tip:** For information on Pencil Tool options, see "pencil tool options" in Illustrator Help.

3   Position the Pencil tool on the top left of the curved path (not on the point) and notice that the x disappears from the pointer. This indicates that you are about to redraw the selected path.

● **Note:** Depending on where you begin to redraw the path and in which direction you drag, you may get unexpected results. Try redrawing if that happens.

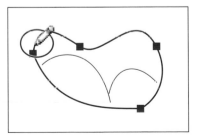

4 Drag to the right to edit the curve of the path. When the pointer is back on the path, release the mouse button to see the shape.

5 Choose Select > All On Active Artboard.

● **Note:** Your curved path result may not look exactly as you see in the figure above. That's OK. If you want, edit the path again, using the Pencil tool.

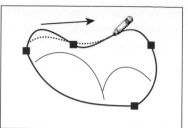

6 Choose Object > Group.

7 With the group selected, double-click the Scale tool (⬚) in the Tools panel. In the Scale dialog box that appears, change the Uniform Scale to **70**% and click OK.

8 Choose Select > Deselect, then File > Save.

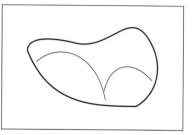

Finishing the violin illustration

To complete the illustration, you'll make some minor modifications and assemble and paint the objects.

Assembling the parts

1 Choose View > Fit All In Window. Choose Essentials from the workspace switcher in the Application bar.

2 Choose View > Show Bounding Box so that you can see the bounding boxes of selected objects as you transform them.

3 Select the Selection tool (▶) in the Tools panel, and move the curved shape group you just edited to the bottom left of the violin, as shown in the figure.

4 Shift-click the edge of the violin shape to select both shapes and then choose Object > Group.

5 Choose Object > Lock > Selection.

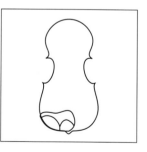

6 With the Selection tool, move the violin neck to the top of the violin body. Using the rulers as a guide, position the neck about an inch from the top of the artboard and align it as close to the center of the violin body as you can.

7 With the violin neck still selected, choose Object > Arrange > Bring to Front.

8 Select the Direct Selection tool (▷) in the Tools panel, and drag a marquee across the bottom of the neck shape. Holding down the Shift key, drag one of the bottom points of the neck shape down. Release the mouse button and then the key. See figure for approximate length.

9 Choose Object > Lock > Selection.

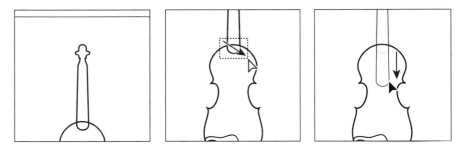

10 With the Selection tool, drag the dashed line group (from the 5 Strings artboard) onto the center of the violin shape. Drag it so that the bottom of the dashed line is above the curved shaped and on the left edge of the violin neck shape. See the figure below for placement.

11 Choose Object > Arrange > Bring To Front.

12 Select the Direct Selection tool in the Tools panel. Click to select the top point of the dashed line group. Begin dragging the top point of the dashed line group up. While dragging, hold down the Shift key, and drag until the point is just below the top of the violin neck. Release the mouse button and then the key.

13 With the Selection tool, click to select the dashed line group. Double-click the Selection tool in the Tools panel to open the Move dialog box.

14 In the Move dialog box, change Horizontal to **.1** in and make sure that Vertical is **0**. Click Copy to copy and move the dashed line group to the right.

15 With the copied line group still selected, choose Object > Transform > Transform Again twice, until there are 4 dotted line groups.

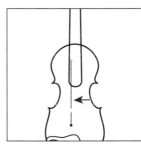 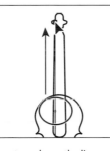 

Drag the line group in to place. Drag to reshape the line. Copy the line group.

16 Choose Select > All On Active Artboard, and then Object > Group.

17 In the Control panel, change the Stroke weight to **1** pt.

18 Select the Zoom tool (🔍) in the Tools panel and click the bottom portion of the dotted line groups three times.

19 Select the Rectangle tool in the Tools panel. Click anywhere in the artwork. In the Rectangle dialog box, change the Width to **.5 in** and the Height to **.18 in**. Click OK.

20 With the Rectangle on the page and selected, press the letter D to set the shape to the default stroke and fill.

● **Note:** You may need to adjust the height of the rectangle so that it fits into the gap between your dashed lines more accurately.

21 With the Selection tool, drag the Rectangle to where you cut the dotted lines. See figure for positioning.

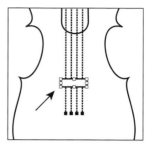

22 Choose View > Fit Artboard In Window.

23 Choose Object > Unlock All, then Select > All On Active Artboard.

24 In the Control panel, choose Align To Artboard (⊞), and then click Horizontal Align Center (⊥).

● **Note:** If you don't see the align options in the Control panel, click the word Align or choose Window > Align.

25 Choose Select > Deselect, and then File > Save.

Painting the artwork

In the color illustration, the fills are painted with custom-made colors called Violin, Neck, and Gray, which are provided in the Swatches panel. To learn more about painting options in Illustrator, see Lesson 6, "Color and Painting."

● **Note:** To change the color of the curved shape, double-click the shape to enter isolation ode and change the color. Then press the Escape key to exit.

1 With the Selection tool (▶), select an object, and then change the Fill color in the Control panel. Apply the swatch named Violin to the violin shape, Gray to the rectangle and the curved shape group, and Neck to the neck shape.

2 Choose File > Save, and keep the file open if you plan to explore on your own.

Exploring on your own

For additional practice with the Pen tool, try tracing over images with it. As you practice with the Pen tool, you'll become more adept at drawing the kinds of curves and shapes you want.

1 Open the practice.ai file in the Lesson05 folder, located in the Lessons folder on your hard disk.

2 Select the Pen tool (✒) and start using the techniques you learned throughout this lesson to recreate the S shape, using the gray shape as a guide.

3 Create 2 copies of the shape and paste them onto the violin. One of them will need to be reflected by selecting the shape and double-clicking the Reflect tool (⋈) in the Rotate tool group in the Tools panel.

4 Choose File > Save, and then File > Close.

Review questions

1 Describe how to draw straight vertical, horizontal, or diagonal lines using the Pen tool.

2 How do you draw a curved line using the Pen tool?

3 How do you draw a corner point on a curved line?

4 Name two ways to convert a smooth point on a curve to a corner point.

5 Which tool would you use to edit a segment on a curved line?

6 How can you change the way the Pencil tool works?

Review answers

1 To draw a straight line, click twice with the Pen tool. The first click sets the starting anchor point, and the second click sets the ending anchor point of the line. To constrain the straight line vertically, horizontally, or along a 45° diagonal, press the Shift key as you click with the Pen tool.

2 To draw a curved line with the Pen tool, click to create the starting anchor point and drag to set the direction of the curve, and then click to end the curve.

3 To draw a corner point on a curved line, press the Alt (Windows) or Option (Mac OS) key and drag the direction handle on the end point of the curve to change the direction of the path. Continue dragging to draw the next curved segment on the path.

4 Use the Direct Selection tool to select the anchor point, and then use the Convert Anchor Point tool to drag a direction handle to change the direction. Another method is to choose a point or points with the Direct Selection tool and then click the Convert Selected Anchor Points To Corner button (⌐) in the Control panel.

5 To edit a segment on a curved line, select the Direct Selection tool and drag the segment to move it, or drag a direction handle on an anchor point to adjust the length and shape of the segment.

6 Double-click the Pencil tool to open the Pencil Tool Options dialog box, where you can change the smoothness, fidelity, and more.

6 COLOR AND PAINTING

Lesson overview

In this lesson, you'll learn how to do the following:

- Use color modes and color controls.

- Create, edit, and paint with colors using the Control panel and shortcuts.

- Name and save colors, create color groups, and build a color palette.

- Use the Color Guide panel and the Edit Colors/Recolor Artwork features.

- Copy paint and appearance attributes from one object to another.

- Create and paint with patterns.

- Work with Live Paint.

 This lesson takes approximately an hour and a half to complete. If needed, remove the previous lesson folder from your hard disk and copy the Lesson06 folder onto it.

Spice up your illustration with colors by taking advantage of color controls in Adobe® Illustrator® CS5. In this information-packed lesson, you'll discover how to create and paint fills and strokes, use the Color Guide panel for inspiration, work with color groups, recolor artwork, create patterns, and more.

Getting started

In this lesson, you will learn about the fundamentals of color and create and edit colors using the Color panel, Swatches panel, and more.

1 To ensure that the tools and panels function as described in this lesson, delete or deactivate (by renaming) the Adobe Illustrator CS5 preferences file. See "Restoring default preferences" on page 3.

2 Start Adobe Illustrator CS5.

● Note: If you have not already done so, copy the resource files for this lesson onto your hard disk from the Lesson06 folder on the Adobe Illustrator CS5 Classroom in a Book CD. See "Copying the Classroom in a Book files" on page 2.

3 Choose File > Open and open the L6end_1.ai file in the Lesson06 folder to view a final version of the label you will paint. Leave it open for reference.

4 Choose File > Open. In the Open dialog box, navigate to the Lesson06 folder in the Lessons folder. Open the L6start_1.ai file.

This file has some components already in it. You will create and apply color as necessary to complete the label.

5 Choose File > Save As. In the Save As dialog box, navigate to the Lesson06 folder and name it **label.ai**. Leave the Save As Type option set to Adobe Illustrator (*.AI) (Windows) or the Format option set to Adobe Illustrator (ai) (Mac OS), and click Save. In the Illustrator Options dialog box, leave the options at their default settings, and then click OK.

Understanding color

When working with color in Illustrator, you first need to understand color modes (also called color models). When you apply color to artwork, keep in mind the final medium in which the artwork will be published (print or web, for instance), so that you can use the correct color model and color definitions. First, you will learn about color modes, and then you will learn the basic color controls.

Color modes

Before starting a new illustration, you must first decide which color mode the artwork should use, CMYK or RGB.

- **CMYK**—Cyan, magenta, yellow, and black are the colors used in four-color process printing. These four colors are combined and overlapped in a screen pattern to create a multitude of other colors. Select this mode for printing.

- **RGB**—Red, green, and blue light are added together in various ways to create an array of colors. Select this mode if you are using images for onscreen presentations or the Internet.

When creating a new document, you select a color mode by choosing File > New and picking the appropriate document profile, such as Print, which uses CMYK for the color mode. You can change the color mode by clicking the arrow to the left of Advanced and selecting a Color Mode.

When a color mode is selected, the applicable panels open displaying colors in either the CMYK or RGB mode. You can change the color mode of a document after a file is created by choosing File > Document Color Mode, and then selecting either CMYK or RGB in the menu.

Understanding the color controls

In this lesson, you will learn about the traditional methods of coloring objects in Illustrator. This includes painting objects with colors and patterns using a combination of panels and tools, including the Control panel, Color panel, Swatches panel, Gradient panel, Stroke panel, Color Guide panel, Color Picker, and the paint buttons in the Tools panel. You'll begin by looking at finished artwork to which color has already been applied.

1   Click the L6end_1.ai document tab at the top of the Document window.

2 Choose 1 from the Artboard Navigation menu in the lower-left corner of the Document window to fit the first artboard in the Document window.

3 Select the Selection tool (⬈), and then click the green shape behind the text "Pizza Sauce."

Note: Depending on your screen resolution, your Tools panel may be displayed in a single-column rather than a double-column.

Objects in Illustrator can have a fill, a stroke, or both. In the Tools panel, notice that the Fill box appears in the foreground, indicating that it is selected. This is the default setting. The Fill box is green for this object. Behind the Fill box, the Stroke box has a yellow outline.

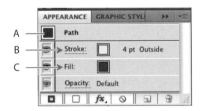

A. Fill box
B. Default Fill And Stroke button
C. Color button
D. Swap Fill And Stroke button
E. Stroke box
F. None button
G. Gradient button

4 Click the Appearance panel icon (●) on the right side of the workspace.

The Fill and Stroke attributes of the selected object also appear in the Appearance panel. You can edit, delete or save appearance attributes as graphic styles, which you can apply to other objects, layers, and groups. You'll use this panel later in this lesson.

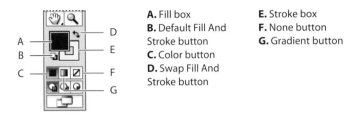

A. Object selected
B. Stroke color
C. Fill color

Tip: Shift-click the color spectrum bar at the bottom of the Color panel to rotate through different color modes like CMYK and RGB.

5 Click the Color panel icon (🎨) on the right side of the workspace. The Color panel displays the current color of the fill and stroke. The CMYK sliders in the Color panel show the percentages of cyan, magenta, yellow, and black. The color spectrum bar is at the bottom of the Color panel.

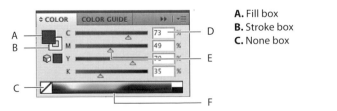

A. Fill box
B. Stroke box
C. None box
D. Color value
E. Color slider
F. Color spectrum bar

The color spectrum bar lets you quickly and visually select a fill or stroke color from a spectrum of colors. You can also choose white or black by clicking the appropriate color box at the right end of the bar.

6   Click the Swatches panel icon (▦) on the right side of the workspace. You can name and save document colors, gradients, and patterns in the Swatches panel, for instant access. When an object has a fill or stroke that contains a color, gradient, pattern, or tint applied in the Swatches panel, the applied swatch is highlighted in the panel.

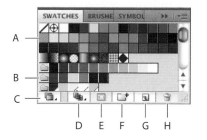

A. Swatch
B. Color group
C. Swatch Libraries menu
D. Show Swatch Kinds menu
E. Swatch Options

F. New Color Group
G. New Swatch
H. Delete Swatch

7   Click the Color Guide panel icon (◗) on the right side of the workspace. Click the green swatch in the upper-left corner of the panel to set the base color as the color of the selected object (labeled A in the figure below). Click the Harmony Rules menu, and choose Complementary 2.

The Color Guide can provide color inspiration while you create your artwork. It helps you pick color tints, analogous colors, and much more. In this panel, you can also access the Edit or Apply Color feature, which lets you edit and create colors.

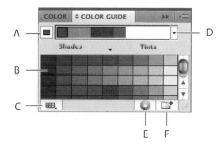

A. Set base color to the current color
B. Color variations
C. Limits the color group to colors in a swatch library

D. Harmony Rules menu and active color group
E. Edit Or Apply Colors
F. Save color group to Swatch panel

8   Click the Color panel icon (🎨). Using the Selection tool (▶), click various shapes in the L6end_1.ai file to see how their paint attributes are reflected in the panel.

9   Leave the L6end_1.ai file open for reference or choose File > Close to close it, without saving.

10 Click the label.ai document tab at the top of the Document window if you did not close the L6end_1.ai document.

Creating color

You are working on artwork in the CMYK color mode, which means that you can create your own color from any combination of cyan, magenta, yellow, and black. You can create color in a variety of ways, depending on the artwork. If you want to create a color that is specific to your company, for instance, you can use a swatch library. If you are trying to match color in artwork, you can use the Eyedropper tool to sample color, or the Color Picker to enter exact values. Next, you will create color using different methods and then apply that color to objects.

Building and saving a custom color

First you will create a color using the Color panel, and then save the color as a swatch in the Swatches panel.

● **Note:** If an object is selected when you create a color, the color is typically applied to the selected object.

1 Choose Select > Deselect to ensure that nothing is selected.

2 Choose 1 from the Artboard Navigation menu in the lower-left corner of the Document window to fit the first artboard in the Document window.

3 If the Color panel is not visible, click the Color panel icon (🎨). If the CMYK sliders are not visible, choose CMYK from the Color panel menu (▼≡).

Click the Stroke box and type these values in the CMYK text fields: C=**19**, M=**88**, Y=**78**, K=**22**.

> ▶ **Tip:** These values are each a percentage of 100.

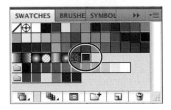

▶ **Tip:** To save a color you made in the Color panel, you can also click the New Swatch button in the Swatches panel to open the New Swatch dialog box.

4 Click the Swatches panel icon (▦), and choose New Swatch from the Swatches panel menu (▼≡).

5 In the New Swatch dialog box, name the color **label background** and, leaving the rest of the options as is, click OK. Notice that the swatch is highlighted in the Swatches panel.

New colors added to the Swatches panel are saved with the current file only. Opening a new file displays the default set of swatches that comes with Adobe Illustrator CS5.

> ▶ **Tip:** If you want to load swatches from one saved document into another, click the Swatch Libraries Menu button (📚) at the bottom of the Swatches panel and choose Other Library. Then locate the document with the swatches that you want to import.

● **Note:** The Swatches panel that appears when you click Fill color in the Control panel is the same as the Swatches panel on the right side of the workspace.

6 With the Selection tool (▶), click the white-filled background shape to select it. Click the Fill box at the bottom of the Tools panel. Click the Swatches panel icon (▦) if the panel is not showing, and select the label background swatch. Choose Select > Deselect.

Next, you will create another swatch using a similar, yet different, method.

7 In the Swatches panel, click the New Swatch (![icon]) button at the bottom of the panel. This creates a copy of the selected swatch and opens the New Swatch dialog box.

8 In the New Swatch dialog box, change the name to **label background stroke** and change the values to C=**19**, M=**46**, Y=**60**, K=**0**. Click OK.

● **Note:** If the shape had still been selected, it would be filled with the new color.

9 With the Selection tool (![icon]), click the shape again to select it. Click the Stroke color in the Control panel. When the Swatches panel appears, select the label background stroke swatch.

10 Change the Stroke Weight in the Control panel to 7 pt. Leave the Swatches panel showing.

Editing a swatch

After a color is created and saved in the Swatches panel, you can edit that color.

Next, you will edit the label background swatch that you just saved.

1 Select the Stroke box in the Tools panel. This expands the Color panel. Click the Swatches panel icon (![icon]) on the right side of the workspace.

2 With the shape still selected, double-click the label background stroke swatch in the Swatches panel. In the Swatch Options dialog box, change the values to C=**2**, M=**15**, Y=**71**, K=**20**. Select Preview to see the changes to the logo shape. Change the K value to **0**, and then click OK.

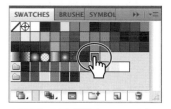

▶ **Tip:** You can position the pointer over a color swatch in the Swatches panel to see a tooltip indicating the name of the swatch.

When you create a swatch and then edit it, the objects that already have that swatch color applied need to be selected to apply the change.

Next, you will change the logo background swatch to a global color. When you edit it, a global color automatically updates throughout the artwork, regardless of whether the objects that use that global color are selected.

3 With the shape still selected, click the Fill box in the Tools panel.

4 Double-click the label background swatch in the Swatches panel to open the Swatch Options dialog box. Select Global, and then click OK.

5 Choose Select > Deselect.

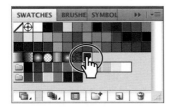

● **Note:** The white triangle in the lower-right corner of a swatch icon (▣) in the Swatches panel indicates a global color.

6 Double-click the label background swatch in the Swatches panel again to open the Swatch Options dialog box. Change the K value (black) to **70**. Select Preview to see the changes. Notice how the shape fill changes, even though the shape is not selected. Click Cancel so the color change is not saved.

7 Choose File > Save.

Using Illustrator swatch libraries

● **Note:** Most, but not all, of the libraries that come with Illustrator are CMYK colors.

Swatch libraries are collections of preset colors such as PANTONE, TOYO, and thematic libraries like Earthtone and Ice Cream. The libraries appear as separate panels and cannot be edited. When you apply color from a library to artwork, the color in the library becomes a swatch that is saved in the Swatches panel for that document. Libraries are a great starting point for creating colors.

Next, you will create a yellow spot color using the PANTONE solid coated library for another shape in the label. When this color is defined, it could be a warm, dark, or light yellow. This is why most printers and designers rely on a color matching system, like the PANTONE system, to help maintain color consistency and to give a wider range of colors in some cases.

Spot versus process colors

You can designate colors as either spot or process color types, which correspond to the two main ink types used in commercial printing.

- A process color is printed using a combination of the four standard process inks: cyan, magenta, yellow, and black (CMYK).

- A spot color is a special premixed ink that is used instead of, or in addition to, CMYK process inks. A spot color requires its own printing plate on a printing press.

Creating a spot color

In this section, you will see how to load a color library, such as the PANTONE color system, and to add a PANTONE (PMS) color to the Swatches panel.

1 In the Swatches panel, click the Swatch Libraries Menu button (![icon]). Choose Color Books > PANTONE Solid Coated. The PANTONE solid coated library appears in its own panel.

2 Choose Show Find Field from the PANTONE Solid Coated panel menu (![icon]). Type **100** in the Find field. PANTONE 100 C is highlighted. Click the highlighted swatch to add it to the Swatches panel. Close the PANTONE Solid Coated panel. The PANTONE color appears in the Swatches panel.

● **Note:** When you exit Illustrator and then relaunch it, the PANTONE library panel does not reopen. To automatically open the panel whenever Illustrator opens, choose Persistent from the PANTONE Solid Coated panel menu.

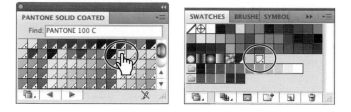

3 Position the pointer on the artboard and, holding down the Spacebar, drag to the right so that you can see both the white-filled shape off the left edge and the content on the first artboard.

4 With the Selection tool (![icon]), click the white-filled shape off the left edge of artboard 1 to select it. From the Fill color in the Control panel, choose the PANTONE 100 C color to fill the shape. Change the Stroke color to None (![icon]).

5 With the shape still selected, Shift-click to select the original red label background shape on the first artboard. Release the Shift key.

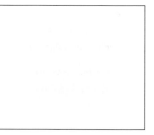

6 Choose View > Fit Artboard In Window.

7 With the Selection tool, click the red shape once more to make it the key object.

● **Note:** To learn more about what key objects are and how to work with them, see Lesson 2, "Selecting and Aligning."

8 In the Control panel, click the Horizontal Align Center button (![icon]) and Vertical Align Center button (![icon]) to align the yellow shape to the red label shape.

● **Note:** If you don't see the Align options, click the word Align in the Control panel to reveal the Align panel.

9 Choose Select > Deselect.

10 Choose File > Save. Keep the file open.

Why does my PANTONE swatch look different from the other swatches in the Swatches panel?

In the Swatches panel, the color type is identified by the icon that appears next to the name of the color. You can identify spot-color swatches by the spot-color icon (⊚) when the panel is in list view or by the dot in the lower corner (⬚) when the panel is in thumbnail view. Process colors do not have a spot-color icon or a dot.

By default, the PANTONE solid coated swatch is defined as a spot color. A spot color is not created from a combination of CMYK inks but is its own solid ink color. A press operator uses a premixed PMS (PANTONE Matching System) color in the press, offering more consistent color.

A triangle indicates that the color is global. If a global color is edited, all color references used in the illustration are updated. Any color can be global, not only PANTONE colors. To learn more about spot colors, choose Help > Illustrator Help and search for "spot colors."

Using the Color Picker

The Color Picker lets you select color in a color field and in a spectrum by either defining colors numerically or by clicking a swatch.

Next, you will create a color using the Color Picker, and then save the color as a swatch in the Swatches panel.

1   With the Selection tool (▶), click one of the white bars in the lower part of the label shape to select the underlying white shape in the lower half of artboard 1.

2   Double-click the Fill box in the Tools panel to open the Color Picker.

▶ **Tip:** You can double-click the Fill box or Stroke box in the Tools panel or Color panel to access the Color Picker.

▶ **Tip:** If you work in Adobe Photoshop, the Color Picker is probably familiar, because Photoshop also has a Color Picker feature.

3   In the Color Picker dialog box, type these values into the CMYK text fields: C=**0**, M=**11**, Y=**54**, and K=**0**.

Notice that the slider in the color spectrum bar and the circle in the color field move as you enter the CMYK values. The color spectrum shows the hue, and the color field shows saturation (horizontally) and brightness (vertically).

4   Select S (saturation) to change the color spectrum displayed in the Color Picker. The color spectrum bar becomes the saturation of the orange color. Drag the color spectrum slider up until the S value is 60%, and then click OK.

The white shape is filled with the yellow/orange color you just made in the Color Picker.

● **Note:** The Color Swatches button in the Color Picker shows you the swatches in the Swatches panel and lets you select one. Then you can return to the color models view you started with by clicking the Color Models button and editing the swatch color values.

5 Change the stroke color in the Control panel to None (⊘).

Next, you will save the color in the Swatches panel.

6 Select the Fill box at the bottom of the Tools panel. This ensures that when you create a new swatch, it is created using the fill of the selected shape.

7 Expand the Swatches panel by clicking its panel icon (▦).

8 Click the New Swatch button (▣) at the bottom of the Swatches panel and name the color **yellow/orange** in the New Swatch dialog box. Select Global, and then click OK to see the color appear as a swatch in the Swatches panel.

9 Choose Select > Deselect, and then File > Save.

Creating and saving a tint of a color

A tint is a lighter version of a color. You can create a tint from a global process color like CMYK or from a spot color.

Next, you will create a tint of the yellow/orange swatch.

1 With the Selection tool, click one of the black bars in the lower half of the artboard. Change the fill color in the Control panel to the yellow/orange color you just made.

2 Click the Color panel icon (🎨) to expand the Color panel.

3 Make sure that the Fill box is selected in the Color panel, and then drag the tint slider to the left to change the tint value to 20%.

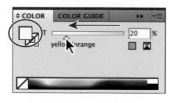

4 Click the Swatches panel icon (▦) on the right side of the workspace. Click the New Swatch button (▣) at the bottom of the panel to save the tint. Notice the tint swatch in the Swatches panel. Position the pointer over the swatch icon to see its name, yellow/orange 20%.

5 Choose File > Save.

Copying attributes

1 Using the Selection tool (▸), select one of the black bars that has not yet been colored, and then choose Select > Same > Fill Color to select the remaining black rectangles.

2 Using the Eyedropper tool (✐), click the painted bar. All the bars that are unpainted pick up the attributes from the painted bar.

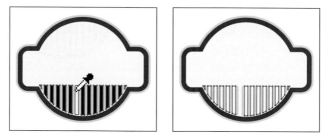

3 With the Selection tool, Shift-click to select the original bar.

4 Choose Object > Group.

5 Choose Select > Deselect, and then File > Save.

Creating color groups

In Illustrator, you can save colors in color groups, which consist of related color swatches in the Swatches panel. Organizing colors by their use, such as grouping all the logo colors, is helpful. Only spot, process, and global colors can be in a group.

Next, you will create a color group using the label colors you've created.

1 In the Swatches panel, click a blank area of the panel to deselect the color swatches. Click the label background swatch (red) and, holding down the Shift key, click the yellow/orange swatch to the right to select four color swatches.

▶ **Tip:** To select multiple colors that are not next to each other in the Swatches panel, Ctrl-click (Windows) or Cmd-click (Mac OS) the swatches you want to select.

2   Click the New Color Group button (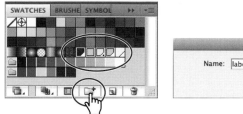) at the bottom of the Swatches panel to open the New Color Group dialog box. Change the Name to **label base** and click OK to save the group.

● **Note:** If objects are selected when you click the New Color Group button, an expanded New Color Group dialog box appears. In this dialog box, you can create a color group from the colors in the artwork and convert the colors to global colors.

Next, you'll edit a color in the group and then add a color to the group.

3   With the Selection tool (▶), click a blank area of the Swatches panel to deselect the color group you just created.

4   In the Swatches panel, double-click the yellow/orange swatch in the label base color group to open the Swatch Options dialog box. Change the values to C=**0**, M=**12**, Y=**54**, and K=**0**. Click OK.

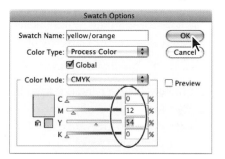

5   Click the yellow/orange 20% swatch and drag it between the PANTONE 100 C swatch and the yellow/orange swatch in the label base color group.

You can still reorder the swatches in the group by dragging them. Try dragging the PANTONE 100 C swatch to the right of the yellow/orange 20% swatch.

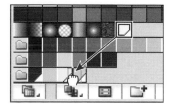

● **Note:** If you drag the PANTONE 100 C swatch too far to the right, you may pull it out of the group. If that happens, you can always drag it back into the group.

6   Choose File > Save.

The colors in the label have now been saved with this document as a color group. You will learn how to edit a color group later in the lesson.

Working with the Color Guide panel

The Color Guide panel can provide you with color inspiration as you create your artwork. Use it to pick harmony rules such as color tints, analogous colors, and much more. In this panel, you can also access the Edit Color/Recolor Artwork feature, which allows you to edit and create colors.

Next, you will use the Color Guide panel to select different colors for a second label, and then you'll save those colors as a color group in the Swatches panel.

1 Choose 2 from the Artboard Navigation menu in the lower-left corner of the Document window.

2 With the Selection tool (), click the red background shape of the label. Make sure that the Fill box is selected in the Tools panel.

● **Note:** The colors you see in the Color Guide panel may be different from what you see in the figure. That is okay.

3 Click the Color Guide panel icon () on the right side of the workspace to open the panel. Click the Set Base Color To The Current Color button ().

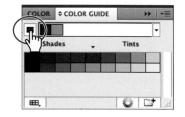

This allows the Color Guide panel to suggest colors based on the color showing in the Set Base Color To The Current Color button.

Next, you'll experiment with the colors in the label.

4 Choose Complementary 2 from the Harmony Rules menu to the right of the Set Base Color To The Current Color button in the Color Guide panel.

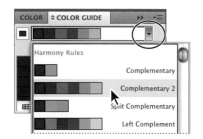

5 Click the Save Color Group To Swatch Panel button () to save the colors in the Right Complement harmony rule in the Swatches panel.

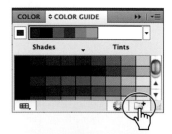

6 Click the Swatches panel icon (). Scroll down to see the new group added. You can apply these colors to the artwork and you can edit them.

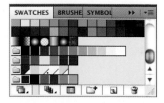

7 Click the Color Guide icon () to open the Color Guide panel.

Next, you'll experiment with the colors.

8 In the color variations in the Color Guide panel, select the fifth color from the left, in the second row. Notice that the logo changes color. Click the Set Base Color To The Current Color button (■) to try a new group of colors using the Complementary 2 harmony rule. Click the Save Group To Swatch Panel button (□⁺) to save the colors in the Swatches panel.

● **Note:** If you choose a different color variation than the one suggested, your color will differ from those in the rest of this section.

9 Choose File > Save.

Editing a color group

Illustrator has many tools for working with color. When you create color groups, either in the Swatches panel or in the Color Guide panel, you can edit them individually or as a group in the Edit Colors dialog box. You can also rename the color group, reorder the colors in the group, add or remove colors, and more. In this section, you will learn how to edit colors of a saved color group using the Edit Color dialog box.

1 Choose Select > Deselect and then click the Swatches panel icon (⊞).

2 Click the folder icon to the left of the last color group, to select the group (you may need to scroll down in the Swatches panel). Notice that the Swatch Options button (▣) changes to the Edit Color Group button (●) when the group (folder) is selected.

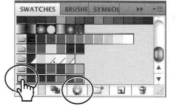

The Swatch Options button (▣) at the bottom of the panel lets you edit a single, selected color.

▶ **Tip:** To edit a color group, you can also double-click the folder icon to the left of the color group in the Swatches panel.

3 Click the Edit Color Group button (●) at the bottom of the Swatches panel to open the Edit Color dialog box.

On the right side of the Edit Color dialog box, under Color Groups, all of the existing color groups in the Swatches panel are listed. On the left side of the dialog box, you can edit the colors of each color group, either individually or as a group.

● **Note:** If artwork is selected when you click the Edit Color Group button in the Swatches panel, the color group applies to the selected object(s). The Recolor Artwork dialog box appears, allowing you to edit colors for and apply colors to the selected object(s).

Next, you will edit the colors for the color group.

4   In the Edit Colors dialog box, the group of colors you are about to edit is shown in the upper-left corner. Select the name Color Group 2 in the field above the Assign button, and rename the group **label 2**. This will be the name of a new color group you save later in the lesson.

5   In the color wheel, you see markers (circles) that represent each color in the group. Drag the large red marker on the right side of the color wheel up and to the right edge of the color wheel.

6   Change the Brightness (☼) by dragging the Adjust Brightness slider to the right, to brighten all the colors at once. Leave the Edit Colors dialog box open.

The Recolor Art selection at the bottom of the Edit Colors dialog box is dimmed because no artwork is selected. If artwork is selected when you open this dialog box, the dialog box is called the Recolor Artwork dialog box, and any edits you make change the artwork as well.

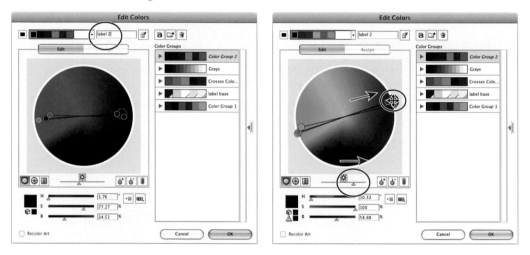

Rename the color group.   Edit the color saturation and brightness.

● **Note:** The larger marker in the color wheel with the double circle is the base color of the color group.

Next, you will edit the colors in the group independently, and then save the colors as a new named group.

7   Click the Unlink Harmony Colors button (⊠) in the Edit Colors dialog box to edit the colors independently. The button will turn into the Link Harmony Colors button (⊠).

The lines between the color markers (circles) and the center of the color wheel become dotted, indicating that the colors can be edited independently.

8 Drag the larger red marker down and to the left, to the edge of the color wheel below the green color markers, to change the red color into a blue.

By moving the color markers away from the center, you increase saturation. By moving the color markers toward the center of the color wheel, you decrease saturation. When a color marker is selected, you can edit the color using the HSB (hue, saturation, and brightness) sliders below the color wheel.

9 Click the Color Mode button (⊞), and choose CMYK from the menu, if the CMYK sliders are not already visible. Click to select one of the green markers in the color wheel, as shown in the figure below, on the right. Change the CMYK values to C=**65**, M=**0**, Y=**80**, and K=**0**. Notice the light green color marker move in the color wheel.

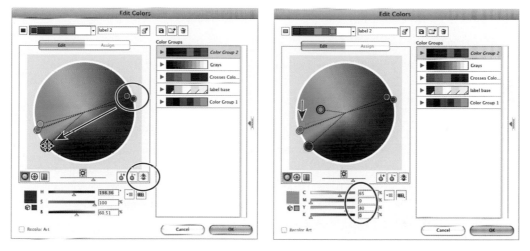

Edit a single color.   Edit another color.

● **Note:** It's okay if the color markers in your Edit Colors dialog box are different from the figure above.

10 Click the Color Mode button (⊞) and choose HSB from the menu, so that next time you edit colors you will be using the HSB sliders.

11 Click the New Color Group button (⊞) at the top of the Edit Colors panel, to save the colors you've edited as a new color group named label 2. The color groups that are available in the document appear on the right side of the Edit Colors dialog box.

▶ **Tip:** To edit a color group and save the changes without creating a new color group, click the Save Changes To Color Group button (⊟).

12 Click OK to close the Edit Colors dialog box and save the label 2 color group in the Swatches panel. If a dialog box appears, click Yes to save the changes to the color group in the Swatches panel.

13 Choose File > Save.

Editing color options

You can use the options in the lower portion of the Edit Colors dialog box to edit color, as described in the figure below.

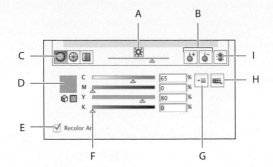

A Show saturation and hue on color wheel.

B Add and subtract color marker tools.

C Color display options (smooth color wheel, segmented color wheel, color bars)

D Color of the selected color marker or color bar

E Selected artwork is recolored when selected (the check box is dimmed when artwork is not selected).

F Color sliders

G Color mode button

H Limit the color group to colors in a swatch library.

I Unlink harmony colors.

Editing colors in artwork

You can also edit the colors in selected artwork, using the Recolor Artwork command. Next, you will edit the colors in the second label, and save the edited colors as a color group.

1 Choose Select > All On Active Artboard.

2 Choose Edit > Edit Colors > Recolor Artwork to open the Recolor Artwork dialog box.

You use the Recolor Artwork dialog box to reassign or reduce the colors in your artwork and to create and edit color groups. All the color groups that you create for a document appear in the Color Groups storage area of the Recolor Artwork dialog box and in the Swatches panel. You can select and use these color groups at any time.

▶ **Tip:** You can also access the Recolor Artwork dialog box by selecting the artwork, and then clicking the Recolor Artwork button (◉) in the Control panel.

3 In the Recolor Artwork dialog box, click the Hide Color Group Storage icon (◄) on the right side of the dialog box.

4 Click the Edit tab to edit the colors in the artwork and using a color wheel.

5 Click the Link Harmony Colors icon (🔘) to edit all the colors at the same time. The icon should now look like this 🔘.

6 Press the Shift key and drag the larger red color circle down into the purple area of the color wheel. Release the mouse button and then the Shift key. Dragging with the Shift key allows you to adjust the color in the color wheel only, not the saturation.

> ▶ **Tip:** If you want to return to the original logo colors, click the Get Colors From Selected Art button (🔳).

> ▶ **Tip:** You can save the edited colors as a color group by clicking the Show Color Group Storage icon (▶) on the right side of the dialog box and then clicking the New Color Group button (📄).

7 Drag the Adjust Brightness slider to the left to make the colors darker overall.

The edit options in the Recolor Artwork dialog box are the same as the options in the Edit Color dialog box. Instead of editing color and creating color groups to apply later, you are dynamically editing colors in the selected artwork. Notice the Recolor Art selection in the lower-left corner of the dialog box. When artwork is selected, you are editing the artwork.

8 Click OK.

9 Choose File > Save.

Next, you will get a color group from a community of users, using the Kuler panel.

Working with the Kuler panel

The Kuler panel is a portal to themed color groups, such as ice cream, created by an online community of designers. You can browse lots of the groups and download themes to edit or use. You can also create themed color groups to share with others.

Next, you will download a themed color group for a soda can and apply color to it.

1 Choose Select > Deselect.

2 Choose 3 Artboard 3 from the Artboard Navigation menu in the lower-left corner of the Document window.

3 Choose Window > Extensions > Kuler.

● **Note:** You need an Internet connection to access the Kuler themes.

● **Note:** Because the themes are constantly updated and are brought into the Kuler panel via the Internet, your Kuler panel may show different themes from those in the figures shown.

4 In the Kuler panel, click the Highest Rated menu and choose Most Popular. The Kuler panel shows you the newest themes, highest rated themes, and more.

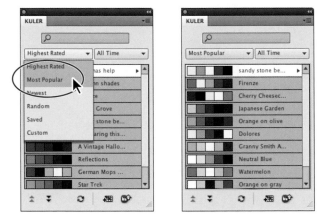

5 To search for themes, type **Italian restaurant** in the Search field at the top of the panel and press Enter or Return. This brings in the themes related to the words Italian restaurant.

6 Click the first Italian restaurant theme in the Browse panel (below the search field). If the Italian restaurant theme does not appear, select another. Click the Add Selected Theme To Swatches button (▦) to add it to the Swatches panel for the open document.

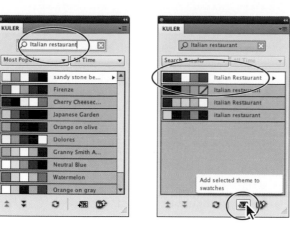

7   Close the Kuler panel.

8   Click the Swatches panel icon (▦) to open the panel if it isn't already open. Notice that the new color group, Italian restaurant, appears in the panel list of swatches (scroll down, if necessary).

9   Choose File > Save.

Kuler panel options

The Kuler™ panel is your portal to groups of colors, or themes, created by an online community of designers. You can use it to browse thousands of themes on Kuler, and then download some to edit or to include in your own projects. You can also use the Kuler panel to share your themes with the Kuler community by uploading them.

The Kuler panel is available in Adobe Photoshop® CS5, Adobe Flash® Professional CS5, Adobe InDesign® CS5, Adobe Illustrator® CS5, and Adobe Fireworks® CS5. The panel is not available in the French versions of these products.

Here are a few more options in the Kuler panel:

View a theme online on Kuler:

1   In the Browse panel, select a theme in the search results.

2   Click the triangle on the right side of the theme and select View Online in Kuler.

Saving frequent searches:

1   Select the Custom option in the first pop-up menu in the Browse panel.

2   In the dialog box that opens, enter your search terms and save them. When you want to run the search, select it from the first pop-up menu.

To delete a saved search, select the Custom option in the pop-up menu and clear the searches you'd like to delete.

—From Illustrator Help

Assigning colors to your artwork

The Assign tab of the Recolor Artwork dialog box lets you assign colors from a color group to your artwork. You can assign colors in several ways, including using a new color group chosen from the Harmony Rules menu. Next, you will assign new colors to a third version of the label.

1 Choose Select > All On Active Artboard.

2 Choose Edit > Edit Colors > Recolor Artwork.

3 Click the Show Color Group Storage icon (▸) on the right side of the dialog box to show the color groups, if they aren't already showing. Make sure that, in the top left of the dialog box, the Assign button is selected.

In the Recolor Artwork dialog box, notice that the colors of the label are listed in the Current Colors column in what is called "Hue-Forward" sorting. That means they are arranged, from top to bottom, in the ordering of the color wheel: red, orange, yellow, green, blue, indigo, and violet.

● **Note:** If the colors in the Kuler group you selected earlier were different than what we selected, the colors in this section will also look a little different and that is okay.

4 Under Color Groups in the Recolor Artwork panel, select the Italian restaurant color group you saved from the Kuler panel.

In the Recolor Artwork dialog box, notice that the colors of the Italian Restaurant color group are assigned to the colors in the label. The Current Color column shows what the color was in the label, and the New column shows what the color has become (or been "reassigned to"). Also, notice that the two yellow colors in the original label are now next to each other and are mapped to a single color. This is because there are only five colors in the Italian Restaurant group and six in the label.

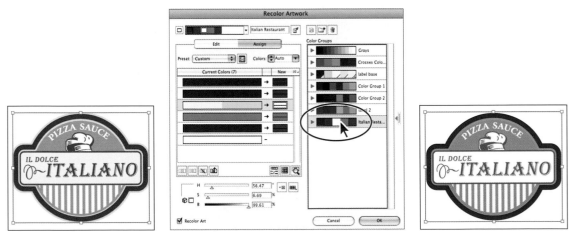

● **Note:** If the colors of the label do not change, make sure that Recolor Art is selected at the bottom of the Recolor Artwork dialog box.

5 Click the Hide Color Group Storage icon (◄) to hide the color groups.

6 In the New column of the Recolor Artwork dialog box, drag the red color on top of the green color below it. This swaps the green and red colors in the artwork order.

7 Drag the colors back to their original order.

The colors in the New column show what you see in the artwork. If you click one of the colors, notice that the HSB sliders at the bottom of the dialog box let you edit that one color.

8 Double-click the darker brown color at the bottom of the New column.

9 In the Color Picker dialog box, click the Color Swatches button to see the document swatches. Select label background in the Color Swatches list. Click OK to return to the Recolor Artwork dialog box.

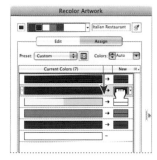 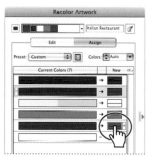 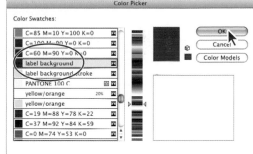

10 Drag the Recolor Artwork dialog box out of the way to see the artwork, if necessary.

Next, you will make a few more changes to the colors in the label, and then save the color edits to the Italian Restaurant color group.

11 Click the arrow between the lighter green color in the Current Color column and the light brown color in the New column. In the artwork, the color on the label changes slightly.

By clicking the arrow between a current color and a new color, you prevent the current color in the row (the light green) from being reassigned to the new color (light brown).

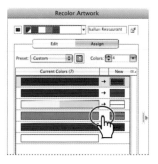

Note: If you want to apply a single color to the selected artwork, you can choose 1 from the Colors menu, above the New column in the Recolor Artwork dialog box. Be sure to finish the steps in this lesson before experimenting with this.

12 Drag the light green bar up on top of the dark brown bar in the current color list. Notice the color change in the artwork.

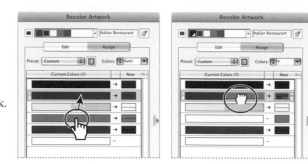

When you drag a color in the current color column onto another row in the same column, you are telling Illustrator to apply the same new color (the green in this case) to both colors. The green color in the New column is split into three sections (). The darkest color in the row (the dark brown gray) is replaced with the green. The lighter green color is replaced with a proportionally lighter tint of the green.

Note: Many kinds of color edits can be made to selected artwork in the Recolor Artwork dialog box. To learn more, search for "working with color groups" in Illustrator Help.

13 Click the Show Color Group Storage icon () to show the color groups on the right side of the dialog box. Click the Save Changes To Color Group button () to save the changes to the color group without closing the dialog box.

14 Click OK. The color changes that you made to the color group are saved in the Swatches panel.

15 Choose Select > Deselect, and then File > Save.

Reassigning colors in artwork

Do any of the following additional methods to reassign colors in selected artwork:

- If a row contains multiple colors and you want to move them all, click the selector bar at the left of the row and drag up or down.

- To assign a new color to a different row of current colors, drag the new color up or down in the New column. (To add a new color to or remove a color from the New column, right-click in the list and choose Add New Color or Remove Color.)

- To change a color in the New column, right-click it and choose Color Picker to set a new color.

- To exclude a row of current colors from being reassigned, click the arrow between the columns. To include it again, click the dash.

- To exclude a single current color from being reassigned, right-click the color and choose Exclude Colors, or click the icon.

- To randomly reassign colors, click the Randomly Change Color Order button. The New colors move randomly to different rows of current colors.

- To add a row to the Current Colors column, right-click and choose Add A Row, or click the icon.

—From Illustrator Help

Adjusting colors

Next, you will change the original label on artboard 1 to use CMYK colors only. You'll need to convert the yellow color PANTONE 100 C to CMYK.

1 Choose 1 from the Artboard Navigation menu in the lower-left corner of the Document window.

2 Choose Select > All On Active Artboard.

3 Choose Edit > Edit Colors > Convert To CMYK. The colors in the selected label, including the yellow PANTONE 100 C, are now CMYK.

   There are many options in the Edit > Edit Colors menu for converting color, including Recolor With Preset. This command lets you change the color of selected artwork using a chosen number of colors, a color library, and a specific color harmony (such as complementary colors). To learn more about adjusting colors this way, search for "reduce colors in your artwork" in Illustrator Help.

● **Note:** Using this method for converting to CMYK does not affect the color swatches in the Swatches panel. It simply converts the selected artwork colors to CMYK.

4 Choose Select > Deselect, and then File > Save.

Painting with patterns and gradients

In addition to process and spot colors, the Swatches panel can also contain pattern and gradient swatches. Illustrator provides sample swatches of each type in the default Swatches panel and lets you create your own patterns and gradients.

● **Note:** To learn more about working with gradients, see Lesson 10, "Blending Colors and Shapes."

Applying existing patterns

A pattern is artwork saved in the Swatches panel that can be applied to the stroke or fill of an object. You can customize existing patterns and design patterns from scratch with any of the Illustrator tools. All patterns start with a single tile that is tiled (repeated) within a shape, starting at the ruler origin and continuing to the right. Next, you will apply an existing pattern to a shape.

1 Choose Window > Workspace > Essentials.

2 Click the Layers panel icon (●) to expand the Layers panel.

3 In the Layers panel, click to select the Visibility column to the left of the layer named pattern.

4 Click the Swatches panel icon (▦). In the Swatches panel, click the Swatch Libraries menu button (▣) at the bottom of the panel and choose Patterns > Decorative > Decorative_Classic to open the pattern library.

5 Using the Selection tool (⬆), select the white shape towards the top of the artboard.

6 In the Control panel, change the Stroke color to None (⬜).

7 Make sure that the Fill box is selected in the Tools panel.

● **Note:** This last step is important. When you apply a pattern swatch, it applies to the stroke or the fill that is selected.

8 Select the Plaid 3 pattern swatch in the Decorative_Classic panel to fill the group of objects with the pattern.

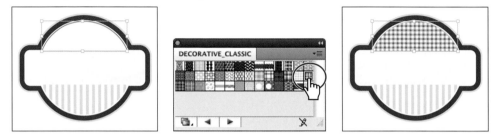

▶ **Tip:** Because some supplied patterns have a clear background, you can create a second fill for the object using the Appearance panel. For more information, see Lesson 13, "Applying Appearance Attributes and Graphic Styles."

9 Close the Decorative_Classic panel.

10 With the shape still selected, double-click the Scale tool (⬛) in the Tools panel to make the pattern larger without affecting the shape. In the Scale dialog box, deselect Scale Strokes & Effects, if necessary. Deselect Objects, which selects Patterns. Change the uniform scale to **150**, and select Preview to see the change. Click OK. This scales the pattern only.

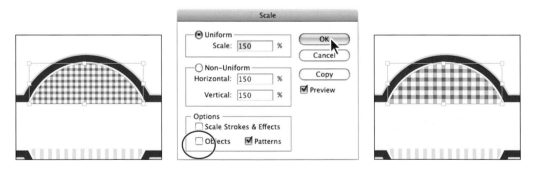

11 Click the Swatches panel icon to collapse the panel.

12 Choose Select > Deselect, then File > Save.

Creating your own pattern

In this section of the lesson, you will create your own custom pattern and add it to the Swatches panel.

1 Select the Rectangle tool (□) in the Tools panel. Click once in a blank area of the artboard to open the Rectangle dialog box. Change the Width to **.4 in** and the Height to **.4 in**, and then click OK.

Rectangle	
Options Width: 28.8 pt Height: .4in	OK Cancel

Notice that the newly rectangle has the same pattern fill as the shape in the previous steps.

2 With the rectangle selected, press the letter D to set the default stroke (black) and fill (white) on the selected shape.

3 With the shape still selected, double-click the Rotate tool (✪) in the Tools panel. In the Rotate dialog box, change the Angle value to **45**, and make sure that the Objects option is selected and that Patterns is deselected. Click OK.

Rotate	
Angle: 45 °	OK Cancel Copy
Options ☑ Objects ☐ Patterns	☑ Preview

4 Select the Selection tool (▶), and make sure that the new shape is still selected.

5 Click the Swatches panel icon (▦) to reveal the Swatches panel and make sure you can see the top of the swatch list. With the Selection tool, drag the selected shape into the Swatches panel. You have created a new pattern.

● **Note:** A pattern swatch can be composed of more than one shape. For instance, to create a flannel pattern for a shirt, you can create three overlapping rectangles or lines, each with varying colors. Then select all three shapes and drag them as one into the Swatches panel.

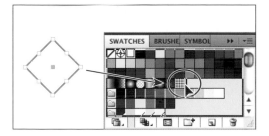

6 Double-click the pattern swatch you added and assign the name **checker**. Click OK.

7 With the Selection tool, click to select the diamond shape on the artboard that you used to make the pattern swatch, and then delete it.

8 Choose File > Save.

Swatch Options	
Swatch Name: checker	OK Cancel
Color Type: Process Color	
☐ Global	
Color Mode:	☐ Preview
C	0 %
M	0 %
Y	0 %
K	0 %

Applying a pattern

You can assign a pattern using a number of different methods. In this lesson, you will use the Swatches panel to apply the pattern. You can also apply the pattern using the Fill color in the Control panel.

1   With the Selection tool (🡑), click the shape filled with the pattern you've just created, near the top of the artboard.

2   Select the checker pattern swatch from the Fill color in the Control panel.

Notice that the pattern is transparent between the diamond shapes.

▶ **Tip:** As you add more custom swatches, you may want to view the Swatches panel by the swatch names. To change the view, choose List View from the Swatches panel menu.

3   Choose Select > Deselect, and then File > Save.

Editing a pattern

To edit a pattern swatch, you need the artwork used to create the swatch. If you've deleted it, you can get it back by dragging the pattern swatch onto the artboard.

Next, you will edit the saved pattern and then update all instances in your artwork.

1   Using the Selection tool (🡑), drag the checker swatch from the Swatches panel to an empty location on the right side of the artboard.

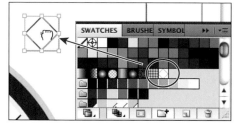

This places the shape you used to make the pattern onto the artboard or canvas.

● **Note:** You may need to zoom in or hold down the Spacebar and drag the artboard down, so that you can see the group better.

2   With the shape selected, notice the word Group, at the left end of the Control panel. Double-click the diamond shape to enter isolation mode and then choose View > Outline.

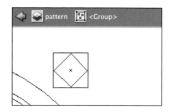

When you create an irregular (non-rectangular) shape, Illustrator displays a rectangle shape behind it to create a rectangular tile.

3   Click to select the square shape and choose white from the Fill color in the Control panel. This eliminates the transparency between the diamond shapes in the pattern.

4   Choose View > Preview.

5 With the Selection tool, click to select the diamond shape. In the Control panel, change the fill color to the red swatch (C=15, M=100, Y=90, K=10). Change the Stroke color to None in the Control panel. Press Escape to hide the Swatches panel.

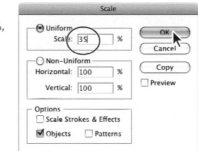

6 Press Escape to exit isolation mode.

Next, you will update the pattern swatch.

7 Choose Select > Deselect, then click the diamond shape with the Selection tool to select the group.

8 Double-click the Scale tool (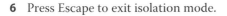) in the Tools panel. Change Uniform Scale to **35%**, make sure that Objects is the only option selected, and then click OK.

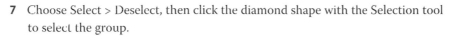

9 Using the Selection tool, select the diamond shape group and press the Alt (Windows) or Option (Mac OS) key and drag it back on top of the existing pattern swatch, called checker, in the Swatches panel. The swatch is updated and the artwork that is filled with the pattern swatch is updated as well.

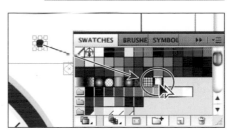

10 On the artboard, select and delete the diamond shape group that you edited to create the updated pattern.

11 Open the Layers panel and make all layers visible by selecting the Visibility column to the left of the "tomato" and "top shapes" layers.

12 Choose Select > Deselect, and then File > Save. Choose File > Close.

Working with Live Paint

Live Paint lets you paint vector graphics intuitively, by automatically detecting and correcting gaps that otherwise would have affected how fills and strokes were applied. Paths divide the drawing surface into areas, any of which can be colored, regardless of whether the area is bounded by a single path or by segments of multiple paths. Painting objects is like filling in a coloring book or using watercolors to paint a pencil sketch.

Live Paint is different from using the Shape Builder tool because Live Paint is "live." This means that the Shape Builder tool edits the underlying shapes, whereas Live Paint does not. To learn more about the Shape Builder tool, see Lesson 3, "Creating and Editing Shapes."

Creating a Live Paint group

Next, you will open a file and paint objects using the Live Paint Bucket tool.

1 Choose File > Open and open the L6start_2.ai file in the Lesson06 folder.

2 Choose File > Save As. In the Save As dialog box, name the file **greetingcard.ai** and navigate to the Lesson06 folder. Leave the Save As Type option set to Adobe Illustrator (*.AI) (Windows) or the Format option set to Adobe Illustrator (ai) (Mac OS), and click Save. In the Illustrator Options dialog box, leave the Illustrator options at their default settings, and then click OK.

3 Use the Selection tool (▸) to drag a selection across the three white flower shapes on the artboard.

4 Choose Object > Live Paint > Make. This creates a Live Paint group that you can now paint using the Live Paint Bucket tool (◔▯).

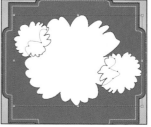

Once a Live Paint group is created, each path remains fully editable. When you move or adjust a path's shape, the colors are automatically reapplied to the new regions that are formed by the edited paths.

▶ **Tip:** You can tell it's a Live Paint group because of the special bounding box around all three shapes.

● **Note:** You may need to press the Escape key to hide the Swatches panel.

5 Select the Live Paint Bucket tool (◔▯) in the Tools panel, which is in the same group as the Shape Builder tool (◔▯). Before painting, click the Fill color in the Control panel and select the yellow/orange swatch in the Swatches panel.

6 Position the pointer over the center of the Live Paint group. As you move over Live Paint objects, they are highlighted and three color swatches appear above the pointer. The swatches represent the three adjacent swatches in the Swatches panel. The center swatch is the last selected color. Click when the center flower shape is highlighted.

▶ **Tip:** You can also drag across multiple shapes to apply color to them at once.

7 Move the pointer to the left, to the overlapping shape. Click the left arrow key twice to highlight the light yellow color in the three swatches above the pointer. Click to apply the color to the flower.

You will repeat the previous step to paint the rest of the flower shapes.

● **Note:** You can also switch to a color other than the one selected in the group by clicking a color in the Swatches panel.

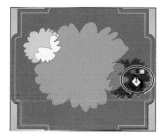

8 Paint the remaining three flower shapes using the colors you see in the figure at right (yellow, pink, and dark pink). Before clicking to apply a color, press the left and right arrow keys to cycle through the colors in the Swatches panel.

Painting strokes with the Live Paint Bucket tool is just as easy as painting fills. First, you need to enable the option to paint strokes.

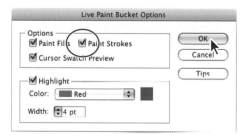

9 Double-click the Live Paint Bucket tool in the Tools panel. This opens the Live Paint Bucket Options dialog box.

Select the Paint Strokes option and then click OK.

● **Note:** To learn more about the options in the Live Paint Bucket Options dialog box, such as the Cursor Swatch Preview (the three swatches that appear above the Live Paint Bucket cursor), and the Highlight options like changing color and width, search for "paint with the Live Paint Bucket tool" in Illustrator Help.

Next you'll remove the inner black strokes from the shapes and retain the outer black strokes.

10 Position the pointer directly over the stroke between the center shape and the light yellow filled shape, as shown in the figure. When the Stroke cursor (🖌) appears, click the left arrow to select None, and then click the stroke to remove the stroke color.

11 Position the pointer directly over the stroke between the center shape and the light pink filled shape, as shown in the figure. When the Stroke cursor appears, click the left arrow to select None, and then click the stroke to remove the stroke color.

12 Choose Select > Deselect to see how the strokes are now painted. Then choose File > Save.

Editing Live Paint regions

When you make a Live Paint group, each path remains editable. When you move or adjust a path, the colors that were previously applied don't just stay where they were, like they do in natural media paintings or image editing software. Instead, the colors are automatically reapplied to the new regions that are formed by the edited paths.

Next, you will edit the paths, and add another shape.

1 Select the Selection tool (▶) in the Tools panel, then hold down the Spacebar and drag the artboard to the right to reveal the flower shape off the left edge of the artboard.

2 Select the flower shape and choose Edit > Copy.

3 Double-click the Hand tool to fit the artboard in the Document window.

4 With the Selection tool, double-click the Live Paint group. This places the document in isolation mode and allows you to edit each shape independently.

5 Choose Edit > Paste. Drag the pasted flower shape down to the lower left, so that it overlaps the center flower, as shown in the figure.

6 Select the Live Paint Bucket tool () in the Tools panel and paint the shapes with the dark green (outside half) and light green (inside half) swatches.

7 Position the pointer directly over the strokes between the center orange shape and the green-filled shape. When the Stroke cursor appears, click the left arrow to highlight None, and then click the stroke to remove the stroke color. Do this for any strokes inside the green-filled shape.

● **Note:** When you move or edit shapes that are part of a Live Paint group, unexpected things can happen. For instance, a stroke may appear where there was none before. Be sure to double-check the shapes to make sure that they look like they should.

8 Select the Selection tool and drag the green-filled flower shape a little up and to the left, to reposition it. Notice how the color fill changes.

9 Select the Direct Selection tool () in the Tools panel, and position the pointer over the small yellow flower in the upper-left corner. Click one of the anchor points on the edge of the center flower (located in the middle of the small yellow flower) and drag to reposition it.

Notice how the paths are still completely editable and the colors are automatically reapplied to the new regions that are formed by the edited paths.

● **Note:** The Selection tool selects an entire Live Paint group. The Direct Selection tool selects the individual paths inside a Live Paint group. For instance, clicking with the Selection tool once selects the entire Live Paint group, and clicking once with the Direct Selection tool or the Group Selection tool selects individual paths that make up the Live Paint group.

Next, that will add a white color to the center of the larger flower so that you can add text and make it readable.

10 Press Ctrl++ (Windows) or Cmd++ (Mac OS) twice to zoom in.

11 Press Escape to exit isolation mode, and then choose Select > Deselect.

12 Expand the Layers panel by clicking the Layers panel icon (●) on the right side of the workspace. Click the Visibility column for the layer named text (just above the eye icon for the layer named live paint).

13 Select the Selection tool and double-click the flower shapes to enter isolation mode.

14 Select the Line Segment tool (\) in the Tools panel. Change the Stroke color to white in the Control panel.

15 Press the Shift key and click the right edge of the small yellow flower. Drag towards the right edge of the large center flower to draw a line. When you're close to the edge (not at the edge) release the mouse button, then the Shift key, as shown in the figure below, to leave a small gap on the right end of the line.

16 Draw another line below that by pressing the Shift key and clicking the right edge of the green flower, and dragging to the right, to the point where the line snaps to the left edge of the light pink shape. The smart guides help you snap the line to the shapes.

● **Note:** If the red outline stops at the top line, try making the top line shorter using the Direct Selection tool.

17 Select the Live Paint Bucket tool in the Tools panel and position the cursor over the center of the large orange flower, between the lines. Note where the red outline shows, and that the bottom line "closes" the bottom of the flower shape. The top line, which is not touching the edge of the flower, may not close the top of the path. This gap is a problem that you will fix next.

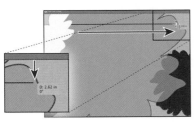

Draw the top line.

Draw the bottom line.

Hover to see the paint area.

Working with Gap Options

Next, you will work with the Gap Options dialog box.

1 Choose Select > All.

2 Choose Object > Live Paint > Gap Options. In the Gap Options dialog box, select Gap Detection, if it is not already selected. The Gap Preview Color is set to highlight any gaps it detects in red.

● **Note:** If you can't get this to work, in the Gap Options dialog box, try changing the Paint Stops At option to Small or Large Gaps, or try resizing the top line so that it snaps to the right edge of the flower.

3 Choose Medium Gaps from the Paint Stops At menu. This stops paint from leaking through some of the gaps as you paint. Look at the artwork to see any gaps highlighted in red. The gap between the top line and the right edge of the flower shape is closed. Click OK.

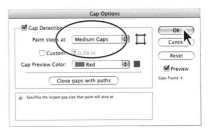

4 Select the Live Paint Bucket tool (⬚), and cross over the space between the two lines you drew. Make sure that white is showing in the swatches above the pointer, and then click to color the space.

5 Select the Live Paint Selection tool (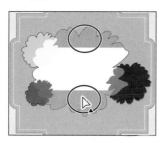) in the Tools panel, beneath the Live Paint Bucket tool. Click the top yellow shape and Shift-click the bottom yellow shape, as shown in the figure. Choose the background gradient from the Fill color in the Control panel.

▶ **Tip:** Within a Live Paint group, you can also select content by dragging across artwork with the Live Paint Selection tool.

6 Select the Gradient tool (⬛) in the Tools panel. Drag from the center of the large flower shape down and to the right, to create a uniform gradient across both shapes.

7 Select the Selection tool, and press Escape to exit isolation mode and see the "Happy Birthday" text on the artboard. Choose View > Fit Artboard In Window.

Select the pieces.   Drag with the Gradient tool.   The final result

8 Choose File > Save, then File > Close.

Exploring on your own

1 Choose File > Open. In the Open dialog box, navigate to the Lesson06 folder in the Lessons folder. Open the file named color.ai.

2 Using the Selection tool, select the letters in the center of the poster.

3 Fill the letters with a color from the Fill color in the Control panel, and then save the color as a swatch in the Swatches panel by Ctrl-clicking (Windows) or Command-clicking (Mac OS) the New Swatch button. Name the color **text**.

4 With the swatch applied to the text fill, create a tint of the text color, and then save it in the Swatches panel.

5 Apply a 3 pt stroke to the text and paint the stroke with the saved tint, making sure that the fill of the text is just the text color, not the tint.

6 Select the Ellipse tool in the Tools panel and create a circle on the artboard. Select a swatch from the Fill color in the Control panel. Create a pattern out of the circle you drew.

7 Apply the pattern to the star shape behind the text.

8 Edit the pattern and resize the pattern fill in the star shapes by double-clicking the Scale tool.

9 Choose File > Close without saving.

Review questions

1 Describe at least three ways to fill an object with color.

2 How can you save a color?

3 How do you name a color?

4 How do you assign a transparent color to an object?

5 How can you choose color harmonies for colors?

6 Name two things that the Edit Colors/Recolor Artwork dialog box allows you to do.

7 How do you add pattern swatches to the Swatches panel?

8 Explain what Live Paint allows you to do.

Review answers

1 To fill an object with color, select the object and the Fill box in the Tools panel. Then do one of the following:

   • Double-click the Fill or Stroke box in the Control panel to access the Color Picker.

   • Drag the color sliders, or type values in the text boxes in the Color panel.

   • Click a color swatch in the Swatches panel.

   • Select the Eyedropper tool, and then click a color in the artwork.

   • Choose Window > Swatch Libraries to open another color library, and then click a color swatch in the Color Library panel.

2 You can save a color for painting other objects in your artwork by adding it to the Swatches panel. Select the color, and do one of the following:

   • Drag it from the Fill box and drop it over the Swatches panel.

   • Click the New Swatch button at the bottom of the Swatches panel.

   • Choose New Swatch from the Swatches panel menu.

   You can also add colors from other color libraries by selecting them in the Color Library panel and choosing Add To Swatches from the panel menu.

3   To name a color, double-click the color swatch in the Swatches panel, or select it and choose Swatch Options from the panel menu. Type the name for the color in the Swatch Options dialog box.

4   To paint a shape with a semitransparent color, select the shape and fill it with any color. Then adjust the opacity percentage in the Transparency panel or Control panel to less than 100%.

5   The Color Guide panel is a tool you can use for inspiration while you create your artwork. The panel suggests color harmonies based on the current color in the Tools panel.

6   You use the Edit Colors/Recolor Artwork dialog box to create and edit color groups, to reassign or reduce the colors in your artwork, and more.

7   Create a pattern (patterns cannot contain patterns themselves), and drag it into the Swatches panel.

8   Live Paint lets you paint vector graphics intuitively by automatically detecting and correcting gaps that otherwise would have affected how fills and strokes were applied. Paths divide the drawing surface up into areas, any of which can be colored, regardless of whether the area is bounded by a single path or by segments of multiple paths. Painting objects with Live Paint is like filling in a coloring book or using watercolors to paint a pencil sketch.

7 WORKING WITH TYPE

Lesson overview

In this lesson, you'll learn how to do the following:

- Import text.

- Create columns of type.

- Change text attributes.

- Use and save styles.

- Sample type.

- Wrap type around a graphic.

- Reshape text with a warp.

- Create text on paths and shapes.

- Create type outlines.

 This lesson will take approximately an hour to complete. If needed, remove the previous lesson folder from your hard disk, and copy the Lesson07 folder onto it.

Text as a design element plays a major role in your illustrations. Like other objects, type can be painted, scaled, rotated, and so on. In this lesson, discover how to create basic text and interesting text effects.

Getting started

You'll be working in one art file during this lesson, but before you begin, restore the default preferences for Adobe® Illustrator® CS5. Then open the finished art file for this lesson to see the illustration.

1 To ensure that the tools and panels function as described in this lesson, delete or deactivate (by renaming) the Adobe Illustrator CS5 preferences file. See "Restoring default preferences" on page 3.

2 Start Adobe Illustrator CS5.

● **Note:** If you have not already done so, copy the resource files for this lesson onto your hard disk from the Lesson07 folder on the Adobe Illustrator CS5 Classroom in a Book CD. See "Copying the Classroom in a Book files" on page 2.

3 Choose File > Open. Locate the file named L7end_1.ai in the Lesson07 folder in the Lessons folder that you copied onto your hard disk.

In this lesson, you will create the text for this poster. Leave it open for reference, or choose File > Close without saving.

4 Choose File > Open. In the Open dialog box, navigate to the Lesson07 folder in the Lessons folder. Open the L7start_1.ai file.

This file already has non-text components in it. You will build all the text elements to complete the poster.

5 Choose File > Save As. In the Save As dialog box, navigate to the Lesson07 folder and name the file **yoga.ai**. Leave the Save As Type option set to Adobe Illustrator (*.AI) (Windows) or the Format option set to Adobe Illustrator (ai) (Mac OS), and click Save. In the Illustrator Options dialog box, leave the Illustrator options at their default settings, and then click OK.

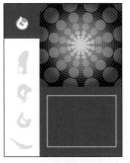

6 Choose View > Smart Guides to deselect smart guides.

7 Choose Window > Workspace > Essentials.

Working with type

Type features are some of the most powerful aspects of Illustrator. You can add a single line of type to your artwork, create columns and rows of text like in Adobe InDesign, flow text into a shape or along a path, and work with letterforms as graphic objects.

You can create text in three different ways: as point type, area type, and text along a path. Following is a short description of each type of text:

- **Point type** is a horizontal or vertical line of text that begins where you click and expands as you enter characters. Each line of text is independent—the line expands or shrinks as you edit it, but doesn't wrap to the next line. Entering text this way is useful for adding a headline or a few words to your artwork.

- **Area type** uses the boundaries of an object to control the flow of characters, either horizontally or vertically. When the text reaches a boundary, it automatically wraps to fit inside the defined area. Entering text this way is useful when you want to create one or more paragraphs, such as for a brochure.

- **Type on a path** flows along the edge of an open or closed path. When you enter text horizontally, the characters are parallel to the baseline. When you enter text vertically, the characters are perpendicular to the baseline. In either case, the text flows in the direction in which points were added to the path.

Next, you will create point type, and then you will create area type. Later in this lesson you will also create type on a path.

Creating point type

When typing text directly into a document, you select the Type tool and click where you'd like the text. When the cursor appears, you can begin typing.

Next, you will enter a subhead on artboard 1 (of 2).

1 Select the Zoom tool (⌕) in the Tools panel and click the bottom yoga figure on the left three times.

2 Select the Type tool (**T**) and click above and to the left of the bottom yoga figure. The cursor appears on the artboard. Type **info@transformyoga.com**.

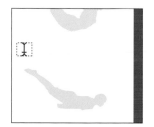

By clicking with the Type tool, you create point type. Point type is a line of text that keeps going until you stop typing or press Return or Enter. It's very useful for headlines.

3 Select the Selection tool (▶) in the Tools panel and notice the bounding box around the text. Drag the bounding point on the right to the right. Notice that the text stretches as you drag.

● **Note:** Point type that is scaled as in step 3 is still printable, but the font size may not be a whole number (such as 12pt).

4 Choose Edit > Undo Scale.

Creating area type

To create area type, you click with the Type tool where you want the text, and drag to create an area type object. When the cursor appears, you can type. You can also convert an existing shape or object to a type object by clicking on or inside the edge of the object with the Type tool.

Next, you will create area type and enter an address.

1 With the Selection tool (▶), hold down the spacebar and drag the artboard down to pan to the top yoga figure in the white area on the left side of the artboard.

2 Select the Type tool (T), and then drag from the upper left to the lower right to create a rectangle above the top yoga figure. The cursor appears in the new type object.

3 Type **1000 Lombard Ave. Central, Washington**. The text wraps inside of the type object.

You will now adjust how the text wraps.

● **Note:** For now, keep the default settings for type formatting.

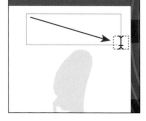

● **Note:** If the text is already wrapping correctly, try dragging the edge of the bounding box to see how it affects the text.

4 Select the Selection tool and notice the bounding box appears that around the address. Drag the right center bounding point to the right and then to the left, noticing how the text wraps within the object. Drag until only the text "1000 Lombard Ave." appears on the first line.

5 Choose Select > Deselect, and then choose File > Save.

Area type versus point type

Illustrator provides visual indications to help you tell the difference between point type and area type. With the Selection tool, click to select text and its bounding box.

Area type has two extra boxes, called ports. Ports are used to thread (flow) text from one type area to another. Working with ports and threading is covered later in this lesson. Point type, when selected, does not have ports; instead, it has a point before the first letter in the first line.

Area type   **Point type**

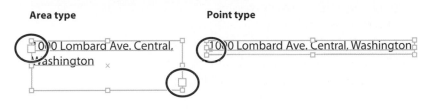

Importing a plain text file

You can import text into artwork from a file that was created in another application. Illustrator supports the following formats for importing text:

- Microsoft Word for Windows 97, 98, 2000, 2002, 2003, and 2007
- Microsoft Word for Mac OS X, 2004, and 2008
- RTF (Rich Text Format)
- Plain text (ASCII) with ANSI, Unicode, Shift JIS, GB2312, Chinese Big 5, Cyrillic, GB18030, Greek, Turkish, Baltic, and Central European encoding

You can also copy and paste text, but formatting can be lost when text is pasted. One of the advantages of importing text from a file rather than copying and pasting it, is that imported text retains its character and paragraph formatting. For example, text from an RTF file retains its font and style specifications in Illustrator.

Next you will place text from a simple text file.

1 Double-click the Hand tool (✋) to fit the artboard in the window. Choose View > Smart Guides to select the smart guides.

2 Before importing text, create an area type object by selecting the Type tool (T) and dragging from the upper-left corner of the guide box that has been provided to the lower-right corner.

3 Choose File > Place. Navigate to the Lesson07 folder in the Lessons folder, select the L7copy.txt file, and click Place.

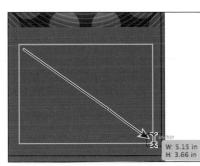

● **Note:** If you place text without creating a type area, the type area that is created automatically. The type area spans most of the artboard, by default.

4 In the Text Import Options dialog box, you can set options prior to importing text. Leave the default settings, and click OK.

The text is now placed in a type object. You will learn how to apply attributes to format text later in this lesson. Also, if you see a red plus sign (⊞) in the lower-right corner of the type object, this indicates that the text does not fit in the type object. You will fix this later in the lesson.

5 Choose File > Save, and leave this file open.

Creating columns of text

You can create columns and rows of text easily by using the Area Type options.

1 If the type object is no longer selected, use the Selection tool (▶) to select it.

● **Note:** If the cursor is still in the type object, you don't have to select the text area with the Selection tool to access the Area Type options.

2 Choose Type > Area Type Options.

3 In the Area Type Options dialog box, select Preview. In the Columns section of the dialog box, change Number to **2**, and click OK.

4 Choose Select > Deselect.

5 Choose File > Save. Leave this document open.

Area type options

You can use the Area Type options to create rows and columns of text. Read about additional options below:

- **Number** specifies the number of rows and columns you want the object to contain.

- **Span** specifies the height of individual rows and the width of individual columns.

- **Fixed** determines what happens to the span of rows and columns if you resize the type area. When this option is selected, resizing the area can change the number of rows and columns, but not their width. Leave this option deselected if you want row and column widths to change when you resize the type area.

- **Gutter** specifies the distance between rows or columns.

- **Inset** controls the margin between the text and the bounding path. This margin is referred to as the inset spacing.

- **First Baseline** controls the alignment of the first line of text with the top of the object.

- **Text Flow** determines how text flows between rows and columns.

—From Illustrator Help

Understanding text flow

For this next section, you will place a Microsoft Word document (.doc) into a rectangle shape to create area type in the second artboard of the currently open file, yoga.ai. This will add text to a postcard that accompanies the poster.

1 Click the Next button in the status bar in the lower left of the Document window to navigate to the second artboard. Choose View > Fit Artboard In Window if the entire postcard is not showing.

2 Select the Rectangle tool (▭) in the Tools panel.

3 Press D to set the default fill (white) and stroke (black).

4 Position the pointer in the upper-left corner of the square guide in the center of the artboard and drag down and to the right to create a rectangle about 1 inch in height. The word "path" appears when the pointer snaps to the guide.

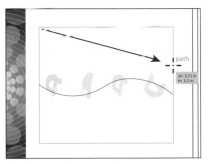

Note: The square that appears after you drag may have a black fill and/or stroke that covers the content. When the shape is converted into a type area, the fill and stroke change to None.

5 Select the Type tool (**T**) and move it over the edge of the rectangle shape. The word "path" appears when you are near the edge of the rectangle. The text insertion cursor is in parentheses (I), indicating that when you click, the cursor will appear inside this shape. Click to insert the cursor.

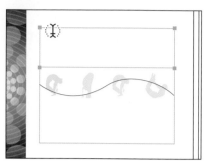

6 With the cursor active in the rectangle, choose File > Place and navigate to the Lesson07 folder in the Lessons folder on your hard disk. Select the file yoga_pc.doc, and then click Place. You are placing a native Microsoft Word document, so you will have additional options to set.

7 In the Microsoft Word Options dialog box, ensure that Remove Text Formatting is deselected to keep the Word formatting. Leave the remaining settings as is. Click OK. The text appears in the square.

Notice the red plus sign that appears in the lower-right corner of the type object. This indicates that the text does not fit in the object. You will fix this in the next section.

Working with overflow text and text reflow

Each area type object contains an in port and an out port. The ports enable you to link to other objects and create a linked copy of the type object. An empty port indicates that all the text is visible and that the object isn't linked. A red plus sign (⊞) in an out port indicates that the object contains additional text, which is called overflow text.

There are two main methods for remedying overflow text:

- Thread the text to another type object
- Resize the type object

Threading text

To thread, or continue, text from one object to the next, you have to link the objects. Linked type objects can be of any shape; however, the text must be entered in an object or along a path, not at a point.

Next, you will thread the overset text to another type object.

1 Use the Selection tool (▶) to select the type object.

2 With the Selection tool, click the out port of the selected type object. The pointer changes to the loaded text icon (⧉).

● **Note:** If you double-click, a new type object appears. If this happens, you can either drag the new object into place, or choose Edit > Undo Link Threaded Text and the loaded text icon reappears.

3 Click below the yoga figures, on the left edge of the guide box and drag down and to the right corner of the guide box.

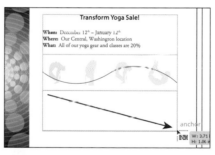

● **Note:** With the loaded text icon, you can simply click the artboard instead of dragging to create a new type object. This creates a much larger type object.

▶ **Tip:** Another way to thread text between objects is to select an area type object, select the object (or objects) you want to link to, and then choose Type > Threaded Text > Create.

4 Choose File > Save.

With the bottom type object still selected, notice the line between the two objects, which is the thread that tells you that the two objects are connected. Notice the out port (▷) of the top type object and the in port (▷) of the bottom type object (both circled in the figure at right). The arrow indicates that the object is linked to another object.

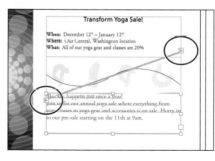

● **Note:** Your text may not look exactly like the figure. That's OK. In the next part of the lesson, you will resize the type objects.

● **Note:** If you delete the second type object (created in step 3), the text is pulled back into the original object as overflow text. Although not visible, the overflow text is not deleted.

Resizing type objects

For this next lesson, you will see how to resize type objects to make room for additional text.

1   Select the Selection tool (⬉) and click the text in the top area type object.

2   Double-click the out port (▣) in the lower-right corner of the type object.

Because the type objects are threaded, double-clicking the out port or the in port breaks the connection between them. Any text threaded between the two type objects flows back into the first object. The bottom object is still there, but it has no stroke or fill.

3   Choose View > Smart Guides to deselect them.

4   Using the Selection tool, drag the bottom middle handle of the bounding box down to the top of the yoga figures. The type object changes in size vertically. Notice that the further you drag down, the more text is revealed.

5   With the Selection tool, click the out port (⊞) in the lower-right corner of the top type object. The pointer changes to the loaded text icon (▦).

6   Choose View > Outline to reveal the bottom type object.

7   Position the loaded text icon (▦) over the edge of the bottom type object until it changes in appearance to (⬚). Click to thread the two objects together.

8   Choose View > Preview.

9   Choose Select > Deselect.

10 With the Selection tool, click to select the top type object. Drag the bottom middle handle up until the text "This sale happens just once a year!" is no longer highlighted in blue. This indicates that it will move to the next type object when the mouse button is released. Release the mouse button to see the text.

When type objects are threaded, you can move them anywhere and still maintain the connection between them. You can even thread between artboards. When type objects are resized, especially those in the beginning of the thread, text can reflow.

11 Choose File > Save.

▶ **Tip:** You can create unique type object shapes by deselecting the type object and choosing the Direct Selection tool (⬚). Drag the edge or corner of the type object to adjust the shape of the path. This method is easier to use when View > Hide Bounding Box is selected. Adjusting the type path with the Direct Selection tool is easiest when you're in Outline view (View > Outline).

● **Note:** If you edit the type object by following the previous tip, choose Edit > Undo before continuing.

Formatting type

In this section, you'll discover how to change text attributes, such as size, font, and style. You can quickly change most attributes in the Control panel.

1 With the yoga.ai file still open, click the Previous button (◄) in the status bar to return to artboard 1 (the poster).

2 Choose View > Fit Artboard In Window if the poster isn't completely visible in the window.

▶ **Tip:** If you double-click text with the Selection or Direct Selection tool, the Type tool becomes selected.

3 Select the Type tool (**T**) in the Tools panel and insert the cursor anywhere in the text in the two column text area that you created earlier.

4 Choose Select > All, or press Ctrl+A (Windows) or Command+A (Mac OS) to select all the text in the type object.

In this next section, you'll learn two different methods for selecting a font.

First, you'll change the font of selected text using the Font menu in the Control panel.

5 Click the arrow to the right of the Font menu and scroll to find and select Adobe Garamond Pro.

● **Note:** The Adobe Garamond Pro font is in the G section of the menu (not the A section). Also, you may see the word Character instead of Font menu listed in the Control panel. Click the word Character to reveal the Character panel.

● **Note:** You may need to click the arrow that appears at the bottom of the font list continue scrolling through the list.

6 With the text still selected, choose Type > Font to see a list of available fonts. Scroll down and select Myriad Pro > Regular. If your font list is long, you may need to scroll quite far to find this font.

7 Make sure that the text is still selected and then follow the instructions below. This next method is the most dynamic method for selecting a font.

- Click the word Character in the Control panel to reveal the Character panel.

- With the font selected in the Character panel, begin typing the name **Minion Pro**. Illustrator filters through the list and displays the name in the field.

- Press Enter or Return to set the font.

8 Click the arrow in the Font Style menu, below the Font menu, to see the available styles for Minion Pro and to make sure Regular is selected.

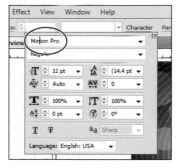

▶ **Tip:** To keep the Character panel open, choose Window > Type > Character.

Font styles are specific to each font family. Although you may have the Minion Pro font family on your system, you may not have the bold and italic styles of that family.

Fonts installed and on the Illustrator CS5 DVD

The following fonts and accompanying documentation are installed, and included in the Documentation folder on the Illustrator CS5 product DVD, or in the packaged download file if you download Illustrator CS5 from the Adobe Store. For trial customers, the fonts are not available until after purchase.

Adobe® Caslon® Pro
Adobe® Garamond® Pro
Adobe Gothic Std
Birch Std
Cooper Black Std
Giddyup Std
Letter Gothic Std
MESQUITE STD
Minion Pro
OCRA Std
Prestige Elite Std
ROSEWOOD STD
Tekton Pro
Kozzuka Gothic Pro
Kozuka Mincho Pro
Adobe Arabic
Adobe Myungjo Std
Adobe Heiti Std

Blackoak Std
Brush Script Std
Chaparral Pro
CHARLEMAGNE STD
Adobe Fangsong Std
Hobo Std
LITHOS PRO
Myriad Pro
Nueva Std
ORATOR STD
Poplar Std
STENCIL STD
TRAJAN PRO
Adobe Hebrew
Adobe Kaiti Std
Adobe Ming Std
Adobe Song Std
Adobe Fan Heiti Std

What is OpenType?

If you frequently send files back and forth between platforms, you should be designing your text files using the OpenType format.

OpenType® is a new cross-platform font file format developed jointly by Adobe and Microsoft. Adobe has converted the entire Adobe Type Library into this format and now offers thousands of OpenType fonts.

The two main benefits of the OpenType format are its cross-platform compatibility (the same font file works on Macintosh and Windows computers), and its ability to support widely expanded character sets and layout features, which provide richer linguistic support and advanced typographic control.

The OpenType format is an extension of the TrueType SFNT format that also can support Adobe® PostScript® font data and new typographic features. OpenType fonts containing PostScript data, such as those in the Adobe Type Library, have an .otf suffix in the font file name, while TrueType-based OpenType fonts have a .ttf file name suffix.

OpenType fonts can include an expanded character set and layout features, providing broader linguistic support and more precise typographic control. Feature-rich Adobe OpenType fonts can be distinguished by the word "Pro," which is part of the font name and appears in application font menus. OpenType fonts can be installed and used alongside PostScript Type 1 and TrueType fonts.

—From Adobe.com/type/opentype

Changing the font size

1   If the two column text is not active, use the Type tool (T) to insert the cursor in the area type object and choose Select > All.

2   Type **13** pt in the Font Size field in the Control panel and press Enter or Return. Notice the text change. Choose 12 pt from the Font Size menu. Leave the text selected.

● **Note:** You may see the word Character instead of the Font Size field in the Control panel. Click the word Character to reveal the Character panel.

The Font Size menu has preset sizes. If you want a custom size, select the value in the Font Size field, enter a value in points, and then press Enter or Return.

▶ **Tip:** You can dynamically change the font size of selected text using keyboard shortcuts. To increase the font size in increments of 2 pts, press Ctrl+Shift+> (Windows), or Command+Shift+> (Mac OS). To reduce the font size, press Ctrl+Shift+< (Windows), or Command+Shift+< (Mac OS).

Changing the font color

You can change the font color of the fill and stroke of selected text. In this example, you will change only the fill.

1 With the text still selected, click the Fill color in the Control panel. When the Swatches panel appears, select White. The text fill changes to white.

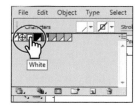

2 With the Type tool, drag to select the first line of text, Transform Yoga, in the area type object, or triple-click the text.

▶ **Tip:** Double-click to select a word; triple-click to select an entire paragraph. The end of a paragraph is defined by a hard return.

3 Change the Fill color in the Control panel to Aqua.

4 Keep the first line of text selected. Select the text in the Font Size field in the Control panel and change the font size by typing **13**. Press Enter or Return.

5 Choose Bold from the Font Style menu in the Control panel to change the font style for the selected text.

6 Choose Select > Deselect.

7 Chose File > Save.

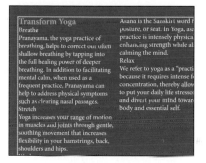

Changing additional text attributes

You can change many additional text attributes in the Character panel, which you can access by clicking the blue, underlined word Character in the Control panel. In this lesson, you will apply some of the many possible attributes, to experiment with the different ways you can format text.

A. Font
B. Font Style
C. Font Size
D. Kerning
E. Horizontal Scale
F. Baseline Shift
G. Underline

H. Language
I. Leading
J. Tracking
K. Vertical Scale
L. Character Rotation
M. Text anti-aliasing
N. Strikethrough

1 With the Type tool, click the address above the top yoga figure on the left side of the artboard. With the cursor in the text, triple-click to select the entire paragraph.

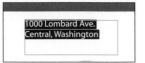

2 Select the Zoom tool (🔍) and click the selected text several times to zoom in.

Tip: To reset the leading value to the default, choose Auto from the Leading menu.

3 Click Character in the Control panel to reveal the Character panel. Click the up arrow to the left of the Leading field a few times to increase the leading to 16 pt. Leading is the vertical space between lines. Keep the Character panel open.

Notice the change in the vertical distance between the lines. Adjusting the leading is useful for fitting text into a text area.

Next, you will change the spacing between letters.

4 With the text still selected, click the Tracking icon in the Character panel to select the Tracking field. Type **60**, and press Enter or Return.

🔴 **Note:** If the text becomes overflow text, as indicated by the red plus sign, you can fit the text into the area type object by decreasing the Tracking value, or by changing the size of the area type object with the Selection tool.

Tracking changes the spacing between characters. A positive value pushes the letters apart horizontally; a negative value pulls the letters closer together.

5 Double-click the Hand tool (✋) in the Tools panel to fit the artboard in the window.

6 Select the Zoom tool in the Tools panel and drag a marquee around the headline Transform Yoga, at the top of the first column in the type object.

7 Select the Type tool (T) in the Tools panel and click to place the cursor at the end of the headline, Transform Yoga.

8 Choose Type > Glyphs to open the Glyphs panel.

The Glyphs panel is used to insert type characters like trademark symbols (™) or bullet points(·). It shows all the characters (glyphs) available for a given font.

Next, you will insert a copyright symbol.

9 In the Glyphs panel, scroll down until you see a copyright symbol (©). Double-click the symbol to insert it at the text insertion cursor. Close the Glyphs panel.

10 With the Type tool, drag to select the copyright symbol (©) you just inserted.

11 Choose Window > Type > Character to open the Character panel.

12 Choose Superscript from the Character panel menu (▼≡).

13 Click with the Type tool between the word Yoga and the copyright symbol to insert the cursor.

14 Choose 75 from the Kerning menu in the Character panel. Close the Character panel group, and choose File > Save.

Kerning is similar to tracking, but it adds or subtracts space between a pair of characters. It's useful for situations such as this one, when you're working with a glyph.

Changing paragraph attributes

As with character attributes, you can set paragraph attributes, such as alignment or indenting, before you enter new type, or reset them to change the appearance of existing type. If you select several type paths and type containers, you can set attributes for them all at the same time.

Now, you'll add more space before all the paragraphs in the column text.

1 Choose View > Fit Artboard In Window.

2 Using the Type tool (T), insert the cursor in either column of the text, and choose Select > All.

3 Click the word Paragraph in the Control panel to open the Paragraph panel.

4 Type **5** in the Space After Paragraph text field (in the bottom-right corner), and press Enter or Return. Setting a spacing value after paragraphs, rather than pressing the Return key, is recommended when working with large type objects.

5 Choose Select > Deselect.

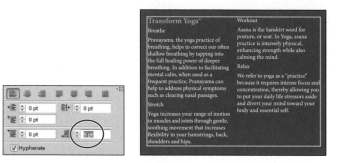

● **Note:** Your text may not look exactly like the figure above. That's okay.

6 With the Type tool, click the address above the top yoga figure on the left side of the artboard to insert the cursor.

7 Click the Align Center button (▣) in the Control panel.

```
1000 Lombard Ave.
Central, Washington
```

● **Note:** If you don't see alignment options in the Control panel, click the blue, underlined word Paragraph to open the Paragraph panel.

8 Choose Select > Deselect.

9 Choose File > Save.

Document setup options

By choosing File > Document Setup, you can access the Document Setup dialog box. In this dialog box, there are many text options, including the Highlight Substituted Fonts and Highlight Substituted Glyphs options, which are in the Bleed And View Options section.

In the Type Options section at the bottom of the dialog box, you can set the document language, change double and single quotes, edit Superscript, Subscript, Small Caps, and more.

Saving and using styles

Styles allow you to format text consistently and are helpful when text attributes need to be globally updated. Once a style is created, you only need to edit the saved style. Then, all text formatted with that style is updated.

Illustrator provides two types of styles:

- **Paragraph**—Retains text and paragraph attributes and applies them to an entire paragraph.

- **Character**—Retains the text attributes and applies them to selected text.

Creating and using a paragraph style

1   Using the Type tool (**T**), select the subhead Breathe. Choose Bold from the Font Style menu in the Control panel.

> ● **Note:** You may see the word Character instead of the Font Style menu in the Control panel. Click the word Character to reveal the Character panel.

2   With the Type tool, place the cursor anywhere in the text Breathe. You do not need to select text to create a paragraph style, but you do have to place the text insertion point in the line of text that has the attributes you are going to save.

3   Choose Window > Type > Paragraph Styles, and choose New Paragraph Style from the panel menu (▼≡).

4   In the New Paragraph Style dialog box, type the name **Subhead**, and click OK. The text attributes used in the paragraph have been saved in a paragraph style named Subhead.

5   Apply the new paragraph style by selecting the text Breathe and then selecting the Subhead style in the Paragraph Styles panel. The text attributes are applied to the selected text.

> ● **Note:** If you see a plus sign (+) to the right of the style name, the style has an override. An override is any formatting that doesn't match the attributes defined by the style, for example, if you changed the font size for the selected paragraph. If you see the plus sign (+), press the Alt (Windows) or Option (Mac OS) key when you select the style name to overwrite existing attributes on the selected text.

Notice the Normal style in the Paragraph Styles panel. When you placed the Word document earlier in this lesson, the Normal style from Word was brought into the Illustrator document.

6 Select the text Stretch, and Alt-click (Windows) or Option-click (Mac OS) the Subhead style in the Paragraph Styles panel. Repeat this step to apply the style to the text, Workout and Relax.

Creating and using a character style

Whereas paragraph styles apply attributes to an entire paragraph, character styles can be applied to selected text only.

1 Using the Type tool (**T**), select the first occurrence of the text Pranayama in the first column of the paragraph text.

2 Choose Bold from the Font Style menu in the Control panel.

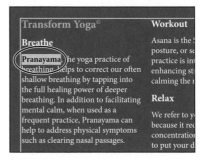

⬤ **Note:** You may see the word Character instead of the Font Style menu in the Control panel. Click the word Character to reveal the Character panel.

Now, you will save these attributes as a character style, and apply it to other instances in the text.

3 In the Paragraph Styles panel group, click the Character Styles panel tab.

4 In the Character Styles panel, Alt-click (Windows) or Option-click (Mac OS) the Create New Style button (◻) at the bottom of the Character Styles panel. Alt or Option-clicking the New Style button lets you name the style as it is added to the panel. You can also double-click a style to name and edit it.

5 Name the style **Bold** and click OK. The style records the attributes applied to your selected text.

Now, you will apply that character style to other text.

6 With the Pranayama text still selected, Alt-click (Windows) or Option-click (Mac OS) the style named Bold in the Character Styles panel to assign the style to that text. This removes any existing attributes from the text that are not part of the character style.

7 Select the next occurrence of Pranayama and apply the Bold style again.

⬤ **Note:** You must select the entire word rather than just placing the cursor in the text.

8 Choose Select > Deselect.

▶ **Tip:** Perhaps you decide that you want to change the color of all text that is formatted with the Bold character style. Using styles (either character or paragraph), you can change the type attributes of the original style, and all instances are updated.

Next, you will change the color of the Bold character style.

9 Double-click the Bold style name in the Character Styles panel. In the Character Style Options dialog box, click the Character Color category on the left side of the dialog box and make sure that the Fill box is selected. Click the Mustard swatch in the Swatches panel that appears.

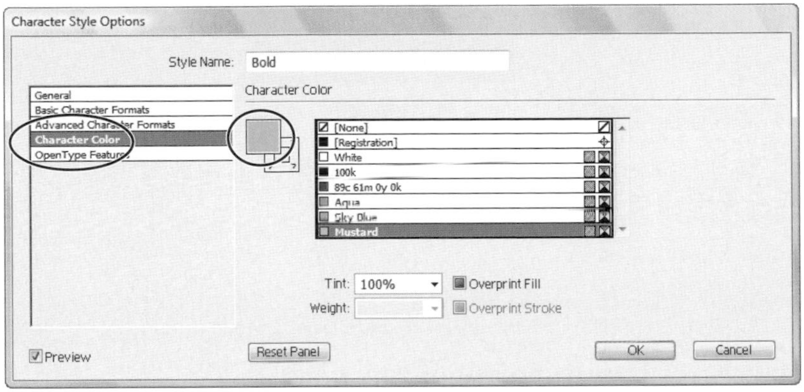

10 Select the Preview checkbox in the lower-left corner of the Character Style Options dialog box if it isn't already selected. As you change the style formatting, the text that uses the Bold style changes automatically.

11 Click OK, and close the Character Style panel group.

12 Choose File > Save. Leave the file open.

Sampling text

Using the Eyedropper tool, you can quickly sample type attributes and apply them to text without creating a style.

1 Choose View > Fit Artboard In Window.

2 With the Zoom tool (Q), drag a marquee across the text "1000 Lombard Ave. Central, Washington," above the top yoga figure on the left.

3 Using the Type tool (T), triple-click to select the paragraph.

4 In the Control panel, change the Fill color to blue (C=89, M=61, Y=0, K=0), the Font to Myriad Pro (if it isn't already selected), and the Font Style to Condensed or something similar.

● **Note:** If the word Central is included in the first line of text, use the Type tool to place the cursor before "Central" and press Shift+Enter or Shift+Return to add a soft return, pushing the text to the next line.

5 Double-click the Hand tool (✋) to fit the artboard in the window.

6 Choose View > Smart Guides to select them.

7 With the Type tool, select the text "info@transformyoga.com" above the bottom yoga figure on the left side of the artboard.

Note: If you position the Eyedropper cursor over text with smart guides selected, a line appears beneath that text, to confirm that you are clicking in the right place to sample formatting.

8 Select the Eyedropper tool (🖊) in the Tools panel and click anywhere in the line of text "1000 Lombard Ave. Central, Washington." A letter T appears above the eyedropper pointer. The attributes are immediately applied to your selected text. If the e-mail address shifts to the left, move it to its original position with the Selection tool.

9 Choose Select > Deselect.

10 Choose File > Save. Leave the file open.

Reshaping text with an envelope warp

Warping text is fun because it allows you to give text a more interesting shape. An envelope warp lets you fit the text into a shape that you create or that is created for you. An envelope is an object that distorts or reshapes selected objects. You can use a preset warp shape or a mesh grid as an envelope, or you can create and edit your own using objects on the artboard.

1 Select the Type tool (T) in the Tools panel. Before typing, in the Control panel, change the font family to Myriad Pro (if it is not already selected), the font style to Bold Condensed, and the font size to **48** pt.

Note: You may want to zoom in.

2 With the Type tool, click the poster below the two columns of text once. Exact placement is not important. A cursor appears.

3 Type the word **transform**.

4 Select the Selection tool (▶). If the text overlaps the text in the two columns above, drag it down until it no longer overlaps. Change the Fill color in the Control panel to White.

▶ **Tip:** With the Type tool selected, you can temporarily switch to the Selection tool by pressing the Ctrl (Windows) or Command (Mac OS) key.

5 Select the text with the Selection tool, and then click the Make Envelope button (🔲) in the Control panel. In the Warp Options dialog box, select Preview. The text appears as an arc.

6 Choose Arc Upper from the Style menu. Drag the Bend slider to the right to see it bend up further. You can experiment with many combinations. Drag the

Horizontal and Vertical Distortion sliders to see the effect on the text. When you are finished experimenting, drag the Distortion sliders to 0%, and click OK.

● **Note:** The Make Envelope button (⬚) does not apply an effect. It just turns the text into an envelope object. The same visual result is achieved by choosing Effect > Warp > Arc Upper. For more information about envelopes, see "Reshape using envelopes" in Illustrator Help.

7 Use the Selection tool to move the envelope object (warped text) until the bottom of the warped text is aligned roughly with the bottom of the two columns of text.

If you want to make any changes, you can edit the text and shape separately. Next, you will edit the text transform, and then the warp shape.

8 With the warped text still selected, click the Edit Contents button (⊠) in the Control panel. This is how you edit the text in the warped shape.

9 Using the Type tool, position the cursor over the warped text. Notice the text transform text is in blue and is underlined. The smart guides show you the original text. Click the text transform to insert the cursor, and then double-click to select it.

● **Note:** If you double-click with the Selection tool instead of the Type tool, you enter isolation mode. Press Escape to exit isolation mode.

10 Type workout and notice the text warps automatically in the arc upper shape. Choose Edit > Undo Typing to return to the original text.

● **Note:** Notice that the text you are editing seems to float in the warped shape, which indicates that the text is being forced into the shape. It is still editable as text.

11 In the Control panel, change the Stroke Weight to **.75** pt, and the Stroke color to Mustard. Press Escape to close the Swatches panel.

Notice that the attributes are applied to the warped text. Next, you will edit the warp shape.

12 With the Selection tool, make sure that the warped text is still selected. Click the Edit Envelope button (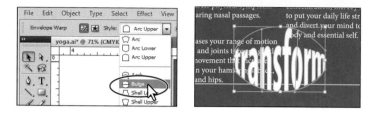) in the Control panel.

13 Choose Bulge from the Select Warp Style menu in the Control panel. Notice the other options in the Control panel, such as Horizontal, Vertical, and Bend. Choose Arc Upper to return to the arc upper shape.

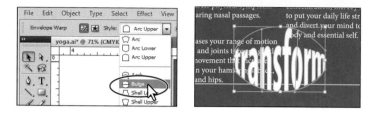

● **Note:** You may have to reposition the warped text to align it with the bottom of the columns of text. Changing the warp style may move the text on the artboard.

14 Select the Direct Selection tool (◻) in the Tools panel. Notice the anchor points around the warped shape. First, click to select the anchor point above the letter "n" in transform. Then, drag the selected point up to change the warp shape.

▶ **Tip:** To take the text out of the warped shape, select the text with the Selection tool and choose Object > Envelope Distort > Release. This gives you two objects: the text and the arc upper shape.

15 Choose Edit > Undo Move to return the shape to the arc upper shape.

Next, you will add a drop shadow effect to the warped text.

16 Switch to the Selection tool and click transform.

17 Choose Effect > Stylize > Drop Shadow from the Illustrator effects. In the Drop Shadow Options dialog box, change Opacity to **30**%, X Offset to **3** pt, Y Offset to **3** pt, and Blur to **3** pt, and click OK.

18 Choose Select > Deselect, and File > Save. Leave the file open.

Wrapping text around an object

You can create interesting and creative results by wrapping text around an object. Next, you will wrap text around the warped text.

1 With the Selection tool, click to select the warped text, transform.

2 Choose Object > Text Wrap > Make. The text in the two columns wraps around the warped text, transform.

⬤ **Note:** To wrap text around an object, the wrap object must be in the same layer as the text and located directly above the text in the layer hierarchy.

3 With the Selection tool, drag the transform text to see the effect on the text in the two columns.

4 If text is flowing in areas where you don't want it, choose Object > Text Wrap > Text Wrap Options. In the Text Wrap Options dialog box, change Offset to **4** and select Preview to see the change. Click OK.

5 Using the Selection tool, reposition the text transform to create a better text flow. For this example, it is okay if some of your text overflows out of the text area.

6 Choose Select > Deselect.

7 Choose File > Save. Keep the file open.

Creating text on open paths

Using the Type tools, you can type on paths and shapes to flow text along the edge of an open or closed path.

1 Click the Next button (▶) in the status bar in the lower left of the Document window to navigate to the second artboard.

2 Choose View > Fit Artboard In Window if the entire postcard is not showing.

3 With the Selection tool (▶), select the wavy path crossing the yoga figures.

▶ **Tip:** To quickly switch to the Selection tool and back to the Type tool, press the Ctrl (Windows) or Command (Mac OS) key.

4 With the Type tool (**T**), cross the cursor over the left side of the path to see an insertion point with an intersecting wavy path (⅄·). Click when this cursor appears. The stroke attributes change to None and a cursor appears. Don't type yet.

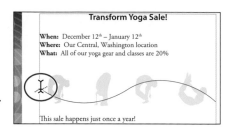

5 Change the font size to **20** pt in the Control panel. Change the Fill color to blue (C=89, M=61, Y=0, K=0). Make sure that the font is Myriad Pro and change the font style to Condensed.

6 Type the word **breathe** and press the spacebar to add a space. Note that the newly typed text follows the path.

7 Choose Type > Glyphs, and find a bullet point in the Glyphs panel. Double-click to insert the bullet point. Keep the Glyphs panel open. Insert a space after the inserted bullet.

8 Type the text **stretch · relax · transform yourself**. Add a space before and after each bullet point.

9 Close the Glyphs panel.

● **Note:** If the text doesn't fit on the path, a small box with a plus sign (+) appears at the bottom of the bounding box. You can make the font size smaller or the line bigger, among other options.

10 Choose Select > Deselect.

● **Note:** Click the word Paragraph if the align options are not visible.

11 Click in the text you just typed with the Type tool. In the Control panel, make sure the Align Center button (≡) is selected to center the text on the path.

● **Note:** You can apply any character and paragraph formatting you want to the text on the path.

12 With the Selection tool, make sure that the text path is still selected. In the Control panel, change Opacity to **60**% to make the text semitransparent.

● **Note:** If you don't see the opacity settings in the Control panel, you can open the Transparency panel by choosing Window > Transparency.

13 Choose Select > Deselect, and then File > Save.

Creating text on closed paths

Now, you will put text on a closed path.

1 Click the Previous button in the status bar in the lower left of the Document window to navigate to the first artboard.

2 Choose View > Fit Artboard In Window if the entire poster is not showing. Select the Zoom tool (🔍) in the Tools panel and click the blue circle with the yoga figure in the upper-left corner of the poster three times to zoom in.

3 With the Selection tool (▶), select the aqua circle behind the yoga figure.

Next, you will copy the blue circle so that you can put text on it. This is necessary because putting text on the existing aqua circle would remove the stroke and fill of that circle. Remember, putting text on a path removes the stroke and fill from the path.

4 Double-click the Scale tool (📐) in the Tools panel to open the Scale dialog box. In the Scale dialog box, change Uniform Scale to **130**, and click Copy to make a copy of the circle. This makes a copy that is 130% larger than the original circle.

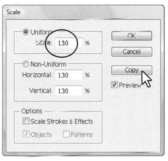

● **Note:** Read more about transforming objects in Lesson 4, "Transforming Objects."

5 Switch to the Type tool. While pressing the Alt (Windows) or Option (Mac OS) key, move the pointer across the left side of the circle. The insertion point with an intersecting wavy path (ϟ) appears. Click, but don't type. The path now has a stroke and fill of None, but the type will have a black fill, and a cursor is on the path.

6 In the Control panel, change the font size to **30** pt, the font to Myriad Pro (if not already selected), the font style to Condensed or something similar, and the Fill color to White.

7 Click the Align Left button (≡) in the Control panel.

8 Type **transform yoga**. The text flows on the circular path.

● **Note:** Instead of using the Alt (Windows) or Option (Mac OS) key, you can select the Type On A Path tool by holding down the Type tool in the Tools panel.

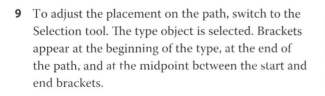

9 To adjust the placement on the path, switch to the Selection tool. The type object is selected. Brackets appear at the beginning of the type, at the end of the path, and at the midpoint between the start and end brackets.

● **Note:** It may look like there are only two brackets. That's because the start and end brackets are next to each other on the left side of the circle.

10 Position the cursor over the center bracket until a small icon (⌐) appears next to the cursor. Drag the center bracket along the outside of the path. Press the Ctrl (Windows) or Command (Mac OS) key to prevent the type from flipping to the other side of the path. Position the text so that it is relatively centered across the top of the circle.

11 With the path type object selected with the Selection tool, choose Type > Type On A Path > Type On A Path Options. In the Type On A Path Options dialog box, select Preview, and then choose Skew from the Effect menu. Select other options from the Effect menu, and then change the effect to Rainbow. Choose Descender from the Align To Path menu. Click OK.

⬤ **Note:** Read more about Type On A Path options in Illustrator Help. Search for, "Creating type on a path."

12 Choose Select > Deselect.

13 Choose File > Save, and leave the file open.

Creating text outlines

When creating artwork for multiple purposes, it is a good idea to create outlines of text so that the file recipient doesn't need to have your fonts installed in order to open and use the file correctly. Always keep your original artwork because you cannot change outline text back to editable text.

1 Click the Next button in the status bar in the lower left of the Document window to navigate to the second artboard.

2 Choose View > Fit Artboard In Window if the entire postcard is not showing.

3 Select the Type tool (T) in the Tools panel and click away from the left edge of the postcard artboard on the canvas.

4 Change the Fill color in the Control panel to blue (C=89, M=61, Y=0, K=0).

5 Type **transform yourself**.

6 Double-click the Rotate tool (⟳) in the Tools panel. In the Rotate dialog box, type **90** in the Angle field. Click OK. The text is rotated 90 degrees counterclockwise.

7 With the Selection tool (▶), position the text in the lower-right corner of the blue background image on the left.

8 Using the Selection tool, Shift-click the upper-right handle of the bounding box of the text and drag to proportionally enlarge the text to the height of the postcard.

● **Note:** If the descender of the letters appear in the white area to the right, then drag the text to the left.

9 Click the word Opacity in the Control panel to open the Transparency panel. Choose Screen from the Blending Mode menu.

Tip: One benefit of creating outlines from text is that it allows you to fill the text with a gradient. If you want a gradient fill and also want to maintain text editing control, select the text with the Selection tool, and choose Effect > Path > Outline Object.

10 With the text area still selected with the Selection tool, choose Type > Create Outlines. The text is no longer linked to a particular font. Instead, it is now artwork, much like any other vector art in your illustration. Choose Select > Deselect.

11 Choose File > Save.

Exploring on your own

Experiment with text features by integrating paths with illustrations. Use the clip art provided in the Lesson07 folder and try some of these type techniques:

- coffee.ai—Using the Pen tool, create paths representing steam rising from the coffee cup. Create text on the wavy paths and apply varying levels of opacity.

- airplane.ai—Complete a banner following the airplane by including your own text.

Take the project further by using this artwork to create a one-page sales flyer that has the following text elements on the page:

- Using the placeholder.txt file in the Lesson07 folder, create a three-column text area.

- Use the graphic of the pizza or plane for a text wrap.

- Create a masthead across the top of your page that has text on a curve.

- Create a paragraph style.

- On the yoga poster, choose View > Outline to see all the paths on the page. Notice a spiral shape at the top of the page. Try adding text to that spiral path and choose Type > Type On A Path > Type On A Path Options to change the attributes.

Review questions

1   Name two methods for creating a text area in Adobe Illustrator CS5.

2   What are two benefits of using an OpenType font?

3   What is the difference between a character and paragraph style?

4   What are the advantages and disadvantages of converting text to outlines?

Review answers

1   The following three methods can be used for creating text areas:

   •   With the Type tool, click the artboard, and start typing when the cursor appears. A text area is created to accommodate the text.

   •   With the Type tool, drag to create a text area. Type when a cursor appears.

   •   With the Type tool, click a path or closed shape to convert it to text on a path or a text area. Alt clicking (Windows) or Option-clicking (Mac OS) when crossing over the stroke of a closed path creates text around the shape.

2   The two main benefits of OpenType fonts are cross-platform compatibility (they work the same on both Windows and Mac OS), and support of widely expanded character sets and layout features, which provide richer linguistic support and advanced typographic control.

3   A character style can be applied to selected text only. A paragraph style is applied to an entire paragraph. Paragraph styles are best for indents, margins, and line spacing.

4   Converting type to outlines eliminates the need to send the fonts along with the file when sharing with others. You can also fill the type with a gradient and create interesting effects on individual letters. However, when you create outlines from text, you should consider the following:

   •   Text is no longer editable. The content and font cannot be changed for outlined text. It is best to save a layer with the original text, or use the Outline Object effect.

   •   Bitmap fonts and outline-protected fonts cannot be converted to outlines.

   •   Outlining text that is less than 10 points in size is not recommended. When type is converted to outlines, the type loses its hints—instructions built into outline fonts to adjust their shape to display or print optimally at many sizes. When scaling type, adjust its point size before converting it to outlines.

   •   You must convert all type in a selection to outlines; you cannot convert a single letter within a string of type. To convert a single letter into an outline, create a separate type area containing only that letter.

8 WORKING WITH LAYERS

Lesson overview

In this lesson, you'll learn how to do the following:

- Work with the Layers panel.
- Create, rearrange, and lock layers, nested layers, and groups.
- Move objects between layers.
- Paste layers of objects from one file into another.
- Merge layers into a single layer.
- Apply a drop shadow to a layer.
- Make a layer clipping mask.
- Apply an appearance attribute to objects and layers.
- Isolate content in a layer.

This lesson will take approximately 45 minutes to complete. If needed, remove the previous lesson folder from your hard disk and copy the Lesson08 folder onto it.

Layers let you organize your work into distinct
levels that can be edited and viewed individually or
together. Every Adobe® Illustrator® document has
at least one layer. Creating multiple layers in your
artwork lets you easily control how artwork is printed,
displayed, and edited.

Getting started

In this lesson, you'll finish the artwork of a wall clock as you explore the various ways to use the Layers panel.

1 To ensure that the tools and panels function as described in this lesson, delete or deactivate (by renaming) the Adobe Illustrator CS5 preferences file. See "Restoring default preferences" on page 3.

2 Start Adobe Illustrator CS5.

● **Note:** If you have not already done so, copy resource files for this lesson onto your hard disk from the Lesson08 folder on the Adobe Illustrator CS5 Classroom in a Book CD. See "Copying the Classroom in a Book files" on page 2.

3 Choose File > Open, and open the L8end_1.ai file in the Lesson08 folder, located in the Lessons folder on your hard disk.

● **Note:** If the Layers panel in your workspace does not look exactly like the figure below, that's okay. At this point, you just need to familiarize yourself with the panel.

Separate layers are used for the objects that make up the clock's frame, face, hands, and numbers, as indicated by the layer names listed in the Layers panel. Below you can see the Layers panel (Window > Layers) and descriptions of the icons.

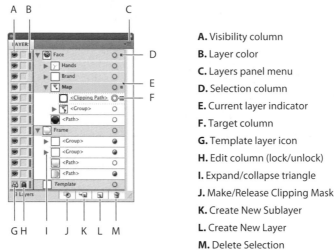

A. Visibility column
B. Layer color
C. Layers panel menu
D. Selection column
E. Current layer indicator
F. Target column
G. Template layer icon
H. Edit column (lock/unlock)
I. Expand/collapse triangle
J. Make/Release Clipping Mask
K. Create New Sublayer
L. Create New Layer
M. Delete Selection

4 Choose View > Fit Artboard In Window. If you like, you can leave the file open as a visual reference. Otherwise, choose File > Close.

To begin working, you'll open an existing art file that is incomplete.

5 Choose File > Open, and open the L8start_1.ai file in the Lesson08 folder, located in the Lessons folder on your hard disk.

6 Choose File > Save As, name the file **clock.ai**, and select the Lesson08 folder. Leave the Save As Type option set to Adobe Illustrator (*.AI) (Windows) or the Format option set to Adobe Illustrator (ai) (Mac OS), and click Save. In the Illustrator Options dialog box, leave the Illustrator options at their default settings, and then click OK.

About layers

When creating complex artwork, it's a challenge to keep track of all the items in your document window. Small items get hidden under larger items, and selecting artwork becomes difficult. Layers provide a way to manage all the items that make up your artwork. Think of layers as clear folders that contain artwork. If you reshuffle the folders, you change the stacking order of the items in your artwork. You can move items between folders and create subfolders within folders.

The structure of layers in your document can be as simple or complex as you want it to be. By default, all items are organized in a single, parent layer. However, you can create new layers and move items into them, or move elements from one layer to another at any time. The Layers panel provides an easy way to select, hide, lock, and change the appearance attributes of artwork. You can even create template layers, which you can use to trace artwork, and exchange layers with Photoshop.

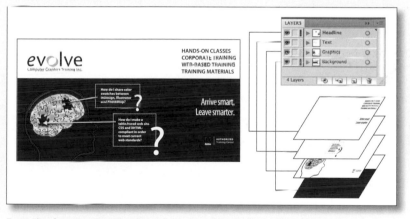

Example of composite art and how layers break out individually.

—From Illustrator Help

Creating layers

By default, every document begins with one layer. As you create artwork, you can rename and add layers at any time. Placing objects on separate layers lets you easily select and edit them. For example, by placing type on a separate layer, you can change the type all at once without affecting the rest of the artwork.

Next, you'll change the default layer name, and then create a layer and a sublayer, and learn the difference between the two.

1 If the Layers panel isn't visible, click the Layers panel icon (⬦) on the right side of the workspace, or choose Window > Layers.

Layer 1 (the default name for the first layer) is highlighted, indicating that it is active. The layer also has a triangle (◥) in the upper-right corner, indicating that objects on the layer can be edited.

2 In the Layers panel, double-click the layer name to open the Layer Options dialog box. Type **Clock** in the Name text field, and then click OK.

Now, you'll create a layer for the clock face elements and a sublayer for the clock numbers. Sublayers help you organize content within a layer.

3 Click the Create New Layer button (⬍) at the bottom of the Layers panel, or choose New Layer from the Layers panel menu (▾☰).

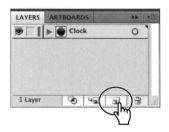

4 Double-click Layer 2. In the Layer Options dialog box, change the name to **Face**, make sure Red is chosen in the Color menu, and then click OK.

The new Face layer is added above the Clock layer and becomes active.

5 Click the layer named Clock once and then Alt-click (Windows) or Option-click (Mac OS) the Create New Sublayer button (⊣▣) at the bottom of the Layers panel to create a new sublayer. The Layer Options dialog box appears. Creating a new sublayer opens the layer to show existing sublayers.

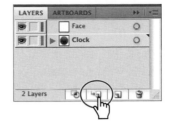

● **Note:** To create a new sublayer without setting options or naming the sublayer, click the Create New Sublayer button without pressing the Alt (Windows) or Option (Mac OS) key. Layers and sublayers that aren't named are numbered in sequence, for example, the second layer is labeled Layer 2.

A sublayer is a layer within another layer. Sublayers are used to organize content within a layer without grouping or ungrouping content.

6 In the Layer Options dialog box, change the name to **Numbers**, and then click OK. The new sublayer appears directly beneath its main layer, Clock, and is selected.

Layers and color

By default, Illustrator assigns a unique color (up to nine colors) to each layer in the Layers panel. The color displays next to the layer name in the panel. The same color displays in the illustration window in the bounding box, path, anchor points, and center point of a selected object.

You can use this color to quickly locate an object's corresponding layer in the Layers panel, and you can change the layer color to suit your needs.

Each layer and sublayer can have a unique color.

—From Illustrator Help

Moving objects and layers

By rearranging the layers in the Layers panel, you can reorder layered objects in your artwork. You can also move selected objects from one layer or sublayer to another. On an artboard, objects on layers higher in the Layers panel list are in front of objects on layers lower in the list.

First, you'll move the clock numbers into their own sublayer.

1   In the Layers panel, click the row for the 11 object and drag it onto the Numbers sublayer. Release the mouse button when you see the large black triangles at either end of the Numbers sublayer. The large triangles indicate that you are adding something to that layer. Notice the arrow that appears to the left of the Numbers sublayer when you release the mouse button. This indicates that the sublayer has content.

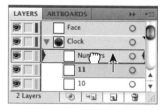

▶ **Tip:** Keeping layers and sublayers closed can make it easier to navigate content in the Layers panel.

2   Click the triangle to the left of the Numbers sublayer thumbnail to open the sublayer and see its contents.

3   Repeat step 1 for each of the remaining number sublayers in the Layers panel. This better organizes the panel and makes it easier to find content later.

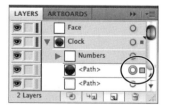

▶ **Tip:** You can use the Shift key to select multiple sublayers and drag them all in at once.

4   Click the triangle to the left of the Numbers sublayer to hide its contents. Hiding layer and/or sublayer contents makes the Layers panel easier to work with.

5   Choose File > Save.

Now, you'll move the clock face artwork to the Face layer, to which you'll later add the map, hands, and brand name of the clock. You'll also rename the Clock layer to reflect the new organization of the artwork.

6   In the artwork, using the Selection tool (▶), click behind the numbers to select the clock face. In the Layers panel, an object named <Path> becomes active, as indicated by the selected-art indicator (■) to the right of the upper <Path> layer.

▶ **Tip:** To select objects behind other objects, you can also press the Ctrl (Windows) or Cmd (Mac OS) key and click multiple times where the objects overlap to select behind. To learn more about selecting behind, see Lesson 2, "Selecting and Aligning."

7 Drag the selected-art indicator (■) on the \<Path\> sublayer in the Layers panel up to the right of the target icon (○) on the Face layer.

This action moves the \<Path\> object to the Face layer. The color of the selection lines in the artwork changes to the color of the Face layer, which is red in this case.

Because the Face layer is on top of the Clock layer and the Numbers sublayer, the clock numbers are covered. Next, you'll move the Numbers sublayer into a different layer and rename the Clock layer.

8 Choose Select > Deselect.

9 In the Layers panel, drag the Numbers sublayer into the Face layer. Release the mouse button when you see the indicator bar with large black triangles at either end of the Face layer in the Layers panel.

Now, you can see the numbers again because they are on the top (Face) layer.

10 Double-click the Clock layer to display the Layer Options dialog box. Change the layer name to **Frame**, and then click OK.

11 Choose File > Save.

Locking layers

As you edit objects on a layer, use the Layers panel to lock other layers and prevent selecting or changing the rest of the artwork.

Now, you'll lock all of the layers except the Numbers sublayer so that you can easily edit the clock numbers without affecting objects on other layers. Locked layers cannot be selected or edited in any way.

1 Click the triangle to the left of the Frame layer to collapse the layer view.

2 Select the edit column to the right of the eye icon on the Frame layer, to lock the layer. The lock icon (🔒) indicates that a layer and all its content are locked.

3 Repeat the previous step for the <Path> sublayer below the Numbers sublayer.

You can unlock individual layers by deselecting the lock icon (🔒). Clicking again in the edit column relocks the layer. Pressing the Alt (Windows) or Option (Mac OS) key as you click in the edit column alternately locks and unlocks all other layers.

Now, you'll change the type size and font of the numbers.

4 Click the Selection column to the right of the Numbers sublayer in the Layers panel to select all the content on that layer.

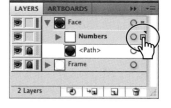

The Numbers sublayer now has a larger green square, indicating that everything on that sublayer is selected. On the artboard, you can see that the numbers are selected as well.

Next, you will change the font, font style, and font size for the selected numbers.

5 In the Control panel, choose Myriad Pro from the Font menu, Semibold from Font Style menu, and type **28** in the Font Size field.

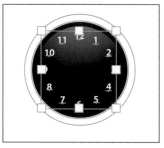

● **Note:** Myriad Pro is an OpenType font that is included with Illustrator CS5.

6 Use the Color panel (🎨) if you want to change the color of the selected numbers.

7 In the Layers panel, deselect the lock icons (🔒) next to the <Path> and Frame layers to unlock them.

8 Choose Select > Deselect.

9 Choose File > Save.

Viewing layers

The Layers panel lets you hide layers, sublayers, or individual objects from view. When a layer is hidden, the content on the layer is also locked and cannot be selected or printed. You can also use the Layers panel to display layers or objects individually, in either preview or outline mode.

▶ **Tip:** Alt (Windows) or Option (Mac OS) click the layer eye icon to hide or show a layer. Hiding layers prevents them from being changed.

Now, you'll edit the frame on the clock, using a painting technique to create a three-dimensional effect on the frame.

1 In the Layers panel, click the Frame layer to select it, and then Alt-click (Windows) or Option-click (Mac OS) the eye icon (👁) to the left of the Frame layer name to hide the other layers.

Alt-click or Option-click the eye icon to hide all other layers.

2 Using the Selection tool (▶), on the artboard, click the inner circle of the frame to select it. Then Shift-click the outer circle to add it to the selection.

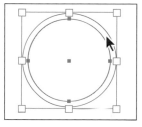

3 With the two circles selected, click Fill color in the Control panel, and then select the clock.frame swatch in the Swatches panel that appears, to paint the circles with a custom gradient.

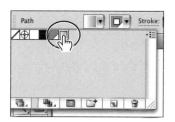 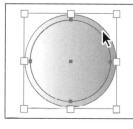

4 Shift-click the outer circle to deselect it. The inner circle remains selected.

5 Select the Gradient tool (▣) in the Tools panel. Position the pointer over the inner circle, just below the top of the circle, so a horizontal bar appears. Click the pointer, then drag in a vertical line straight down, to change the direction of the gradient. Release the mouse button.

The Gradient tool works only on selected objects that are filled with gradients. To learn more about the Gradient tool, see Lesson 10, "Blending Colors and Shapes."

● **Note:** When you first select the Gradient tool, a horizontal line appears in the selected circle. This is the default direction of the gradient fill.

6 Choose Select > Deselect, and then File > Save. Try selecting the outer circle and changing the direction of the gradient with the Gradient tool.

7 In the Layers panel, choose Show All Layers from the panel menu (▼≡).

As you edit objects in layered artwork, you can display individual layers in outline mode, keeping the other layers in preview mode.

8 Ctrl-click (Windows) or Command-click (Mac OS) the eye icon (👁) next to the Face layer to switch to outline mode for that layer.

This action lets you see the gradient-filled circle behind the clock face. Displaying a layer in outline mode is also useful for viewing the anchor points or center points on objects without selecting them.

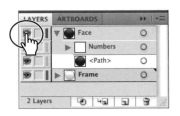

Ctrl-click (Windows) or Command-click (Mac OS) the eye icon to enter outline mode.

9 Control-click (Windows) or Command-click (Mac OS) the eye icon (👁) next to the Face layer to return to preview mode for that layer. Choose Select > Deselect.

Pasting layers

To complete the clock, you'll copy and paste the remaining pieces of artwork from another file. You can paste a layered file into another file and keep the layers intact.

1 Choose File > Open, and open the Details.ai file, located in the Lesson08 folder in the Lessons folder on your hard disk.

2 To see how the objects in each layer are organized, Alt-click (Windows) or Option-click (Mac OS) the eye icons for each layer in the Layers panel to show one layer and hide the others. You can also click the triangles (▶) to the left of the layer names to expand and collapse the layers for further inspection.

When you're finished, make sure that all the layers are showing and that they are collapsed.

3 Choose Select > All, and then Edit > Copy to select and copy the clock details to the clipboard.

4 Choose File > Close to close the Details.ai file without saving any changes. If a warning dialog box appears, click No (Windows) or Don't Save (Mac OS).

5 In the clock.ai file, choose Paste Remembers Layers from the Layers panel menu (▼≡). A check mark next to the option indicates that it's selected.

Selecting the Paste Remembers Layers option indicates that when multiple layers from another file are pasted into the artwork, they're added as individual layers in the Layers panel. If the option is not selected, all objects are pasted into the active layer.

6 Choose Edit > Paste In Front to paste the details into the clock. Choose Select > Deselect.

The Paste In Front command pastes the objects from the clipboard to a position relative to the original position in the Details.ai file. The Paste Remembers Layers option causes the Details.ai layers to be pasted as four separate layers at the top of the Layers panel (Highlight, Hands, Brand, Map).

Now, you will reposition some of the layers.

7 Close any open layers by toggling the arrow to the left of the layer names. Move the Frame layer above the Highlight layer, and then the Face layer above the Frame layer. If necessary, drag the bottom of the Layers panel down to reveal all the layers.

▶ **Tip:** As you drag layers in the Layers panel, the panel scrolls up or down for you. You can also drag the bottom or lower-right corner of the Layers panel to make it taller.

Release the mouse button when the indicator bar with black triangles extends the full column width above the Frame and Highlight layers so that you want to create a separate layer, not a sublayer. If any content is still selected on the artboard, choose Select > Deselect.

Now, you'll move the Hands and Brand layers into the Face layer, and the Highlight layer in front of the Frame layer.

8 In the Layers panel, select the Highlight layer, and drag it up between the Face and Frame layers.

 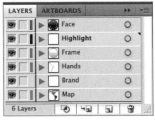 

9 Click the arrow to the left of the Face layer to show the sublayers.

10 Click the Hands layer, then Shift-click the Brand layer to select both.

11 Drag the selected layers up between the Numbers and <Path> sublayers. When the insertion bar appears between those sublayers, release the mouse button to make the Hands and Brand layers into sublayers of the Face layer.

● **Note:** You may want to resize the Layers panel by dragging the bottom of the Layers panel down so it is easier to see the layers.

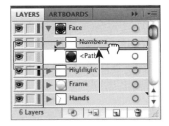 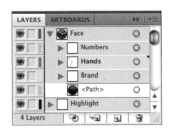 

12 Choose File > Save.

Creating clipping masks

The Layers panel lets you create clipping masks to control whether artwork on a layer (or in a group) is hidden or revealed. A clipping mask is an object or group of objects whose shape masks artwork below it so that only artwork within the shape is visible.

Now, you'll create a clipping mask with the circle shape in the Face layer. You'll group it with the Map sublayer so that only the map shows through the circle shape.

1 Drag the bottom of the Layers panel down to reveal all the layers.

2 In the Layers panel, drag the Map layer up until the double lines of the insertion bar are highlighted above the <Path> sublayer within the Face layer. Release the mouse button.

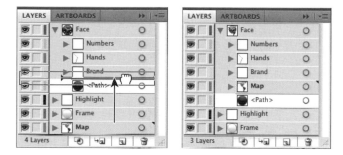

In the Layers panel, a masking object must be above the objects it masks. Because you want to mask only the map, you'll copy the circular <Path> object to the top of the Map sublayer before you create the clipping mask.

3 Click the selection column in the Layers panel to the right of the <Path> sublayer. Notice that the path is selected on the artboard.

4 Press the Alt (Windows) or Option (Mac OS) key, and click and drag the selected-art indicator (■) on the <Path> sublayer straight up to the right of the target icon (○) on the Map sublayer.

5 Choose Select > Deselect.

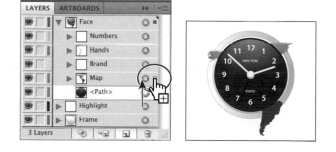

6 Click the triangle (▶) to the left of the Map sublayer in the Layers panel to expand the layer view.

7 Make sure that the <Path> sublayer is at the top of the Map sublayer (above the <Group> sublayer), moving it if necessary. (Clipping masks must be the first object in a layer or group.)

● **Note:** Deselecting the artwork on the artboard is not necessary to complete the next steps, but it can be helpful for viewing the artwork.

8 Select the Map sublayer to highlight it in the Layers panel.

● **Note:** You may not be able to see the entire name, <Clipping Path>, in the Layers panel.

9 Click the Make/Release Clipping Mask button (⬚) at the bottom of the Layers panel. Notice that all the sublayer dividing lines are now dotted and the first path name has changed to <Clipping Path>. The name is also underlined to indicate that it is the masking shape. On the artboard, the <Path> sublayer has clipped the parts of the map that extended outside of the clock face.

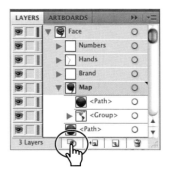  

10 In the Layers panel, click the triangle next to the Map sublayer name to collapse it.

11 Choose File > Save.

Merging layers

● **Note:** Layers can only merge with other layers that are on the same hierarchical level in the Layers panel. Likewise, sublayers can only merge with other sublayers that are in the same layer and at the same hierarchical level. Objects can't be merged with other objects.

To streamline your artwork, you can merge layers. Merging layers combines the contents of all selected layers into one layer.

1 Click the Numbers sublayer in the Layers panel to highlight it, and then Shift-click to highlight the Hands sublayer.

Notice that the current layer indicator (◀) shows the last highlighted layer as the active layer. The last layer you select determines the name and color of the merged layer.

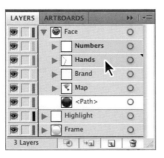

2 Choose Merge Selected from the Layers panel menu (▾≡) to merge the Numbers sublayer into the Hands sublayer.

The objects on the merged layers retain their original stacking order, and are added above the objects in the destination layer.

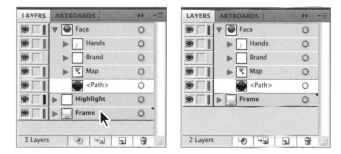

3 Click the Highlight layer to select it, and then Shift-click the Frame layer.

4 Choose Merge Selected from the Layers panel menu (▾≡) to merge the objects from the Highlight layer into the Frame layer.

5 Choose File > Save.

To consolidate layers and groups

Merging and flattening layers are similar in that they both let you consolidate objects, groups, and sublayers into a single layer or group. With merging, you can select which items you want to consolidate; with flattening, all visible items in the artwork are consolidated in a single layer. With either option, the stacking order of the artwork remains the same, but other layer-level attributes, such as clipping masks, aren't preserved.

- To flatten layers, click the name of the layer into which you want to consolidate the artwork. Then select Flatten Artwork from the Layers panel menu.

—From Illustrator Help

Applying appearance attributes to layers

You can apply appearance attributes such as styles, effects, and transparency to layers, groups, and objects using the Layers panel. When an appearance attribute is applied to a layer, any object on that layer takes on that attribute. If an appearance attribute is applied only to a specific object on a layer, it affects only that object, not the entire layer. To learn more about working with appearance attributes, see Lesson 13, "Applying Appearance Attributes and Graphic Styles."

You will apply an effect to an object on one layer. Then you'll copy that effect to another layer to change all objects on that layer.

1 In the Layers panel, collapse the Face layer and expand the Frame layer to reveal all its content.

2 Click to select the bottom <Path> sublayer in the Frame layer.

● **Note:** Clicking the target icon also selects the object(s) on the artboard.

3 Click the target icon (○) to the right of the lower <Path> sublayer name. Clicking the target icon indicates that you want to apply an effect, style, or transparency change.

4 Choose Effect > Stylize > Drop Shadow from the Illustrator Effects. In the Drop Shadow dialog box, leave the settings at their default values, and then click OK. A drop shadow appears on the outer edge of the clock.

● **Note:** There are two Stylize commands in the Effect menu. Choose the top Stylize menu command, which is in the Illustrator Effects.

Notice that the target icon (●) is now shaded on the lower <Path> sublayer, indicating that the object has appearance attributes applied to it.

5 Click the Appearance panel icon (●) on the right side of the workspace to reveal the Appearance panel. If the Appearance panel isn't visible, choose Window > Appearance. Notice that Drop Shadow has been added to the list of appearance attributes for the selected object.

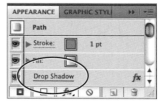

6 Change Stroke Weight to **0** pt in the Control panel.

7 Choose Select > Deselect.

You will now use the Layers panel to copy an appearance attribute into a layer and then edit it.

8 Click the Layers panel icon on the right side of the workspace to open the Layers panel. Click the arrow to the left of the Face layer to reveal its contents. If necessary, drag the bottom of the Layers panel down to display the entire list. Make sure that the triangles to the left of the Hands, Brand, and Map sublayers are toggled closed.

9 With the Selection tool (▶), click the clock hands in the artwork to select them.

10 Choose Locate Object from the Layers panel menu (▾≣). This selects and scrolls to the group (<Group> appears in the Layers panel) that contains the clock hands in the Layers panel. You may need to scroll in the Layers panel for the next step.

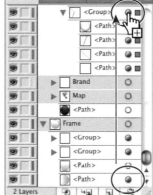

11 Press the Alt (Windows) or Option (Mac OS) key and drag the shaded target icon of the bottom <Path> sublayer in the Frame layer to the target icon of the clock hands <Group> sublayer, without releasing the mouse button. The hand pointer with a plus sign indicates that the appearance is being copied.

● **Note:** You can drag and copy the shaded target icon to any layer or sublayer, to apply the properties found in the Appearance panel.

12 When the target icon of the <Group> sublayer turns light gray, release the mouse button and then the Alt or Option key. The drop shadow is now applied to the entire <Group> sublayer, as indicated by the shaded target icon.

Now, you'll edit the drop shadow attribute for the type and clock hands to tone down the effect.

13 Click the triangle to the left of the <Group> sublayer under the Hands layer to toggle it closed.

14 In the Layers panel, click the target icon (◎) for the <Group> sublayer that contains the clock hands. This automatically selects the objects on the <Group> sublayer and deselects the object on the Frame layer.

15 Click the Appearance panel icon (●) on the right side of the workspace to reveal the Appearance panel. In the Appearance panel, click the words Drop Shadow, scrolling down if necessary.

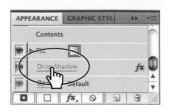

16 In the Drop Shadow dialog box, change X Offset, Y Offset and Blur to **3** pt. Click OK.

17 Choose Select > Deselect.

18 Choose File > Save.

For information on opening layered Photoshop files in Illustrator and working with layered Illustrator files in Photoshop, see Lesson 15, "Combining Illustrator CS5 Graphics with Other Adobe Applications."

Isolating layers

When a layer is in isolation mode, objects on that layer are isolated so that you can easily edit them without affecting other layers. Next, you will enter isolation mode for a layer and make some simple edits.

1 Open the Layers panel by clicking the Layers panel icon.

2 Click the triangles to the left of the sublayers in the Layers panel to close them all. Make sure that the sublayers of the Face layer are showing.

3 Click to select the Map sublayer in the Layers panel.

4 Choose Enter Isolation Mode from the Layers panel menu (▼≡).

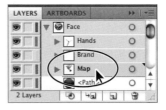

In isolation mode the contents of the Map sublayer appear on top of all the objects on the artboard. The rest of the content on the artboard is dimmed and locked.

The Layers panel now shows a layer called
Isolation Mode and a sublayer that contains
the map content.

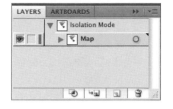

5   Select the Selection tool (▶), and click the map on
    the artboard to select it.

6   Choose View > Smart Guides to deselect them
    temporarily.

7   Drag the map up to position it toward the top of the
    dark inner circle.

8   Press Escape to exit isolation mode. Notice that the
    content is no longer locked and the Layers panel
    reveals all the layers and sublayers again.

9   Chose Select > Deselect.

Now that the artwork is complete, you may want to
combine all the layers into a single layer and delete
the empty layers. This is called flattening artwork.

Delivering finished artwork in a single layer file can prevent accidents, such as
hiding layers and omitting parts of the artwork during printing.

▶ **Tip:** To flatten specific layers without deleting hidden layers, select the layers you want to flatten,
and then choose Merge Selected from the Layers panel menu.

For a complete list of shortcuts that you can use with the Layers panel, see
"Keyboard shortcuts" in Illustrator Help.

10 Choose File > Save.

11 Choose File > Close.

Exploring on your own

When you print a layered file, only the visible layers print, in the same order in which they appear in the Layers panel, with the exception of template layers, which do not print even if they're visible. Template layers are locked, dimmed, and non-printing layers. Objects on template layers neither print nor export.

Now that you know how to work with layers, try creating layered artwork by tracing an image on a template layer. is For practice, you can use the bitmap photo image of a goldfish, or your own artwork or photo images.

1　Choose File > New to create a new file for your artwork.

2　Choose File > Place. In the dialog box, select the goldfish.ai file, located in the Lesson08 folder, in the Lessons folder on your hard disk; alternatively, locate your file containing the artwork or image you want to use as a template. Click Place to add the placed file to Layer 1.

3　Create the template layer by choosing Template from the Layers panel menu or choosing Options for Layer 1 and selecting Template in the Layer Options dialog box.

4　Click the Create New Layer button to create a new layer on which to draw.

5　With Layer 2 active, use any drawing tool to trace over the template, creating new artwork.

6　Create additional layers to separate and edit various components of the new artwork.

7　If you want, delete the template layer after you finish to reduce the size of the file.

▶ **Tip:** For information on custom views, search for "Use multiple windows and views" in Illustrator Help.

Review questions

1   Name two benefits of using layers when creating artwork.

2   How do you hide layers? How do you show individual layers?

3   Describe how to reorder layers in a file.

4   How can you lock layers?

5   What is the purpose of changing the selection color for a layer?

6   What happens if you paste a layered file into another file? Why is the Paste Remembers Layers option useful?

7   How do you move objects from one layer to another?

8   How do you create a layer clipping mask?

9   How do you apply an effect to a layer? How can you edit that effect?

10 What is the purpose of entering isolation mode?

Review answers

1   The benefits of using layers when creating artwork include: protecting artwork that you don't want to change, hiding artwork that you aren't working with so that it's not distracting, and controlling what prints.

2   To hide a layer, click to deselect the eye icon to the left of the layer name. Select the blank, leftmost column (the Visibility column) to show a layer.

3   You reorder layers by selecting a layer name in the Layers panel and dragging the layer to its new location. The order of layers in the Layers panel controls the document's layer order—topmost in the panel is frontmost in the artwork.

4   You can lock layers in several different ways:

    • You can click in the edit column to the left of the layer name. A lock icon appears, indicating that the layer is locked.

    • You can choose Lock Others from the Layers panel menu to lock all layers but the active layer.

    • You can hide a layer to protect it.

5   The selection color controls how selected anchor points and direction lines are displayed on a layer, and helps you identify the different layers in your document.

6   The paste commands paste layered files or objects copied from different layers into the active layer, by default. The Paste Remembers Layers option keeps the original layers intact when the objects are pasted.

7   Select the objects you want to move, and drag the selected-art indicator (to the right of the target icon) to another layer in the Layers panel.

8   Create a clipping mask on a layer by selecting the layer and clicking the Make/Release Clipping Mask button. The topmost object in the layer becomes the clipping mask.

9   Click the target icon for the layer to which you want to apply an effect. Then choose an effect from the Effect menu. To edit the effect, make sure that the layer is selected, and then click the name of the effect in the Appearance panel. The effect's dialog box opens, and you can change the values.

10   Isolation mode isolates objects so that you can easily select and edit content on a single layer or sublayer.

9 WORKING WITH PERSPECTIVE DRAWING

Lesson overview

In this lesson, you'll learn how to do the following:

- Understand perspective drawing.

- Use and edit grid presets.

- Draw and edit objects in perspective.

- Edit grid planes and content.

- Create and edit text in perspective.

- Attach symbols to perspective.

 This lesson will take approximately an hour and a half to complete. If needed, remove the previous lesson folder from your hard disk and copy the Lesson09 folder onto it.

In Adobe® Illustrator® CS5, you can easily draw or render artwork in perspective using the Perspective Grid. The Perspective Grid allows you to approximately represent a scene on a flat surface, as it is naturally perceived by the human eye. For example, you can render a road or a pair of railway tracks, which seem to meet or vanish in the line of vision.

Getting started

You'll explore working with the Perspective Grid, adding content to it, and editing on the Perspective Grid.

Before you begin, you'll restore the default preferences for Adobe Illustrator. Then you'll open the finished art file for this lesson to see what you'll create.

1   To ensure that the tools and panels function as described in this lesson, delete or rename the Adobe Illustrator CS5 preferences file. See "Restoring default preferences" on page 3.

2   Start Adobe Illustrator CS5.

● **Note:** If you have not already done so, copy the resource files for this lesson onto your hard disk from the Lesson09 folder on the Adobe Illustrator CS5 Classroom in a Book CD. See "Copying the Classroom in a Book files" on page 2.

3   Choose File > Open, and open the L9end_1.ai file in the Lesson09 folder, located in the Lessons folder on your hard disk.

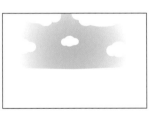

4   Choose View > Zoom Out to make the finished artwork smaller if you want to leave it on your screen as you work. (Use the Hand tool (🖑) to move the artwork where you want it in the window.) Leave the file open for reference, or choose File > Close.

5   Choose File > Open, and open the L9start_1.ai file in the Lesson09 folder, located in the Lessons folder on your hard disk.

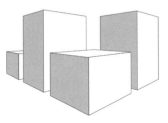

6   Choose File > Save As, name the file **city.ai** in the Lesson09 folder. Leave the Save As Type option set to Adobe Illustrator (*.AI) (Windows) or the Format option set to Adobe Illustrator (ai) (Mac OS), and click Save. In the Illustrator Options dialog box, leave the Illustrator options at their default settings, and then click OK.

Understanding perspective

In Illustrator CS5, you can easily draw or render artwork in perspective using a feature set that works based on established laws of perspective drawing. Perspective in drawing is an approximate representation, on a flat surface, of an image as it is seen by the eye. Objects drawn in perspective are characterized primarily by the following features:

- They are drawn smaller as their distance from the observer increases.

- The perspective objects are foreshortened, which means that an object or distance appears shorter than it actually is because it is angled toward the viewer.

Understanding the Perspective Grid

The Perspective Grid allows you to approximately represent a scene on a flat surface, as it is naturally perceived by the human eye. For example, you can render a road or a pair of railway tracks, which seem to meet or vanish in the line of vision. The Perspective Grid allows you to create and render artwork in perspective.

● **Note:** It may be helpful to refer back to the Perspective Grid options shown in this figure as you progress through the lesson.

1 Choose Essentials from the workspace switcher in the Application bar.

2 Choose View > Fit Artboard In Window.

3 Select the Perspective Grid tool (▦) in the Tools panel. This shows the default, two point Perspective Grid on the artboard.

The figure below shows the Perspective Grid and its parts. As you go through this lesson, you will learn about each part.

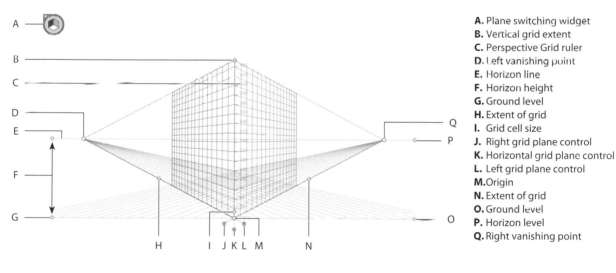

A. Plane switching widget
B. Vertical grid extent
C. Perspective Grid ruler
D. Left vanishing point
E. Horizon line
F. Horizon height
G. Ground level
H. Extent of grid
I. Grid cell size
J. Right grid plane control
K. Horizontal grid plane control
L. Left grid plane control
M. Origin
N. Extent of grid
O. Ground level
P. Horizon level
Q. Right vanishing point

Working with the Perspective Grid

In order to begin working with content in perspective, it is helpful to see and set up the Perspective Grid the way you want.

Using a preset grid

To begin the lesson, you'll work with the Perspective Grid, starting with some Illustrator presets.

The Perspective Grid, by default is set up as a two-point perspective. You can easily change that using presets. The Perspective Grid tool is used to edit and move the grid. You use the Perspective Grid to draw and snap content in perspective, although the grid is non-printing. Illustrator can have up to three points of perspective.

▶ **Tip:** You can show the Perspective Grid without selecting the Perspective Grid tool, by choosing View > Perspective Grid > Show Grid.

1   Choose View > Perspective Grid > One Point Perspective > [1P-Normal View]. Notice that the grid changes to a one-point perspective.

A one-point perspective can be very useful for drawing roads, railway tracks, or buildings viewed so that the front is directly facing the viewer.

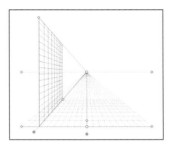

2   Choose View > Perspective Grid > Three Point Perspective > [3P-Normal View]. Notice that the grid changes to a three-point perspective.

Three-point perspective is usually used for buildings seen from above or below. In addition to showing vanishing points for each wall, there is now a point showing those walls receding into the ground or high in space.

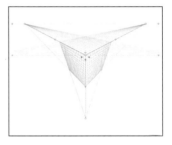

3   To return the grid back to a two-point perspective, choose View > Perspective Grid > Two Point Perspective > [2P-Normal View].

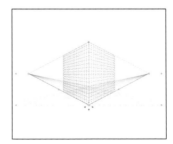

Editing the Perspective Grid

Next, you'll learn how to edit the Perspective Grid. To edit the grid, you can either select the Perspective Grid tool or edit using the Define Grid menu item. You can make changes to the grid if you have content on the grid, although it may be easier to establish the grid settings before you add content. You can create only one grid per Illustrator document.

1 With the Perspective Grid showing two-point perspective and the Perspective Grid tool (▦) selected, drag the horizon line point down below the bottom of the blue sky to move the horizon down, as shown in the figure. The measurement label should show approximately 147 pt.

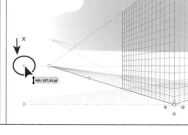

● **Note:** Throughout this section, the pink X in the figures shows where to drag from.

● **Note:** The gray lines in some of these figures indicate the initial position of the Perspective Grid, before it was adjusted.

The location of the horizon line indicates the observer's eye level.

2 With the Perspective Grid tool, drag the left ground level point up to move the whole Perspective Grid. Drag until the horizon line you adjusted in the previous step is lined up with the bottom of the blue sky.

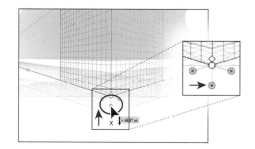

The ground level point allows you to drag the Perspective Grid to different parts of the artboard or to a different artboard altogether.

● **Note:** As you drag the Perspective Grid by the ground level point, notice that you can move it in any direction. Make sure that it is still more or less centered horizontally on the artboard.

3 With the Perspective Grid tool, drag the horizontal grid plane control point up about 68 pt so that it's closer to the horizon line.

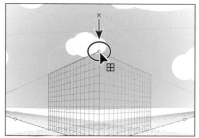

▶ **Tip:** The location of the ground level in relation to the horizon line will determine how far above or below eye level the object will be viewed.

4 With the Perspective Grid tool, click and drag the Vertical Grid Extent point down to shorten the vertical extent.

Making the vertical extent shorter can be a way to minimize the grid if you are drawing objects that are less precise, as you will see later in the lesson.

5 Choose File > Save. Changes you make to the Perspective Grid are saved with this document only.

Setting the grid up for your drawing is an important step. Next, you will access these changes using the Define Grid menu.

▶ Tip: After setting the Define Perspective Grid settings, you can save them as a preset to access later. In the Define Perspective Grid dialog box, change the settings, and then click the Save Preset button.

▶ Tip: To learn more about the Define Perspective Grid dialog box, search for "Define grid presets" in Illustrator Help.

6 Choose View > Perspective Grid > Define Grid.

7 In the Define Perspective Grid dialog box, change the Units to Inches, and change the Gridline Every value to **.3** in. Change the Viewing Distance to **7** in. The Viewing Distance is the distance between the observer and the scene.

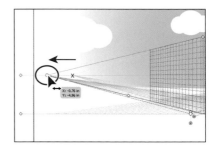

Notice that you can change the Scale of the grid, which you might want to do if real world measurements are involved. You can also edit settings like Horizon Height and Viewing Angle, which you can also edit on the artboard using the Perspective Grid tool. Leave the Grid Color & Opacity settings at their defaults. When you have finished making changes, click OK.

8 With the Perspective Grid tool, drag the left vanishing point about −.75 in to the left until it reaches the left horizon line point. Notice that this changes only the left (blue) grid on the two-point Perspective Grid.

9 Choose Edit > Undo Perspective Grid Edit. You are able to undo most changes made to the Perspective Grid.

10 Choose View > Perspective Grid > Lock Station Point. This locks the left and right vanishing points so that they move together.

11 With the Perspective Grid tool, drag the left vanishing point about −.75 in to the left again, until it reaches the left Horizon Line point. Notice that this now changes both grids on the two-point Perspective Grid.

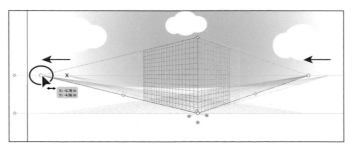

12 Choose File > Save.

13 Choose View > Perspective Grid > Lock Grid. This option restricts the grid movement and other grid editing features that use the Perspective Grid tool. You can change only the visibility and the grid plane position, which you will work with later in this lesson.

● **Note:** When you select another tool besides the Gradient Perspective tool, you cannot edit the Perspective Grid. Also, if the Perspective Grid is locked, you can edit it by choosing View > Perspective Grid > Define Grid.

Now that the grid is locked into the correct position, you will begin creating your cityscape by adding content to it.

Drawing objects in perspective

To draw objects in perspective, use the line group tools or rectangle group tools (except for the Flare tool), while the grid is visible. Before you begin drawing using any of these tools, you need to select a grid plane to attach the content to, using the Plane Switching Widget or keyboard shortcuts.

The Plane Switching Widget

When you select the Perspective Grid, a Plane Switching Widget also appears in the upper left corner of the Document window, by default. You can use this widget to select the active grid plane.

In Perspective Grid, an active plane is the plane on which you draw an object to project the observer's view of that portion of the scene.

—From Illustrator Help

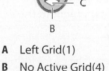

A Left Grid(1)
B No Active Grid(4)
C Horizontal Grid(2)
D Right Grid(3)

▶ **Tip:** The numbers in parentheses (Left Grid(1), for instance) refer to the keyboard shortcut assigned to that grid.

Next, you will draw several objects in perspective on the Perspective Grid.

1 Click the Layers panel icon (●) to expand the Layers panel. Click the eye icon (●) to the left of the Background layer to hide its contents on the artboard. Click to select the Left face layer so that the new content you will create is on that layer.

2 Click the Layers panel icon (●) to collapse the panel.

3 Select the Rectangle tool (□) in the Tools panel.

4 Click the Left Grid in the Plane Switching Widget.

Whichever grid plane is selected in the widget is the grid plane on the Perspective Grid to which you'll add content.

Left Grid(1)

● **Note:** With practice, you'll develop the habit of checking which grid plane is active before drawing or adding content.

Tip: When drawing in perspective, you can still use the usual keyboard shortcuts for drawing objects, such as Shift-drag or Alt-drag.

5   Position the pointer over the top of the Perspective Grid where the two planes meet. Notice the cursor (◄|) has an arrow pointing to the left, indicating that you are about to draw on the left grid plane. Drag down and to the left, to the bottom orthogonal line, as shown in the figure. Note that it's okay if your measurements are a little different from those shown.

When drawing on the grid plane, objects do not snap to the grid lines by default. However, smart guides do help to snap to corners and edges.

6   With the rectangle selected, change the Fill color in the Control panel to medium gray (C=0, M=0, Y=0, K=40).

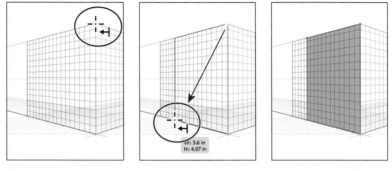

Start drawing.   Create the rectangle.   Change the color fill.

Next, you will draw another rectangle to create the other side of a building, this time snapping it to the Perspective Grid.

7   Choose View > Perspective Grid > Snap To Grid.

8   Press Ctrl++ (Windows) or Cmd++ (Mac OS) twice to zoom into the Perspective Grid. Snapping to the grid doesn't work if you are zoomed out too far.

Note: To learn more about working with layers see Lesson 8, "Working with Layers."

9   Click the Layers panel icon (◆) to expand the Layers panel. Click to select the layer named Right face so that the new content is on that layer.

10 With the Rectangle tool still selected, click Right Grid(3) in the Plane Switching Widget, to draw in perspective on the right grid plane. Notice that the cursor (|►) now has an arrow pointing to the right, indicating that you are about to draw on the right grid plane. Drag down and to the right, starting at the same top point as for the last rectangle you drew. When the measurement label shows a width of

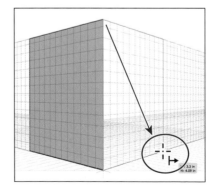

approximately 3.3 in and the pointer reaches the bottom of the right grid plane, release the mouse button.

11 With the rectangle selected, change the Fill color in the Control panel to a light gray (C=0, M=0, Y=0, K=10).

12 Click the X in the upper-left corner of the Plane Switching Widget to hide the Perspective Grid and see your artwork.

▶ **Tip:** You can also choose View > Perspective Grid > Hide Grid to hide the grid.

13 Choose View > Fit Artboard In Window.

Next, you will draw a rectangle that will serve as a door for the building. But first you must show the grid again, to continue drawing in perspective.

14 Press Shift+Ctrl+I (Windows) or Shift+Cmd+I (Mac OS) to show the grid.

▶ **Tip:** You can also show the Perspective Grid by selecting the Perspective Grid tool, or choosing View > Perspective Grid > Show Grid.

15 Select the Rounded Rectangle tool (⬛) in the Tools panel by holding down the Rectangle tool (⬛) and positioning the pointer over the center of the rectangle you just created. Click once to open the Rectangle dialog box. Change the Width to **1.5** in and the Height to **.9** in.

Change the Corner Radius to **.1** in, and then click OK. This will be a window in the building.

16 Press Ctrl++ (Windows) or Cmd++ (Mac OS) three times to zoom in.

17 Select the Selection tool (▶), and drag the rectangle down and to the left, to position it at the bottom left of the light gray rectangle.

If you use the Selection tool to drag an object that was drawn in perspective, it maintains its original perspective, but it doesn't change to match the Perspective Grid.

18 Choose Edit > Undo Move to return it to its original position.

Selecting and transforming objects in perspective

You can select objects in perspective using the Perspective Selection tool (▶). The Perspective Selection tool uses the active plane settings to select the objects.

Next you will move and resize the rectangle you just drew.

1 Select the Perspective Selection tool (▶) in the same tools group as the Perspective Grid tool in the Tools panel. Drag the rounded rectangle down and to the left, in the lower-left corner of the light gray rectangle.

Notice that it snaps to the grid as you drag it.

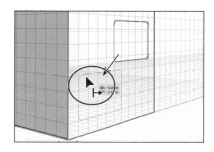

2 With the rectangle still selected, change the Fill color in the Control panel to the window gradient.

3 With the Perspective Selection tool still selected, click the dark gray rectangle on the left grid plane to select it. Notice that the left grid plane is now selected in the Plane Switching Widget.

4 Select the Zoom tool (🔍) in the Tools panel and drag a marquee across the lower-left corner of the medium-gray rectangle on the left grid plane.

▶ **Tip:** You can open the Transform panel (Window > Transform) and make the height of both rectangles the same in the Transform panel.

5 Select the Perspective Selection tool, then drag the lower-left corner up and to the left, following the bottom grid plane line that leads to the left vanishing point. See the figure below for help. When the measurement label shows a width of about 4.5 in, release the mouse button.

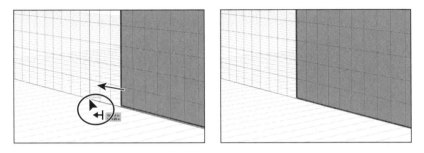

● **Note:** The size does not have to match exactly, as long as the shape is snapped to the Perspective Grid. The height of your rectangles may be different than what you see in the figure.

Scale objects in perspective

You can scale objects in perspective using the Perspective Selection tool. While scaling objects in perspective, the following rules apply:

• Scaling is done in the object's plane. When you scale an object, the height or distance is scaled based on the object's plane and not the current or active plane.

• For multiple objects, scaling is done for objects that are on the same plane. For example, if you select multiple objects on the right and left plane, then all the objects that are on the same plane as the object whose bounding box is used for scaling, are scaled.

• Objects that have been moved perpendicularly, are scaled on their respective plane and not the current or active plane.

—From Illustrator Help

Next, you will duplicate an object in perspective, as well as move an object perpendicular to an existing object.

6 Choose View > Fit Artboard In Window.

7 With the Perspective Selection tool selected, holding down Alt+Shift (Windows) or Option+Shift (Mac OS), drag to the right the light gray rectangle on the right grid plane. When the measurement label shows a distance (dX) of approximately 4.75 in, release the mouse button and then the modifier keys.

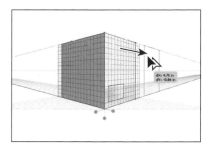

You will use this copy as the face of another building. As with other types of drawings, the Alt or Option key duplicates the object and the Shift key constrains the movement.

With the rectangle copy in place and in perspective, you will now adjust the Perspective Grid so that the grid pattern covers the new shape. You'll do this by editing the grid extent.

8 Select the Perspective Grid tool (▦) in the Tools panel.

9 Press Ctrl++ (Windows) or Cmd++ (Mac OS) twice to zoom in.

Notice that the grid pattern in the Perspective Grid starts to expand to the right and left.

10 Choose View > Perspective Grid > Unlock Grid, which enables you to edit the grid.

11 With the Perspective Grid tool, position the pointer over the right grid extent widget and drag to the left until it reaches the right edge of the copied rectangle, as shown in the figure below. The pink x in the figure below indicates the approximate starting location of the right grid extent widget.

Next, you will adjust the grid cell size.

12 Drag the grid cell widget down a bit until the grid cell size becomes smaller.

Notice that if you drag too far down, the left and right extent of the grid moves away from its accompanying vanishing point. Dragging up would increase the size of the grid cells.

● **Note:** Gridlines are set to display on-screen when there is a 1-pixel gap in them. Progressive zooming in will bring in to view more gridlines that are closer to the Vanishing Point.

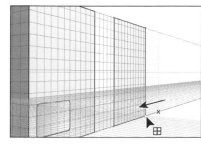

Drag the grid extent widget.

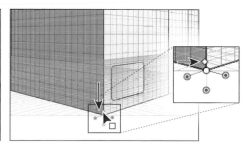

Edit the grid cell size.

13 Select the Selection tool, and click to select the medium-gray rectangle on the left grid plane. Change the Fill color in the Control panel to the building face 1 color. Click to select the second rectangle you created (the other face of the same building) and change the color in the Control panel to building face 2.

14 Choose File > Save.

Now that the copied rectangle is in place and the grid cells display correctly, you will copy the rectangle on the left grid plane so that it becomes the left face of the newly-copied rectangle. Next, you will see how to move an object parallel to its current location.

1 Select the Perspective Selection tool (➤.) in the Tools panel. Click to select the red-colored rectangle on the left grid plane. Holding down the number 5 key, drag the rectangle to the left a bit. Release the mouse and then the 5 key.

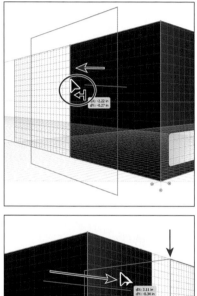

This action moves the object in parallel to its current location.

2 Choose Edit > Undo Perspective Move.

3 With the Perspective Selection tool selected, hold down the Alt (Windows) or Option (Mac OS) key and the number 5 key, and drag the same rectangle to the right. Drag to position it as the left face of the second building. When in position, release the mouse and then the modifier keys.

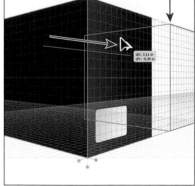

This duplicates the object and places it at the new location without changing the original object. In Draw Behind mode this action, creates the object behind the original object.

4 With the new copy still selected, choose Object > Arrange > Send To Back. Change the Fill color of the new object in the Control panel to a medium gray.

Next, you will make a copy of the rounded rectangle "window," and then move it to the left grid plane of the red building by pressing a keyboard shortcut to switch planes while dragging.

5 With the Perspective Selection tool selected, select the blue window on the right face of the building. Choose Edit > Copy, and then Edit > Paste In Front.

6 Drag a copy of the rounded rectangle window to the left with the Perspective Selection tool. As you drag, press, then release number 1 to switch the window to the left grid plane. Drag the window to the lower-left corner of the red rectangle on the left (which is the left side of the red building).

● **Note:** While dragging you may need to press the number 1 a few times.

7 Choose Edit > Cut.

8 Click the Layers panel icon (●) to expand the Layers panel. In the Layers panel make sure that the Left face layer is selected. Click the Layers panel icon to collapse the panel again.

9 Choose Edit > Paste In Front.

● **Note:** If the rounded rectangle doesn't appear on top of all other objects, choose Object > Arrange > Bring To Front.

10 With the rounded rectangle still selected, press the right arrow key, and then the up arrow key. Notice that pressing the arrow keys snaps the rounded rectangle to the Perspective Grid. Using the arrow keys, position the window in the lower-left corner of the red rectangle, as shown in the figure.

● **Note:** The grid size determines the distance an object is moved using the arrow keys.

11 Click to select the original rounded rectangle on the right grid plane so that it is the only thing selected. Position it on the same grid lines (relatively) as the copy, using the arrow keys to snap it to the grid, as shown in the figure.

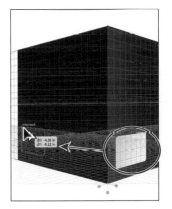
Copy and position the rectangle.

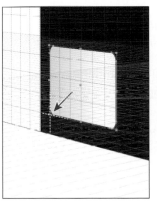
Use the arrow keys to position the left grid rectangle.

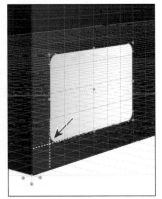
Use the arrow keys to position the right grid rectangle.

12 Press Ctrl+Shift+I (Windows) or Cmd+Shift+I (Mac OS) to temporarily hide the Perspective Grid.

13 Choose Select > Deselect, then File > Save.

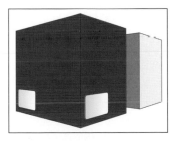

Attaching objects to perspective

If you have already created objects, Illustrator provides an option to attach the objects to an active plane on the Perspective Grid. You will now add an existing sign for a coffee shop to one of the sides of a building.

1 Choose View > Perspective Grid > Show Grid to show the grid.

2 Choose View > Fit All In Window to see the two artboards.

3 Select the Selection tool (▶) and click to select the Coffee sign on the artboard on the right. Drag the sign close to the right of the gray building you've created in perspective. After you've placed the sign, click once somewhere on a blank area of the main artboard with the grid. This puts the focus on the artboard with the Perspective Grid.

4 Choose View > Fit Artboard In Window.

5 Press Ctrl++ (Windows) or Cmd++ (Mac OS) twice to zoom into the Perspective Grid and artwork.

Next, you will add the selected sign to the right side of the red building, and put it into perspective along with the rest of the artwork on the main artboard.

▶ **Tip:** You can also select the active plane by pressing keyboard shortcuts: 1=Left Grid, 2=Horizontal Grid, 3=Right Grid, and 4=No Active Grid.

6 Select the Perspective Selection tool (▶) in the Tools panel. Click the Left Grid(1) in the Plane Switching Widget to make sure that the sign will be added to the left plane grid.

● **Note:** This is an important step that can be easily forgotten!

▶ **Tip:** Instead of dragging the object onto the plane using the Perspective Selection tool, you can also select the object with the Perspective Selection tool, choose the plane using the Plane Switching Widget, and then choose Object > Perspective > Attach to Active Plane.

7 With the Perspective Selection tool, drag the sign so that the top of the sign aligns with the top of the Vertical Grid Extent.

The artwork is added to the grid that is selected in the Plane Switching Widget.

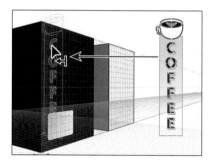

● **Note:** The coffee sign is a group of objects. You can just as easily attach a single object to the Perspective Grid.

8 With the sign still selected, choose Edit > Cut.

9 Click the Layers panel icon (▧) on the right side of the workspace to expand the Layers panel. Click to select the Right face layer. Choose Edit > Paste In Place. This pastes the sign on the Right face layer.

10 Click the Layers panel icon to collapse the panel.

With the coffee sign attached to the left grid plane, you will now move it perpendicular to its current location, so that it is on the right side of the building.

11 With the Perspective Selection tool, hold down the number 5, and drag the coffee sign to the right until it reaches the right side of the red rectangle, as shown in the figure. Release the mouse button and then the modifier key.

12 With the Perspective Selection tool, hold down the Shift key and drag the bottom, middle point of the sign up to make it smaller. When the measurement label shows a Height of about 2.4 or 2.5 inches, stop dragging. Release the mouse button, and then the Shift key.

Drag the sign into position.   Scale the sign.

● **Note:** If your sign is too close or too far from the red building after resizing, then you can drag to position it better using the Perspective Selection tool.

13 Choose Select > Deselect, then File > Save.

Editing planes and objects together

You can edit the grid planes in perspective either before or after there is artwork on them in perspective. You can move objects perpendicularly by dragging them or move a grid plane using grid plane controls to move objects perpendicularly.

Next, you will edit the grid planes and the artwork.

1 With the Perspective Selection tool (➤) still selected, drag the right grid plane control to the right until approximately D:1in appears in the measurement label, as shown in the figure. This moves the right grid plane, but not the objects on it.

● **Note:** Throughout this section, a pink X in the figures shows where to drag from.

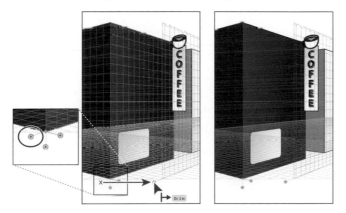

2 Choose Edit > Undo Perspective Grid Edit to return the grid plane to its original position.

3 With the Perspective Selection tool still selected, hold down the Shift key, drag the right grid plane control to the right until the measurement label shows about 1 in. Release the mouse button, and then the Shift key.

The Shift key moves the grid plane and the artwork on the grid perpendicular to their original positions.

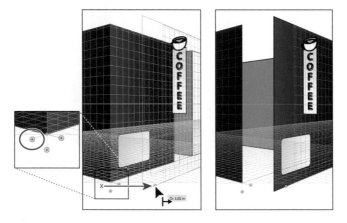

▶ **Tip:** Dragging a grid plane control while pressing Shift+Alt (Windows) or Shift+Option (Mac OS) drags a copy of the objects with the grid plane.

Dragging a grid plane control is not very precise. For more precision, you can move the right grid plane control according to values you enter, which you will do next.

4 Double-click the same right grid plane control you just dragged. Change the Location to **.5 in**, and then select Move All Objects. Click OK.

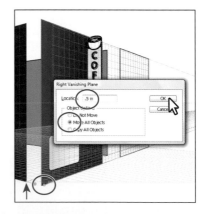

In the Right Vanishing Plane dialog box, the Do Not Move option allows you to move the grid plane and not the objects on it. Copy All Objects allows you to move the grid plane and bring a copy of the objects on the grid plane with it.

The location starts at 0, which is at the station point. The station point is indicated by the small green diamond above the horizontal grid control (an arrow is pointing to it in the figure).

Next, you will move the left grid plane using the same method.

5 Double-click the left grid plane control. Change the Location to **–.4 in**, and then select Move All Objects. Click OK.

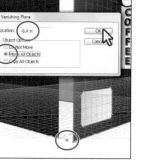

The grid planes move to the right when you enter a positive value and to the left when you enter a negative value.

Now the grid planes and objects are where they need to be, except for the coffee sign and the left side of the second, gray building, which you will move later. You will now add a flat corner rectangle to the red building.

6 Click the Layers panel icon (⬢) on the right side of the workspace to expand the Layers panel. Click to select the Center face layer.

7 Click the Layers panel icon to collapse the panel.

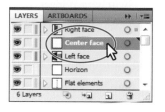

8 Select the Rectangle tool (▭) from the same group as the Rounded Rectangle tool in the Tools panel. Click No Active Grid in the Plane Switching Widget. This allows you to draw without perspective.

9 Starting from the upper-right corner of the red rectangle on the left grid plane, drag down and to the right to the lower-left corner of the red rectangle on the right grid plane, as shown in the figure below.

● **Note:** The corners of the rectangles may not line up perfectly. If you want to ensure that they do, you can select the Perspective Selection tool and select each rectangle. Then, with the smart guides on, the corner points to snap to each other.

10 With the rectangle still selected, change the Fill color to building corner in the Control panel.

11 Choose Select > Deselect, then File > Save.

Now that the red building is taking shape, you will reposition the coffee sign, and draw some rectangles to attach the sign the face of the building. This will require that you move a grid plane to match the coffee sign.

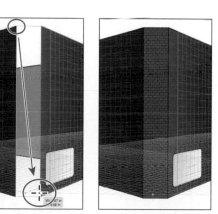

1   Select the Perspective Selection tool (⬊) in the Tools panel. Click to select the Coffee sign. Choose Object > Perspective > Move Plane To Match Object.

This moves the left plane grid to match the perspective of the sign. This allows you to draw or add more content in the same plane as the coffee sign.

● **Note:** If you wanted to simply move the coffee sign in perspective with the Perspective Selection tool, you would not have to move the grid plane to match it.

2   Choose Select > Deselect. Select the Zoom tool (🔍) in the Tools panel and drag a marquee around the coffee sign to zoom into it.

3   Making sure that the Left Grid is selected in the Plane Switching Widget, select the Rectangle tool in the Tools panel.

▶ **Tip:** You can hide or reposition the Plane Switching Widget by double-clicking the Perspective Grid tool (▦) or the Perspective Selection tool (⬊) and then changing the options in the Perspective Grid Options dialog box.

Next, you will draw some rectangles between the sign and the building, to attach the sign to the building.

4   Starting on the left edge of the coffee sign, drag down and to the left to create a small rectangle, as shown in the figure below. This acts as one attachment point for the sign.

5   With the rectangle still selected, change the Fill color in the Control panel to light blue.

6   Select the Perspective Selection tool (⬊) in the Tools panel. Holding down Shift+Alt (Windows) or Shift+Option (Mac OS), drag the new rectangle down, to create a copy towards the bottom of the sign. Release the mouse button and then the modifier keys. You may need to zoom in further.

7   With the new rectangle copy still selected, Shift-click the first rectangle you just drew and the coffee sign and then choose Object > Group.

▶ **Tip:** Effects can be applied to objects in perspective. For instance, you could apply a 3D extrude effect (Effect > 3D > Extrude & Bevel) to the coffee sign group.

8   Holding down the Shift key, drag the sign group to the right so that it looks like it's attached to the building. The sign position does not have to match the figure below exactly.

9 Choose View > Fit Artboard In Window.

10 With the Perspective Selection tool, click to select the red rectangle representing the left side of the building. Choose Object > Perspective > Move Plane To Match Object.

11 Choose Select > Deselect.

▶ **Tip:** To return the left grid plane to the building face, you can also double-click the left grid plane control and change the Location to –.4 in, select Do Not Move, and then click OK.

Next, you'll move the medium gray rectangle that represents the left part of the second building into the proper position. In order to see a grid plane as you drag the rectangle into position, you can temporarily align the left grid plane to the object.

12 Press Ctrl++ (Windows) or Cmd++ (Mac OS) twice to zoom into the Perspective Grid and artwork.

13 With the Perspective Selection tool, click to select the medium gray rectangle behind the coffee sign, as shown in the figure below.

● **Note:** If it is difficult selecting the medium gray rectangle behind the coffee sign, you may need to choose View > Outline to select it by the edge, and then choose View > Preview.

14 Holding down the Shift key, position the pointer over the lower-right corner point on the medium gray rectangle. Release the Shift key.

The left grid plane is temporarily aligned with the medium gray rectangle, which means that you can draw or add content to the grid on that plane. You can position the pointer over any of the corner points while holding the Shift key to do the same thing.

● **Note:** Smart guides need to be turned on (View > Smart Guides) in order for you to position the plane automatically, using the Shift key.

15 Drag the middle, right point on the medium gray rectangle to the right, so that it aligns with the edge of the light gray rectangle.

● **Note:** You do not need to position the grid plane in order to resize or reposition an object in perspective, using the Perspective Selection tool.

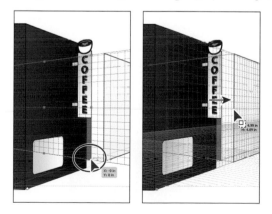

After dragging the rectangle, notice that the left grid plane returns to its original position. This is a way to temporarily reposition a grid plane.

16 Choose Select > Deselect, and then File > Save.

Automatic plane positioning

Using the automatic plane positioning options, you can select to move the active plane temporarily when you mouse over the anchor point or gridline intersection point by pressing the Shift key.

The automatic plane positioning options are available in the Perspective Grid Options dialog box. To display this dialog box, double-click the Perspective Grid tool (▦) or the Perspective Selection tool (▸) in the Tools panel.

—From Illustrator Help

Adding and editing text in perspective

You cannot directly add text to a perspective plane when the grid is visible. However, you can bring text into perspective after creating it in normal mode. Next, you will add a sign above one of the windows.

Note: You may want to zoom into the artwork by pressing Ctrl++ (Windows) or Cmd++ (Mac OS) twice.

1 Click the Layers panel icon (◆) to expand the Layers panel. In the Layers panel make sure that the Left face layer is selected. Click the Layers panel icon to collapse the panel again.

2 Select the Type tool (**T**) in the Tools panel.

3 Click in a blank space on the artboard and type **Coffee**.

Note: If you don't see the font formatting options in the Control panel, click the word Character in the Control panel to reveal the Character panel.

4 Select the text with the Type tool and change the Font to Myriad Pro, the Font Size to **48** pt, and the Font Style to Bold in the Control panel.

5 Select the Perspective Selection tool (▸) in the Tools panel. Press the number 1 on your keyboard to select the Left Grid, and then drag the text above the rounded rectangle window on the left wall.

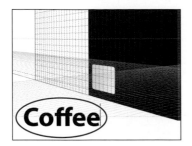

Create the Coffee text.

Drag the text into perspective.

Next, you will edit the text while it is in perspective.

6 With the text object still selected, double-click the text with the Perspective Selection tool. This enters isolation mode, allowing you to edit the text instead of the perspective object.

▶ **Tip:** You can also enter isolation mode to edit text by clicking the Edit Text button (⬛) in the Control panel.

7 In isolation mode, the Type tool (**T**) is selected automatically. Insert the cursor after the "Coffee" text, press the spacebar, and then type **Shop**. Press the Escape key twice to exit isolation mode and return to the perspective object.

▶ **Tip:** To exit isolation mode, you can also click the gray arrow twice that appears below the document tab at the top of the Document window.

8 Using the Perspective Selection tool, hold down the Shift key and drag the upper-right corner of the text object up and to the right, to make it a bit larger. We made the width approximately 3.8 in. Release the mouse button, and then the modifier key.

Edit the Coffee text.

Resize the text.

9 Click the Graphic Styles panel icon (⬛) on the right side of the workspace. With the text object selected, click the graphic style named "Text" in the Graphic Styles panel. Click the Graphic Styles panel icon to collapse the panel.

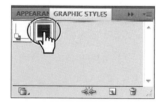

● **Note:** To learn more about working with graphic styles, see Lesson 13, "Applying Appearance Attributes and Graphic Styles."

This applies a 3D Extrude effect as well as strokes, fills, and a drop shadow effect to the text object. You can apply many kinds of effects, strokes, fills, and more to text in perspective.

10 Choose View > Fit Artboard In Window.

11 Press Ctrl+Shift+I (Windows) or Cmd+Shift+I (Mac OS) to temporarily hide the Perspective Grid.

12 Choose Select > Deselect, and then File > Save.

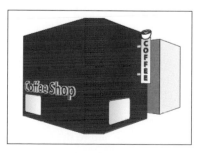

Working with symbols in perspective

● **Note:** To learn more about symbols, see Lesson 14, "Working with Symbols."

Adding symbols to a perspective plane when the grid is visible is a great way to add repeating items, such as windows. Like text, you can bring symbols into perspective after creating them in normal mode. Next, you will add some windows to the red building from a window symbol that is already created.

Adding Symbols to the Perspective Grid

1   Press Ctrl+Shift+I (Windows) or Cmd+Shift+I (Mac OS) to show the Perspective Grid and then press Ctrl++ (Windows) or Cmd++ (Mac OS) twice to zoom into the Perspective Grid and artwork.

2   Select the Perspective Selection tool (➤◉), and then click the left side of the red building on the left grid plane.

Next, you'll attach a window to the left plane grid and put it on the Left face layer.

● **Note:** Clicking the left side of the building does two things: it switches planes in the Plane Switching Widget to the left grid plane, and it selects the Left face layer in the Layers panel (because that is the layer that the red rectangle is on).

3   Click the Symbols panel icon (♣) on the right side of the workspace to expand the Symbols panel. Drag the window1 symbol from the Symbols panel onto the left face of the red building. Notice that it is not in perspective.

4   Drag the window with the Perspective Selection tool to above the Coffee Shop text to attach it to the left grid plane. Then, drag the window towards the upper-left corner of the left side of the red building. Snap it to the grid.

● **Note:** Make sure that the window is close to the top of the building, since you will be adding another row of windows below this one. See the figure for position.

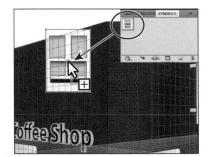

Drag the symbol onto the artboard.   Drag it into perspective.

Transforming Symbols in perspective

1   With the Perspective Selection tool (➤◉), double-click the window on the left grid plane. A dialog box appears, telling you that you are about to edit the symbol definition. This means that if you edit the content, it will change all of the window symbols on the artboard, which are called instances. Click OK.

2   Select the Selection tool (▶) in the Tools panel. Choose Select > All On Active Artboard. Holding down the Shift key, drag the lower-right corner of the window up and to the left, to make it smaller. When the measurement label shows a width of about .6 in, release the mouse button and then the Shift key.

3 Press the Escape key to exit isolation mode. Notice that the window is now smaller.

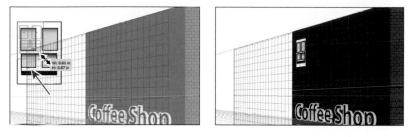

The window on the grid needs be aligned with the rounded rectangle window shape at the bottom of the building face. To do that, you will reposition the grid origin. If you shift the origin, the x and y coordinates of the horizontal plane and the x coordinate of vertical planes are affected. When you select an object in perspective while the grid is visible, the x and y coordinates displayed in the Transform and Info panels change with the shift in the origin.

4 Select the Perspective Selection tool in the Tools panel. Click to select the rounded rectangle window on the left side of the red building, below the Coffee Shop text. Choose Window > Transform to open the Transform panel. Notice the X and Y measurements.

5 Select the Perspective Grid tool (⊞)in the Tools panel. Position the pointer over the origin point at the bottom of the center, brick face of the red building on the grid. The cursor (▶) will show a small circle next to it. Drag the origin point to the lower-left corner of the red rectangle of the left grid plane.

▶ **Tip:** You can show rulers on the Perspective Grid by choosing View > Perspective Grid > Show Rulers. This shows you a ruler on each grid plane in the units set in the Define Grid dialog box.

This sets the 0,0 point (origin) for the x and y coordinates of the horizontal plane and the x coordinate of vertical planes to that new origin point.

6 Select the Perspective Selection tool in the Tools panel. Click to select the rounded rectangle window and then click the lower-left reference point in the Transform panel (▦). Change the X value to **.3 in**.

7 Select the window above the rounded rectangle and change the X value to **.3 in**. This will align the left edge of both objects to each other at a distance you specified from the origin.

● **Note:** To reset the origin point, you can select the Perspective Grid tool in the Tools panel, and double-click the origin point.

Drag the origin point.   Reposition the window.   Reposition the other window.

8 Close the Transform panel.

9 Holding down the Shift+Alt (Windows) or Shift+Option (Mac OS) keys, drag the window to the right until the measurement label shows approximately 1 inch for the dX. Release the mouse button, and then the keys. This creates a copy of the window in perspective.

10 Choose Object > Transform > Transform Again to repeat the transformation. Press Ctrl+D (Windows) or Cmd+D (Mac OS) once to repeat the transformation again. Notice that the copies are in perspective.

● **Note:** When you Shift-click the window(s) you may accidentally move them. If this happens, choose Edit > Undo Perspective Move and try again.

11 With the Perspective Selection tool, Shift-click the windows in a row to select them all.

12 Holding down the Shift+Alt (Windows) or Shift+Option (Mac OS) keys, drag the selected windows down, to just above the Coffee Shop text. Release the mouse button, and then release the modifier keys. This creates a copy of the windows in perspective, making a total of eight windows.

Drag a copy of the window.　　Repeat the transformation.　　Drag a copy of the windows.

13 Choose Select > Deselect.

14 With the Perspective Selection tool, starting above the left side of the red building, drag a marquee across the four windows on the right, above the word "Shop." Shift-click the red rectangle on the left grid plane to deselect it.

 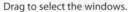

Drag to select the windows.　　Shift-click to deselect.

The next step requires several key commands in a precise order, so read carefully.

15 With the four windows selected, drag them to the right. Don't release the mouse button yet. Press the number 3 key to switch to the right grid plane. Hold down the Alt (Windows) or Option (Mac OS) key, and continue dragging the windows close to the upper-left corner of the right side of the red building. Try to align the left edges of the windows with the round rectangle on the right grid plane. When they are in position, release the mouse button, and then the modifier key. Leave the windows selected.

The copied windows are on another layer that is beneath the rectangle on the right side of the building. You need to move the copied windows to the same layer.

Drag and switch planes.   Drag a copy of the windows.

16 Choose Edit > Cut.

17 Click the Layers panel icon (⬢) on the right side of the workspace to expand the Layers panel. Click the Right face layer to select it.

18 Choose Edit > Paste In Place.

19 Choose Select > Deselect.

20 Choose View > Fit Artboard In Window, and then choose File > Save.

Release content from perspective

There will be times when you want to use objects that are currently in perspective elsewhere or you want to detach an object from a grid plane. Illustrator allows you to release an object from the associated perspective plane and make it available as normal artwork. That's what you'll do next.

1 With the Perspective Selection tool (⬛) selected, click to select the Coffee Shop text on the left side of the red building.

2 Choose Object > Perspective > Release With Perspective.

3 Choose Select > Deselect.

4　With the Perspective Selection tool, Shift-drag the left grid plane control to the left until the measurement label shows a distance of approximately –1 in. Release the mouse button, and then the modifier key. This shows that the Coffee Shop text does not move with the grid, since the text has been released from the grid.

5　Choose Edit > Undo Perspective Grid Edit, then choose Edit > Undo Release With Perspective.

6　In the Layers panel icon click the visibility column to the left of the Background layer to show it.

7　Choose Select > Deselect, then File > Save.

Exploring on your own

To explore more, you will create a sidewalk, and doors.

1　Click the Layers panel icon (⬦) to expand the panel. Click the Horizon layer to select it.

2　Select the Rectangle tool, and press the number 2 key to select the Horizontal Grid. Position the pointer about an inch below the bottom edge of the brick building face, and drag up to the horizon line. This will be a sidewalk. Select the Perspective Selection tool (▸) and drag the corner points of the rectangle so that it looks similar to the gray shape beneath the buildings in the figure below.

3　Change the Fill color of the sidewalk to a gray in the Control panel.

4　Click to select the Left face layer in the Layers panel.

5　With the Rectangle tool (▭), create a door for the red building on the left grid plane.

6　Choose File > Save, and then choose File > Close.

Review questions

1 There are three preset grids. Describe briefly what each could be used for.

2 How can you show or hide the Perspective Grid?

3 Before drawing content on a grid plane, what must be done to ensure that the object is on the correct grid plane?

4 Describe the steps required to move content from one grid plane to another.

5 What does double-clicking a grid plane control allow you to do?

6 How do you move an object perpendicular to the grid?

Review answers

1 A one-point perspective can be very useful for roads, railway tracks, or buildings viewed so that the front is directly facing the viewer. Two-point perspective is useful for drawing a cube, like a building, or two roads going off into the distance and typically has two vanishing points. Three-point perspective is usually used for buildings seen from above or below. In addition to vanishing points for each wall, there is a vanishing point showing those walls receding into the ground or high in space in three-point perspective.

2 You can hide or show the Perspective Grid by selecting the Perspective Grid tool (▦) in the Tools panel, by choosing View > Perspective Grid > Show Grid/Hide Grid, or by pressing Ctrl+Shift+I (Windows) or Cmd+Shift+I (Mac OS).

3 The correct grid plane must be selected by choosing it in the Plane Switching Widget, by using the following keyboard commands: Left Grid (1), Horizontal Grid (2), Right Grid (3), or No Active Grid (4), or selecting content on the grid you want to choose with the Perspective Selection tool (▶).

4 With the object(s) selected, begin dragging them, without releasing the mouse button yet. Press the number 1, 2, 3, or 4 key, (depending on which grid you intend to attach the object(s) to) to switch to the grid plane of your choice.

5 Double-clicking a grid plane control allows you to move the plane. You can specify whether to move the content associated with the plane, and whether to copy the content as the plane moves.

6 With the Perspective Selection tool, hold down the number 5 key, and drag the object perpendicular to the plane.

10 BLENDING COLORS AND SHAPES

Lesson overview

In this lesson, you'll learn how to do the following:

- Create and save gradients.

- Add colors to a gradient.

- Adjust the direction of a gradient blend.

- Adjust the opacity of color in a gradient blend.

- Create smooth-color blends between objects.

- Blend the shapes of objects in intermediate steps.

- Modify a blend, its path, shape, and color.

 This lesson will take approximately an hour to complete. If needed, remove the previous lesson folder from your hard disk and copy the Lesson10 folder onto it.

Gradient fills are graduated blends of two or more colors. Using the Gradient tool and Gradient panel, you can create or modify a gradient fill. With the Blend tool, you can blend the shapes and colors of objects together into a new blended object, or a series of intermediate shapes.

Getting started

You'll explore various ways to create your own color gradients, and blend colors and shapes together using the Gradient panel and the Blend tool.

Before you begin, you'll restore the default preferences for Adobe® Illustrator® CS5. Then you'll open the finished art file for this lesson to see what you'll create.

1   To ensure that the tools and panels function as described in this lesson, delete or rename the Adobe Illustrator CS5 preferences file. See "Restoring default preferences" on page 3.

2   Start Adobe Illustrator CS5.

● **Note:** If you have not already done so, copy the resource files for this lesson onto your hard disk from the Lesson10 folder on the Adobe Illustrator CS5 Classroom in a Book CD. See "Copying the Classroom in a Book files" on page 2.

3   Choose File > Open, and open the L10end_1.ai file in the Lesson10 folder, located in the Lessons folder on your hard disk.

The text, background, steam, and coffee liquid are all filled with gradients. The objects that make up the colored beans on the coffee cup, and the coffee beans to the left of the cup, have been blended to create new objects.

4   Choose View > Zoom Out to make the finished artwork smaller, if you want to leave it on your screen as you work. (Use the Hand tool (✋) to move the artwork where you want it in the window.) If you don't want to leave the image open, choose File > Close.

To begin working, you'll open an existing art file.

5   Choose File > Open, and open the L10start_1.ai file in the Lesson10 folder, located in the Lessons folder on your hard disk.

6   Choose File > Save As, name the file **coffee.ai**, and select the Lesson10 folder in the Save In menu. Leave the Save As Type option set to Adobe Illustrator (*.AI) (Windows) or the Format option set to Adobe Illustrator (ai) (Mac OS), and then click Save. In the Illustrator Options dialog box, leave the Illustrator options at their default settings, and then click OK.

Working with gradients

A gradient fill is a graduated blend between two or more colors. You can create your own gradients, or you can use the gradients provided with Adobe Illustrator, and then edit them and save them as swatches for later use.

You can use the Gradient panel (Window > Gradient) or the Gradient tool (▣) to apply, create, and modify gradients. In the Gradient panel, the Gradient Fill box displays the current gradient colors and gradient type. When you click the Gradient Fill box, the selected object is filled with the gradient. The Gradient menu (▣) lists the default and saved gradients.

A. Gradient Fill box	**F.** Location
B. Reverse Gradient	**G.** Gradient type
C. Gradient slider	**H.** Aspect ratio
D. Color stop	**I.** Angle
E. Opacity	**J.** Delete Stop

By default, the panel includes a start and end color stop. You can add more color stops by clicking below the gradient slider. Double-clicking a color stop opens a panel where you can choose a color from swatches, color sliders, or the eyedropper.

In the Gradient panel, the left gradient stop under the gradient slider marks the starting color; the right gradient stop marks the ending color. A gradient stop is the point at which a gradient changes from one color to the next.

Creating and applying a linear gradient

To begin the lesson, you'll create a gradient fill for the background.

1   Choose Essentials from the workspace switcher in the Application bar.

2   Choose View > Fit Artboard In Window.

3   Using the Selection tool (▶), click to select the larger, top rectangle with rounded corners in the background of the artboard.

The background is painted with a brown color fill and a red stroke, as shown in the Fill and Stroke boxes toward the bottom of the Tools panel. The Gradient box below the Fill and Stroke boxes shows the last used gradient. The default gradient fill is a black-and-white gradient. If you select a gradient-filled object or a gradient swatch in the Swatches panel, the gradient fill in the Tools panel changes to the fill of the selected object or swatch.

4 Click the Gradient box (▣) near the bottom of the Tools panel.

The default black-and-white gradient appears in the Fill box, and is applied to the fill of the selected background shape.

5 Choose Window > Gradient if the Gradient panel is not visible on the right side of the workspace.

6 In the Gradient panel, double-click the white, leftmost gradient stop to select the starting color of the gradient. The tip of the gradient stop appears darker to indicate that it's selected.

A new panel appears when you double-click a color stop. In this panel, you can change the color of the stop, using swatches or the Color panel.

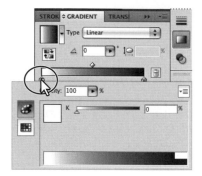

7 In the panel that appears below the Gradient panel, click the Swatches button (▦). Click to select the swatch named Light Brown. Notice the gradient change on the artboard. Press Escape or click in a blank area of the Gradient panel to return to the Gradient panel.

8 Double-click the black color stop in the Gradient panel to edit the color.

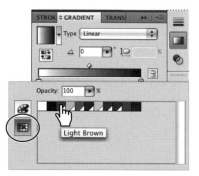

▶ **Tip:** To move between text fields, press Tab. Press Enter or Return to apply the last value typed.

9 In the panel that appears below the Gradient panel, click the Color button (🎨) to open the Color panel. Choose CMYK from the Color panel menu (▾☰) if it is not already showing. Change the values to C=**45**, M=**62**, Y=**82**, and K=**44**. Press Escape or click in a blank area of the Gradient panel to return to the Gradient panel.

Next, you'll save the gradient in the Swatches panel.

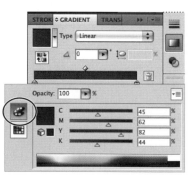

10 To save the gradient, click the Gradient menu button (⧉), and then click the Add To Swatches button (💾) at the bottom of the panel that appears.

The Gradient menu lists all the default and pre-saved gradients that you can choose.

Next, you will rename the gradient swatch in the Swatches panel.

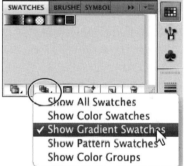

▶ Tip: You can save a gradient by selecting an object with a gradient fill, clicking the Fill box in the Tools panel, and then clicking the New Swatch button (🔲) at the bottom of the Swatches panel.

11 Click the Swatches panel icon on the right side of the workspace to open the Swatches panel. In the Swatches panel, double-click New Gradient Swatch 1 to open the Swatch Options dialog box. Type **Background** in the Swatch Name field, and then click OK.

12 To display only gradient swatches in the Swatches panel, click the Show Swatch Kinds Menu button (🔳) at the bottom of the Swatches panel, and choose Show Gradient Swatches from the menu.

13 With the rectangle still selected in the artboard, try some of the different gradients by clicking them in the Swatches panel. Click the Background gradient you just saved to make sure it is applied before continuing to the next step.

Show All Swatches
Show Color Swatches
✓ Show Gradient Swatches
Show Pattern Swatches
Show Color Groups

Notice that some of the gradients have several colors. You'll learn how to make a gradient with multiple colors later in this lesson.

14 Click the Show Swatch Kinds Menu button (🔳) at the bottom of the Swatches panel and choose Show All Swatches from the menu.

15 Choose Select > Deselect.

16 Choose File > Save.

Adjusting the direction and angle of a gradient blend

Once you have painted an object with a gradient fill, you can adjust the direction, origin, and the beginning and end points of the gradient using the Gradient tool.

Now, you'll adjust the gradient fill in the background shape.

1 Use the Selection tool (◣) to select the same rectangle in the background.

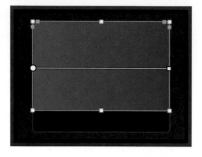

2 Select the Gradient tool (▮▮) in the Tools panel.

The Gradient tool works only on selected objects that are filled with a gradient. Notice the horizontal gradient annotator (bar) that appears in the middle of the rectangle. The bar indicates the direction of the gradient. The larger circle shows the starting point of the gradient, and the smaller square is the ending point.

▶ **Tip:** You can hide the gradient annotator (bar) by choosing View > Hide Gradient Annotator. To show it again, choose View > Show Gradient Annotator.

● **Note:** If you move the pointer to different areas of the gradient slider, the appearance of the pointer may change. This indicates that different functionality has been activated.

3 Position the pointer over the gradient annotator. It turns into the gradient slider, much like the one in the Gradient panel. You can use the gradient slider to edit gradient colors and more, without opening the Gradient panel.

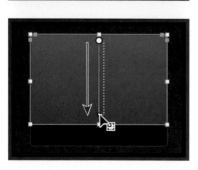

4 With the Gradient tool, Shift-click the top of the rectangle and drag down to change the position and direction of the starting and ending colors of the gradient.

Holding down the Shift key constrains the gradient to 45 degree angles.

Practice changing the gradient in the rectangle. For example, drag inside the rectangle to create a short gradient with distinct color blends; drag a longer distance outside the rectangle to create a longer gradient with more subtle color blends. You can also drag up to transpose the colors and reverse the direction of the blend.

Next, you will rotate and reposition the gradient.

5   With the Gradient tool, position the
    pointer just off the small white square at
    the bottom of the gradient annotator. A
    rotation icon (⟳) appears. Drag to the right
    to rotate the gradient in the rectangle.

    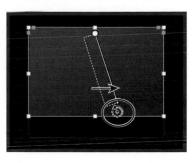

    The gradient annotator and the gradient
    rotate, but the gradient bar stays in the
    center of the rectangle when you release
    the mouse button.

Next, you will change the rotation in the Gradient panel.

6   Click the Gradient icon (▭) on the right side
    of the workspace to show the Gradient panel,
    if it isn't already showing. Change the rotation
    angle in the Angle field to **−90**, to return the
    gradient to vertical. Press Enter or Return to set
    the value.

    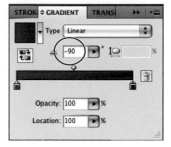

7   With the background rectangle still selected,
    choose Object > Lock > Selection.

8   Choose File > Save.

● **Note:** Entering the
gradient rotation in
the Gradient panel,
rather than adjusting it
directly on the artboard,
is useful when you want
to achieve consistency
and precision.

Creating a radial gradient

You can create linear or radial gradients. Both types of gradient have a starting and
ending color. With a radial gradient, the starting color (leftmost color stop) of the
gradient defines the center point of the fill, which radiates outward to the ending
color (rightmost color stop). Next, you will create and edit a radial gradient.

1   Open the Layers panel by clicking the
    Layers panel icon (◉) on the right side of
    the workspace. Click to select the Visibility
    column to the left of the Coffee Cup layer (you
    may need to scroll in the Layers panel).

    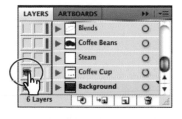

2   Use the Selection tool (▶) to select the
    brown-filled ellipse at the top of the coffee
    cup. This is the coffee in the cup.

3   Select the Zoom tool (🔍) in the Tools panel
    and click the coffee cup several times to
    zoom in.

4 With the ellipse selected, click the Gradient box (◼) at the bottom of the Tools panel to apply the last selected gradient (the Background gradient). The Gradient panel appears on the right side of the workspace.

The linear gradient that you created and saved earlier fills the ellipse. Next, you will change the linear gradient to a radial gradient, and then edit it.

5 In the Gradient panel, choose Radial from the Type menu to convert the gradient to a radial gradient. Keep the ellipse selected.

Changing colors and adjusting the gradient

Once you have filled an object with a gradient, you can use the Gradient tool to add or edit the gradients, including changing the direction, color, and origin. You can also move the start and end points of a gradient.

Next, you will use the Gradient tool to adjust the color of each color stop.

1 With the Zoom tool (🔍) selected, click once to zoom into the ellipse at the top of the coffee cup.

2 With the Gradient tool (▭), position the pointer over the gradient bar to reveal the gradient slider, which has a dashed circle around it, indicating that it is a radial gradient. Double-click the rightmost color stop to edit the color. In the panel that appears, click the Color button (🎨), if it's not already selected.

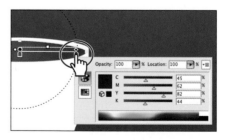

3 Shift-click the Cyan slider and drag a bit to the right to darken the color overall. Press Escape to close the panel.

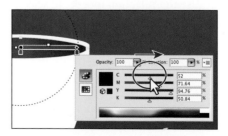

4 In the gradient slider, double-click the leftmost color stop. In the panel that appears, click the Color button (![icon]) and change the tint to 50% by dragging the tint slider to the left (or by typing **50** into the Tint field). Press Escape to close the panel.

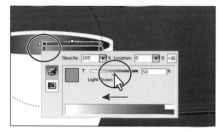

Next, you will change the aspect ratio, origin, and radius for the gradient.

5 In the Gradient panel, change Aspect Ratio to **20**, and press Enter or Return to set the ratio.

● **Note:** The aspect ratio is a value between 0.5 and 32767%. As the aspect ratio gets smaller, the ellipse flattens and widens.

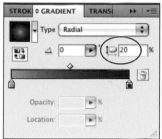

The aspect ratio changes a radial gradient into an elliptical gradient. This makes the coffee appear more realistic.

Next, you will edit the aspect ratio using the Gradient tool.

6 With the Gradient tool, click the top black circle on the dotted path and drag up to change the aspect ratio.

When you release the mouse button, notice the gradient in the ellipse on the artboard. If the Gradient panel isn't showing, click the Gradient panel icon. The Aspect Ratio is now larger than the 20 set previously.

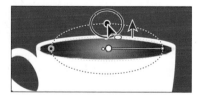

7 Drag the top black circle on the dotted path back down so that the Aspect Ratio is roughly 14% in the Gradient panel.

Next, you will drag the gradient slider to reposition the gradient in the ellipse.

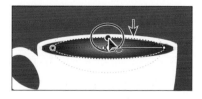

8 With the Gradient tool, click the gradient slider and drag down a little bit to move the gradient in the ellipse.

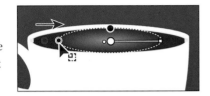

9 Choose Edit > Undo Gradient to move it back.

10 Choose File > Save.

You will now change the radius and origin of the gradient.

▶ **Tip:** To change the radius, you can also drag the second color stop to the right or left.

11 With the Gradient tool, position the pointer over the ellipse to reveal the gradient slider. Click the black circle on the left of the dotted path and drag to the right to make the radius smaller. This shortens the transition between the leftmost and rightmost color stops.

Try dragging the black circle on the left of the dotted path to the left and to the right to see the effect on the gradient. Make sure to drag it to match the figure above once you are done experimenting.

Next, you'll change the origin of the gradient.

12 With the Gradient tool, click the small white dot to the left of the leftmost color stop and drag to the left. This dot repositions the center of the gradient (the leftmost color stop) without moving the entire gradient bar, and changes the radius of the gradient.

Every gradient has at least two color stops. By editing the color mix of each stop and by adding color stops either in the Gradient panel or using the Gradient tool, you can create custom gradients.

Now, you'll add a third color to the coffee ellipse, and then you'll edit it.

13 With the Gradient tool, position the pointer slightly below the bottom edge of the gradient slider. The pointer changes to a white arrow with a plus sign (⬚₊). Click just below the middle of the gradient slider to add another color stop.

14 Double-click the new color stop to edit the color. In the panel that appears, click the Swatches button (▦), and select the Brown swatch. Press Escape to close the panel.

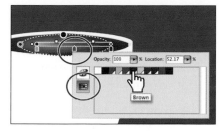

Now that you have three color stops, you will adjust the colors by reordering them.

15 With the Gradient tool, click the leftmost color stop and drag to the right, stopping before the middle color stop.

16 Drag the middle color stop all the way to the left end of the gradient slider to swap the two colors.

Drag the leftmost color stop to the right, and the middle color stop to the left.

17 Choose Select > Deselect, and then File > Save.

Applying gradients to multiple objects

You can apply a gradient to multiple objects by first selecting all the objects, then applying a gradient color, and then dragging across the objects with the Gradient tool.

Now, you'll paint type that has been converted to path outlines with a linear gradient fill, and then edit the colors in it.

1 Choose View > Fit Artboard In Window.

2 Click the Layers panel icon (◉) to open the Layers panel. Click to select the Visibility column to the left of the Logo layer (you may need to scroll up in the Layers panel). Click the eye icon (👁) to the left of the Background layer to deselect visibility for that layer.

● **Note:** The text, coffee beans, and ellipse are still showing.

● **Note:** To convert type to path outlines, select it with the Selection tool, and choose Type > Create Outlines. See Lesson 7, "Working with Type," for more information.

● **Note:** Notice that each letter is filled with the gradient independently. You can adjust this with the Gradient tool.

3 Use the Selection tool (▶) and click to select the text, "Mike's Coffee."

The Mike's Coffee type has already been converted to path outlines so that you can fill it with a gradient.

The Mike's Coffee shapes are grouped together. By grouping the letters, you can fill each letter at once with the same gradient. Grouping them also lets you edit the gradient fill globally.

4 Click the Gradient panel icon (◼) on the right side of the workspace to open the Gradient panel. Click the Gradient menu button (▯), and then select Linear Gradient from the Gradient menu. This applies a white-to-black gradient.

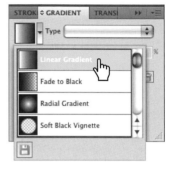

5 In the Gradient panel, double-click the leftmost color stop to select it, so that you can adjust the starting color of the gradient. Click the Swatches button (▦), and select the Light Red swatch. Press Escape to close the panel.

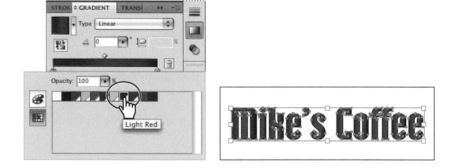

Now, you'll adjust the gradient on the letters so that it blends across all the letters, and then add intermediate colors to the gradient to create a fill with multiple blends between colors.

6 Select the Gradient tool (◼) in the Tools panel. Shift-click the letters and drag across them from top to bottom, as shown in the figure below, to apply the gradient to all the letters.

Next, you will add a color to the gradient by adding a color stop. When you add a color stop, a new diamond appears above the gradient slider to mark the color's new midpoint.

7 In the Gradient panel, click the color bar below the gradient slider to add a stop between the other gradient stops.

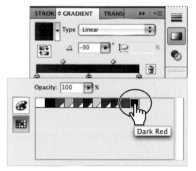

8 Double-click the new color stop to edit the color. In the panel that appears, click the Swatches button and select the Dark Red swatch. Press Escape to close the panel.

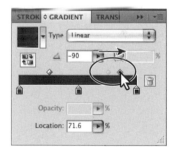

9 To adjust the midpoint between colors, drag the diamond icon between the dark red and black color stops to the right. This gives the gradient more red and less black.

● **Note:** You can delete a color in a gradient by dragging its gradient stop downward and out of the Gradient panel.

Next, you will reverse the gradient colors.

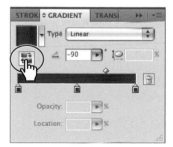

10 With the text still selected, click the Reverse Gradient button (⊞) in the Gradient panel. The leftmost and rightmost color stops switch positions. You can also reverse the colors in a gradient by drawing in the opposite direction with the Gradient tool.

Another way to apply a color to a gradient is to sample the color from the artwork, using the Eyedropper tool, or drag a color swatch onto a color stop.

11 Click the center gradient stop in the Gradient panel.

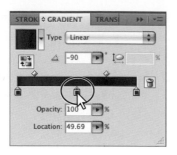

12 Select the Eyedropper tool () in the Tools panel. In the artwork, Shift-click the coffee bean on the far right of where the coffee cup was.

Shift-clicking with the Eyedropper tool applies the color sample to the selected gradient box in the gradient, rather than replacing the entire gradient with the color in the selected artwork. Try sampling other areas of the artwork, finishing with the purple-brown color in the rightmost coffee bean.

Next, you'll save the new gradient.

13 Click the Gradient menu button (), and then click the Add To Swatches button () at the bottom of the panel that appears.

14 Open the Layers panel by clicking the Layers panel icon on the right side of the workspace. Click to select the Visibility column to the left of the Background layer.

15 Choose Select > Deselect, and then File > Save.

Adding transparency to gradients

You can define the opacity of colors used in gradients. By specifying different opacity values for the different color stops in your gradient, you can create gradients that fade in or out and show or hide underlying images. Next, you will create a mirror reflection of the coffee cup and apply a gradient that fades to transparent.

1 Using the Selection tool (▶), click to select the coffee cup.

2 Choose Object > Transform > Transform Each. In the Transform Each dialog box, click the bottom, middle point of the reference point locator (▦). Select Reflect X and change Rotate Angle to **180**. Select Preview to see the changes. Click Copy to reflect, rotate, and copy the coffee cup.

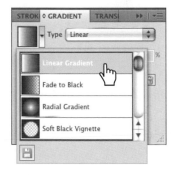

3 With the copy of the coffee cup still selected, open the Gradient panel by clicking the Gradient panel icon. Click the Gradient menu button (▤), and then select Linear Gradient. This fills the coffee cup with a white-to-black gradient.

▶ **Tip:** There are two gradients with transparency, Fade To Black and Soft Black Vignette in this document. These are great starting points for fading to transparency.

4 In the Angle field, change the value to **−90**. Double-click the rightmost color stop (the black color). In the panel that appears, click the Swatches button (▦) and select the white color swatch.

5 Press Escape or click in a blank area of the Gradient panel to return to the Gradient panel.

● **Note:** You'll see the purpose of the white to white gradient in the next step, when you will change the transparency of the rightmost color stop to 0%, so that the coffee cup appears to fade away.

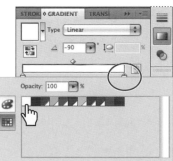

6 Click the rightmost color stop. Type **0** in the Opacity field or click the arrow to the right of the field and drag the slider all the way to the left. Press Enter or Return.

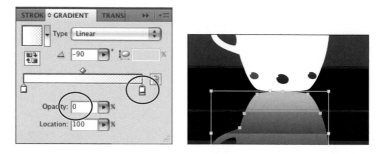

7 Click the leftmost color stop in the Gradient panel and change Opacity to **70**.

8 Select the Gradient tool () in the Tools panel. Holding down the Shift key, drag from the top of the selected coffee cup reflection to just above the outer edge of the dark red rectangle in the background.

You can have a lot of creative fun working with gradients and transparency. Try changing the opacity for the color stops in the coffee cup and changing the direction and distance with the Gradient tool.

9 Choose Select > Deselect.

10 Click the Gradient panel icon (⬛) on the right side of the workspace to collapse the Gradient panel.

11 Choose File > Save.

Working with blended objects

You can blend two distinct objects to create and distribute shapes evenly between two objects. The two shapes you blend can be the same or different. You can also blend between two open paths to create a smooth transition of color between objects, or you can combine blends of colors and objects to create color transitions in the shape of a particular object.

When you create a blend, the blended objects are treated as one object, called a blend object. If you move one of the original objects, or edit the anchor points of the original object, the blend changes accordingly. You can also expand the blend to divide it into distinct objects.

Blend between two of the same shape

Blend between same shape, different colors

Blend between two different shapes and colors

Blend along a path

Smooth color blend between two stroked lines

Blend options for the Blend tool

There are three types of spacing options for a blend: Smooth Color, Specified Steps, and Specified Distance. Each is explained below:

- **Smooth Color:** Lets Illustrator auto-calculate the number of steps for the blends. If objects are filled or stroked with different colors, the steps are calculated to provide the optimum number of steps for a smooth color transition. If the objects contain identical colors, or if they contain gradients or patterns, the number of steps is based on the longest distance between the bounding box edges of the two objects.

- **Specified Steps:** Controls the number of steps between the start and end of the blend.

- **Specified Distance:** Controls the distance between the steps in the blend. The distance specified is measured from the edge of one object to the corresponding edge on the next object (for example, from the rightmost edge of one object to the rightmost edge of the next). The Orientation options determine the orientation of blended objects.

- **Align to Page**: Orients the blend perpendicular to the x axis of the page.

- **Align to Path**: Orients the blend perpendicular to the path.

—From Illustrator Help

Creating a blend with specified steps

Now, you'll use the Blend tool to create a series of blended shapes. You'll use three different-colored shapes that make up the design on the coffee cup by specifying the number of steps in the blend.

1 Double-click the Blend tool (🖎) in the Tools panel to open the Blend Options dialog box.

2 Choose Specified Steps from the Spacing menu, and change the number of steps to **2**. Click OK.

▶ **Tip:** You can also make a blend by selecting objects and choosing Object > Blend > Make.

3 Using the Blend tool, position the pointer over the coffee bean on the far left. Click when the pointer displays an X (🖎ₓ). Then, hover over the red coffee bean in the middle until the pointer displays a plus sign (🖎₊), indicating that you can add an object to the blend. Click the red coffee bean to add it. There is now a blend between these two objects.

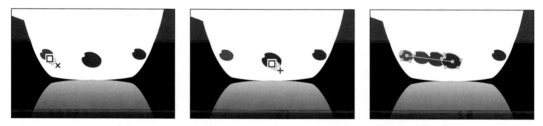

4 Click the rightmost coffee bean with the Blend tool pointer (displaying the plus sign) to add it to the blend and complete the blended path.

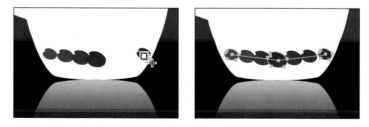

● **Note:** To end the current path and continue blending other objects on a separate path, first click the Blend tool in the Tools panel, and then click the other objects.

Modifying the blend

Now, you'll modify the blend object using the Blend Options dialog box. You'll also use the Convert Anchor Point tool to edit the shape of the path, called the spine, that the coffee beans blend along.

1   With the blended beans still selected, choose Object > Blend > Blend Options. In the Blend Options dialog box, change the Specified Steps to **1**, and then click OK.

▶ **Tip:** To edit the blend options for an object, you can also select the blend, and then double-click the Blend tool.

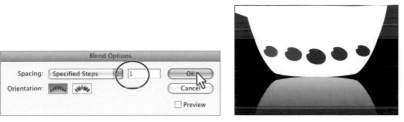

2   Choose Select > Deselect.

3   Select the Direct Selection tool (⟨⟩) in the Tools panel. Click the center of the red, center coffee bean to select that anchor point. In the Control panel, click the Convert Selected Anchor Points To Smooth button (⌐) to smooth the curve. With the Direct Selection tool, drag the anchor point down.

● **Note:** You are editing the spine. However you edit the spine, the blend objects will follow.

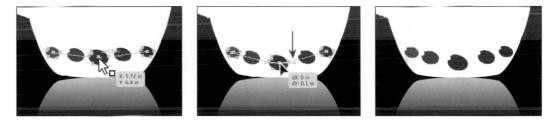

To edit the spine of a blend, select the anchor point, convert it to a smooth point, and drag.

4   Choose Select > Deselect.

▶ **Tip:** A quick way to reshape the spine of a blend is to wrap it around another path or object. Select the blend, select the other object or path, and then choose Object > Blend > Replace Spine.

You can modify the blend instantly by changing the shape, color, or position of the original objects. Next, you will edit the color and position of the middle, red coffee bean and see the effect on the blend.

▶ **Tip:** When you converted the bottom anchor point to a smooth point, the spacing changed between the coffee beans. To even out the spacing, convert the leftmost and rightmost anchor points on the spine to smooth points and then adjust the direction lines with the Direct Selection tool.

5   Select the Zoom tool (🔍) in the Tools panel and drag a marquee across the beans to zoom in on them.

6 With the Selection tool (▶), click the blended objects to select them.

7 Double-click the red coffee bean in the center of the blend to enter isolation mode. This temporarily ungroups the blended objects and lets you edit each original bean (not the beans created by blending), as well as the spine. Click to select the red coffee bean.

8 Choose View > Outline to see the pieces of the blend. Choose View > Preview to see the filled objects again.

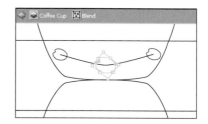

9 Change the fill color of the selected bean to the swatch called Light Green in the Control panel. Notice that the rest of the blend changes.

10 With the Selection tool, press Shift+Alt (Windows) or Shift+Option (Mac OS), and drag a corner bounding point of the selected coffee bean to make the bean bigger.

Try changing the shape of the coffee bean by rotating it and using the Direct Selection tool (▷).

11 Press Escape to exit isolation mode.

12 With the Selection tool, click to select the blended objects again. Choose Object > Blend > Reverse Spine. This reverses the order of the beans. Keep the blended objects selected.

The blended objects are considered a single blend object. If you need to edit all the coffee beans (including the beans that the blend created), you can expand the blend. Expanding the blend converts the blend to individual objects. You can no longer edit the blend as a single object because it has become a group of beans.

Next, you will expand the beans.

13 Choose Object > Blend > Expand. With the beans still selected, notice the word Group on the left side of the Control panel.

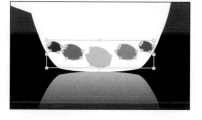

The blend is now a group of individual shapes that you can edit independently.

14 Choose Select > Deselect.

15 Choose File > Save.

Creating smooth color blends

You can choose several options for blending the shapes and colors of objects to create a new object. When you choose the Smooth Color blend option, Illustrator combines the shapes and colors of the objects into many intermediate steps, creating a smooth graduated blend between the original objects.

Now, you'll combine two shapes for a coffee bean into a smooth color blend.

1 Chose View > Fit Artboard In Window.

2 Expand the Layers panel, and click to select the Visibility column to the left of the Blends layer and the Coffee Beans layer.

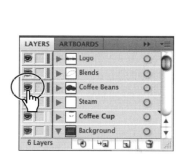

You are going to blend colors to make the coffee bean look more realistic.

3 Click the eye icon (👁) to deselect visibility for the Coffee Beans layer, so that it's easier to see the two objects you will blend next. Leave the Layers panel expanded, unless it gets in the way.

4 Select the Zoom tool (🔍) in the Tools panel and drag a marquee around the curved lines that appear to the left of the coffee cup.

5 Double-click the Blend tool (🝏) in the Tools panel to open the Blend Options dialog box.

6 Choose Smooth Color from the Spacing menu to set up the blend options, which remain set until you change them. Click OK.

▶ **Tip:** To release, or remove, a blend from the original objects, select the blend and choose Object > Blend > Release.

Next, you'll create a smooth color blend from the two lines to the left of the coffee cup. Both objects have a stroke and no fill. Objects that have strokes blend differently than those that have no stroke.

7 Position the Blend tool pointer over the top line until it displays an X (⊡ₓ), then click. Click the bottom line with the Blend tool pointer that displays a plus sign (⊡₊) to add it to the blend. You've created a smooth blend between the lines.

8 Choose Select > Deselect.

▶ **Tip:** Creating smooth color blends between paths can be difficult in certain situations. For instance, if the lines intersect or the lines are too curved, unexpected results can occur.

When you make a smooth color blend between objects, Illustrator automatically calculates the number of intermediate steps necessary to create the transition between the objects. Once you've applied a smooth color blend to objects, you can edit it. Next, you will edit the paths that make up the blend.

9 Using the Selection tool (▶), double-click the color blend to enter isolation mode. Click to select one of the paths, and change the stroke color in the Control panel to any color you want. Notice how the colors are blended. Choose Edit > Undo Apply Swatch to return to the original stroke color.

10 Double-click away from the blend paths to exit isolation mode.

11 In the Layers panel, click to select visibility for the Coffee Beans layer and the Steam layer to make those objects visible on the artboard.

12 To complete the bean, select the blended paths with the Selection tool and choose Edit > Copy, and then Edit > Paste to paste a copy of the blend.

13 Move the blend to the bottom part of the same coffee bean, to the left of the coffee cup.

14 Select the Rotate tool (⟳) in the Tools panel. Drag to rotate the blend so that it fits into the bottom part of the bean. You will need to switch to the Selection tool to move the blend into position.

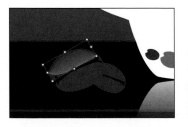
Copy the blend.

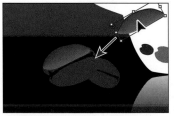
Paste and move into position.

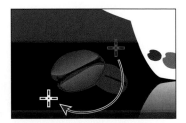
Rotate and position the blend.

15 Choose View > Fit Artboard In Window.

16 Choose Select > Deselect, and then File > Save.

Exploring on your own

There are many ways to be creative with gradients and blends. To explore more, you will create a blend for coffee steam. Then you'll create a new document for a more complex path that you will blend.

1   With the Steam layer visible, select the steam on the artboard with the Selection tool (▶).

2   Choose Essentials from the workspace switcher in the Application bar.

3   Expand the Gradient panel and select Fade To Black from the Gradient menu.

4   Select the Gradient tool (▬) in the Tools panel and position the pointer over the steam. Drag from the top of the steam to the bottom of the steam to change the direction of the gradient.

5   Add a color stop so that three appear in the gradient slider.

6   Change the color of each color stop to white by double-clicking each, using the Gradient tool. Change Opacity to **10** for the topmost color stop and **5** for the bottommost color stop.

Try changing the color and opacity of each color stop.

7   Choose File > Save, then File > Close.

Next, you'll create a more complex blend.

1   Choose File > New to create a new document. Draw a straight line using the Line Segment tool.

2   Select the line, remove the fill, paint the stroke with a color, and increase the stroke weight to **20** pt.

3   If the Stroke panel is not showing, choose Window > Stroke. With the line selected, select the Dashed Line option. Type **25** in the first dash field, and press Enter or Return.

4   Choose Object > Path > Outline Stroke.

Notice that the stroke color and fill color values have switched, so now you can fill the object with a gradient.

5   Fill the object with a gradient of your choice.

6   Copy and paste the object, moving them apart with the Selection tool. Double-click the Blend tool (▣) in the Tools panel. Choose Smooth Color in the Blend Options dialog box and click OK. Click each of the two objects with the Blend tool to create the blend. Practice editing the individual objects in the blend.

Review questions

1 What is a gradient fill?

2 Name two ways to fill a selected object with a gradient.

3 What is the difference between a gradient fill and a blend?

4 How do you adjust the blend between colors in a gradient?

5 Name two ways you can add colors to a gradient.

6 How do you adjust the direction of a gradient?

7 Describe two ways to blend the shapes and colors of objects.

8 What is the difference between selecting a smooth color blend and specifying the number of steps in a blend?

9 How do you adjust the shapes or colors in the blend? How do you adjust the path of the blend?

Review answers

1 A gradient fill is a graduated blend between two or more colors, or between tints of the same color.

2 Select an object and do one of the following:

- Click the Gradient box in the Tools panel to fill an object with the default white-to-black gradient or with the last selected gradient.

- Click a gradient swatch in the Swatches panel.

- Make a new gradient by clicking a gradient swatch in the Swatches panel and mixing your own in the Gradient panel.

- Use the Eyedropper tool to sample a gradient from an object in your artwork, and then apply it to the selected object.

3 The difference between a gradient fill and a blend is the way that colors combine together—colors blend together within a gradient fill and between objects in a blend.

4 You drag the diamond icons or color stops of the gradient in the Gradient panel.

5 In the Gradient panel, click beneath the gradient bar to add a gradient stop to the gradient. Then use the Color panel to mix a new color or, in the Swatches panel,

Alt-click (Windows) or Option-click (Mac OS) a color swatch. You can select the Gradient tool in the Tools panel and position the pointer over the gradient-filled object. You can also click beneath the gradient slider that appears in the Gradient panel or in the artwork with the Gradient tool selected, to add a color stop.

6 Drag with the Gradient tool to adjust the direction of a gradient. Dragging a long distance changes colors gradually; dragging a short distance makes the color change more abrupt. You can also rotate the gradient using the Gradient tool, and change the radius, aspect ratio, and starting point.

7 You can blend the shapes and colors of objects by doing one of the following:

   • Clicking each object with the Blend tool to create a blend of intermediate steps between the objects, according to preset blend options.

   • Selecting the objects and choosing Object > Blend > Blend Options to set the number of intermediate steps, and then choosing Object > Blend > Make to create the blend.

   Objects that have painted strokes blend differently than those with no strokes.

8 When you choose Smooth Color blend, Illustrator automatically calculates the number of intermediate steps necessary to create a seamlessly smooth blend between the selected objects. Specifying the number of steps lets you determine how many intermediate steps are visible in the blend. You can also specify the distance between intermediate steps in the blend.

9 You can use the Direct Selection tool to select and adjust the shape of an original object, thus changing the shape of the blend. You can change the colors of the original objects to adjust the intermediate colors in the blend. Use the Convert Anchor Point tool to change the shape of the path, or spine, of the blend by dragging anchor points or direction handles on the spine.

11

WORKING WITH BRUSHES

Lesson overview

In this lesson, you'll learn how to do the following:

- Use the four brush types: Art, Calligraphic, Pattern, and Bristle.

- Apply brushes to paths created with drawing tools.

- Paint and edit paths with the Paintbrush tool.

- Change the brush color and adjust brush settings.

- Create new brushes from Adobe® Illustrator® artwork.

- Work with the Blob Brush tool and the Eraser tool.

 This lesson takes approximately an hour to complete. If needed, remove the previous lesson folder from your hard disk and copy the Lesson11 folder onto it.

The variety of brush types in Adobe Illustrator CS5 lets you create a myriad of effects simply by painting or drawing using the Paintbrush tool or the drawing tools. You can work with the Blob Brush tool, as well as choose from the Art, Calligraphic, Pattern, Bristle, and Scatter brushes, or create new ones based on your artwork.

Getting started

In this lesson, you will learn how to work with the Blob Brush tool and the Eraser tool. You will also learn how to use the four brush types in the Brushes panel, and change brush options and create your own brushes. Before you begin, you'll restore the default preferences for Adobe Illustrator CS5. Then you'll open the finished art file for the first part of this lesson to see the finished artwork.

1 To ensure that the tools and panels function as described in this lesson, delete or deactivate (by renaming) the Adobe Illustrator CS5 preferences file. See "Restoring default preferences" on page 3.

2 Start Adobe Illustrator CS5.

● **Note:** If you have not already done so, copy the resource files for this lesson onto your hard disk, from the Lesson11 folder on the Adobe Illustrator CS5 Classroom in a Book CD. See "Copying the Classroom in a Book files" on page 2.

3 Choose File > Open, and open the L11end_1.ai file in the Lesson11 folder, located in the Lessons folder on your hard disk.

4 If you like, choose View > Zoom Out to make the finished artwork smaller, and then adjust the window size and leave the artwork on your screen as you work. (Use the Hand tool (✋))
to move the artwork where you want it in the Document window.) If you don't want to leave the artwork open, choose File > Close.

To begin working, you'll open an existing art file.

5 Choose File > Open to open the L11start_1.ai file in the Lesson11 folder in the Lessons folder on your hard disk.

6 Choose File > Save As. In the Save As dialog box, name the file **bookcover.ai**, and choose the Lesson11 folder. Leave the Save As Type option set to Adobe Illustrator (*.AI) (Windows) or the Format option set to Adobe Illustrator (ai) (Mac OS), and then click Save. In the Illustrator Options dialog box, leave the Illustrator options at their default settings, and then click OK.

Working with brushes

Using brushes, you can decorate paths with patterns, figures, brush strokes, textures, or angled strokes. You can modify the brushes provided with Illustrator and create your own brushes.

You can apply brush strokes to existing paths, or you can use the Paintbrush tool to draw a path and apply a brush stroke simultaneously. You can change the color, size, and other features of a brush. You can also edit paths after brushes are applied.

Types of brushes

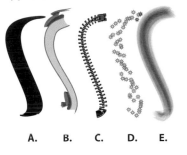

A. B. C. D. E.

A. Calligraphic brush
B. Art brush
C. Pattern brush
D. Scatter brush
E. Bristle brush

There are five types of brushes that appear in the Brushes panel (Window > Brushes): Calligraphic, Art, Pattern, Scatter, and Bristle. In this lesson, you will discover how to work with all of these except for the Scatter type of brush.

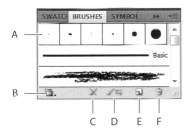

A. Brushes
B. Brush Libraries Menu
C. Remove Brush Stroke

D. Options Of Selected Object
E. New Brush
F. Delete Brush

Using Calligraphic brushes

Calligraphic brushes resemble strokes drawn with the angled point of a calligraphic pen. Calligraphic brushes are defined by an elliptical shape whose center follows the path. You can use these brushes to create the appearance of hand-drawn strokes made with a flat, angled pen tip.

Next, you'll use a Calligraphic pen to create the bunting on the train car.

Calligraphic brush examples.

1   Choose View > Fit Artboard In Window.

2   Click the Brushes panel icon (🖌) on the right side of the workspace to expand the Brushes panel.

3   In the Brushes panel, choose List View from the panel menu (▼≡).

4   Open the Brushes panel menu (▼≡) and deselect Show Art Brushes, Show Bristle Brushes, and Show Pattern Brushes, leaving only the Calligraphic brushes visible in the Brushes panel.

● **Note:** A check mark next to the brush type in the Brushes panel menu indicates that the brush type is visible in the panel.

5 In the Control panel, click the Stroke color and choose the light orange swatch. Change the Stroke Weight to **2** pt, and make sure that the fill color is None. Calligraphic brushes use the current stroke color when you apply the brushes to artwork.

6 Double-click the Pencil tool (✏) in the Tools panel. In the Pencil Tool Options dialog box, change the Smoothness to **100**%. Click OK.

7 Position the pointer in the upper-left corner of the red train car shape and draw two "u"s on the train car, from left to right, in one continuous motion. This will be the bunting on the car.

8 With the shape you drew selected, click the 5 pt. Oval brush in the Brushes panel to apply it to the line. Notice that the stroke weight changes in the Control panel.

Draw the bunting.

Apply the brush.

The result.

Editing a brush

To change the options for a brush, you can double-click the brush in the Brushes panel. Edits will apply to the current document only, and can change the artwork to which the brush has been applied, you can decide. Now you'll change the appearance of the 5 pt. Oval brush.

● **Note:** The edits you make will change the brush for this document only.

1 In the Brushes panel, double-click the 5 pt. Oval brush to display the Calligraphic Brush Options dialog box.

You can change the following options: the angle of the brush, relative to a horizontal line; the roundness (from a flat line to a full circle); the diameter (from 0 to 1296 points), to change the shape that defines the brush's tip; and the appearance of the stroke that the brush makes.

▶ **Tip:** The preview window in the dialog box (below the Name field) shows the changes that you make to the brush.

2 In the Name text field, type **30 pt. Oval**. Enter **135** for the angle, **10**% for roundness, and **30** pt for the diameter. Select Preview and notice that the Calligraphic brush strokes in the artwork change. Click OK.

3 In the warning dialog box, click Apply To Strokes to apply the change to the artwork that has the brush applied.

Since you are editing the brush in the Brushes panel, Apply To Strokes allows you to update the strokes on the artboard that have this brush applied.

4 Choose Select > Deselect, then choose File > Save.

Using a fill color with brushes

When you apply a brush to an object's stroke, you can also apply a fill color to paint the interior of the object with a color. When you use a fill color with a brush, the brush objects appear on top of the fill color in places where the fill and the brush objects overlap. Now, you'll fill the bunting shape you created with a fill color.

Path with a fill color and a brush applied to the stroke.

1 With the Selection tool (![arrow]), select the bunting shape that you drew.

2 Click the Fill color in the Control panel, and select the CMYK Cyan swatch.

3 Click outside the artwork to deselect it.

Remove a brush stroke

You can easily remove a brush stroke applied to artwork where you don't want it. Now, you'll remove the brush stroke on the path above the duck, on the train engine. This path has the 5 pt. Oval path you edited applied to it.

1 With the Selection tool (![arrow]), click the dark gray path above the duck.

2 Click the Remove Brush Stroke button (✗) at the bottom of the Brushes panel.

3 Change the Stroke Weight to 10 pt in the Control panel.

4 Choose File > Save.

Using Art brushes

Art brushes, which include arrow brushes, decorative brushes, artistic brushes, and others, stretch a brush shape (such as Rough Charcoal) or object shape evenly along the length of the path. Art brushes include strokes resembling various graphic media, such as the Charcoal-Feather brush.

Art brush examples.

Drawing with the Paintbrush tool

Now, you'll use the Paintbrush tool to apply an art brush to the bear to make it look fuzzy. As mentioned earlier, the Paintbrush tool allows you to apply a brush as you draw.

1   Choose Essentials from the workspace switcher in the Application bar.

2   Select the Zoom tool (🔍) in the Tools panel and drag a marquee around the teddy bear to zoom in on it.

3   Select the Selection tool (▶) in the Tools panel and click to select the bear. This selects the layer that the bear is on, so that any artwork you paint will be on the same layer. Choose Select > Deselect.

4   Change the Stroke color to bear brown and the Fill color to None in the Control panel.

● **Note:** A check mark next to the brush type in the Brushes panel menu indicates that the brush type is visible in the panel.

5   Click the Brushes panel icon (🖌) on the right side of the workspace. Open the Brushes panel menu (▾≡) and deselect Show Calligraphic Brushes. Then select Show Art Brushes to make the brushes visible in the Brushes panel.

6   Click the Brush Libraries Menu button (📖) at the bottom of the Brushes panel and choose Artistic > Artistic_ChalkCharcoalPencil.

7   In the Artistic_ChalkCharcoalPencil panel, choose List View from the panel menu. Click Charcoal - Thick in the list to add the brush to the Brushes panel for this document. Close the Artistic_ChalkCharcoalPencil panel.

You are going to paint around the outside of the bear to give the edges a roughened (fuzzy) look.

8   Select the Paintbrush tool (🖌) in the Tools panel, and then click the Charcoal - Thick brush in the Brushes panel. Change the Stroke Weight to **.5** pt in the Control panel. Draw a long, upward stroke to create the left side of the bear's face, starting at the shoulder and stopping at the ear. Don't worry if your stroke doesn't follow the edges exactly. Drag across the top of the head from left ear to right ear. Finish by dragging a long downward stroke to create the right side of the bear's face, starting at the bottom of the right ear and stopping at the right shoulder.

9   Select the Selection tool (▶) in the Tools panel. Double-click the left ear twice to enter isolation mode. Click to select the lighter brown part of the ear.

10 Click the Charcoal - Thick brush in the Brushes panel to apply it. Change the Stroke Weight to **.5** pt and the Fill color to bear brown in the Control panel.

11 Press Escape to exit isolation mode. Repeat the steps for the other ear.

12 Choose Select > Deselect, then choose File > Save.

Editing paths with the Paintbrush tool

Now, you'll use the Paintbrush tool to edit a selected path.

1 Click to select the last path you drew on the right side of the bear's face with the Selection tool.

2 Select the Paintbrush tool (✐) in the Tools panel. Position the pointer near the bottom of the selected path and drag down and to the left to extend the path a bit under the bear's chin. Make sure the pointer is over the selected path to begin with.

The selected path is edited from the point where you began drawing.

3 Press and hold the Ctrl (Windows) or Command (Mac OS) key to toggle to the Selection tool, and select the first path you drew with the Paintbrush tool (on the left side of the bear's face).

4 With the Paintbrush tool still selected, move the pointer near the bottom of the selected path and drag down and to the right to extend the path a bit under the bear's chin. See the figure below for placement.

▶ **Tip:** You can also edit paths drawn with the Paintbrush tool using the Smooth tool (✐) and the Path Eraser tool (✐), located under the Pencil tool (✐) in the Tools panel.

5 Choose Select > Deselect, and then choose File > Save.

Next, you will edit the Paintbrush tool options.

▶ **Tip:** Increase the value of the Smoothness option in the Paintbrush Tool Options dialog box to smooth the path by using fewer points as you draw.

6 Double-click the Paintbrush tool (🖌) to display the Paintbrush Tool Options dialog box. Select Keep Selected, and then click OK.

The Paintbrush Tool Options dialog box changes the way the Paintbrush tool functions. Because you selected Keep Selected, the paths now remain selected after you finish drawing them.

7 With the Paintbrush tool selected, position the pointer over the left shoulder and drag down and to the left, to trace around the arm on the left. Paint all the way around the arm and down the side of the bear.

● **Note:** You can release the mouse button at certain points, and then continue painting the path. The path remains selected because of the Keep Selected option you set in the Paintbrush Tool Options dialog box.

8 With the Paintbrush tool selected, position the pointer over the right shoulder and drag down and to the right, to trace around the arm on the right. Paint all the way around the arm and down the side of the bear.

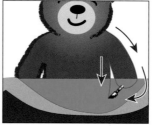

● **Note:** When the Keep Selected option is deselected, you can edit a path by selecting it with the Selection tool (▶) or by selecting a segment or point on the path with the Direct Selection tool (▷), and then redrawing over the path with the Paintbrush tool.

9 Double-click the Paintbrush tool in the Tools panel. In the Paintbrush Tool Options dialog box, deselect the Keep Selected option, and then click OK.

Now the paths will not remain selected after you finish drawing them, and you can draw overlapping paths without altering previously drawn paths.

10 Choose Select > Deselect. Choose Select > Object > Brush Strokes. This will select all of the objects with a brush stroke applied, on all artboards.

11 Select the Selection tool in the Tools panel. Shift-click the bunting to deselect it.

12 Click several other brushes in the Brushes panel to see the effects. When you have finished, click the Charcoal - Thick brush again to reapply that brush. Make sure the Stroke Weight is .5 pt in the Control panel.

The selected paths.

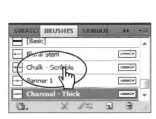
Try another brush.

The result.

▶ **Tip:** Don't forget the large number of brushes that come with Illustrator. To access them, click the Brush Libraries Menu button (⬛) in the lower-left corner of the Brushes panel.

13 Click outside the artwork to deselect it.

14 Choose File > Save.

Create an Art brush

You can create new calligraphic, scatter, art, pattern, and bristle brushes based on your settings. For scatter, art, and pattern brushes, you must first create the artwork you want to use. In this section, you'll use artwork provided with the lesson to create a new Art brush. The art brush will be used to create a logo for the train engine.

1 Choose View > Fit Artboard In Window.

2 Choose 2 from the Artboard Navigation menu in the lower-left corner of the Document window. This will fit the second artboard in the Document window.

3 Using the Selection tool (▶), click to select the group of stars.

Next, you will make an art brush from the selected artwork. You can make an art brush from vector artwork, but that artwork must not contain gradients, blends, other brush strokes, mesh objects, bitmap images, graphs, placed files, masks, or text that has not been converted to outlines.

4 Click the New Brush button (⬛) at the bottom of the Brushes panel. This creates a new brush from the selected artwork.

5 In the New Brush dialog box, select Art Brush and then click OK.

Note: To learn about guidelines for creating brushes, see "Create or modify brushes" in Illustrator Help.

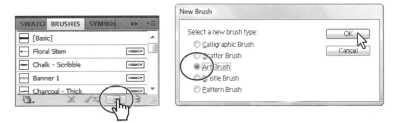

6 In the Art Brush Options dialog box, change the Name to **train logo**. Click OK.

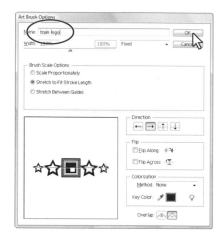

7 Choose 1 from the Artboard Navigation menu in the lower-left corner of the Document window.

8 Select the Selection tool in the Tools panel, and click to select the circle around the "RR" on the engine.

9 Select the Zoom tool (🔍) in the Tools panel, and drag a marquee across the circle and the RR in the center of the engine to zoom in to it.

10 Click the train logo brush in the Brushes panel to apply it.

Notice that the original artwork is stretched around the shape. This is the default behavior of an art brush.

Edit an Art brush

Next, you will edit the train logo art brush.

▶ **Tip:** To learn more about the Art Brush Options dialog box, see "Art brush options" in Illustrator Help.

1 With the circle still selected, double-click the train logo brush in the Brushes panel to open the Art Brush Options dialog box. Select Preview to see the changes as you make them. Change the Width to **120**%. This will increase the size of the artwork relative to its original width. Select Stretch Between Guides, then change the Start to **17** pt and the End to **18** pt. Select Flip Along and then click OK.

Note: If the stars on your circle are not at the bottom of the circle, you can rotate the circle with the Rotate tool (↻) in the Tools panel, to match position shown in the figure.

2 In the warning dialog box, click Apply To Strokes to apply the change to the artwork that has the brush applied.

3 Choose View > Fit Artboard In Window.

4 Choose Select > Deselect, then choose File > Save.

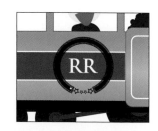

Using Bristle brushes

Bristle brushes allow you to create strokes with the appearance of a natural brush with bristles. You'll start by adjusting options for the brush to change how it appears in the artwork, and then paint with the Paintbrush tool to create a fire effect.

Bristle brush examples.

Changing bristle brush options

As you've seen earlier, you can change the appearance of a brush by adjusting its settings in the Brush Options dialog box, either before or after brushes have been applied to the artwork. When you paint with a bristle brush, it creates vector paths. It is usually best to adjust bristle brush settings prior to painting since it can take some time to update the brush strokes.

1 In the Brushes panel, choose Show Bristle Brushes from the panel menu (▼≡), and then deselect Show Art Brushes.

2 Double-click the Filbert brush to open the Brush Options dialog box for that brush. Leave the dialog box open for the next step.

▶ **Tip:** Illustrator comes with a series of default Bristle brushes. Click the Brush Libraries Menu button (▨) at the bottom of the Brushes panel and choose Bristle Brush > Bristle Brush Library.

3 In the Bristle Brush Options dialog box, leave the Shape set at Flat Curve, and press the Tab key to move to the next field. Set the following values:

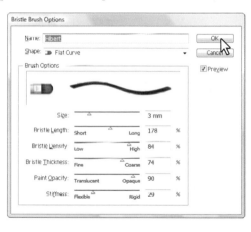

- Make sure that Size is 3 mm. The brush size is the diameter of the brush.

- Change the Bristle Length to **178**. The bristle length starts from the point where the bristles meet the handle of the bristle tip.

- Change the Bristle Density to **84**. The bristle density is the number of bristles in a specified area of the brush neck.

- For Bristle Thickness, set the value to **74**. The bristle thickness can vary from fine to coarse (between 1% and 100%).

- For Paint Opacity, change the value to **90**. This option lets you set the opacity of the paint being used.

● **Note:** To learn more about the Bristle Brush Options dialog box and its settings, see "Using the Bristle brush" in Illustrator Help.

- For Stiffness, change the value to **29**. Stiffness implies the rigidity of the bristles.

4 Click OK.

Painting with a Bristle brush

Now, you'll use the Filbert brush to draw some fire. Painting with a Bristle brush can create a very organic stroke. In order to constrain the painting, you will paint inside a shape. This will mask the painting to be in the shape of the flame.

1   Select the Zoom tool (🔍) in the Tools panel and drag a marquee around the flame shape next to the dinosaur, to zoom in on it.

2   Select the Selection tool (▶) in the Tools panel and click to select the flame shape. This selects the layer that the shape is on, so that any artwork you paint will be on the same layer.

● **Note:** To learn more about the drawing modes, see Lesson 3, "Creating and Editing Shapes."

3   Click the Draw Inside button (◉) at the bottom of the Tools panel.

● **Note:** If the Tools panel appears as one column, click and hold down the Drawing Modes button at the bottom of the Tools panel, then choose a drawing mode from the menu that appears.

4   Choose Select > Deselect to deselect the flame shape. You can still draw inside the shape, as indicated by the dotted lines on the corners of the shape.

5   Select the Paintbrush tool (🖌) in the Tools panel. Choose the Filbert brush from the Brush Definition menu in the Control panel.

6   Change the Fill color to None and Stroke color to flame red in the Control panel.

▶ **Tip:** If you want to edit paths as you draw, you can select the Keep Selected option in the Paintbrush Tool Options for the Paintbrush tool, or select paths with the Selection tool. You don't need to completely fill the shape.

7   Position the pointer at the upper-left tip of the flame shape. Drag down and to the right to loosely follow the top edge of the flame shape. Release the mouse button when you pass the lower-right tip of the flame shape.

When you release the mouse button, notice that the path you just painted is masked by the flame shape.

8   Use the Paintbrush tool (🖌) to provide some texture by drawing more strokes inside the flame shape, using the Filbert brush.

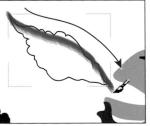 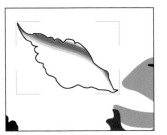 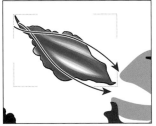

Paint with the bristle brush.   The masked path   The result

▶ **Tip:** If you don't like what you just painted, you can choose Edit > Undo Bristle Stroke.

Next, you will edit the brush, and paint with another color to build the flame by layering paths on each other.

9   Change the Stroke color to flame orange in the Control panel.

10 Double-click the Filbert brush in the Brushes panel. In the Bristle Brush Options dialog box, change the Paint Opacity to **30**, and then click OK.

11 Click Leave Strokes in the dialog box that appears. This changes the brush settings without changing the red flame you already painted.

12 Draw some more paths on top of the red flames using the Paintbrush tool. Focus the orange paths you draw close the dinosaur's mouth.

13 Change the Stroke color to flame yellow in the Control panel.

14 Double-click the Filbert brush in the Brushes panel. In the Bristle Brush Options dialog box, change the Bristle Density to **18** and the Stiffness to **60**. Click OK.

15 Click Leave Strokes in the dialog box that appears.

16 Draw some more paths on top of the orange flames, using the Paintbrush tool. Focus the yellow paths you draw close the dinosaur's mouth.

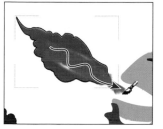
Apply some orange flame.

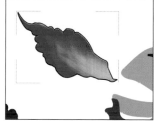
Finish the flame with yellow.

17 Choose View > Outline.

18 Choose Select > Object > Bristle Brush Strokes to select all of the paths created with the Paintbrush tool using the Filbert bristle brush.

19 Choose Object > Group, then View > Preview.

20 Click the Draw Normal button at the bottom of the Tools panel.

21 Select the Selection tool in the Tools panel. Click the edge of the flame shape so it's the only selected object.

22 Click the Edit Clipping Path button (◻) in the Control panel. Change the Stroke color to None in the Control panel.

23 Choose Select > Deselect, then choose File > Save.

The Bristle Brush and graphic tablets

When you use Bristle brush with a graphic tablet, Illustrator interactively tracks the movements of the stylus over the tablet. It interprets all aspects of its orientation and pressure input at any point along a drawing path. Illustrator provides the output that is modeled on the stylus's x-axis position, y-axis position, pressure, tilt, bearing, and rotation.

A cursor annotator that simulates the tip of an actual brush is displayed when using a tablet and stylus that support rotation. This annotator does not appear when other input devices such as a mouse are used. The annotator is also disabled while using the precise cursors.

Note: *Use the Wacom Intuos 3 or higher tablet with Art (6D) pen to explore the full capabilities of the Bristle brush. Illustrator can interpret all 6-degrees of freedom that this device combination provides. However, other devices including the Wacom Grip pen and Art brush pen may not be able to interpret some attributes such as rotation. These uninterpreted attributes are treated as constants in the resulting brush strokes.*

While using a mouse, only x and y-axis movements are recorded. Other inputs, such as tilt, bearing, rotation, and pressure remain fixed resulting in even and consistent strokes.

For Bristle brush strokes, feedback is displayed when you drag the tool. This feedback provides an approximate view of the final stroke.

Note: *Bristle brush strokes are made up of several overlapping, filled transparent paths. These paths, like any other filled path in Illustrator, interact with the paint of other objects, including other bristle bush paths. However, the fill for strokes does not self-interact. Therefore, layered, individual, bristle brush strokes build up and interact with each other, but a single stoke scrubbed back and forth in place does not interact with itself and build up.*

—From Illustrator Help

Using Pattern brushes

Pattern brushes paint a pattern made up of separate sections, or tiles. When you apply a Pattern brush to artwork, different tiles of the pattern are applied to different sections of the path, depending on where the section falls on the path—the end, middle, or corner. There are hundreds of interesting pattern brushes that you can choose from when creating your own projects, from dog tracks to cityscapes. Next, you'll open an existing Pattern Brush library and choose a train track pattern to create tracks.

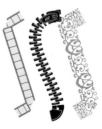

Pattern brush examples.

1 Choose View > Fit Artboard In Window.

2 In the Brushes panel, choose Show Pattern Brushes from the panel menu (▼≡) and deselect Show Bristle Brushes.

3 Click the Brush Libraries Menu button (📖) and choose Borders > Borders_Novelty. A brush library panel with various borders appears.

4 Scroll to the bottom of the Brushes panel and click the Train Tracks brush to add it to the panel. Close the Borders_Novelty brush library panel.

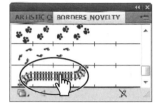

Next, you will apply the brush, and then edit its properties.

5 Click the Layers panel icon (◆) on the right side of the workspace to expand the Layers panel.

6 Click the visibility column to the left of the Railroad tracks layer to show the path for the tracks on the artboard. Click the Layers panel icon to collapse the panel.

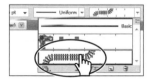

7 Select the Selection tool (▶) in the Tools panel. Click the path that appears below the train to select it.

8 Choose the Train Tracks pattern brush from the Brush Definition menu in the Control panel to apply the pattern brush.

9 Change the Stroke Weight to **4** pt in the Control panel.

Notice that the train tracks follow the curve precisely. A pattern brush has tiles, as described earlier, that correspond to parts of the path.

Next, you will edit the brush properties for the selected train tracks.

10 Click the Brushes panel icon (🖌) on the right side of the workspace to expand the panel. Click the Options Of Selected Object button (✏≡) at the bottom of the Brushes panel to edit the brush options for only the selected train tracks on the artboard. This opens the Stroke Options (Pattern Brush) dialog box.

11 Change the Scale to **120%** either by dragging the slider beneath the field to the right or by typing in the value. Click OK.

When you edit the brush options of the selected object, you only see some of the brush options. The Stroke Options (Pattern Brush) dialog box is used to edit the properties of the brushed path without updating the corresponding brush.

12 Choose Select > Deselect, and then File > Save.

Creating a Pattern brush

You can create a Pattern brush in several ways. For a simple pattern applied to a straight line, for instance, you can select the object that you're using for the pattern and click the New Brush button (◲) at the bottom of the Brushes panel. To create a more complex pattern to apply to objects with curves and corners, you must first create swatches in the Swatches panel from the artwork that you are using for the Pattern brush tiles, and then create the new brush. For example, to create a pattern brush that will be used on a straight line with corners, you might need to create three swatches, one for the straight line, another for the inside corner and another for the outside corner. Next, you'll create swatches to be used in a pattern brush.

1 Click the Layers panel icon (◈) on the right side of the workspace to expand the Layers panel.

2 Click the visibility column to the left of the Frame layer to show its contents.

3 Click the Swatches panel icon (▦) to expand the Swatches panel, or choose Window > Swatches.

Now, you'll create a pattern swatch.

4 Choose 2 from the Artboard Navigation menu in the lower-left corner of the Document window.

5 With the Selection tool (▶), drag the flower into the Swatches panel. The new pattern swatch appears in the Swatches panel.

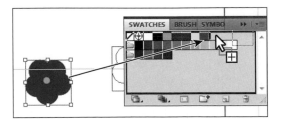
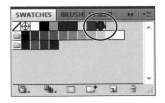

6 Choose Select > Deselect.

7 In the Swatches panel, double-click the pattern swatch that you just created. In the Swatch Options dialog box, name the swatch **Corner**, and then click OK.

8 Repeat steps 5 through 7 to create a pattern swatch of the orange circle located to the left of the flower on the artboard. Name the swatch **Side**.

▶ **Tip:** For more information on creating pattern swatches, see "About patterns" in Illustrator Help.

To create a new Pattern brush, you apply swatches from the Swatches panel to tiles in the Brush Options dialog box. Now, you'll apply the pattern swatches that you just made to tiles, to create a new Pattern brush.

9 Click the Brushes panel icon (🔧) to expand the panel.

10 Choose Select > Deselect if there is content selected.

This is an important step! Any content selected will be part of the brush.

11 In the Brushes panel, click the New Brush button (🔳).

12 In the New Brush dialog box, select Pattern Brush.

Notice that you can't select the Art Brush or Scatter Brush. That is because artwork needs to be selected in the document first. Click OK.

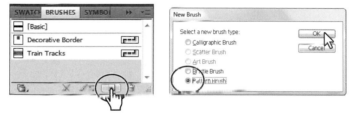

Now, you'll apply the swatches to the tiles for the new Pattern brush.

13 In the Pattern Brush Options dialog box, name the brush **Border**.

14 Make sure that, in the pattern swatches list, located below Spacing, the Side Tile box is selected. Below the tile boxes, select Side. The Side swatch appears in the Side tile box.

The Pattern Brush Options dialog box shows the tiles in the new brush you are making. The first tile on the left is the side tile, which is used to paint the middle sections of a path. The second tile is the outer corner tile. The third tile is the inner corner tile.

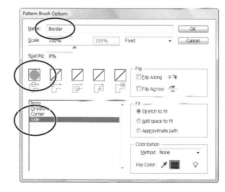

▶ **Tip:** Position the pointer over the tile squares in the Pattern Brush Options dialog box to see a tooltip indicating which tile it is.

Pattern brushes can have up to five tiles—the side, start, and end tiles, plus an outer corner tile and an inner corner tile to paint sharp corners on a path. Some brushes have no corner tiles because the brush is designed for curved paths.

In the next part of this lesson, you'll create your own Pattern brush that has corner tiles. Next, you'll apply the Corner swatch to the outer corner and inner corner tiles for the new Pattern brush.

15 In the Pattern Brush Options dialog box, select the Outer Corner Tile box (the second tile box from the left). In the pattern swatches list, select Corner. The Corner swatch appears in the Outer Corner Tile box.

16 Select the Inner Corner Tile box (the middle tile box). In the pattern swatches list, select the Corner swatch. The Corner swatch appears in the Inner Corner Tile box. Click OK.

● **Note:** When you create a new brush, the brush appears in the Brushes panel of the current document only.

You won't create a start or end tile for the new brush, because you'll apply the new brush to a path in the artwork next. When you want to create a Pattern brush that includes start and end tiles, you add those tiles the same way as you did the side and corner tiles.

The Border brush appears in the Brushes panel.

▶ **Tip:** To save a brush and reuse it in another file, you can create a brush library with the brushes you want to use. For more information, see "Work with brush libraries" in Illustrator Help.

Applying a Pattern brush

In this section, you'll apply the Border brush to a rectangular border around the artwork. When you use drawing tools to apply brushes to artwork, you first draw the path with the drawing tool, and then select the brush in the Brushes panel to apply the brush to the path.

1 Click the First artboard button (◀) in the lower-left corner of the Document window to return to the first artboard and fit it in the Document window.

2 With the Selection tool (▶) selected, click the white stroke of the rectangle on the border.

3 In the Tools panel, click the Fill box and make sure that None (⊘) is selected. Then click the Stroke box and select None (⊘).

4 Choose Thumbnail View from the Brushes panel menu (▼≣).

Notice that pattern brushes in Thumbnail view are segmented in the Brushes panel. Each segment corresponds to a pattern tile. The side tile is repeated in the Brushes panel thumbnail preview.

5 With the rectangle selected, click the Border brush in the Brushes panel.

The rectangle is painted with the Border brush, with the side tile on the sides and the corner tile on the corners.

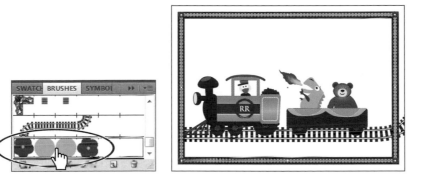

Now, you'll edit the Border brush.

6   In the Brushes panel, double-click the Border pattern brush to open the Pattern Brush Options dialog box.

7   In the Pattern Brush Options dialog box, change the Scale to **70**%, the Spacing to **120**%, and select Add Space To Fit. Click OK.

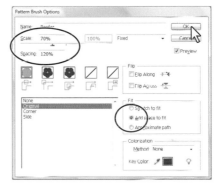

8   In the Brush Change Alert dialog box, click Apply To Strokes to update the border on the artboard.

9   With the Selection tool selected, click to select the arch right above the duck's head. Click the Border brush in the Brushes panel to apply it.

Notice that the flowers are not applied to the path. The path is painted with the side swatch from the Border brush, to which the side tile is applied. Because the path does not include sharp corners, the outer corner and inner corner tiles are not applied to the path.

10 Choose Edit > Undo Apply Pattern Brush to remove the brush from the arch.

● **Note:** Earlier in the lesson you learned how to remove a brush from an object by clicking the Remove Brush Stroke button (✖) in the Brushes panel. In this case, you chose Edit > Undo Apply Pattern Brush instead, because clicking the Remove Brush Stroke button would strip the previous formatting from the arch, leaving it with a default fill and stroke.

Changing the color attributes of brushes

The colors that a scatter, art, or pattern brush paints depend on the current stroke color and the colorization method of the brush. If you have not set a colorization method, the default color for that brush is used. For example, the train logo art brush was applied with its default color (not the current stroke of black), because its colorization method was set to None.

To colorize Art, Pattern, and Scatter brushes, there are three editing options you can use in the Brush Options dialog box: Tints, Tints and Shades, and Hue Shift. To learn more about each of these colorization methods, search for "Colorization options" in Illustrator Help.

● **Note:** Brushes colorized with a stroke color of white may appear entirely white. Brushes colorized with a stroke color of black may appear entirely black. Results depend on which brush colors were originally chosen.

Changing a brush color using Tints colorization

Now, you'll change the color of the train logo art brush using the Tints colorization method.

1 In the Brushes panel, choose Show Art Brushes from the panel menu (▼≡) and deselect Show Pattern Brushes.

2 With the Selection tool (▶), click to select the train logo (the circle with the train logo art brush applied) below the duck.

3 Pressing the Shift key, click the Stroke color in the Control panel to open the Color panel.

4 Click in the color spectrum bar to select a color. We chose an orangish-red color.

5 In the Brushes panel, double-click the train logo brush to view the Art Brush Options dialog box. Select Preview to see the changes you will make, then move the dialog box off to the side so that you can see your artwork as you work.

You must choose a colorization method before you can change the brush color. Brushes set to the Tints, Tints And Shades, or Hue Shift colorization method, automatically apply the current stroke color to the brush when you use it in the artwork.

6 In the Colorization section of the Art Brush Options dialog box, choose Tints from the Method menu.

The selected path with the train logo brush applied is colorized and displays the brush stroke in tints of the stroke color. Portions of the art that are black become the stroke color, portions that aren't black become tints of the stroke color, and white remains white.

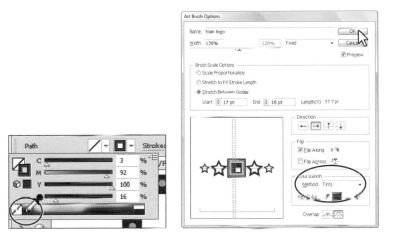

● **Note:** The Tints And Shades colorization method displays the brush stroke in tints and shades of the stroke color. Tints and Shades maintains black and white, and everything between becomes a blend from black to white through the stroke color.

7 If desired, choose the Tints And Shades colorization method from the menu in the Art Brush Options dialog box to preview the change. Choose the Tints method and then click OK. In the warning dialog box, click Apply To Strokes to apply the colorization change to the strokes in the artwork.

You can also choose to change only subsequent brush strokes and leave existing strokes unchanged. When you select a colorization method for a brush, the new stroke color applies to selected brush strokes and to new paths painted with the brush.

8 Click the Color panel icon (🎨) on the right side of the workspace to expand the panel. Click the Stroke Box to bring it forward, and then click the color spectrum bar in several different places to try applying other stroke colors to the selected artwork.

9 When you are satisfied with the color of the train logo, click away from the artwork to deselect it.

10 Choose File > Save.

Changing the brush color using Hue Shift colorization

Now, you'll apply a new color to the Banner 1 brush in the Brushes panel.

1 Click the Layers panel icon (⬢) on the right side of the workspace to expand the Layers panel. Click the visibility column to the left of the Text layer to show its contents.

2 Select the Zoom tool (🔍) in the Tools panel, and drag a marquee around the Golden Book Award seal to zoom into it.

3 With the Selection tool (▸), click to select the circle in the seal with the brush applied.

4 Click the Brushes panel icon (🖌) to expand the panel. Double-click the Banner 1 brush in the Brushes panel to reveal the Art Brush Options dialog box. Note that the Banner 1 brush is set to a None Colorization method by default.

▶ **Tip:** To learn more about how the different colorization methods affect artwork, click the light bulb icon (💡) in the Art Brush Options dialog box.

5 In the Art Brush Options dialog box, select Preview if not already selected. In the Colorization section choose Hue Shift from the Method menu.

You typically choose Hue Shift for brushes that use multiple colors. Everything in the artwork that is the key color changes to the new stroke color when the stroke color is changed.

6 In the Colorization section of the Art Brush Options dialog box, click the Key Color Eyedropper (🖋) and position the pointer over an orange color in the preview area (to the left of the Colorization settings) and then click, as shown in the figure below.

The key color you just sampled (the orange) will be used the next time you apply a stroke color to the artwork after you've closed the dialog box.

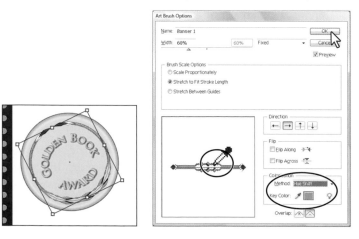

The orange parts of the path with the brush applied are now colorized with the current stroke color. This color appears when you apply the Hue Shift colorization method.

7   Click OK. In the warning dialog box, click Apply To Strokes to apply the colorization change to the strokes in the artwork. You can also choose to change only subsequent brush strokes and leave existing strokes unchanged.

When you select a colorization method for a brush, the new stroke color applies to selected brush strokes and to new paths painted with the brush.

8   Change the Stroke color to flame red in the Control panel. Try other stroke colors for the selected brush strokes before finally choosing flame yellow, as shown in the figure at right.

9   Choose Select > Deselect, then choose File > Save.

Working with the Blob Brush tool

You can use the Blob Brush tool to paint filled shapes that intersect and merge with other shapes of the same color. With the Blob Brush tool, you can draw with Paintbrush tool artistry. Unlike the Paintbrush tool, which lets you create open paths, the Blob Brush tool lets you create a closed shape with a fill only (no stroke) that you can then edit with the Eraser or Blob Brush tool. Shapes that have a stroke cannot be edited with the Blob Brush tool.

Path created with the
Paintbrush tool

Shape created with the
Blob Brush tool

Next, you will use the Blob Brush tool to create a part of the smoke coming from the train engine.

Drawing with the Blob Brush tool

The Blob Brush tool uses the same default brush options as calligraphic brushes.

1 Choose Essentials from the workspace switcher in the Application bar.

2 Choose View > Fit Artboard In Window.

3 Click the Layers panel icon (🖼) on the right side of the workspace to expand the Layers panel. Click the eye icon to the left of the Text layer to hide its contents, then click the visibility column to the left of both the Background layer and the Smoke layer. Click the Smoke layer to select it.

● **Note:** When drawing with the Blob Brush tool, if a fill and stroke are set before drawing, the stroke becomes the fill of the shape made by the Blob Brush tool. If only a fill is set before drawing, it becomes the fill of the shape created.

4 Change the fill color to white and the stroke color to None (⬜) in the Control panel.

5 Double-click the Blob Brush tool (🖌) in the Tools panel. In the Blob Brush Tool Options dialog box, select the Keep Selected option and change the Size to **30** pt in the Default Brush Options area. Click OK.

6 Position the pointer just above the black smoke stack to the left of the duck. Drag in a zigzag pattern up and to the right to create some smoke.

7 Choose Select > Deselect. Next, you will edit the smoke shape you created, to give it a more stylized look.

Merging paths with the Blob Brush tool

● **Note:** When you draw with the Blob Brush tool, you create filled, closed shapes. Those shapes can contain any type of fill, including gradients, solid colors, patterns, and more.

Besides drawing new shapes with the Blob brush tool, you can use it to intersect and merge shapes of the same color. Next, you will merge the smoke you just created and the white ellipse to the right of it to create one big smoke shape.

1 Click the Appearance panel icon (⬤) on the right side of the workspace to expand the panel. In the Appearance panel menu (▼≡), deselect New Art Has Basic Appearance. When this option is deselected, the Blob Brush tool uses the attributes of the selected artwork.

2 With the Selection tool (▶), click the smoke you just drew and Shift-click the white ellipse to the right of the smoke shape.

3 In the Appearance panel, click the word Path at the top of the panel, so that the drop shadow you apply next isn't applied to the fill or stroke only.

4 Choose Effect > Stylize > Drop Shadow. In the Drop Shadow dialog box, change Opacity to **35**%, X Offset to **3** pt, Y Offset to **3** pt, and Blur to **2** pt. Click OK.

5 Choose Select > Deselect.

6 With the Blob Brush tool selected in the Tools panel, make sure that you see the same attributes as the smoke shapes (a white fill, no stroke, and a drop shadow) in the Appearance panel. Drag from inside the smoke shape you created to the inside of the ellipse to the right, connecting the two shapes.

● **Note:** Notice that the drop shadow is applied to the entire shape as you draw and edit.

● **Note:** Objects merged with the Blob Brush tool need to have the same appearance attributes, have no stroke, be on the same layer or group, and be adjacent to each other in the stacking order.

7 Continue drawing with the Blob Brush tool to make the smoke look more like a cloud. When you release the mouse button, the drop shadow is applied.

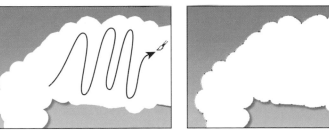

8 With the Blob Brush tool, add more shape to the ellipse part of the smoke on the right side to make it more cloud-like.

● **Note:** Objects merged with the Blob Brush tool need to have the same appearance attributes and no stroke, be on the same layer or group, and adjacent to each other in the stacking order.

9 Choose Select > Deselect, and then File > Save.

Editing with the Eraser tool

As you draw and merge shapes with the Blob Brush tool, you may draw too much and want to edit what you've done. Use the Eraser tool to mold the shape and correct any changes you don't like.

▶ **Tip:** As you draw with the Blob Brush and Eraser tools, it is recommended that you use shorter strokes and release the mouse button often. You can undo the edits that you make, but if you draw in one long stroke without releasing the mouse button, an undo removes the entire stroke.

● **Note:** Selecting the shape before the selecting the Eraser tool limits the Eraser tool so that it erases only the selected shape.

1 With the Selection tool (◣), click to select the smoke shape.

2 Select the Eraser tool (◢) in the Tools panel. Proceed slowly with the next steps and remember that you can always stop and undo.

3 With the Eraser tool, drag along the bottom of the smoke shape to remove some of the smoke.

The Blob Brush and Eraser tools have pointers that include a circle, indicating the diameter of the brush. Next, you will change the brush size to help edit the smoke shape.

4 Press the right bracket key (]) several times to increase the size of the brush.

5 Try switching between the Blob Brush tool and the Eraser tool to edit the smoke.

● **Note:** You may need to select the Selection tool and reposition the text, "Ted and Fuego Take a Train" to center the text on the smoke.

6 Click the Layers panel icon (🝊) on the right side of the workspace to expand the Layers panel. Click the visibility column to the left of the Text layer.

7 Choose File > Save. Leave the file open for the Exploring on your own section.

The Blob Brush tool guidelines

When using the Blob Brush tool, keep the following guidelines in mind:

• To merge paths, they must be adjacent in stacking order.

• The Blob Brush tool creates paths with a fill and no stroke. If you want your Blob Brush paths to merge with existing artwork, make sure that the artwork has the same fill color and no stroke.

• When drawing paths with the Blob Brush tool, new paths merge with the topmost matching path encountered. If the new path touches more than one matching path within the same group or layer, all of the intersecting paths are merged together.•

• To apply paint attributes (such as effect or transparency) to the Blob Brush tool, select the brush and set the attributes in the Appearances panel before you start drawing.

• You can use the Blob Brush tool to merge paths created by other tools. To do this, make sure that the existing artwork does not have a stroke; then set up the Blob Brush tool to have the same fill color, and draw a new path that intersects all of the paths that you want to merge together.

—From Illustrator Help

Exploring on your own

There are many ways to be creative with brushes. Try practicing with the Bristle brush next.

1 Select the smoke shape with the Selection tool (▶).

2 Click the Draw Inside button at the bottom of the Tools panel.

● **Note:** If you cannot select Draw Inside, it may be because the cloud is now a group. Choose Object > Ungroup, then choose Select > Deselect. Click the cloud shape again to select it.

3 Choose Select > Deselect.

4 Click the Brushes panel icon (🌵) to expand the panel. Click the Brush Libraries Menu button (🖼.) and choose Bristle Brush > Bristle Brush Library from the menu.

5 Click a bristle brush in the Bristle Brush Library panel.

6 Select the Paintbrush tool (✎) in the Tools panel. Change the Stroke color to a light gray in the Control panel. Practice adding some texture to the inside of the smoke shape.

Experiment with the bristle brush settings.

7 Choose File > Save, and then File > Close.

● **Note:** A warning dialog box may appear telling you that the document contains multiple Bristle Brush paths with transparency. For this lesson, click OK.

Practice applying brushes to paths that you create with drawing tools, just as you applied the Pattern brush to a rectangle earlier in the lesson.

1 Choose File > New, and create a document to use for practice.

2 Click the Brushes Libraries Menu button (🖼.) in the Brushes panel, and choose Decorative > Decorative_Scatter.

3 Use the drawing tools (the Pen or Pencil tool, and any of the basic shape tools) to draw objects. Use the default fill and stroke colors when you draw.

4 With one of the objects selected, click a brush in the Decorative Scatter panel to apply the brush to the object's path.

When you select a Scatter brush, it is automatically added to the Brushes panel.

5 Repeat step 4 for each object you drew.

6 In the Brushes panel, double-click one of the Scatter brushes that you used in Step 4 to display the Scatter Brush Options dialog box. Change the color, size, or other features of the brush. After you close the dialog box, click Apply To Strokes to apply your changes to the brush in the artwork.

Review questions

1 Describe each of the five brush types: Art, Calligraphic, Pattern, Bristle, and Scatter.

2 What is the difference between applying a brush to artwork using the Paintbrush tool and applying a brush to artwork using one of the drawing tools?

3 Describe how to edit paths with the Paintbrush tool as you draw. How does the Keep Selected option affect the Paintbrush tool?

4 How do you change the colorization method for an Art, Pattern, or Scatter brush? (Remember, you don't use colorization methods with Calligraphic or Bristle brushes.)

5 For which brushes must you have artwork selected on the artboard before you can create a brush?

6 What does the Blob Brush tool allow you to create?

Review answers

1 The following are the five brush types:

- Art brushes stretch artwork evenly along a path. Art brushes include strokes that resemble graphic media, such as the Charcoal-Feather brush used to create the tree. Art brushes also include objects, such as the Arrow brush.

- Calligraphic brushes are defined by an elliptical shape whose center follows the path. They create strokes that resemble hand-drawn lines made with a flat, angled calligraphic pen tip.

- Pattern brushes paint a pattern made up of separate sections, or tiles, for the sides, ends, and corners of the path. When you apply a pattern brush to artwork, the brush applies different tiles from the pattern to different sections of the path, depending on where the section falls on the path.

- Bristle brushes allow you to create brush strokes with the appearance of a natural brush with bristles.

- Scatter brushes scatter an object, such as a leaf, along a path. You can adjust the size, spacing, scatter, and rotation options to change the appearance of the brush.

2 To apply brushes using the Paintbrush tool, you select the tool, choose a brush in the Brushes panel, and draw on the artboard. The brush is applied directly to the paths as you draw. To apply brushes using a drawing tool, you select the tool and draw in the

artwork. Then you select the path in the artwork and choose a brush in the Brushes panel. The brush is applied to the selected path.

3 To edit a path with the Paintbrush tool, drag over a selected path to redraw it. The Keep Selected option keeps the last path selected as you draw with the Paintbrush tool. Leave the Keep Selected option selected (the default setting) when you want to easily edit the previous path as you draw. Deselect the Keep Selected option when you want to draw layered paths with the paintbrush without altering previous paths. When Keep Selected is deselected, you can use the Selection tool to select a path and then edit it.

4 To change the colorization method of a brush, double-click the brush in the Brushes panel to open the Brush Options dialog box. Use the Method menu in the Colorization section to select another method. If you choose Hue Shift, you can use the default color displayed in the dialog box preview, or you can change the key color by clicking the Key Color Eyedropper, and clicking a color in the preview. Click OK to accept the settings, and close the Brush Options dialog box. Click Apply To Strokes in the alert dialog box if you want to apply the changes to existing strokes in the artwork.

Existing brush strokes are colorized with the stroke color that was selected when the strokes were applied to the artwork. New brush strokes are colorized with the current stroke color. To change the color of existing strokes after applying a different colorization method, select the strokes and select a new stroke color.

5 For Art and Scatter brushes, you need to have artwork selected in order to create a brush using the New Brush button in the Brushes panel.

6 Use the Blob Brush tool to edit filled shapes that you can intersect and merge with other shapes of the same color, or to create artwork from scratch.

12 APPLYING EFFECTS

Lesson overview

In this lesson, you'll learn how to do the following:

- Use various effects like Pathfinder, Distort & Transform, Offset Path, and Drop Shadow effects.

- Use Warp effects to create a banner logotype.

- Use Photoshop effects to add texture to objects.

- Create 3D objects from 2D artwork.

- Map artwork to the surfaces of 3D objects.

 This lesson will take approximately an hour to complete. If needed, remove the previous lesson folder from your hard disk and copy the Lesson12 folder onto it.

Effects change the look of an object. Effects are live, which means you can apply an effect to an object and then modify or remove it at any time using the Appearance panel. Using effects, it's easy to apply drop shadows, turn two-dimensional artwork into three-dimensional shapes, and much more.

Getting started

In this lesson, you'll create objects using various effects. Before you begin, you'll need to restore the default preferences for Adobe® Illustrator®. Then you'll open a file containing the finished artwork to see what you'll create.

1 To ensure that the tools and panels function exactly as described in this lesson, delete or rename the Adobe Illustrator CS5 preferences file. See "Restoring default preferences" on page 3.

2 Start Adobe Illustrator CS5.

● **Note:** If you have not already done so, copy the resource files for this lesson onto your hard disk from the Lesson12 folder on the Adobe Illustrator CS5 Classroom in a Book CD. See "Copying the Classroom in a Book files" on page 2.

3 Choose File > Open, and open the L12end_1.ai file in the Lesson12 folder, located in the Lessons folder on your hard disk.

This file displays a completed illustration of a soda can.

4 Choose View > Zoom Out to make the finished artwork smaller. Adjust the window size, and leave it on your screen as you work. (Use the Hand tool (✋) to move the artwork where you want it in the window.) If you don't want to leave the image open, choose File > Close.

To begin working, you'll open an existing art file.

5 Choose File > Open, and open the L12start_1.ai file in the Lesson12 folder, located in the Lessons folder on your hard disk.

6 Choose File > Save As, name the file **sodacan.ai**, and select the Lesson12 folder in the Save In menu. Leave the Save As Type option set to Adobe Illustrator (*.AI) (Windows) or the Format option set to Adobe Illustrator (ai) (Mac OS), and click Save. In the Illustrator Options dialog box, leave the Illustrator options at their default settings, and then click OK.

Using live effects

The Effect menu commands alter the appearance of an object without changing the base object. Applying an effect automatically adds the effect to the object's appearance attribute. You can apply more than one effect to an object. You can edit, move, delete, or duplicate an effect at any time in the Appearance panel. To edit the points that the effect creates, you must first expand the object.

There are two types of effects in Illustrator: vector effects and raster effects. In Illustrator, click the Effect menu item.

Object with a drop shadow effect applied.

> **● Note:** When you apply a raster effect, the original vector data is rasterized using the document's raster effects settings, which determine the resolution of the resulting image. To learn about document raster effects settings, search for "Document raster effects settings" In Illustrator Help.

- **Illustrator (vector) effects**: The top half of the Effects menu contains vector effects. You can apply these effects only to vector objects or to the fill or stroke of a bitmap object in the Appearance panel. The following vector effects can be applied to both vector and bitmap objects: 3D effects, SVG filters, Warp effects, Transform effects, Drop Shadow, Feather, Inner Glow, and Outer Glow.

- **Photoshop (raster) effects**: The bottom half of the Effects menu contains raster effects. You can apply them to either vector or bitmap objects.

Applying an effect

Effects are applied using the Effect menu or the Appearance panel and can be applied to objects or groups. In this part of the lesson, you are first going to learn how to apply an effect to a soda can label, then you will apply an effect using the Appearance panel.

1 Choose Essentials from the workspace switcher in the Application bar to reset the workspace.

2 Choose View > Smart Guides to deselect them.

3 With the Selection tool (▶), click the text shapes Sparkling Soda on the artboard.

4 With the group selected, choose Effect > Stylize > Drop Shadow.

5 In the Drop Shadow dialog box, change the X Offset, Y Offset, and Blur to **3** pt. Select Preview to see the drop shadow applied to the text shapes. Click OK.

6 With the Selection tool, click the cherries to select the group.

7 With the group selected, click the Appearance panel icon (⊙) on the right side of the workspace to expand the Appearance panel.

In the Appearance panel, you will see the word Group at the top of the panel, indicating that a group is selected. Effects can be applied to grouped objects.

8 Click the Add New Effect button (*fx.*) at the bottom of the Appearance panel. You'll see the same options as in the Effect menu.

9 Choose Stylize > Drop Shadow from the Illustrator Effects section of the menu that appears.

10 In the Drop Shadow dialog box, change the Opacity to **40** and leave the X Offset, Y Offset, and Blur set at 3 pt. Select Preview to see the drop shadow applied to the text shapes. Click OK.

In the Appearance panel, notice that Drop Shadow is now listed below Group.

11 Choose Select > Deselect.

12 Choose File > Save.

Next, you will edit the two drop shadow effects.

Editing an effect

Effects are live, so they can be edited after they are applied to an object. You can edit the effect in the Appearance panel by selecting the object with the effect applied, then either clicking the name of the effect or double-clicking the attribute row in the Appearance panel. This displays the dialog box for that effect. Changes you make to the effect update in the artwork. In this section, you will edit the drop shadow effect applied to the cherries.

1   With the Selection tool (▶), click the grouped cherry shapes and make sure that the Appearance panel is showing. If it isn't, choose Window > Appearance or click its panel icon (◉).

    Notice the drop shadow effect listed in the Appearance panel.

2   Click the blue underlined Drop Shadow in the Appearance panel. In the Drop Shadow dialog box, change Opacity to **60**% and select Preview to see the change. Try different settings to see their effects (we set the Blur at 5), and then click OK.

Click Drop Shadow.

Edit the Drop Shadow settings.   The result

Next, you will remove an effect from the "Sparkling Soda" text shapes.

3   With the Selection tool, click the Sparkling Soda text shapes.

4   In the Appearance panel, click to the right or left of the blue, underlined name Drop Shadow to highlight the attribute row for the Drop Shadow effect, if it's not already highlighted. After highlighting the attribute row, click the Delete Selected Item button (🗑) at the bottom of the panel.

Note: Be careful not to click the blue, underlined name Drop Shadow, which will open the Drop Shadow dialog box.

5 With the Selection tool, click to select the cherries group again.

6 Choose Object > Ungroup.

● **Note:** When you ungroup the cherries, you will still see the word Group at the top of the Appearance panel. That's because each cherry is its own group.

Notice that the drop shadow effect is gone from the cherries. When an effect is applied to a group, it affects the group as a whole. If the objects are no longer grouped together, then the effect no longer applies.

7 Choose Edit > Undo Ungroup and the drop shadow reappears.

8 Choose Select > Deselect, then File > Save.

Styling text with effects

You can make a warp from objects in your artwork, or you can use a preset warp shape or mesh object as an envelope. Next, you will use a warp effect to warp the text at the bottom of the label.

1 Select the Selection tool (▶) in the Tools panel, and then select the "NET WT..." type at the bottom of the label.

2 Choose Effect > Warp > Arc Lower.

3 In the Warp Options dialog box, to create an arcing effect, set Bend to **35**%. Select Preview to preview the changes. Try choosing other styles from the Style menu, and then return to Arc Lower. Try adjusting the Horizontal and Vertical Distortion sliders to see the effect. Make sure that the Distortion values are returned to **0**, and then click OK.

● **Note:** To learn more about the Appearance panel, see Lesson 13, "Applying Appearance Attributes and Graphic Styles."

4 With the warped text still selected, click the visibility icon (👁) to the left of the Warp: Arc Lower row in the Appearance panel to turn off visibility for the effect. Notice how the text is no longer warped on the artboard.

5 Select the Type tool (**T**) in the Tools panel, and select and change the "375" text on the page to **380**.

6 Select the Selection tool, then click the visibility icon (👁) to the left of the Warp: Arc Lower row in the Appearance panel, to turn on visibility for the effect. Notice how the text is once again warped.

● **Note:** You selected the Selection tool again in this step because you originally applied the effect to the text object with the Selection tool.

7 Choose Select > Deselect.

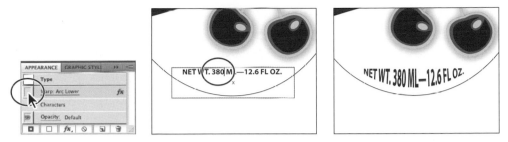

Turn off the Warp effect.   Edit the text on the artboard.   The result with the effect on

▶ **Tip:** It is not necessary to turn the visibility off for the Warp effect before editing the text on the artboard, but doing so makes it easier.

Next, you will apply effects to the text shapes "CHERRY BLAST" at the top of the soda label.

8 With the Selection tool (▶), click the CHERRY BLAST type shapes to select the group.

9 Choose Effect > Warp > Rise.

10 In the Warp Options dialog box, leave the Horizontal option selected and change the Bend to **20%**. Click OK.

Notice how the selected text shapes (in blue) still look like the original shapes, but are actually warped. This shows how a live effect allows you to print the text shapes with the Rise effect applied, but does not change the underlying object.

11 If the Appearance panel is not visible, choose Window > Appearance.

Notice that the Appearance panel lists the Warp: Rise effect that has been applied to the text shapes.

Next, you will hide the selection anchor points so that you can focus on the outcome.

12 With the CHERRY BLAST text shapes still selected, choose View > Hide Edges.

13 In the Control panel, change the Fill to the banner color and leave the stroke at black, 1 pt.

14 Choose Edit > Copy.

15 With the text shapes still selected, choose Object > Hide > Selection.

16 Choose Edit > Paste In Front.

17 With the copy selected, change the fill to the scribble swatch and the stroke color to None in the Control panel.

Next, you will apply the Scribble effect to the text shapes.

18 With the text shapes selected, choose Effect > Stylize > Scribble.

19 In the Scribble dialog box, choose Tight from the Settings menu. Select Preview to see the change. Change the Angle to **10**, the Path Overlap to **−3** pt, and leave the remainder of the settings at default. Click OK.

20 Choose Object > Show All.

21 Choose Select > Deselect, then File > Save.

Editing shapes with a Pathfinder effect

Pathfinder effects are similar to working with Pathfinder commands in the Pathfinder panel, except they are applied as effects and do not change the underlying content.

Next, you will apply a Pathfinder effect to several shapes.

1   With the Selection tool (▶), Shift-click to select both the red banner shape beneath the SPARKLING SODA text shapes and the oval in the background.

2   Choose Object > Group.

    You grouped the objects together because Pathfinder effects may only be applied to groups, layers, or type objects.

3   Choose Effect > Pathfinder > Intersect to create a shape that shows where the two shapes intersect.

    ● **Note:** If you see a warning dialog box when you choose Effect > Pathfinder > Intersect, it's because you didn't group the objects first.

4   In the Appearance panel notice that the Intersect effect appears in the Appearance panel. Clicking Intersect allows you to change the Pathfinder effect and edit the Intersect effect.

    ● **Note:** To remove the Intersect effect from a group that you just applied, click the Intersect effect in the Appearance panel, and then click the Delete Selected Item button (🗑) at the bottom of the panel.

    ● **Note:** You'll learn more about the Appearance panel in Lesson 13, "Applying Appearance Attributes and Graphic Styles."

5   With the group still selected, choose View > Outline.

    The two shapes are still there and completely editable since this is a live effect being applied.

    ● **Note:** To intersect shapes, you can also use the Pathfinder panel, which will expand the shapes immediately, by default. Using the Effect menu lets you edit shapes independently.

Group the objects.

Apply the Pathfinder effect.

Choose View > Outline.

Next, you will copy the oval shape from the group of shapes with the Pathfinder effect applied.

6 With the Selection tool, double-click the edge of the oval shape to enter isolation mode. This allows you to edit just the two shapes that are part of the group.

● **Note:** You are double-clicking the edge because shapes in isolation mode have no fill, so they can't be selected by clicking in the center.

7 Click the edge of the oval shape to select it. Choose Edit > Copy.

8 Press Escape to exit isolation mode. Choose Select > Deselect.

9 Choose Edit > Paste In Front to paste a copy on top of the other objects.

10 Choose View > Preview and leave the oval shape selected.

11 Choose File > Save.

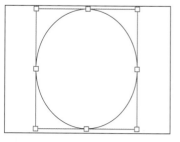

Offsetting paths

Next, you will edit the oval shape by adding multiple strokes to it. You will then edit the multiple strokes by offsetting them against the oval shape. This process allows you to create the appearance of multiple stacked shapes.

1 With the oval shape selected, change the stroke color to green, the fill color to the green gradient labeled center, and the stroke weight to **5** pt in the Control panel.

2 Click the Layers panel icon (◆) on the right side of the workspace to expand the Layers panel. Click the visibility column to the left of the Background layer to reveal the background shape.

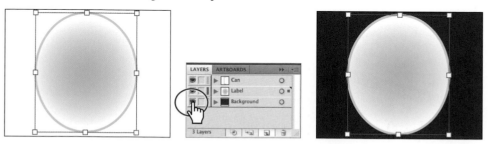

Next, you will add another stroke to the shape, then edit the gradient fill.

3 Click the Appearance panel icon (●) to expand the panel. With the green shape still selected and the stroke row selected in the Appearance panel, click the Add New Stroke button (■) at the bottom of the Appearance panel. A new stroke appears in the panel, but the shape looks the same.

The shape now has two strokes that are the same color and same weight directly on top of each other.

4   In the Appearance panel, change the stroke weight for the selected (highlighted) Stroke to **9** pt.

5   Click the Stroke Color in the Appearance panel and select the white swatch in the Swatches panel. Press Enter or Return to close the Swatches panel and return to the Appearance panel.

You can add multiple strokes to an object and apply different effects to each one, giving you the opportunity to create unique and interesting artwork.

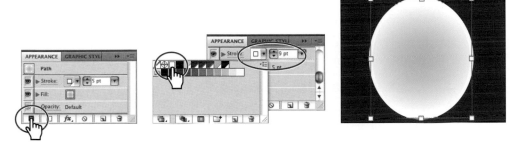

Add a new stroke.   Change the stroke weight and color.   The result

● **Note:** You'll learn more about the Appearance panel in Lesson 13, "Applying Appearance Attributes and Graphic Styles."

6   With the white Stroke selected in the Appearance panel, click the Add New Effect (*fx.*) button at the bottom of the Appearance panel. Choose Path > Offset Path.

7   In the Offset Path dialog box, change the Offset to **16** pt, and click OK.

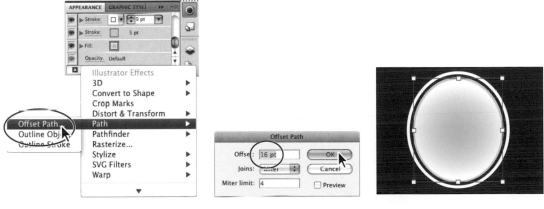

Choose Path > Offset Path.   Set the Offset Path option.   The result

8 In the Appearance panel, click the arrow to the left of the word Stroke (9 pt) to toggle it open. Notice that Offset Path is subset underneath Stroke. This indicates that the Offset Path is applied to only that Stroke.

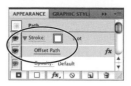

9 Click the word Path at the top of the Appearance panel. This will allow the drop shadow you add in the next step to apply to the entire shape rather than just the offset stroke.

● **Note:** You may need to scroll up in the Appearance panel or resize the panel for easier viewing.

10 Click the Add New Effect (*fx*) button at the bottom of the Appearance panel and choose Stylize > Drop Shadow.

11 In the Drop Shadow dialog box change Opacity to **30**%, X Offset to **0** pt, Y Offset to **0** pt, and Blur to **5** pt. Click OK.

Click Path.

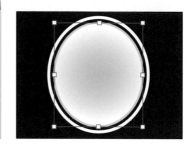

Edit the Drop Shadow options.   The result

▶ **Tip:** Notice the Color square in the Drop Shadow dialog box. Clicking this square will open the Color Picker and allow you to edit the drop shadow color or choose a color from the Swatches panel or other color book.

12 Choose Select > Deselect, then File > Save.

Applying a Photoshop effect

As described earlier in the chapter, the effects in the bottom half of the Effects menu are Photoshop effects (raster effects). You can apply them to either vector or embedded bitmap objects. Raster effects are effects that generate pixels rather than vector data. Raster effects include SVG Filters, all of the effects in the bottom section of the Effect menu, and the Drop Shadow, Inner Glow, Outer Glow, and Feather commands in the Effect > Stylize submenu.

Next, you will apply a Photoshop effect to the background of the label.

1 With Selection tool (![pointer]), click to select the oval shape with the white stroke applied. In the Appearance panel, click the white Stroke row to select it. Be careful not to click the word Stroke.

● **Note:** After you apply the raster effect, the background shape is composed of pixels rather than vector data.

You are going to apply a Photoshop effect to the white stroke.

2 Choose Effect > Texture > Texturizer to open the Effect Gallery. In the Texturizer settings on the right, change the Texture to Sandstone, the Scaling to **140**, the Relief to **8**, and, from the Light menu, choose Bottom.

In the Effect Gallery, you can apply a single raster effect or multiple raster effects to an object. The raster effects are in the middle panel, organized in folders that correlate to the menu item in the Effect menu. You can try more effects and adjust their settings if you like. Click OK to set the Texturizer options.

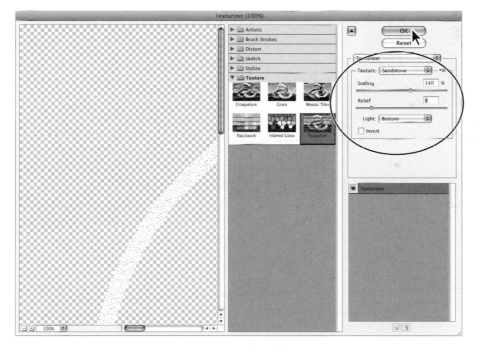

Now that the artwork is complete, you will scale it, and then save it as a symbol in the Symbols panel. Then you'll apply it to a 3D soda can that you'll create.

3 With the Selection tool selected, hold down the Shift key and click the red rectangle in the background to select both shapes. Choose Object > Arrange > Send To Back.

4 Choose Select > All On Active Artboard. Choose Object > Group.

5 With the Group selected, double-click the Scale tool (![scale]) in the Tools panel.

6 In the Scale dialog box, change the Uniform Scale value to **60** and select Scale Strokes & Effects. Click OK.

● **Note:** If you scale content and do not select Scale Strokes & Effects, the stroke weights and effects will stay the same when you scale the content.

▶ **Tip:** To learn more about symbols, see Lesson 14, "Working with Symbols."

7 Click the Symbols panel icon (♣), or choose Window > Symbols to expand the Symbols panel. Select the Selection tool, and drag the selected content onto the Symbols panel to create a symbol. In the Symbol Options dialog box, name the symbol **soda label**, and select Graphic as the symbol type. Click OK.

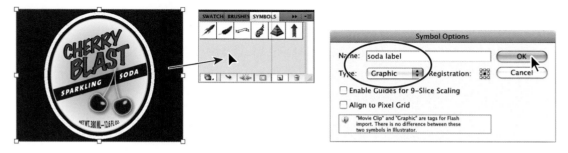

8 Choose Select > Deselect, and then File > Save. Keep the file open.

Document Raster Effects Settings

Whenever you apply a raster effect, Illustrator uses the document's raster effects settings to determine the resolution of the resulting image. It's important to check the document raster effects settings before you start working with effects.

You set rasterization options for a document when creating a new document or by choosing Effect > Document Raster Effects Settings. In the Document Raster Effects Settings dialog box, for all raster effects in a document or when you rasterize a vector object, you can set the Color Model, Resolution, Background, Anti-alias, Create Clipping Mask, and Add Around Object. To learn more about Document Raster Effects Settings, search for "About raster effects" in Help.

—From Illustrator Help

Working with a 3D effect

Using the 3D effect, you can control the appearance of 3D objects with lighting, shading, rotation, and other attributes. In this part of the lesson, you'll use two-dimensional shapes as the foundation for creating three-dimensional objects.

There are three types of 3D effects you can apply:

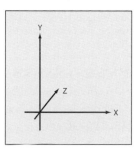

- **Extrude & Bevel**: Extends a 2D object along the object's z axis to add depth to the object. For example, if you extrude a 2D ellipse, it becomes a cylinder.

- **Revolve**: Sweeps a path or profile in a circular direction around the global y axis (revolve axis) to create a 3D object.

- **Rotate**: Uses the z axis to rotate 2D artwork in 3D space and change the artwork's perspective.

The 3D effect takes advantage of the x, y, and z axes.

Extrude & bevel

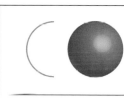

Revolve

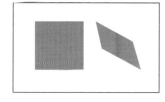

Rotate

Creating a revolved object

In this part of the lesson, you will explore one of the 3D effects called Revolve. You will create a soda can from an existing path on the second artboard, using the Revolve effect.

1 Choose Window > Workspace > Essentials.

2 Click the Artboards panel icon (🗗) to expand the Artboards panel.

3 Double-click Artboard 2 in the panel to fit the artboard in the Document window. Click the Artboards panel icon to collapse the panel.

4 Choose Select > All On Active Artboard.

This path is half of the shape of a soda can. When you apply the revolve effect to it, it will be revolved around the right or left edge to create a 360 degree shape.

5 Click the Stroke color in the Control panel and choose None (◻).

● **Note:** The stroke color overrides the fill color of the object when revolved.

6 Click the Fill color in the Control panel and select White.

7 Choose Effect > 3D > Revolve. In the 3D Revolve Options dialog box, choose Front from the Position menu. Select Preview to see the changes. You may need to reposition the 3D Revolve Options dialog box to see the artwork.

● **Note:** Depending on the complexity of the shape being revolved and the speed of the machine you are working on, making changes in the 3D Revolve Options dialog box can take some time. It may be helpful to deselect Preview, make some changes, then select Preview again. That way the shape does not have to "redraw" on the artboard every time a change is made in the dialog box.

▶ **Tip:** The Angle determines the degree of revolution. To create a "cut-away" look, you can change the degree to less than 360.

8 For the Offset From option, choose Right Edge. This is the edge that your arc revolves around. The result varies dramatically depending on the side that you choose and whether you have a stroke or fill applied to the original object. Click OK.

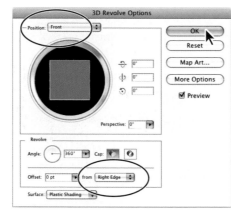

Choose which edge to revolve around.   Revolve with Left Edge selected.   Revolve with Right Edge selected.

9 Choose File > Save, and keep the file open.

3D Revolve options

In the 3D Options dialog box for the Revolve 3D effect, there are several other options worth mentioning:

- **Angle:** Sets the number of degrees to revolve the path, between 0 and 360.

- **Cap:** Specifies whether the object appears solid (Revolve Cap On) or hollow (Revolve Cap Off).

- **Offset:** Adds distance between the revolve axis and the path, to create a ring-shaped object, for instance. You can enter a value between 0 and 1000.

—From Illustrator Help

Changing the lighting of a 3D object

The Revolve effect allows you to add one or more lights, vary the light intensity, change the object's shading color, and move lights around the object.

In this section, you will change the strength and direction of the light source.

1 With the soda can shape selected, click 3D Revolve in the Appearance panel. If the Appearance panel is not visible, choose Window > Appearance. You may also need to scroll in the Appearance panel, or resize it for easier viewing.

2 Select Preview in the 3D Revolve Options dialog box, and click More Options.

You can create custom lighting effects on your 3D object. Use the preview window in the lower left of the 3D Revolve Options dialog box to reposition the lighting and change the shade color.

3 Choose Diffuse Shading from the Surface menu.

4 In the preview window (the shaded sphere), drag the white square that represents the light source to the left. This changes the direction of the lighting. Click the New Light button (image) to add another light source to the soda can. Drag the second light source down and to the right.

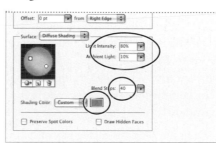

Try positioning them in different arrangements, and move the dialog box out of the way to see the artwork.

5 Choose Custom from the Shading Color menu. Click the colored square to the right of Custom to open the Color Picker. In the Color Picker, change the color to a medium gray (C=0, M=0, Y=0, K=50). Click OK to close the Color Picker and return to the 3D Revolve Options dialog box.

6 In the 3D Revolve Options dialog box, change Light Intensity to **80**% and the Ambient Light to **10**%. Leave the dialog box open.

Ambient light controls the brightness on the surface of the 3D object uniformly.

7 Change the Blend Steps to **40** and click OK when it is done processing.

8 Choose File > Save.

● **Note:** Depending on the speed of the machine you are working on, it may take some time to process changes made in the 3D Revolve Options dialog box.

Surface shading options

In the 3D Options dialog box for Extrude & Bevel and Revolve, Surface lets you choose options for shading surfaces such as:

- **Wireframe:** Outlines the contours of the object's geometry and makes each surface transparent.
- **No Shading:** Adds no new surface properties to the object. The 3D object has the same color as the original 2D object.
- **Diffuse Shading:** Makes the object reflect light in a soft, diffuse pattern.
- **Plastic Shading:** Makes the object reflect light as if it were made of a shiny, high-gloss material.

Note: *Depending on what option you choose, different lighting options are available. If the object only uses the 3D Rotate effect, the only Surface choices available are Diffuse Shading or No Shading.*

—From Illustrator Help

Mapping a symbol to the 3D artwork

You can map artwork from Illustrator and also import artwork from other applications, such as Photoshop. The artwork you map needs to be 2D artwork that's stored in the Symbols panel. Symbols can be any Illustrator art object, including paths, compound paths, text, raster images, mesh objects, and groups of objects. In this part of the lesson, you will map the soda label that you previously saved as a symbol to the soda can.

1 With the soda can still selected, click 3D Revolve in the Appearance panel. Drag the 3D Revolve Options dialog box off to the side so that you can see the soda can artwork. Make sure that Preview is also selected.

2 Click the Map Art button in the 3D Revolve Options dialog box.

When you map art to a 3D object, you first need to choose which surface to map the art to. Every 3D object is composed of multiple surfaces. For example, an extruded square becomes a cube that is made of six surfaces: the front and back faces, and the four side faces. Next, you will choose which surface to map the artwork to.

3 Drag the Map Art dialog box off to the side. Click the Next Surface button (▶) until "4 of 4" appears in the surface field. In the artwork, notice that Illustrator is highlighting the wireframe and the selected surface in red.

4 Choose soda label from the Symbol menu. Select Preview, if not already selected.

● **Note:** If you select the wrong surface, choose Clear and map to another surface.

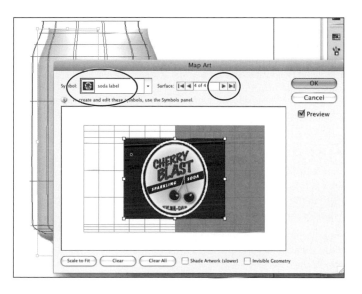

5 Deselect Preview in the Map Art dialog box to speed up the next few steps.

6 Drag the symbol into the light area of the map in the Map Art dialog box.

   A light gray color marks surfaces that are currently visible. A dark gray color marks surfaces that are hidden by the object's current position.

7 Select Shade Artwork (Slower). Select Preview to see the artwork with the symbol mapped to it. You may want to reposition or resize the artwork. Then click OK to close the Map Art dialog box.

8 In the 3D Revolve Options dialog box, click the Fewer Options button, and then click the left edge of the blue square and drag to the right to spin the 3D object along the y-axis. With Preview selected, when you release the mouse button the object on the artboard will update. Click OK.

▶ **Tip:** If you don't like the position or size of the symbol artwork, you can click the Clear button at the bottom of the dialog box to clear the symbol artwork from the current surface.

▶ **Tip:** You can interact with the symbol in the Map Art dialog box using the normal bounding box controls to move, scale, or rotate the object.

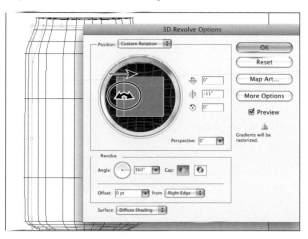

To map artwork to a 3D object

When mapping 3D objects, consider the following:

- Because the Map Art feature uses symbols for mapping, you can edit a symbol instance and then automatically update all surfaces that are mapped with it.

- You can interact with the symbol in the Map Art dialog box with normal bounding box controls to move, scale, or rotate the object.

- The 3D effect remembers each mapped surface on an object as a number. If you edit the 3D object or apply the same effect to a new object, there may be fewer or more sides than the original. If there are fewer surfaces than the number of surfaces defined for the original mapping, the extra artwork will be ignored.

- Because a symbol's position is relative to the center of an object surface, if the geometry of the surface changes, then the symbol will be remapped relative to the new center of the object.

- You can map artwork to objects that use the Extrude & Bevel or Revolve effect, but you can't map artwork to objects that only use the Rotate effect.

—From Illustrator Help

The texture now wraps around the soda can. Next, you will edit the soda can path and the color.

9 With the Selection tool selected, and the 3D object selected, change the Fill color to Black in the Control panel.

Notice that the entire shape changes color, except where the symbol artwork is mapped to the surface. At this point, if necessary, you can edit the shape that you started with. If you need to rotate the 3D object, in this situation it is best done in the 3D Revolve Options dialog box.

▶ **Tip:** If you need to edit the shape, it is recommended that you deselect the visibility column of the 3D Revolve (Mapped) effect in the Appearance panel first. Then, when you are finished editing the shape, click the visibility column to show the 3D Revolve (Mapped) effect again.

10 Choose View > Show Edges to show the edges for later lessons.

11 Choose File > Save. Keep the file open for the Exploring on Your Own section, or choose File > Close.

Printing Resources

To make optimum decisions about printing, you should understand basic printing principles, including how the resolution of your printer or the calibration and resolution of you monitor can affect the way your artwork appears when printed. Illustrator's Print dialog box is designed to help you through the printing workflow. Each set of options in the dialog box is organized to guide you through the printing process. For information on working in the print dialog box, see "Print dialog box options" in Illustrator Help.

For information on working with color management in Illustrator, see "Printing with color management" in Illustrator Help.

For information on the optimal ways to print a document, including information on Color Management, PDF workflows, and more, visit the following site:

- http://www.adobe.com/studio/print/

For information on the printing in the Creative Suite, visit the following site:

- http://www.adobe.com/designcenter/cs4/articles/cs4_printguide.html

For a guide to working with and printing transparency in the Creative Suite, visit the following site:

- http://www.adobe.com/designcenter/creativesuite/articles/cs3ip_transguide.html

Exploring on your own

Next, you will work with another effect to add a nice touch to the sodacan.ai file you still have open.

1 Choose 1 from the Artboard Navigation menu in the lower-left corner of the Document window.

2 With the Selection tool, click to select the symbol instance on the artboard. Click the Break Link button in the Control panel to edit the shapes.

3 Choose Select > Deselect.

4 Click the oval shape with the white stroke to select it.

5 Choose Effect > Convert To Shape > Rounded Rectangle.

6 In the Shape Options dialog box, select the Relative option, and then change Extra Width and Extra Height to **0**. Select Preview, and then adjust the corner radius to the desired corner radius. Click OK.

7 Choose File > Save, and then File > Close.

Create an additional item for the artwork in this lesson.

1   Choose File > Open, and locate the L12start_2.ai file in the Lesson12 folder.

2   Select the Selection tool (▶), and then Select > All.

3   Drag the artwork into the Symbols panel.

4   In the Symbol Options dialog box, change the name to **Soap**, and choose Graphic from the Type menu. Click OK.

5   With the artwork still selected, choose Edit > Clear, or press the Delete key.

6   Select the Rectangle tool (▢), and click the artboard once. Type **325 pt** for the width and **220 pt** for the height. Click OK.

7   Choose Effect > 3D > Extrude & Bevel, and experiment with different positions and settings.

    ● **Note:** Changing the Bevel option can greatly increase the complexity of the 3D object and the number of surfaces to map artwork to.

8   Click Map Art, and map the Soap symbol that you created to one surface of the box.

9   Close both dialog boxes when you are finished.

Take the illustration further by creating your own symbols and applying them to the other faces of the box.

10 Choose File > Close and don't save the file.

Review questions

1 Name two ways to apply an effect to an object.

2 Where can the effects applied to an object be edited, once they are applied?

3 What are the three types of 3D effects that are available? Give an example of why you would use each one.

4 How can you control lighting on a 3D object? Does the lighting of one 3D object affect other 3D objects?

5 What are the steps to map artwork to an object?

Review answers

1 You can apply an effect to an object by selecting the object, and then choosing the effect from the Effect menu. You can also apply an effect by selecting the object, then clicking the Add New Effect button(*fx.*) in the Appearance panel, and then choosing the effect from the menu that appears.

2 You can edit effects in the Appearance panel.

3 The types of 3D effects are Extrude & Bevel, Revolve, and Rotate.

   • **Extrude & Bevel:** Uses the z axis to give a 2D object depth by extruding the object. For example, a circle becomes a cylinder.

   • **Revolve:** Uses the y axis to revolve an object around an axis. For example, an arc becomes a circle.

   • **Rotate:** Uses the z axis to rotate 2D artwork in 3D space and change the artwork's perspective.

4 By clicking the More Options button in any of the 3D dialog boxes, you can change the light, the direction of the light, and the shade color. Settings for the light of one 3D object do not affect the settings for other 3D objects.

5 Map artwork to an object by following these steps:

   a Select the artwork to be used as a symbol and Alt-click (Windows) or Option-click (Mac OS) the New Symbol button in the Symbols panel.

   b Select the object and choose Effect > 3D > Extrude & Bevel or Effect > 3D > Revolve.

   c Click Map Art.

   d Navigate to the surface by clicking the Next Surface or Previous Surface buttons. Select the symbol from the Symbol menu. Close both dialog boxes.

13 APPLYING APPEARANCE ATTRIBUTES AND GRAPHIC STYLES

Lesson overview

In this lesson, you'll learn how to do the following:

- Create and edit an appearance attribute.

- Add a second stroke to an object.

- Reorder appearance attributes and apply them to layers.

- Copy, turn on and off, and remove appearance attributes.

- Save an appearance as a graphic style.

- Apply a graphic style to an object and a layer.

- Apply multiple graphic styles to an object or layer.

 This lesson will take approximately an hour to complete. If needed, remove the previous lesson folder from your hard disk and copy the Lesson13 folder onto it.

Without changing the structure of an object, you can change its look using appearance attributes, including fills, strokes, effects, transparency and blending modes. You can save appearance attributes as graphic styles and apply them to another object. You can also edit an object that has a graphic style applied to it, and then edit the graphic style—an enormous time-saver!

379

Getting started

In this lesson, you'll enhance the design for a web page by applying appearance attributes and graphic styles to the type, background, and buttons. Before you begin, you'll restore the default preferences for Adobe® Illustrator® CS5. Then you will open the finished art file for this lesson to see what you'll create.

1 To ensure that the tools and panels function as described in this lesson, delete or deactivate (by renaming) the Adobe Illustrator CS5 preferences file. See "Restoring default preferences" on page 3.

2 Start Adobe Illustrator CS5.

● **Note:** If you have not already done so, copy the resource files for this lesson onto your hard disk from the Lesson13 folder on the Adobe Illustrator CS5 Classroom in a Book CD. See "Copying the Classroom in a Book files" on page 2.

3 Choose File > Open. Locate the L13end_1.ai file in the Lesson13 folder in the Lessons folder that you copied onto your hard disk to view the finished artwork. In this lesson, you will apply styling to the web buttons and other objects. Leave the file open for reference, or choose File > Close.

The design for the completed web page includes several graphic styles and effects, including gradients, semi-transparent type, drop shadows, and texturized and shaded graphics.

● **Note:** If a color profile warning dialog box appears, click OK.

4 Open the L13start_1.ai file in the Lesson13 folder, located in the Lessons folder on your hard disk.

● **Note:** If a color profile warning dialog box appears, click OK.

5 Choose File > Save As. In the Save As dialog box, navigate to the Lesson13 folder and open it. Name the file **tech_design.ai**. Leave the Save As Type option set to Adobe Illustrator (*.AI) (Windows) or the Format option set to Adobe Illustrator (ai) (Mac OS), and click Save. In the Illustrator Options dialog box, leave the Illustrator options at their default settings, and then click OK.

Using appearance attributes

You can apply appearance attributes to any object, group, or layer by using effects and the Appearance panel and Graphic Styles panel. An appearance attribute is an aesthetic property—such as a fill, stroke, transparency, or effect—that affects the look of an object, but does not affect its basic structure. An advantage of using appearance attributes is that they can be changed or removed at any time without changing the underlying object or any other attributes applied to the object.

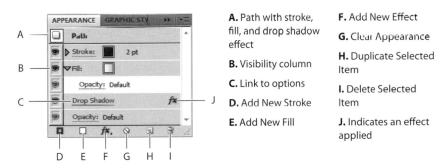

A. Path with stroke, fill, and drop shadow effect

B. Visibility column

C. Link to options

D. Add New Stroke

E. Add New Fill

F. Add New Effect

G. Clear Appearance

H. Duplicate Selected Item

I. Delete Selected Item

J. Indicates an effect applied

For example, if you apply the Drop Shadow effect to an object, you can change the drop shadow distance, blur, or color. You can also copy that effect and apply it to other shapes, groups, or layers. You can even save it as a graphic style and use it for other objects or files.

The Appearance panel contains the following types of editable attributes:

- Stroke (weight, color, and effects)
- Fill (type, color, transparency, and effects)
- Transparency, including opacity and blending mode
- Effect menu

Editing and adding appearance attributes

You'll start by selecting an arrow shape and adding to its basic appearance using the Appearance panel.

1   Choose Window > Workspace > Essentials.

2   In the tech_design.ai file, using the Selection tool (🡒), select the top green arrow shape in the Home button.

3 Click the Appearance panel icon (●) on the right side of the workspace, and click the Stroke attribute row to select it. Do not click the blue underlined word Stroke. Click to the right or left of the word.

Selecting the Stroke attribute row lets you change just the stroke in the artwork.

4 Click the word Opacity in the Control panel to reveal the Transparency panel. In the Transparency panel, choose Multiply from the menu of blending modes. Change Opacity to **50**%. Press Enter or Return to close the Transparency panel.

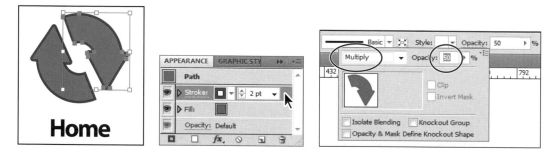

5 With the Selection tool, press Ctrl+spacebar (Windows) or Command+spacebar (Mac OS) and click the arrow shape several times to zoom in to about 200%. Inspect the stroke around the arrow to see how it has changed. The effect of the Multiply blending mode is similar to drawing on a page with transparent marker pens.

Strokes are centered on a path outline—half of the stroke color overlaps the filled arrow shape, and half of the stroke color overlaps the white background.

Next, you will edit the stroke of the arrow using the Appearance panel.

6 In the Appearance panel, expand the stroke attributes by clicking the triangle (▶) to the left of the word Stroke in the panel list.

7 Click the word Opacity to open the Transparency panel.

8 In the Transparency panel, change Opacity to **70**%. Click the Opacity attribute row in the Appearance panel to hide the Transparency panel.

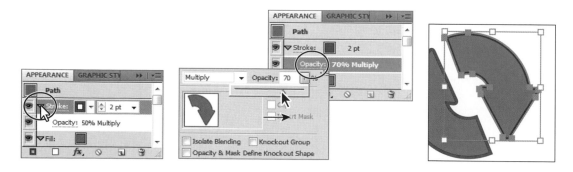

9 Click 2 pt in the Appearance panel to edit the value. Change Stroke Weight to 4 pt. If you want, you can change the stroke color as well.

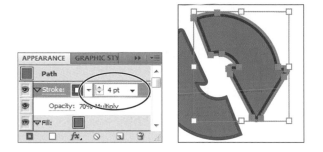

10 Choose File > Save.

Reordering appearance attributes

Now, you'll change the appearance of the Multiply blending mode by rearranging the attributes in the Appearance panel.

1 Resize the Appearance panel so that you can view all its contents. Click the triangle (▶) to the left of the word Stroke to hide the stroke properties. If the Fill properties are showing as well, click the triangle (▶) to the left of the word Fill to hide the fill properties.

2 Drag the Fill attribute above the Stroke attribute. (This technique is similar to dragging layers in the Layers panel to rearrange the stacking order.)

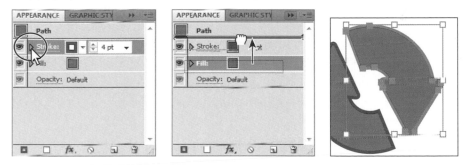

Moving the Fill attribute above the Stroke attribute changes the look of the Multiply blending mode on the stroke. Half the stroke is covered. Blending modes work only on objects that are beneath them in the stacking order.

Adding an additional stroke and fill

You'll now add another stroke to the object, using the Appearance panel. Applying another stroke is a way to add interesting design elements to your artwork.

1 With the arrow shape selected, click the Add New Stroke button (■) at the bottom of the Appearance panel. A stroke is added to the top of the list of appearance attributes. It has the same color and stroke weight as the first stroke.

2 For the new stroke, change Stroke Weight to **2** pt in the Appearance panel.

▶ **Tip:** Other ways to close panels, such as the Color panel, that appear in the Appearance panel include pressing Escape or clicking the Stroke attribute row.

3 Shift-click the Stroke Color to open the Color panel instead of the Swatches panel. Choose RGB from the panel menu (▾☰). Change the RGB values to R=**76**, G=**0**, and B=**121**. Press Enter or Return to close the Color panel and return to the Appearance panel.

You are using the RGB color mode because you are working with a web document.

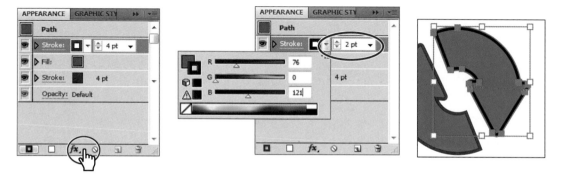

Next, you will add an effect to change the offset of the stroke by bringing it toward the center of the arrow.

4 With the top Stroke attribute row still selected, click the Add New Effect button (*fx.*) at the bottom of the Appearance panel. Choose Path > Offset Path from the menu that appears.

5 Select Preview in the Offset Path dialog box to see the effect of offsetting as you change the values. Change Offset to **−3 px**, and then click OK.

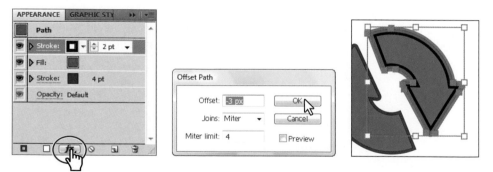

6 In the Appearance panel, click the arrow to the left of the top Stroke to reveal the Offset Path and Opacity effects. Deselect the eye icon (👁) to the left of Offset Path to hide that effect. Notice that the arrow on the artboard changes. Select the Visibility column to view the Offset Path again.

By clicking the eye icon in the Appearance panel, you disable an attribute without deleting it.

▶ **Tip:** You can view all hidden attributes by choosing Show All Hidden Attributes from the Appearance panel menu.

Next, you'll rearrange the order of the appearance attributes to prepare for adding live effects.

7 In the Appearance panel, click the triangle to the left of the 2 pt Stroke attribute to collapse the attribute, and then drag the 4 pt Stroke attribute between the Fill attribute and the 2 pt Stroke attribute.

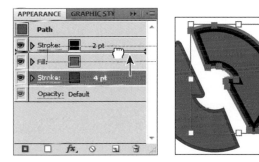

8 Choose File > Save, and keep the arrow selected.

Using graphic styles

A graphic style is a saved set of appearance attributes that you can reuse. By applying graphic styles, you can quickly and globally change the appearance of objects and text.

The Graphic Styles panel (Window > Graphic Styles) lets you create, name, save, apply, and remove effects and attributes to objects, layers, and groups. You can also break the link between an object and an applied graphic style to edit that object's attributes without affecting other objects that use that same graphic style.

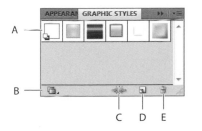

A. Graphic styles

B. Graphic Styles Libraries menu

C. Break Link To Graphic Style

D. New Graphic Style

E. Delete Graphic Style

For example, if you have a map that uses a shape to represent a city, you can create a graphic style that paints the shape green and adds a drop shadow. You can then use that graphic style to paint all the city shapes on the map. If you decide to use a different color, you can change the fill color of the graphic style to blue. All the objects that use that graphic style are then updated to blue.

Creating and saving a graphic style

Now, you'll save and name a new graphic style using the appearance attributes you just specified for the arrow shape in the Home button. You will then apply the same appearance attributes to the other arrow shape.

1 Choose Essentials from the Workspace switcher in the Application bar, to reset the workspace.

● **Note:** Even though Essentials is already selected, selecting it again will reset the workspace.

2 Click the Graphic Styles panel icon (⬛) on the right side of the workspace to open the Graphic Styles panel.

3 Drag the Graphic Styles panel by the panel tab so that it is free-floating in the workspace. Resize the Graphic Styles panel so that all the default styles are visible and there is empty space at the bottom, if necessary.

4 With the arrow shape on the artboard still selected, in the Appearance panel, drag the Path appearance thumbnail into the Graphic Styles panel.

5 When a small box appears on the inside of the panel, release the mouse button. The box indicates that you are adding a new style to the panel.

   The path thumbnail in the Appearance panel changes to "Path: Graphic Style."

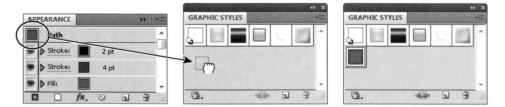

6 In the Graphic Styles panel, double-click the new graphic style thumbnail. In the Graphic Style Options dialog box, name the new style **Home button**. Click OK.

   Notice in the Appearance panel that "Path: Graphic Style" has changed to "Path: Home button." This indicates that a graphic style called Home button is applied to the selected object.

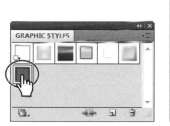

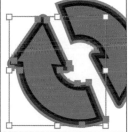

7   Choose Select > Deselect, and then File > Save.

Applying a graphic style to an object

Graphic styles can be easily applied to other objects. Next, you will apply the graphic style of the right arrow shape to the left arrow in the Home button.

1   With the Selection tool (⬉), click to select the other green arrow.

2   Click the Home button graphic style in the Graphic Styles panel to apply its attributes to the other arrow.

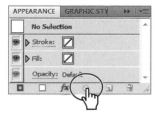

3   Choose Select > Deselect, and then File > Save.

Applying a graphic style to a layer

When a graphic style is applied to a layer, everything added to that layer has that same style applied to it. Now, you'll create a new graphic style and apply it to a layer. Then you'll create new shapes on that layer to see the effect of the style.

1   Choose Essentials from the workspace switcher in the Application bar.

2   Expand the Appearance panel (⬤) on the right side of the workspace, and click the Clear Appearance button (⊘) at the bottom of the panel. Select the No Selection appearance name or thumbnail at the top of the panel.

The Clear Appearance button removes all appearance attributes applied to an object, including any stroke or fill. By clicking the Clear Appearance button with nothing selected, you are setting the default appearance for new shapes.

3 In the Appearance panel, click the Add New Effect button (*fx.*) and choose Stylize > Drop Shadow from the Illustrator Effects. Change Opacity to **50%**, X Offset to **3** pt, Y Offset to **3** pt, and Blur to **3** pt. Click OK.

● **Note:** When you type in 3 pt in a field, you *may* notice that it converts to 3 px when you click in another field. That is because the unit of measurement for the document was set to pixels.

4 In the Appearance panel, notice that Drop Shadow appears in the list. Drag the bottom of the Appearance panel down to expose more of the panel.

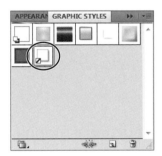

When creating a new style, the Graphic Style panel automatically uses the current appearance attributes displayed in the Appearance panel.

5 Click the Graphic Styles panel icon (⬛) on the right side of the workspace to expand the panel. Alt-click (Windows) or Option-click (Mac OS) the New Graphic Style button (⬛), and name the new style **Drop Shadow**. Click OK.

Now, you'll target the Blog button layer to apply a drop shadow to all the shapes on that layer. Targeting selects the path(s) on that layer in the artwork.

6 Click the Layers panel icon (⬤) on the right side of the workspace to open the Layers panel.

7 In the Layers panel, click the triangle (▶) to the left of the Blog button layer to expand the layer. Then click the target icon (○) to the right of the Blog button layer name. If you can't see the selected shapes on the artboard, you can hold down the spacebar and drag to the left.

● **Note:** You may need to scroll down in the Layers panel.

8 In the Graphic Styles panel, click the Drop Shadow style to apply the style to the layer and all its contents. Keep the shapes selected on the artboard.

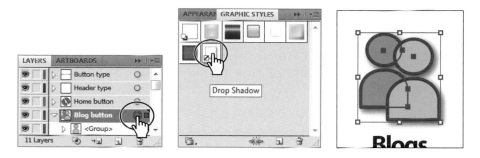

9 Double-click the Scale tool (![scale icon]) in the Tools panel. Change Uniform Scale to **70%**, and then click OK.

10 Choose Select > Deselect, and then File > Save.

Now, you'll test the layer effect by adding a shape to the Blog button layer.

11 Select the Zoom tool (![zoom icon]) in the Tools panel, and click the blog shapes twice to zoom in.

12 Select the Ellipse tool (![ellipse icon]) from the same group as the Rectangle tool (![rectangle icon]) in the Tools panel.

13 Make sure that Fill color in the Control panel is set to None (![none icon]), Stroke Color is black, and Stroke Weight is **3** pt.

14 With the Blog button layer still selected, press the Shift key and draw a circle on top of the blog shapes that is about 82 px in height and width.

● **Note:** To see the size as you draw in the measurement label, make sure that the smart guides are selected (View > Smart Guides).

15 Choose Object > Arrange > Send To Back to send the ellipse behind the blog shapes. With the Selection tool, position the circle so that it is approximately centered behind the blog shapes. Keep the ellipse selected.

Because the Drop Shadow style contains only an effect, and no stroke or fill, the objects added to the layer retain their original stroke and fill attributes.

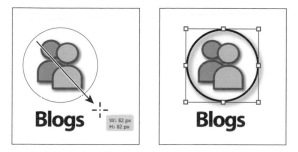

Next, you will edit the drop shadow applied to the layer.

16 Click the Appearance panel icon (⊙) on the right side of the workspace to open the Appearance panel.

In the Appearance panel, notice the name "Layer: Drop Shadow" at the top of the panel. The Appearance panel shows that the ellipse is on a layer with a drop shadow applied to it.

▶ **Tip:** You can also select the Blog button layer target icon in the Layers panel, and then edit the effect in the Appearance panel.

17 Click the words Layer: Drop Shadow to access the Drop Shadow effect applied to the layer.

18 Click the underlined words Drop Shadow in the Appearance panel and, in the Drop Shadow dialog box, change X Offset to **2** pt, and Y Offset to **2** pt. Select Preview to see the subtle change. Click OK.

19 Choose View > Fit Artboard In Window.

20 Choose Select > Deselect, then choose File > Save.

Target icons

The target icon on the Layers panel indicates whether an item in the layer hierarchy has any appearance attributes and whether it is targeted.

(◎) Indicates the item is targeted but has no appearance attributes beyond a single fill and a single stroke.

(○) Indicates the item is not targeted and has no appearance attributes beyond a single fill and a single stroke.

(◉) Indicates the item is not targeted but has appearance attributes.

(◎) Indicates the item is targeted and has appearance attributes.

—From Illustrator Help

▶ **Tip:** It is a good idea to use the Layers panel to select the objects or layers to which you want to apply styles. Effects and styles vary, depending on whether you're targeting a layer or an object, or a group within a layer.

Applying existing graphic styles

You can apply graphic styles to your artwork from libraries that come with Illustrator CS5. Now, you'll finish the button designs by adding an existing style to the Chat button layer.

1 Click the Layers panel icon (◈) on the right side of the workspace to open the Layers panel.

2 In the Layers panel, click the triangle (▷) to left of the Blog button layer to collapse it. Scroll down in the Layers panel, if necessary, and then click the triangle (▷) to left of the Chat button layer to expand the layer.

3 Select the <Path> sublayer. Then click the target icon (O) to the right of the <Path> sublayer.

4 Select the yellow swatch (R=253, G=195, B=17) from the Fill color in the Control panel.

● **Note:** If you target a layer or sublayer by mistake, Ctrl-click or Command-click the target icon to deselect it.

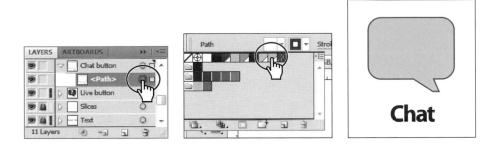

Now, you'll apply a graphic style to the Chat button. The graphic style contains a color fill, which you'll apply to the chat object in place of the existing yellow color.

5 With the target icon (O) for the <Path> sublayer still selected in the Layers panel, click the Style menu in the Control panel. Right-click (Windows) or Control-click (Mac OS) and hold down the mouse button on the Chat style in the Graphic Styles panel to preview the graphic style on the chat bubble.

Previewing a graphic style is a great way to see what how the graphic style will affect the selected object, without actually applying it.

● **Note:** If the Style menu doesn't appear in the Control panel, open the Graphic Styles panel by clicking its icon on the right side of the workspace.

6 Click the Chat graphic style to apply it to the chat bubble.

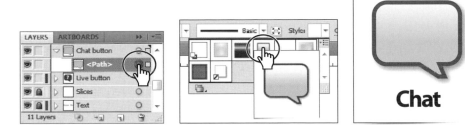

7 Choose File > Save.

Next, you'll apply an existing graphic style to some text.

8 Choose Select > Deselect.

9 With the Selection tool (▶), drag a marquee across the button labels (the text below the buttons) to select them.

Tip: Use the arrows at the bottom of the Illuminate Styles library panel to load the previous or next graphic styles library in the panel.

10 Choose Override Character Color from the Graphic Styles panel menu (▼≡), if it's not already selected. Click the Graphic Styles Libraries Menu button (▦⌄), and choose the Illuminate Styles library.

When you apply a graphic style to type, the text fill overrides the fill color of the graphic style. To prevent that, choose Override Character Color.

11 Choose Use Text For Preview from the Illuminate Styles panel menu (▼≡).

12 In the Illuminate Styles library panel, right-click (Windows) or Control-click (Mac OS) and hold down the mouse button on the Charcoal Highlight graphic style to preview the graphic style on the text. Click the Charcoal Highlight graphic style to apply it.

Note that, if Override Character Color had been deselected, the fill would still be black.

● **Note:** When you click a graphic style from a library, the graphic style is added to the Graphic Styles panel for that document.

13 Close the Illuminate Styles library panel.

14 Choose Select > Deselect, and then File > Save.

Adding to an existing graphic style

You can apply a graphic style to an object that already has a graphic style applied. This can be useful if you want to add properties to an object from another graphic style. The formatting becomes cumulative.

1 With the Selection tool (▶), click to select the red Live Help button shape (not the question mark).

Next, you'll make a change to the shape, and then create a new graphic style out of its appearance attributes.

2 Click the Appearance panel tab in the Graphic Styles panel group to show the panel. Select the red Fill attribute, and click the Duplicate Selected Item button (▤) at the bottom of the panel. This creates a copy of the fill above the original in the Appearance panel.

Tip: To see larger swatches, choose Large Thumbnail View from the Nature_Animal Skins panel menu.

3 Click the Fill color of the new Fill attribute, which is automatically selected in the Appearance panel, to open the Swatches panel. Click the Swatch Libraries menu button (▦⌄) at the bottom of the panel. Choose Patterns > Nature > Nature_Animal Skins. Select the pattern named Tiger to apply it to the fill.

4 Close the Nature_Animal Skins panel.

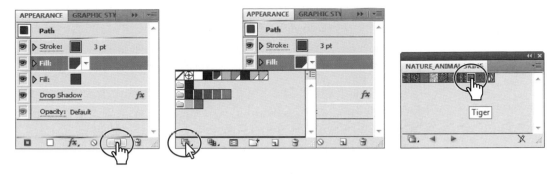

5 With the Tiger fill row selected in the Appearance panel, change Opacity to **30**% in the Control panel.

6 Click the Graphic Styles panel tab to show the graphic styles. Alt-click (Windows) or Option-click (Mac OS) the New Graphic Style button (🔳). In the Graphic Style Option dialog box, name the style **Help**. Click OK.

Next, you will apply the Bevel Soft graphic style to the live help button shape that is still selected.

7 In the Graphic Styles panel, click to apply the Bevel Soft graphic style to the button shape.

Notice that the fills and the stroke are no longer visible. Graphic styles replace the formatting on selected objects by default.

8 Choose Edit > Undo Graphic Styles.

9 Alt-click (Windows) or Option-click (Mac OS) the Bevel Soft graphic style.

Notice that the fills and stroke are preserved and that the bevel is applied as well. Alt-clicking (Windows) or Option-clicking (Mac OS) adds the graphic style formatting to the existing formatting.

10 Open the Appearance panel. Deselect the eye icon () to the left of the Drop Shadow attribute to hide it.

11 Choose Select > Deselect, and then File > Save.

Applying an appearance to a layer

You can also apply simple appearance attributes to layers. For example, to make everything on a layer 50% opaque, target that layer, and change the opacity.

Next, you'll target a layer and change its blending mode to soften the effect of the type.

1 In the Layers panel, click the downward triangle next to any open layers to collapse them.

2 Scroll to the Columns layer, and then click its target icon (○).

3 Select the K=50 swatch from the Fill color in the Control panel, and change Opacity to **20**% in the Control panel as well.

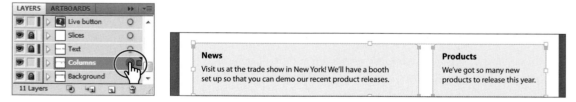

4 Choose Select > Deselect.

5 Choose File > Save.

Copying, applying, and removing graphic styles

When you create several graphic styles and appearances, you may want to use them on other objects in your artwork. You can use the Graphic Styles panel, the Appearance panel, the Eyedropper tool (🖊), or the Live Paint Bucket tool (🪣) to apply and copy appearance attributes.

Next, you'll apply a style to one of the objects using the Appearance panel.

6 With the Selection tool (▶), click one of the arrow shapes for the Home button to select it.

7 In the Appearance panel, drag the appearance thumbnail labeled Path: Home button onto the larger speaker shape of the Forums button to apply those attributes to it.

● **Note:** Be sure to drag the thumbnail, not the text.

You can apply styles or attributes by dragging them from the Graphic Styles panel or the Appearance panel onto any object. The object doesn't have to be selected.

8 Choose Select > Deselect.

Next, you'll apply a style by dragging it directly from the Graphic Styles panel onto an object.

9 With the Selection tool, drag the Charcoal Highlight graphic style thumbnail in the Graphic Styles panel onto the larger speaker shape in the Forums button artwork.

10 Release the mouse button to apply the style to the shape.

11 Drag the same graphic style to the smaller speaker shape to the left in the forums button to apply it. See the figure for placement.

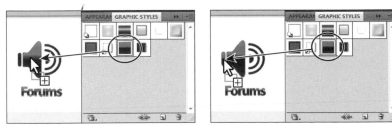

Now, you'll use the Layers panel to copy an attribute from one layer to another.

12 Expand the Layers panel to see all the layers. Click the Blog button layer to select it. Alt-drag (Windows) or Option-drag (Mac OS) the appearance indicator from the Blog button layer onto the appearance indicator of the Header type layer.

Using Alt or Option as you drag copies one layer effect onto another, which is indicated by the hand pointer with the plus sign. To move an appearance or style from one layer or object to another, drag the appearance indicator.

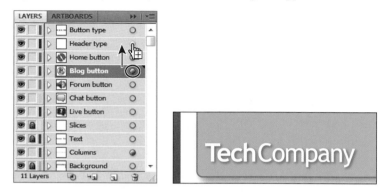

Alt-drag or Option-drag the appearance attributes from one layer to another.

Now, you'll remove an appearance from a layer using the Layers panel.

13 In the Layers panel, click the target icon to the right of the Blog button layer.

14 Drag the target icon to the Trash button at the bottom of the Layers panel to remove the appearance attribute.

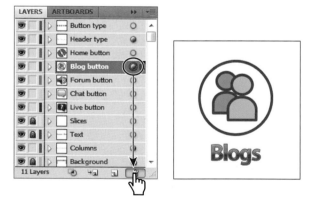

You can also remove attributes of a selected object or layer in the Appearance panel. To do this, select the object and then choose Reduce To Basic Appearance from the panel menu. This returns the object to its original state (including any stroke or fill), as it was before the appearance attribute or style was applied.

15 Choose File > Save, and then File > Close.

Exploring on your own

Now that you've learned the basic steps for creating and using appearances and graphic styles, you can experiment with different combinations of appearance attributes to fashion interesting special effects. Try combining different styles to produce new ones.

For example, here's how to merge two existing styles to create a brand new style:

1   Choose File > New to create a new file. In the New Document dialog box, make sure that Print is chosen from the New Document Profile menu, and then click OK.

2   Choose Window > Graphic Styles to open the panel.

3   In the Graphic Styles panel, select the Round Corners 10 pt style.

● **Note:** If the Round Corners 10 pt style does not appear in the Graphic Styles panel, then click the Graphic Styles Library Menu button and choose Image Effects > Yellow Glow.

4   Add another style to the selected style by Ctrl-clicking (Windows) or Command-clicking (Mac OS) the style named Illuminate Yellow.

● **Note:** If the Illuminate Yellow style does not appear in the Graphic Styles panel, then click the Graphic Styles Library Menu button (▣) and choose Type Effects > Twine and repeat the previous two steps.

5   Choose Merge Graphic Styles from the Graphic Styles panel menu.

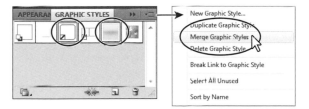

6   Name the new style **merged style** in the Graphic Style Options dialog box, and then click OK.

7   On the artboard, draw a shape or create text, select the content with the Selection tool, and then apply the merged style.

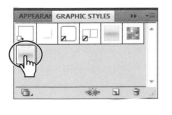

8   Choose File > Close without saving the file.

Review questions

1 Name two types of appearance attributes.

2 How do you add a second stroke to an object?

3 What's the difference between applying a graphic style to a layer versus applying it to an object?

4 How do you add to an existing graphic style?

5 How do you remove an appearance attribute using the Layers panel?

Review answers

1 The Appearance panel contains the following types of editable attributes:

- Fill attributes (fill type, color, transparency, and effects)

- Stroke attributes (stroke type, brush, color transparency, and effects)

- Transparency attributes (opacity and blending mode)

- Effects from the Effect menu

2 Click the Add New Stroke button in the Appearance panel, or choose Add New Stroke from the Appearance panel menu. A stroke is added to the top of the appearance list. It has the same color and stroke weight as the original stroke.

3 After a graphic style is applied to a layer, everything you add to that layer has that style applied to it. For example, if you create a circle on Layer 1 and then move that circle to Layer 2, which has a Drop Shadow effect applied, the circle adopts that effect.

When a style is applied to a single object, other objects on that layer are not affected. For example, if a triangle object has a Roughen effect applied to its path, and you move it to another layer, it retains the Roughen effect.

4 When a graphic style is applied to an object, Alt-click (Windows) or Option-click (Mac OS) a new graphic style in the Graphic Styles panel.

5 In the Layers panel, click the target icon of a layer. Drag the target icon to the Delete Selection button in the Layers panel to remove the appearance attribute. You can also remove the appearance attribute of a selected object or layer using the Appearance panel. Select the object and choose Reduce To Basic Appearance from the Appearance panel menu to return the object to its original state.

14 WORKING WITH SYMBOLS

Lesson overview

In this lesson, you'll learn how to do the following:

- Apply symbol instances.

- Create a symbol.

- Modify and redefine a symbol.

- Use the symbolism tools.

- Store and retrieve artwork in the Symbols panel.

- Work with symbols and Adobe Flash.

 This lesson will take approximately an hour to complete. If needed, remove the previous lesson folder from your hard disk and copy the Lesson14 folder onto it.

The Symbols panel lets you apply multiple objects by painting them on the page. Symbols used in combination with the symbolism tools offer options that make creating repetitive shapes, such as grass, easy and fun. You can also use the Symbols panel as a database to store artwork and map symbols to 3D objects. Symbols can also be used in export to SWF and SVG.

Getting started

In this lesson, you'll finish the artwork for a poster. Before you begin, restore the default preferences for Adobe® Illustrator®. Then open the file containing the finished artwork to see what you are going to create.

1 To ensure that the tools and panels function as described in this lesson, delete or deactivate (by renaming) the Adobe Illustrator CS5 preferences file. See "Restoring default preferences" on page 3.

2 Start Adobe Illustrator CS5.

● **Note:** If you have not already done so, copy the resource files for this lesson onto your hard disk from the Lesson14 folder on the Adobe Illustrator CS5 Classroom in a Book CD. See "Copying the Classroom in a Book files" on page 2.

3 Choose File > Open, and open the L14end_1.ai file in the Lesson14 folder in the Lessons folder on your hard disk.

If you want to view the finished poster as you work, choose View > Zoom Out, and adjust the window size. Use the Hand tool (✋) to move the artwork where you want it in the window. If you don't want to leave the image open, choose File > Close.

4 Choose File > Open to open the L14start_1.ai file in the Lesson14 folder, located in the Lessons folder on your hard disk.

5 Choose File > Save As. In the Save As dialog box, name the file **poster.ai** and navigate to the Lesson14 folder. Leave the Save As Type option set to Adobe Illustrator (*.AI) (Windows) or the Format option set to Adobe Illustrator (ai) (Mac OS), and click Save. In the Illustrator Options dialog box, leave the Illustrator options at their default settings, and then click OK.

6 Choose Window > Workspace > Essentials.

7 Double-click the Hand tool (✋) to fit the artboard in the window.

Working with symbols

A symbol is a reusable art object that is stored in the Symbols panel (Window > Symbols). For example, if you create a symbol from an object in the shape of a blade of grass, you can then quickly add multiple instances of that grass symbol to your artwork, which saves you from having to draw each individual blade of grass. All instances of the grass symbol are linked to the associated symbol in the Symbols panel, so you can easily alter them using symbolism tools.

When you edit the original symbol, all instances of the grass that are linked to it are updated. You can turn that grass from brown to green instantly! Not only do symbols save time, but they greatly reduce file size. They can also be used in conjunction with Adobe Flash to create SWF files or artwork for Flash.

Illustrator comes with a series of symbol libraries, which range from tiki icons to hair and fur. You can access the symbol libraries in the Symbols panel or by choosing Window > Symbol Libraries.

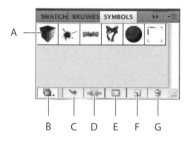

A

A. Symbols
B. Symbol Libraries menu
C. Place Symbol Instance
D. Break Link To Symbol

E. Symbol Options
F. New Symbol
G. Delete Symbol

● **Note:** The Symbols panel at left is the default Symbols panel for a new Illustrator print document.

B C D E F G

Using existing Illustrator symbol libraries

You will start by adding some sushi from an existing symbol library to the artwork.

1 Choose View > Smart Guides to deselect smart guides.

2 Click the Layers panel icon (🔶) on the right side of the workspace to expand the Layers panel. Click the sushi layer to make sure it is selected. Make sure that all of the layers are collapsed by clicking the arrows to the left of the layer names as well.

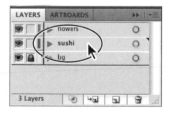

When adding symbols to a document, whatever layer is selected when they are added is the layer they become a part of.

3 Choose Window > Symbols, or click the Symbols panel icon (♣) on the right side of the workspace to expand the panel.

4 In the Symbols panel, click the Symbol Libraries Menu button (⬚⌄) at the bottom of the panel, and choose Sushi. The Sushi library opens as a free-floating panel.

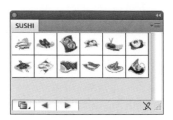

This library is external to the file that you are working on, but you can import any of the symbols into the document and use them in the artwork.

5 Position the pointer over the symbols in the Sushi panel to see their names as tooltips. Click the Futo symbol to add it to the Symbols panel for the document. Close the Sushi panel.

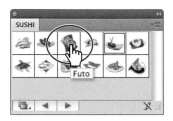

Every document has a default set of symbols in the Symbols panel. When you add symbols to the panel, they are saved with the active document only.

▶ **Tip:** If you want to see the symbol names rather than the symbol pictures, choose Small List View or Large List View from the Symbols panel menu (▾≡).

6 Using the Selection tool (�>), drag the Futo symbol from the Symbols panel onto the right side of the plate, on the artboard. Drag another onto the artboard to the left of the existing Futo symbol.

The symbol you dragged onto the artboard creates instances of the Futo symbol. Next, you will resize one of the symbol instances on the page.

● **Note:** Although you can transform symbol instances in many ways, specific properties of instances cannot be edited. For example, the fill color is locked because it is controlled by the original symbol in the Symbols panel.

7 Using the Selection tool, click to select the rightmost Futo symbol instance. Holding down the Shift key, drag the upper-right corner of the instance down and to the left to make it smaller, while constraining its proportions. Release the mouse button and then the modifier key.

With the symbol instance selected on the artboard, notice that in the Control panel you see the word Symbol, and symbol related options.

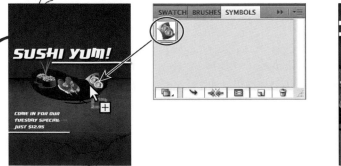

Next, you will edit the original sushi symbol so that both instances are affected. There are several ways to edit a symbol, and in this section we will focus on one.

8 With the Selection tool (▶), double-click the smaller of the Futo symbol instances on the page.

A warning dialog box appears, stating that you are about to edit the original symbol and that all instances will update. Click OK to continue. This takes you into isolation mode, so you can't edit any other objects on the page.

▶ **Tip:** Another way to edit a symbol is to select the symbol instance on the artboard, and then click the Edit Symbol button in the Control panel.

The Futo symbol instance you double-clicked appears to change in size. That's because you are looking at the original symbol, not the resized symbol instance on the page. You can now edit the shapes that make up the symbol.

9 With the Selection tool, double-click the Futo instance to ungroup it.

▶ **Tip:** You may want to zoom in on the Futo sushi symbol instances.

10 Click to select the reddish shape that looks like a plate beneath the sushi pieces. Press the Delete key to remove it. Do the same for the two curved black lines.

11 With the Selection tool, double-click off the sushi content or click the Exit Isolation Mode button (◀) in the upper-left corner of the artboard until you exit isolation mode, so that you can edit the rest of the content. Notice that both Futo instances now reflect the changes you just made.

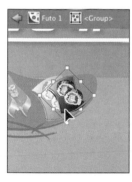 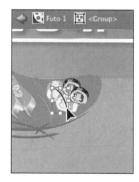 

12 Choose File > Save, and leave the document open.

Creating symbols

● **Note:** You can only use placed art that is embedded to create a symbol.

Illustrator also lets you create your own symbols. You can make symbols from objects, including paths, compound paths, text, raster images, mesh objects, and groups of objects. Symbols can even include active objects, such as brush strokes, blends, effects, or other symbol instances.

Now, you will create your own symbol from existing artwork.

1   Choose View > Draw_flower. This takes you to a zoomed in view off the right side of the artboard.

2   Click the Layers panel icon (◆) on the right side of the workspace to expand the Layers panel. Click the flowers layer to make sure it is selected. You will place the next series of symbol instances on this layer.

3   With the Selection tool, drag a marquee across the two pink shapes off the right edge of the artboard to select them both.

4   Click the Symbols panel icon (♣) to expand the panel. With the Selection tool, drag the selected shapes into a blank area of the Symbols panel.

5   In the Symbol Options dialog box, change the name to **Cherry Blossom Bud** and select Graphic as the Type. Click OK to create the symbol.

● **Note:** By default, the selected artwork becomes an instance of the new symbol. If you don't want the artwork to become an instance of the symbol, press the Shift key as you create the new symbol.

Symbol options

In the Symbol Options dialog box, you will encounter several options that are related to working with Adobe Flash®. These options are briefly described below, and will be addressed more fully later in this lesson.

- Select Movie Clip for type. Movie Clip is the default symbol type in Flash and in Illustrator.
- Specify a location on the Registration grid where you want to set the symbol's anchor point. The location of the anchor point affects the position of the symbol within the screen coordinates.
- Select Enable Guides For 9-Slice Scaling if you want to utilize 9-Slice scaling in Flash.

—From Illustrator Help

After creating the Cherry Blossom Bud symbol, the original cherry blossom shapes off the right edge of the artboard are converted to a symbol instance. You can leave it there or delete it.

6 Choose View > Fit Artboard In Window.

7 Choose File > Save.

Editing a symbol

In this next section, you will add several instances of the Cherry Blossom Bud symbol to the artwork. Then you will edit the symbol in the Symbols panel, and all instances will be updated.

1 Select the Zoom tool (🔍) in the Tools panel and click twice on the right end of the tree branch at the top of the artboard.

2 Using the Selection tool, drag an instance of the Cherry Blossom Bud symbol onto the right end of the branch at the top of the page.

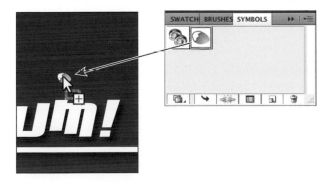

3 Drag another instance of the symbol from the Symbols panel onto the limbs of the top tree branch. See the figure below for placement.

Next, you will learn how to add more instances of a symbol that's already on the artboard, using a modifier key.

4 With the Selection tool (▶), press the Alt (Windows) or Option (Mac OS) key and drag one of the Cherry Blossom Bud instances already on the artboard to create a copy of the instance. When the new instance is in position, release the mouse button and then the modifier key. You should now have a total of three Cherry Blossom Bud instances.

5 Use this same method to create a total of 7 instances on the top tree branch. See the figure for approximate positioning.

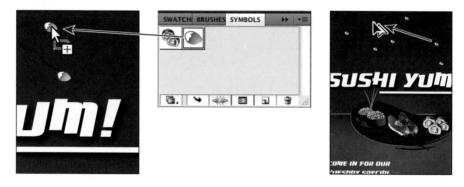

6 In the Symbols panel, double-click the Cherry Blossom Bud symbol to edit it. A temporary instance of the symbol appears in the center of the Document window.

Editing a symbol by double-clicking the symbol in the Symbols panel hides all artboard content except the symbol.

7 Press Ctrl++ (Windows) or Cmd++ (Mac OS) several times to zoom in.

8 With the Selection tool, click to select the smaller, white filled shape. Change the stroke to None and the Fill to Pink in the Control panel.

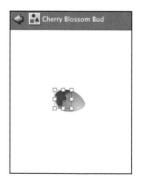

9 Choose Select > All, or drag across the shapes with the Selection tool.

10 Choose Object > Transform > Transform Each to open the Transform Each dialog box. In the Transform Each dialog box, change the Horizontal and Vertical Scale to **80** and the Angle to **–20**. Click OK.

This allows you to scale all of the symbol instances at once, rather than having to scale each individually. You could make other changes to the symbol artwork in a similar manner.

11 Double-click outside the symbol instance artwork on the artboard, or click the Exit Isolation Mode button (◀) in the upper-left corner of the artboard to see all the artwork. Press Ctrl+0 (Windows) or Cmd+0 (Mac OS) to fit the artboard in the window.

The symbol instances have now all been updated with the smaller bud.

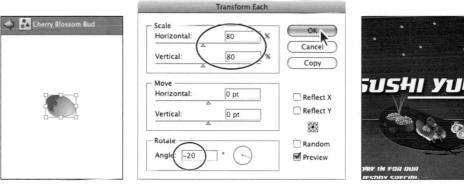

Select the symbol shapes.   Transform the content.   The result

12 Choose File > Save.

Breaking a link to a symbol

At times, you will need to edit specific instances on the artboard. Because the symbolism tools only let you make certain kinds of changes, you may sometimes need to break the link between a symbol and an instance. This creates a group of unlinked instances (if the object is composed of more than one object) on the artboard. You can then ungroup them and edit the individual objects.

Next, you will break the link to one of the Cherry Blossom Bud instances.

1 With the Selection tool (▶) selected, click to select one of the symbol instances of the bud on the page. In the Control panel, click the Break Link button.

This object is now a series of paths, as indicated by the word Path on the left side of the Control panel. You should be able to see the anchor points of the shapes.

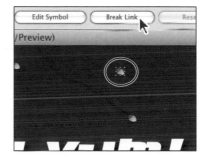

▶ **Tip:** You can also break the link to a symbol instance by selecting the symbol instance on the artboard, and then clicking the Break Link To Symbol button (⬆) at the bottom of the Symbols panel.

● **Note:** It's okay if the color of your selection is different from the color shown in the figure.

2 Select the Zoom tool (🔍) and drag a marquee across the selected content to zoom in.

3 With the two shapes selected, choose Edit > Edit Colors > Saturate.

4 Change the Intensity to **–60** and select Preview in the Saturate dialog box. Click OK.

 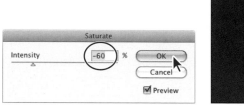 

5 Choose File > Save and keep the artwork selected.

Replacing symbols

Next, you will create a symbol from the modified bud shapes, and then replace a few of the Cherry Blossom Bud symbol instances with the new symbol.

1 Choose View > Fit Artboard In Window.

2 With the Selection tool (▸) drag the modified shapes into the Symbols panel. In the Symbol Options dialog box, change the name to **Cherry Blossom Bud 2** and the Type to Graphic. Click OK.

3 With the Selection tool, select a Cherry Blossom Bud instance on the artboard. In the Control panel, click the arrow to the right of the Replace Instance With Symbol field, to open the Symbols panel. Click the Cherry Blossom Bud 2 symbol.

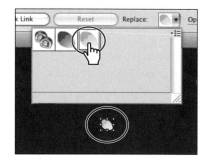

4 Choose Select > Deselect.

5 Choose File > Save. Keep the file open.

Symbol layers

When you edit a symbol using any of the methods described, open the Layers panel and you will see that the symbol has its own layering.

Similar to working with groups in isolation mode, you see the layers associated with that symbol only, not the document's layers. In the Layers panel, you can rename, add, delete, show/hide, and reorder content for a symbol.

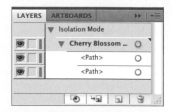

Renaming symbols

Using the Symbols panel, you can easily rename a symbol, which updates all the symbol instances in the artwork as well. Next, you will rename the Futo symbol.

1 With the Selection tool (▶) click to select one of the Futo symbol instances on the artboard (the first sushi symbol you dragged onto the page).

2 In the Symbols panel, make sure that the Futo symbol is selected. Click the Symbol Options button (▣) at the bottom of the Symbols panel.

3 In the Symbol Options dialog box, change the name to **sushi** and the Type to Graphic. Click OK.

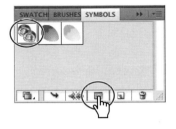

Working with the symbolism tools

The Symbol Sprayer tool (🛋) in the Tools panel allows you to spray symbols on the artboard, creating symbol sets. A symbol set is a group of symbol instances that you create with the Symbol Sprayer tool. You can create mixed sets of symbol instances by using the Symbol Sprayer tool with one symbol and then using it again with another symbol.

Spraying symbol instances

Next, you will draw a flower, save it as a symbol, then use the Symbol Sprayer tool to apply flowers to your illustration.

1 Choose View > Draw_flower.

2 Select the Rounded Rectangle tool (▢) in the Tools panel. Click once, off the right edge of the artboard. In the Rounded Rectangle dialog box, change the Width to **55 pt**, the Height to **30 pt**, and the Corner Radius to **25 pt**. Click OK.

3 With the rounded rectangle selected, press the letter D to apply the default fill of white and a 1pt black stroke.

4 Select the Zoom tool (🔍) and click three times on the rounded rectangle.

5 Select the Rotate tool (⟳) in the Tools panel. Holding down the Alt (Windows) or Option (Mac OS) key, position the pointer just to the right of the center point of the rounded rectangle and click.

6 In the Rotate dialog box change the angle to **72** and click Copy.

7 Press Ctrl+D (Windows) or Cmd+D (Mac OS) three times to repeat the transformation and create a total of five rounded rectangles.

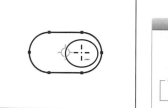

Position the pointer.

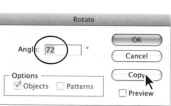

Rotate the initial rectangle.

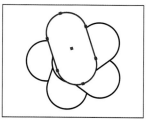

Repeat the transformation.

8 With the Selection tool, drag across the rounded rectangle shapes. Choose Window > Pathfinder to open the Pathfinder panel. Click the Unite button to merge all of the shapes into one. Close the Pathfinder panel group.

9 With the united shape selected, change the fill color to Flower (the pink gradient) and the stroke to None in the Control panel.

10 Click the Symbols panel icon (♣) on the right side of the workspace to open the Symbols panel. Drag the flower shape into the Symbols panel. In the Symbol Options dialog box, change the name to **Flower** and the Type to Graphic. Click OK. Delete the original flower shape off the right edge of the artboard.

11 Choose View > Fit Artboard In Window.

12 Select the Symbol Sprayer tool (🔧) in the Tools panel. Make sure the Flower symbol is selected in the Symbols panel.

● **Note:** A higher intensity value increases the rate of change—the Symbol Sprayer tool sprays more, and faster. The higher the symbol set density value, the more tightly packed the symbols are as you spray them.

13 Double-click the Symbol Sprayer tool (🔧) in the Tools panel. In the Symbolism Tools Options dialog box, change Intensity to **3** and Symbol Set Density to **7**, if not already done. Click OK.

14 Starting on the left side of the artboard, over the tree, click and drag a little up and down, from left to right with the Symbol Sprayer, much like using an airbrush or can of spray paint, to create flowers on the tree branch. Release the mouse button when you see about 5 flowers on the artboard.

Notice the bounding box around the Flower symbol instances, identifying it as a symbol set. As you spray, the instances are grouped together as a single object. If a symbol set is selected when you begin to spray with the Symbol Sprayer tool, the symbol instances that you are spraying are added to the selected symbol set. You can easily delete an entire symbol set by selecting it and then pressing the Delete key.

Spray the symbols.   The result

15 Choose Select > Deselect.

16 With the Symbol Sprayer tool, drag across the top tree branch again, to add a few more flower instances.

Notice that after releasing the mouse button, you see a bounding box around only the new flower instances. To add symbol instances to an existing symbol set, you must first select the set.

17 Choose Edit > Undo Spraying to remove the last Flower symbol set.

18 With the Selection tool, click to select the Flower symbol set at the top of the artboard.

19 Select the Symbol Sprayer tool and add more flowers to the tree branch. Try clicking and releasing, instead of clicking and dragging, to add one flower at a time.

20 Choose File > Save and leave the symbol set selected.

In the next section, you will use the Symbolism tools to alter the look of individual symbol instances.

▶ **Tip:** If you don't like the placement of a flower, you can choose Edit > Undo Spraying to remove the instances you sprayed in the previous click.

Editing symbols with the Symbolism tools

In the next steps, you will edit the flowers in the flower symbol set using the Symbolism tools in the Tools panel.

1 With the flower symbol set and the Symbol Sprayer tool still selected, position the pointer over one of the flowers. Press the Alt (Windows) or Option (Mac OS) key and click to delete one of the instances in the set.

▶ **Tip:** If the Symbol Sizer tool is sizing too quickly, double-click the Symbol Sizer tool in the Tools panel and try lowering the Intensity and Density values in the Symbolism Tools Options dialog box.

2 Select the Symbol Sizer tool ( ) from the Symbol Sprayer tool group in the Tools panel. Position the pointer over some of the flowers and click and hold the mouse button to increase the size of some of the flowers. In the same area of flowers, press the Alt (Windows) or Option (Mac OS) key while you are using the Symbol Sizer tool to reduce the size of the selected instances.

3 Make some of the flowers smaller than the rest, varying the sizes.

▶ **Tip:** To affect fewer Flower symbol instances at a time, press the left bracket key ([) several times to make the brush diameter smaller.

Resize some of the flowers.   The result

● **Note:** The Symbol Sizer works better when you click and release symbol instances, rather than holding down the mouse button.

Now, you will rotate some of the symbols.

● **Note:** Arrows appear as you rotate, indicating the direction of rotation.

4 Select the Symbol Spinner tool ( ) from the Symbol Sizer tool group. Position the pointer over a flower in the symbol set, and then drag left or right to rotate.

The more you move the pointer, the more rotation occurs.

Drag to rotate flowers.   The result

5 Select the Symbol Shifter tool (⚙) in the
Tools panel. With the symbol set still selected,
press the right bracket key (]) several times to
increase the size of the brush. Click the Flower
symbol instances and drag to shift them.

6 Choose Select > Deselect.

7 Choose File > Save.

▶ **Tip:** There are lots
of Symbolism tools for
you to experiment with,
including the Symbol
Stainer tool (⚙), which
allows you to apply a
stain to selected symbol
instances in the
symbol set.

What do the symbolism tools do?

Symbol Shifter tool (⚙)—Moves symbol instances around. It can also change the
relative stacking order of symbol instances in a set.

Symbol Scruncher tool (⚙)—Pulls symbol instances together or apart.

Symbol Sizer tool (⚙)—Increases or decreases the size of symbol instances.

Symbol Spinner tool (⚙)—Orients the symbol instances in a set. Symbol instances
located near the pointer orient in the direction you move the pointer. As you drag
the mouse, an arrow appears above the pointer to show the current orientation of
the symbol instances.

Symbol Stainer tool (⚙)—Colorizes symbol instances. Colorizing a symbol
instance changes the hue toward the tint color while preserving the original lumi-
nosity, so black or white objects don't change at all.

Symbol Screener tool (⚙)—Increases or decreases the transparency of the symbol
instances in a set.

Symbol Styler tool (⚙)—Applies the selected style to the symbol instance. You can
switch to the Symbol Styler tool when using any other symbolism tool by clicking a
style in the Styles panel.

Copy and edit symbol sets

A symbol set is treated as a single object. In order to edit the instances in it, you use the symbolism tools in the Tools panel. You can, however, duplicate symbol instances and use the symbolism tools to make the duplicates look different.

Next, you will duplicate the flower symbol set, and position it at the bottom of the artboard.

1 Click the Layers panel icon (⬢) to expand the Layers panel. Make sure that the bg layer is locked, as indicated by a lock icon (🔒) to the right of the eye icon (👁). Click the Layers panel icon to collapse the panel.

2 Select the Selection tool (▶) and drag a marquee across all of the symbols content at the top of the artboard, including the Flower symbol set and the flower buds.

▶ **Tip:** If you want to select all instances of the same symbol in the artwork and they are not part of a symbol set, select a single instance of the symbol and, then choose Select > Same > Symbol Instance.

3 Choose Object > Group.

4 Press the Alt (Windows) or Option (Mac OS) key and drag a copy of the instances to the bottom, right of the artboard. When it is in position, release the mouse button and then the modifier key.

5 Choose Object > Transform > Transform Each. In the Transform Each dialog box, select Reflect X and Reflect Y. Click OK.

● **Note:** There are many transformations that you can make to a symbol set. You can also drag a point in the bounding box of a symbol set with the Selection tool to resize it.

6 With the copied symbol set at the bottom still selected, double-click the Rotate tool (🔄) in the Tools panel. In the Rotate dialog box, change the Angle to **23** and then click OK.

7 With the Selection tool, drag the symbol instance group into position on top of the bottom tree limb.

8 Choose Select > Deselect, then File > Save.

Storing and retrieving artwork in the Symbols panel

Saving frequently used logos or other artwork as symbols lets you access them quickly. In this next part of the lesson, you will take symbols that you've created and save them as a new symbol library that you can share with other documents or users.

● **Note:** Symbol libraries are saved as Adobe Illustrator (.ai) files.

1 In the Symbols panel, click the Symbol Libraries Menu button (📖▾), and then choose Save Symbols.

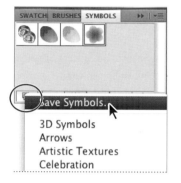

   ● **Note:** When saving symbols as a separate library, the document that contains the symbols should be open and active in the Document window.

2 In the Save Symbols As Library dialog box, choose a location such as your Desktop to place the symbol library file. Name the library file **sushi_poster.ai**. Click Save.

● **Note:** When you first open the Save Symbols As Library dialog box, Illustrator takes you to the default Symbols folder, where you can store the libraries that you create. Illustrator recognizes any libraries stored here and lets you choose them from the Symbol Libraries menu later.

▶ **Tip:** If you save the library in the default folder, you can make subfolders and create a folder structure that suits you. You can then easily access them using the Symbol Libraries Menu button or by choosing Window > Symbol Libraries.

3 Without closing the poster.ai file, create a new document by choosing File > New. Leave the default settings, and then click OK.

4 In the Symbols panel, click the Symbol Libraries Menu button (📖▾) and choose Other Library at the bottom of the menu. Navigate to the folder where you saved the sushi_poster.ai library, select it, and then click Open.

   The sushi_poster library appears as a free-floating panel in the workspace. You can dock it or leave it where it is. It stays open as long as Illustrator is open. When you close Illustrator, and then relaunch it, this panel does not reopen.

5 Drag any of the Symbols from the sushi_poster library panel onto the page.

6 Choose File > Close and do not save the new file. Keep the poster.ai file open if you plan on continuing to the Exploring On Your Own section.

Mapping a symbol to 3D artwork

You can apply any 2D artwork stored as a symbol in the Symbols panel to selected surfaces on a 3D object. To learn about mapping symbols to 3D artwork, see Lesson 12, "Applying Effects."

Symbols and Flash integration

Illustrator also provides excellent support for SWF and SVG file type export. When you export to Flash, you can set the symbol type to Movie Clip. In Adobe Flash, you can choose another type if necessary. You can also specify 9-slice scaling in Illustrator so that the movie clips scale appropriately when used for user interface components.

You can move Illustrator artwork into the Flash editing environment or directly into the Flash Player. You can copy and paste artwork, save files as SWF, or export artwork directly to Flash. In addition, Illustrator provides support for Flash dynamic text and movie clip symbols.

A generic symbol workflow in Illustrator is similar to a symbol workflow in Flash:

- Step 1: Symbol creation

  When you create a symbol in Illustrator, the Symbol Options dialog box lets you name the symbol and set options specific to Flash: movie clip symbol type (which is the default for Flash symbols), Flash registration grid location, and 9-slice scaling guides. In addition, you can use many of the same symbol keyboard shortcuts in Illustrator and Flash, such as F8 to create a symbol.

- Step 2: Isolation mode for symbol editing

- Step 3: Symbol properties and links

- Step 4: Static, dynamic, and input text objects

Next, you will create a button, save it as a symbol, and then edit the symbol options.

1 Choose Window > Workspace > Essentials.

2 Choose File > New.

3 In the New Document dialog box, choose Web from the New Document Profile menu. Keep the rest of the options at their default settings, and then click OK.

4 Choose File > Save As. In the Save As dialog box, name the file **buttons.ai** and navigate to the Lesson14 folder. Leave the Save As Type option set to Adobe Illustrator (*.AI) (Windows) or the Format option set to Adobe Illustrator (ai) (Mac OS), and then click Save. In the Illustrator Options dialog box, leave the Illustrator options at their default settings, and then click OK.

5 Click the Symbols panel icon (♣) to expand the panel.

6 Drag the blue Bullet - Forward symbol from the Symbols panel onto the artboard.

▶ **Tip:** As mentioned previously in this lesson, many more symbols come with Illustrator. You can find them by clicking the Symbol Libraries Menu button at the bottom of the Symbols panel.

7 With the Selection tool (▶), Shift-click the upper-right corner of the button and drag to make it larger, releasing the mouse button and then the key.

8 With the button still selected, change the Instance Name in the Control panel to **Home** and press Enter or Return.

The Instance Name is optional when working in Illustrator and is used to identify one symbol instance from another. Entering an instance name for each button is useful if you choose to import the Illustrator content to the stage in Flash (File > Import > Import To Stage).

9 With the button selected, drag it to the right, and then press Shift+Alt (Windows) or Shift+Option (Mac OS) to create a copy. Release the mouse button first, and then the modifier keys. In the Control panel, type **Info** in the Instance Name field and press Enter or Return.

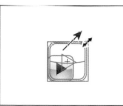
Resize the symbol instance.

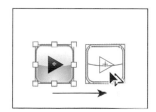
Name the instance.

Duplicate the instance.

10 With one of the buttons still selected, click the Symbol Options button (▣) in the Symbols panel. Make sure that Movie Clip, Enable Guides For 9-Slice Scaling, and Align To Pixel Grid are selected. Click OK.

Next, you'll adjust the 9-slice scaling guides.

11 With the Selection tool, double-click the leftmost button to enter isolation mode. When the warning dialog box appears, click OK.

12 Select the Zoom tool (🔍) in the Tools panel and click three times on the leftmost button to zoom in. Choose Select > All.

Choosing Select > All allows you to see the anchor points in the shapes. When you adjust the 9-slice scaling guides, you want to try to position them to indicate the scalable part of the object (usually not the corners).

13 With the Selection tool, drag the rightmost guide to the left, just past the left edge of the black arrow, as shown in the figure.

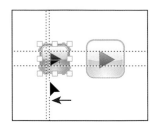

You can use 9-slice scaling (scale-9) to specify component-style scaling for graphic style and movie clip symbols.

14 With the Selection tool, double-click away from the buttons to exit isolation mode.

15 Choose View > Fit Artboard In Window, then File > Save.

Understanding Flash Symbol Options

Movie Clip: Use movie clip symbols to create reusable pieces of animation (in Flash). Movie clips have their own multiframe Timeline that is independent from the main Timeline— think of them as nested inside a main Timeline that can contain interactive controls, sounds, and even other movie clip instances. You can also place movie clip instances inside the Timeline of a button symbol to create animated buttons. In addition, movie clips are scriptable with ActionScript®.

Align to Pixel Grid: To create a pixel-aligned symbol, select the Align to Pixel Grid option from the Symbol Options dialog box. Symbols aligned to pixel grid remain aligned to the pixel grid at all locations of the artboard, in their actual size.

9-slice scaling: You can use 9-slice scaling (scale-9) to specify component-style scaling for graphic style and movie clip symbols. This type of scaling lets you create movie clip symbols that scale appropriately for use as user interface components, as opposed to the type of scaling typically applied to graphics and design elements.

The symbol is conceptually divided into nine sections with a grid-like overlay, and each of the nine areas is scaled independently. To maintain the visual integrity of the symbol, corners are not scaled, while the remaining areas of the image are scaled (as opposed to being stretched) larger or smaller, as needed.

—From Illustrator Help

For the next section, you need to have Adobe Flash CS5 installed on your machine.

1 Open Adobe Flash CS5.

2 Choose File > New. In the New Document dialog box, make sure that the General tab is selected and that ActionScript 3.0 is also selected in the list. Click OK.

3 Choose File > Import > Import To Library in Adobe Flash. Navigate to the buttons.ai file you just saved in Illustrator and click the Import To Library button. The Import "buttons.ai" To Library dialog box appears.

This dialog box lets you select which artboard to import, which layers to import, how to import the content, and more. The Import Unused Symbols option at the bottom of the dialog box brings all the symbols in the Illustrator Symbols panel into the Flash Library panel. This can be very useful if, for instance, you are developing a series of buttons for a site.

4 Click OK.

5 Open the Library panel by clicking the Library panel tab on the right side of the workspace. Click the arrow to the left of the folder names to reveal the assets as well as the Bullet - Forward symbol in the Illustrator Symbols folder.

6 Drag the Bullet - Forward symbol onto the stage.

● **Note:** There are several ways to get Illustrator CS5 content into Flash CS5. You can also copy and paste from Illustrator to Flash (using the default Paste preferences) or choose File > Import > Import To Stage. Import to stage places the two buttons on the stage, and each instance name appears in the Property panel when the buttons are independently selected. The content is also added to the Library panel.

7 Choose File > Close to close the Flash file, and don't save changes. Close Flash, and return to Illustrator.

Pasting Illustrator artwork into Flash

Another option for getting content from Illustrator CS5 to Flash CS5 is to copy and paste content into Flash from Illustrator. When you paste into Flash CS5, the Paste dialog box appears. You can paste

a simple bitmap or paste using the AI File Importer preferences. The latter option works like the File > Import > Import To Stage command, although the Import "buttons.ai" To Stage dialog box does not appear.

When you paste Illustrator artwork into Flash, the following attributes are preserved:

Paths and shapes	Scalability
Stroke weights	Gradient definitions
Text (specify Flash text)	Linked images
Symbols	Effects

—From Illustrator Help

Exploring on your own

Try to integrate symbols into illustrations with repeated artwork from a map that contains everything from repeated icons and road signs to creative and customized bullets for text. Symbols make it easy to update logos in business cards or name tags, or any artwork created with multiple placements of the same art.

To place multiple symbol instances, do the following:

1 Select the artwork that you want to use as a symbol.

2 Using the Selection tool, drag the art into the Symbols panel. Delete the original art when it is in the Symbols panel.

3 To add an instance to the artboard, drag the symbol from the Symbols panel to the artboard.

4 Drag as many instances of the symbol as you like, or press the Alt (Windows) or Option (Mac OS) key and drag the original instance to clone it to other locations.

The symbols are now linked to the original symbol in the Symbols panel. If a symbol is updated, all placed instances are updated.

Review questions

1 What are three benefits of using a symbol?

2 Name the symbolism tool that is used for rotating symbol instances in a symbol set.

3 If you are using a symbolism tool on an area that has two different symbols applied, which one is affected?

4 How do you update an existing symbol?

5 What is something that cannot be used as a symbol?

6 How do you access symbols from other documents?

7 Name two ways to bring symbols from Illustrator to Flash.

Review answers

1 Three benefits of using symbols are:

- You can easily apply multiple shapes.

- You can edit one symbol, and all instances are updated.

- You can map artwork to 3D objects (covered in depth in Lesson 12, "Applying Effects").

2 The Symbol Spinner tool changes the rotation of a symbol instance in a symbol set.

3 If you are using a symbolism tool over an area that has two different symbol instances, the symbol active in the Symbols panel is the only instance affected.

4 To update an existing symbol, double-click the symbol icon in the Symbols panel or double-click an instance of the symbol on the artboard. Then you can make edits in isolation mode.

5 Unembedded images cannot be used as symbols.

6 You can access symbols from saved documents either by clicking the Symbol Libraries Menu button (🗐) at the bottom of the Symbols panel and choosing Other Library from the menu that appears; by choosing Other Library from the Symbols panel menu; or by choosing Window > Symbol Libraries > Other Library.

7 Copy and paste the symbol(s) from Illustrator to Flash, choose File > Import > Import To Stage, or choose File > Import > Import To Library.

15 COMBINING ILLUSTRATOR CS5 GRAPHICS WITH OTHER ADOBE APPLICATIONS

Lesson overview

In this lesson, you'll learn how to do the following:

- Differentiate between vector and bitmap graphics.

- Place linked and embedded Adobe® Photoshop® graphics in an Adobe Illustrator® file.

- Create and edit a clipping mask.

- Create a clipping mask from compound paths.

- Make an opacity mask to display part of an image.

- Sample color in a placed image.

- Replace a placed image with another, and update the document.

- Export a layered file to Adobe Photoshop.

 This lesson takes approximately an hour to complete. If needed, remove the previous lesson folder from your hard disk and copy the Lesson15 folder onto it.

You can easily add an image created in an image editing program to an Adobe Illustrator file. This is an effective method for seeing how a photograph looks incorporated in a line drawing, or for trying out Illustrator special effects on bitmap images.

Getting started

Before you begin, you'll need to restore the default preferences for Adobe Illustrator CS5. Then you'll open the finished art file for this lesson to see what you'll create.

1   To ensure that the tools and panels function as described in this lesson, delete or deactivate (by renaming) the Adobe Illustrator CS5 preferences file. See "Restoring default preferences" on page 3.

2   Start Adobe Illustrator CS5.

● **Note:** If you have not already done so, copy the resource files for this lesson onto your hard disk from the Lesson15 folder on the Adobe Illustrator CS5 Classroom in a Book CD. See "Copying the Classroom in a Book files" on page 2.

3   Choose File > Open. Locate the file named L15end_1.ai in the Lesson15 folder in the Lessons folder that you copied onto your hard disk. This is a postcard for a technology expo, and you will add and edit graphics in this lesson. Leave it open for reference, or choose File > Close.

Now, you'll open the start file from Adobe Bridge CS5.

Working with Adobe Bridge

Bridge is an application that installs when you install either an Adobe® Creative Suite® 5 component, such as Illustrator, or the entire Adobe Creative Suite 5. It allows you to browse content visually, manage metadata, and more.

● **Note:** The first time Adobe Bridge launches, a dialog box may appear asking if you want the Bridge to start at login. Click Yes if you want it to launch at startup. Click No to manually launch Bridge when you need it.

1   Choose File > Browse In Bridge to open Bridge.

2   In the Favorites pane on the left, click Desktop and navigate to the L15start_1.ai file in the Lesson15 folder. Click the file in the middle, Content pane.

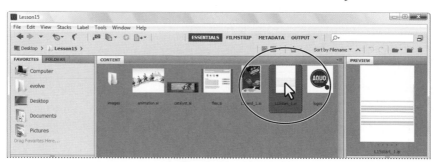

3   At the bottom of the Content pane, drag the slider to the right to increase the size of the thumbnails in the Content pane.

4 At the top of Bridge, click Filmstrip. This changes the appearance of the workspace to a filmstrip view that provides a larger preview of the selected object. Click Essentials to return to the original workspace.

5 At the bottom of the Content pane, drag the slider to the left until you see all the thumbnails in the Content pane.

6 With the L15start_1.ai file still selected in the Content pane, click the Metadata panel tab on the right side of the workspace (if not already selected) to see the metadata associated with the selected file. This can be camera data, document swatches, and more. Click the Keywords panel tab to reveal the Keywords panel.

Keywords can be associated with objects such as images, which will allow them to be searched for by those keywords.

7 In the Keywords panel, click the plus at the bottom to create a keyword. Type **rivertown** into the keyword field and press Enter or Return. Click to select the box to the left of the keyword, if not already selected. This associates the keyword with the selected file.

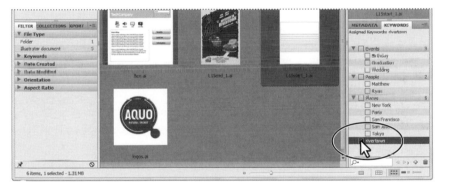

8 Choose Edit > Find. In the Find dialog box, choose Keywords from the first menu in the Criteria section. Type **rivertown** in the rightmost field of the Criteria options. Leave the middle field set to contains and click Find.

The Find results appear in the Content pane.

9 Click the x in the upper right corner of the Content pane, to the right of the New Search button, to close the find results and return to the folder.

Previewing files and working with metadata and keywords are just a few of the many features available in Bridge. To learn more about working with Bridge, choose Help > Illustrator Help and search for Adobe Bridge.

10 Double-click the file L15start_1.ai in the Content pane to open the file in Illustrator. Leave Bridge open.

11 Choose View > Fit Artboard In Window.

12 Choose Window > Workspace > Essentials to reset the Essentials workspace.

13 Choose File > Save As. In the Save As dialog box, navigate to the Lesson15 folder and open it. Name the file **movieposter.ai**. Leave the Save As Type option set to Adobe Illustrator (*.AI) (Windows) or the Format option set to Adobe Illustrator (ai) (Mac OS), and then click Save. In the Illustrator Options dialog box, leave the Illustrator options at their default settings, and then click OK.

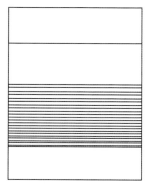

Combining artwork

You can combine Illustrator artwork with images from other graphics applications in a variety of ways for a wide range of creative results. Sharing artwork between applications lets you combine continuous-tone paintings and photographs with line art. Even though Illustrator lets you create certain types of raster images, Adobe Photoshop excels at many image-editing tasks. The images can then be placed in Illustrator.

This lesson steps you through the process of creating a composite image, including combining bitmap images with vector art and working between applications. You will add photographic images created in Photoshop to a postcard created in Illustrator. Then you'll adjust the color in the photo, mask the photo, and sample color from the photo to use in the Illustrator artwork. You'll update a placed image, and then export your postcard to Photoshop.

Vector versus bitmap graphics

Illustrator creates vector graphics, also called draw graphics, which contain shapes based on mathematical expressions. Vector graphics consist of clear, smooth lines that retain their crispness when scaled. They are best for illustrations, type, and graphics that need to be scaled to different sizes, such as logos.

Logo is drawn as vector art, and retains its crispness when scaled to a larger size.

Bitmap graphics, also called raster images, are based on a grid of pixels and are created by image editing applications, such as Photoshop. When working with bitmap images, you edit groups of pixels rather than objects or shapes. Because bitmap graphics can represent subtle gradations of shade and color, they are appropriate for continuous-tone images, such as photographs or artwork created in painting programs. A disadvantage of bitmap graphics is that they lose definition and appear jagged when scaled up.

Logo is rasterized as bitmap art, and loses its definition when enlarged.

In deciding whether to use Illustrator or a bitmap image program such as Photoshop for creating and combining graphics, consider the elements of the image and how the image will be used.

In general, use Illustrator if you need to create art or type with clean lines that looks good at any magnification. In most cases, you'll also want to use Illustrator for laying out a single-page design, because Illustrator offers more flexibility than Photoshop when working with type, and reselecting, moving, and altering images. You can create raster images in Illustrator, but its pixel-editing tools are limited. Use Photoshop for images that need pixel editing, color correcting, painting, and other special effects. Use InDesign for laying out anything from a postcard to a multiple chapter book, such as this Classroom in a Book.

Placing Adobe Photoshop files

You can bring artwork from Photoshop into Illustrator using the Open command, the Place command, the Paste command, and drag-and-drop.

Illustrator supports most Photoshop data, including layer comps, layers, editable text, and paths. This means that you can transfer files between Photoshop and Illustrator without losing the ability to edit the artwork. Adjustment layers for which visibility is deselected in Photoshop are imported into Illustrator, although they are inaccessible. When exported back to Photoshop, the layers are restored.

● **Note:** Illustrator includes support for Device N rasters. For instance, if you create a Duotone image in Photoshop and place it in Illustrator, it separates properly and prints the spot colors.

In this lesson, you'll begin by placing a Photoshop file that contains a layer mask created in Photoshop. A layer mask is a way to mask, or hide, art in an image so that areas can be transparent. Placed files can be embedded or linked. When embedded files are added to the Illustrator file, the Illustrator file size increases to reflect the addition of the placed file. Linked files remain separate external files, and a link to the external file is placed in the Illustrator file. Linking to files can be a great way to ensure that image updates are reflected in the Illustrator file. The linked file must always accompany the Illustrator file or the link will break and the placed file will not appear in the Illustrator artwork.

Placing a Photoshop file

1 In Illustrator CS5, choose Window > Layers to open the Layers panel.

2 In the Layers panel, select the Content layer, and then click the visibility column to show the contents of that layer.

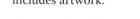

When you place an image, it is added to the selected layer. You'll use the Content layer for the placed image. The layer already includes artwork.

3 Choose File > Place.

4 Navigate to the car.psd file in the images folder inside the Lesson15 folder, and select it. Do not double-click the file or click Place yet.

5 Make sure that Link is selected in the Place dialog box.

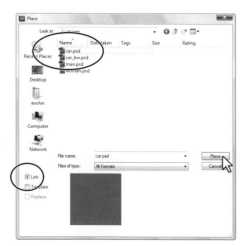

By default, placed Photoshop files are linked to their source file. So if the source file is edited, the placed image in Illustrator is updated. If you deselect the Link option, you embed the PSD file in the Illustrator file.

6   Click Place.

Notice that the image is placed in the center of the Document window. It is selected, has bounding points and an X in the center of the image. Also notice the Control panel. With the image selected, you see the words Linked File, indicating that the image is linked to its source file, and other information about the image. Clicking Linked File in the Control panel opens the Links panel which you'll do later in the lesson.

Now, you'll move and transform the placed image.

Duplicating and editing a placed image

You can duplicate placed images just as you do other objects in an Illustrator file. You can then modify the copy of the image independently of the original.

Next, you will edit the car.psd image and duplicate it in the Layers panel.

1   With the Selection tool (▶) selected and the image already selected, drag the image down and to the right so that it is positioned towards the top of the red "road."

2   Holding down the Shift key, use the Selection tool to drag the upper-right bounding point toward the center of the image until the width is approximately 5.8 in.

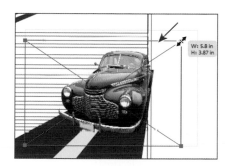

▶ **Tip:** To transform a placed image, you can also open the Transform panel (Window > Transform) and change settings there.

After resizing the image, notice that the PPI value in the Control panel is approximately 165. The PPI (Pixels Per Inch) refers to the resolution of the image. Working in Illustrator, if you make an image smaller, the resolution of the image increases. If you make an image larger, the resolution decreases.

● **Note:** Transformations performed on a linked image in Illustrator, and any resulting resolution changes, do not change the original image. The changes apply only to the image within Illustrator.

3 With the Selection tool, position the pointer off the upper-right bounding point. The rotate arrows should appear. Drag up and to the left to rotate the image about 4 degrees. With smart guides on, you'll see a measurement label.

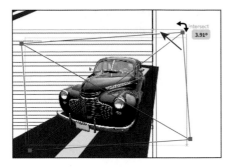

4 Choose File > Save, and leave the car.psd image selected.

Next, you will duplicate the car.psd image and make edits to the copy.

5 In the Layers panel, click the arrow (▷) to the left of the Content layer to expand it. Notice the car.psd sublayer.

6 With the car selected on the artboard, choose Edit > Copy, then Edit > Paste In Place. This pastes a new car.psd image on top of the copied image and selects it on the artboard.

7 In the Layers panel, double-click the new car.psd sublayer (the one on top in the Layers panel) and rename it **small car.psd** in the Options dialog box. Then click OK.

8 With the copied car image still selected on the artboard, double-click the Scale tool (⬚) in the Tools panel. In the Scale dialog box, change the Uniform Scale value to **40** and click OK.

9 Select the Selection tool (▶) and, in the Layers panel, click the visibility column to the left of the Frame layer to show the artwork. Drag the small car.psd sublayer onto the Frame layer. Click the arrow (▷) to the left of the Content layer to collapse it.

10 With the Selection tool, drag the small car on the artboard to the left of the text at the bottom of the poster. The smaller car image should be on top of the cream colored border. Exact positioning is not important. You may want to reposition the small car so that it is not on the text.

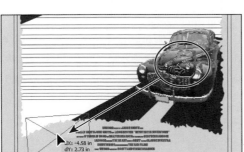

11 Choose Select > Deselect, and then File > Save.

Embed a Photoshop image with Layer comps

Designers often create multiple compositions, or comps, of a page layout to show their clients. Using layer comps in Photoshop, you can create, manage, and view multiple versions of a layout in a single Photoshop file.

A layer comp is a snapshot of a state of the Layers panel in Photoshop. Layer comps record the following information about a layer:

- Visibility—whether a layer is showing or hidden

- Position in the document

- Appearance—whether a layer style is applied to the layer and blending mode

You create a layer comp in Photoshop by making changes to the layers in your document and clicking the Create New Layer Comp button in the Layer Comps panel. You view comps by applying them in the document. You can export layer comps to separate files, to a single PDF file, to a web photo gallery, or choose one when placing the Photoshop file into Illustrator.

Next, you will place a Photoshop file with layer comps, and embed it in the Illustrator file.

1 Choose View > Fit Artboard In Window, in case you zoomed in on the artwork in previous steps.

2 In the Layers panel, click the eye icon (👁) in the Content and Frame layers visibility column to hide both layer contents. Click to select the Woman layer.

3 Choose File > Place.

4 Navigate to the woman.psd file in the images folder inside of the Lesson15 folder. Do not double-click the file or click Place yet.

5 Deselect Link in the Place dialog box, if it is selected.

● **Note:** Deselecting the Link option embeds the PSD file in the Illustrator file. The Photoshop Import Options dialog box appears only when you deselect this option.

6 Click Place.

● **Note:** When placing an image, it is placed in the center of the Document window. That is why you fit the artboard in the window, so that it will place the image centered on the artboard.

7 In the Photoshop Import Options dialog box, select Blue woman, black bg from the Layer Comp menu, and then select Show Preview to preview the artwork.

8 Select Convert Layers To Objects and select Import Hidden Layers to import all the document layers from Photoshop. Click OK.

● **Note:** If a color warning dialog box appears, such as Paste Profile Mismatch, click OK.

Rather than flatten the file, you want to convert the Photoshop layers to objects, because the woman.psd file contains four layers and one layer mask. You will use them later in the lesson.

9 In the Layers panel, click the arrow (▷) to the left of the Woman layer to expand it. Drag the bottom of the panel down, if necessary, so that you can see more of the layers. Click the arrow to the left of the woman.psd sublayer to expand it.

Notice all the sublayers of woman.psd. These sublayers were Photoshop layers in Photoshop and appear in the Layers panel in Illustrator because you chose not to flatten the image when you placed it. Also notice that, with the image still selected on the page, the Control panel shows the word Group on the left side and includes a link to Multiple Images. When you place a Photoshop file with layers and you choose to convert the layers to objects in the Photoshop Import Options dialog box, Illustrator treats the layers as separate images in a group.

10 Deselect the eye icon (👁) to the left of the Blue sublayer to hide the sublayer. Click the visibility column to the left of the Blue sublayer to show it again. Deselect the eye icon (👁) to the left of the woman.psd sublayer to hide it.

The rectangles should be the only visible objects on the artboard.

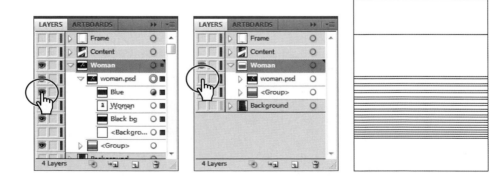

Applying color edits to a placed image

You can use color edits in a variety of ways to modify colors in placed images that are embedded. You can convert to a different color mode (such as RGB, CMYK, or grayscale) or adjust individual color values. You can also saturate (darken) or desaturate (lighten) colors, or invert colors (create a color negative).

Next, you'll adjust colors in an image you will first place. Later in the lesson, you'll apply a mask to this image.

▶ **Tip:** For information on color modes and modifying colors with color edits, see "About colors in digital graphics" and "Apply an effect" in Illustrator Help.

1 In the Layers panel, click the visibility column in the Content layer to show the contents, and then select the Content layer.

2 Choose File > Place.

3 Navigate to the man.psd file in the images folder inside the Lesson15 folder and select it. Do not double-click the file or click Place yet.

4 Select Link in the Place dialog box, and then click Place.

● **Note:** As long as the file is open, the Link option is sticky. That means the next time you place an image, the Link option will automatically apply.

5 With the Selection tool (▶), click the word Transform in the Control panel. Make sure that the center point in the Reference Point indicator (▦) is selected. In the Transform panel that appears, change the X value to **1.8 in** (make sure to type in the "in") and the Y value to **3.3 in** and press Enter or Return.

This positions the man.psd image in the upper-left corner. Notice that the man appears to be cut out. That is a layer mask that was created in Photoshop and recognized by Illustrator.

● **Note:** Depending on your screen resolution, the Transform options may appear in the Control panel, or you may need to choose Window > Transform to open the panel.

In order to edit colors in the image, the image needs to be embedded in the Illustrator file. If the file is linked, the edits you are about to do can be done in Photoshop and then updated in Illustrator. But sometimes you may want to embed the image so that you don't have to worry about keeping track of a linked image.

6 With the man.psd still selected on the artboard, click the Embed button in the Control panel. This opens the Photoshop Import Options dialog box, where you can choose a layer comp or other options. Make sure Flatten Layers to a Single Image is selected, and then click OK.

In the Control panel you will now see the word Embedded.

7 With the image still selected, choose Edit > Edit Colors > Adjust Color Balance.

8 In the Adjust Colors dialog box, drag the sliders or enter values for the CMYK percentages to change the colors in the image. You can press Tab to move between the text fields. We used the following values to create more of a red cast: C=**−70**, M=**30**, Y=**0**, and K=**27**. Feel free to experiment a little. Select Preview so that you can see the color changes.

● **Note:** To see the results, you may need to select and deselect Preview as you change options in the Adjust Colors dialog box.

9 When you are satisfied with the color of the image, click OK.

● **Note:** If you later decide to adjust the colors of the same image by choosing Edit > Edit Colors > Adjust Color Balance, the color values will be set to 0 (zero).

10 Choose Select > Deselect, then File > Save.

Masking an image

Masks crop an image so that only a portion of the image appears through the shape of the mask. Only vector objects can be clipping masks; however, any artwork can be masked. You can also import masks created in Photoshop files as you've seen earlier. The clipping mask and the masked object are referred to as the clipping set.

Applying a clipping mask to an image

In this short section, you'll create a clipping mask for the man.psd image.

1   With the Selection tool (▶), click the man.psd image to select it. Click the Mask button in the Control panel. This applies a clipping mask to the image in the shape and size of the image.

● **Note:** You can also apply a clipping mask by choosing Object > Clipping Mask > Make.

▶ **Tip:** Another way to create a mask is to use the Draw Inside mode. This mode allows you to draw inside the selected object. The Draw Inside mode can eliminate the need to perform multiple tasks such as drawing and altering stacking order or drawing, selecting, and creating a clipping mask. To learn more about the drawing modes, see Lesson 3, "Creating and Editing Shapes."

2   In the Layers panel, click the arrow (▷) to the left of the Content layer to reveal its contents, if not already done so. You may need to drag the bottom of the Layers panel down or scroll in the panel. Click the arrow to the left of the top <Group> Sublayer to reveal its contents as well.

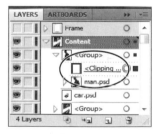

Notice the <Clipping Path> sublayer. This is the mask you created by clicking the Mask button in the Control panel. The <Group> sublayer is the clipping set that contains the mask and the object that is masked.

Next, you will edit this mask.

Editing a mask

1   With the image still selected, notice the Edit Clipping Path button (◻) and the Edit Contents button (◉) that appear on the left side of the Control panel.

2   Click the Edit Contents button (◉) and, in the Layers panel, notice that the man.psd is now selected. Click the Edit Clipping Path button (◻) and notice that the <Clipping Path> is selected in the Layers panel.

When an object is masked, you can edit either the mask or the object that is masked. Use these two buttons to select which to edit.

3 With the Edit Clipping Path button (⬜) selected in the Control panel, use the Selection tool to drag the bottom, middle bounding point of the selected mask up a bit, as shown in the figure below. Notice that the bottom part of the image is hidden (masked).

4 Select the Direct Selection tool (▷) in the Tools panel. Click the bottom, left point first to select it, and then drag straight down until it snaps to the red object in the background. Drag the bottom, right bounding point straight up until it snaps to the same red object in the background.

Resize the mask.

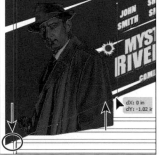
Reshape the mask.

The result.

5 Use the Selection tool to click the man.psd image to select it. In the Control panel, click the Edit Contents button (◉) to edit the man.psd image, not the mask. With the Selection tool, drag the man down a bit. Notice that you are moving the image and not the mask. Choose Edit > Undo Move.

With the Edit Contents button (◉) selected, you can apply many transformations to the image, including scaling, moving, rotating, and more.

6 Choose Select > Deselect, then File > Save.

Masking an object with multiple shapes

In this section, you'll create a mask for the woman.psd image from multiple rectangles. This will give the effect of the woman being hidden by window blinds. In order to create a clipping mask with multiple shapes, the shapes need to be converted to a compound path.

1 In the Layers panel, click the arrow (▷) to the left of the Content layer to collapse it, and then click the eye icon to hide its contents. Click the visibility column to the left of the woman.psd sublayer to see it on the artboard.

2 With the Selection tool, click to select the woman image on the artboard and choose Object > Arrange > Send To Back.

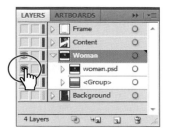

3   With the Selection tool, click one of the rectangles on the artboard. This selects the group of rectangles.

4   Choose Object > Compound Path > Make. Notice that the group of rectangles are placed onto one sublayer, called <Compound Path> in the Layers panel. Leave the new compound path selected.

▶ **Tip:** To make the rectangles into a compound path, you can also right-click the group of rectangles or Control-click and choose Make Compound Path.

The Compound Path command creates a single compound object from two or more objects. Compound paths act as grouped objects. The Compound Path command lets you create complex objects more easily than if you used the drawing tools or the Pathfinder commands.

● **Note:** In order to make a compound path from multiple objects, they don't need to be grouped first.

Next, you'll mask the woman.psd image with the compound path you just made.

5   With the compound path still selected, Shift-click the woman image on the artboard to select both. Right-click (Windows) or Ctrl-click (Mac OS) the compound path and choose Make Clipping Mask.

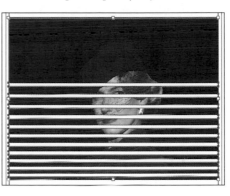

▶ **Tip:** You can also make a clipping mask from text.

Notice the Edit Clipping Path button (◙) and the Edit Contents button (◔) in the Control panel.

▶ **Tip:** You can also choose Object > Clipping Mask > Make.

6   Choose File > Save and leave the masked image selected.

Release a mask

You may at some point no longer want a mask to hide parts of the masked object. You can always release a mask from the clipping set so that it no longer is a mask.

•   With the image still selected, choose Object > Clipping Mask > Release. This releases the mask (compound path) and the image so that they are separate objects once again.

When a mask is released, it typically has no stroke and no fill.

▶ **Tip:** You can also right-click (Windows) or Ctrl-click (Mac OS) the rectangle compound path and choose Release Clipping Mask.

Creating an opacity mask

An opacity mask is different from a clipping mask, because it allows you to not only mask an object, but also alter the transparency of artwork. An opacity mask is made and edited using the Transparency panel.

In this section, you'll create an opacity mask from the compound path so that the woman.psd image appears through the mask.

1 Click the Transparency panel icon (◐) on the right side of the workspace to expand the Transparency panel.

2 Choose Select > Deselect.

3 Choose View > Outline. In Outline mode, click to select the edge of the compound path with the Selection tool (▶). Choose View > Preview to return to Preview mode.

4 Press the letter D to set the default stroke and fill.

Note: The object that is to become the opacity mask (the masking object) needs to be the top selected object in the artboard. If it is a single object like a rectangle, it does not need to be a compound path. If the opacity mask is to be made from multiple objects, they need to be grouped.

The color of the masking object matters. If there is no color fill, then nothing will appear when it is used as an opacity mask. Where the opacity mask is white, the artwork is fully visible. Where the opacity mask is black, the artwork is hidden. Shades of gray in the mask result in varying degrees of transparency in the artwork.

5 Choose Select > All On Active Artboard to select the compound shape and the woman.psd image.

6 In the Transparency panel menu (▼≡), choose Make Opacity Mask. Make sure that the Clip option is selected in the Transparency panel.

The woman.psd image is now masked with the compound path, as indicated by the dashed underline beneath the layer name in the Layers panel, if you were to open it. Right now, the opacity mask doesn't appear to be any different than a clipping mask. You will see that it has many more options.

Next, you'll adjust the opacity mask that you just created.

7 In the Transparency panel, Shift-click the mask thumbnail (as indicated by the white rectangles on the black background) to disable the mask. Notice that a red x appears on the mask in the Transparency panel and that the entire woman.psd image reappears in the Document window.

▶ **Tip:** To disable and enable an opacity mask, you can also choose Disable Opacity Mask or Enable Opacity Mask from the Transparency panel menu.

● **Note:** You need to open the Transparency panel on the right side of the workspace because the Transparency panel in the Control panel closes when you interact with the artwork.

8 In the Transparency panel, Shift-click the mask thumbnail to enable the opacity mask again.

9 Click to select the mask thumbnail on the right side of the Transparency panel.

Clicking the opacity mask in the Transparency panel, selects the mask (the compound path) on the artboard. If the mask isn't selected, click to select it with the Selection tool. You cannot now edit other artwork. Also notice that the document tab shows (<Opacity Mask>/ Opacity Mask), indicating that you are now editing the mask.

10 Click the Layers panel icon (◆) on the right side of the workspace to reveal the Layers panel. In the Layers panel, notice that layer <Opacity Mask> appears. Click the toggle arrow (▷) to the left of the <Opacity Mask> layer to expand it.

11 With the mask selected, in the Control panel, click the fill color and select a black to white linear gradient, called BW Gradient.

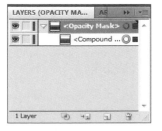

12 Select the Gradient tool (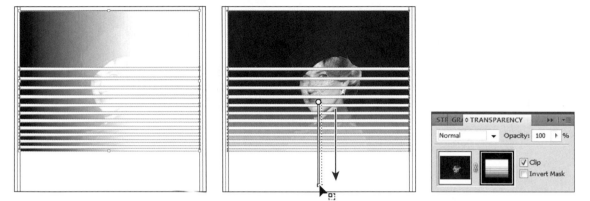) in the Tools panel. Holding down the Shift key, click about half way down from the top of the compound shape and drag down past the bottom of the shapes, as shown in the figure below. Release the mouse button, and then release the Shift key.

13 Click the Transparency panel icon (🖢) and notice how the mask changes in the Transparency panel.

Next, you'll move the image but not the opacity mask. With the image thumbnail selected in the Transparency panel, both the image and the mask are linked together, by default, so that if you move the image on the artboard, the mask moves as well.

Note: You only have access to the link icon when the image thumbnail, not the mask thumbnail, is selected in the Transparency panel.

14 In the Transparency panel, click the image thumbnail so that you are no longer editing the mask. Click the link icon (🔗) between the image thumbnail and the mask thumbnail. This allows you to move just the image or the mask, but not both.

Opacity mask is not linked to art

Note: You need to stop opacity mask editing before you can work with other artwork.

15 With the image selected on the artboard, choose Object > Transform > Reflect. In the Reflect dialog box, make sure that Vertical is selected, and then click OK.

Note: The position of the woman does not have to match the figure exactly.

16 With the Selection tool, drag the woman. psd image down and to the left, as shown in the figure.

17 In the Transparency panel, click the blank space between the image thumbnail and the mask thumbnail (where the link icon (🔗) was). This links the image and the mask again so that they move together.

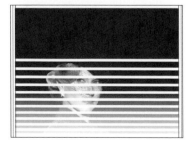

18 Choose Select > Deselect, then choose File > Save.

Sampling colors in placed images

You can sample, or copy, the colors in placed images to apply the colors to other objects in the artwork. Sampling colors enables you to easily make colors consistent in a file that combines Photoshop images and Illustrator artwork.

In this section, you'll use the Eyedropper tool to sample colors from a placed image, and apply the colors to another object.

1 In the Layers panel, make sure that all the layers are collapsed, and then click the visibility column to the left of the Frame, Content, and Background layers to show their contents on the artboard.

2 Select the Zoom tool (🔍) in the Tools panel and drag a marquee around the text at the bottom of the poster to zoom in.

3 Select the Selection tool (▶), and double-click twice on the studio9 logo at the bottom of the artboard. This allows you to enter isolation mode and select just the logo from the group. Click to select the logo.

4 Press Ctrl+– (Windows) or Cmd+– (Mac OS) several times to zoom out until you can see the bottom half of the woman's face.

5 Select the Eyedropper tool (💧) in the Tools panel, and Shift-click the image of the woman to sample and apply the blue color from the top layer in the layered woman.psd file. You can try sampling the color of different images and content if you want.

The color you sample is applied to the selected logo.

> **Note:** Using the Shift key with the Eyedropper tool allows you to apply only the sampled color to the selected object. If you don't use the Shift key, you apply all appearance attributes to the selected object.

> **Note:** You may want to zoom in to the selected studio9 logo to see the color change.

6 Press Escape to exit isolation mode, and then choose View > Fit Artboard In Window.

7 Choose Select > Deselect, and then choose File > Save.

Replacing a placed, linked image

You can easily replace a placed image with another image to update a document. The replacement image is positioned exactly where the original image was, so no realignment is necessary. If you scaled the original image, you may have to resize the replacement image to match the original image.

Now, you'll replace the smaller car.psd image with a grayscale version of the image.

1 Choose File > Save As. In the Save As dialog box, navigate to the Lesson15 folder and open it. Name the file **movieposter2.ai**. Leave the Save As Type option set to Adobe Illustrator (*.AI) (Windows) or the Format option set to Adobe Illustrator (ai) (Mac OS), and then click Save. In the Illustrator Options dialog box, leave the Illustrator options at their default settings, and then click OK.

Include Linked Files option in the Illustrator Options dialog box

In the Illustrator Options dialog box, selecting Include Linked Files will embed any files that are linked to the Illustrator artwork. It should be left unselected if you are saving artwork with linked files.

2 With the Selection tool, click the smaller car.psd image in the lower-left corner of the artboard. In the Control panel, click the blue, underlined Linked File. This opens the Links panel.

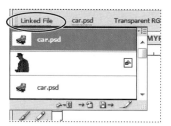

In the Links panel, notice that some of the images listed have no names. That is typically because they are embedded. The embed icon (🔲) also indicates that the images are embedded.

▶ **Tip:** You can also open the Links panel separately by choosing Window > Links.

3 In the Links panel, car.psd is selected. Click the Go To Link button (➡🗂) at the bottom of the Links panel to center the linked image on the artboard and select it if it wasn't already selected. Make sure that car.psd is still selected in the Links panel, and then click the Relink button (➡🔲) at the bottom of the panel.

4 In the Place dialog box, navigate to the car_bw.psd image in the images folder in the Lesson15 folder and select it. Make sure that the Link option is selected. Click Place to replace the small car image with the new one.

The replacement image (car_bw.psd) appears on the artboard in place of the car.psd image. When you replace an image, the color adjustments that you made to the original image are not applied to the replacement. However, masks applied to the original image are preserved. Any layer modes and transparency adjustments that you've made to other layers also may affect the image's appearance.

5 Choose Select > Deselect, then choose View > Fit Artboard In Window.

6 Choose File > Save.

If you want to learn how to open and manipulate a layered Illustrator file in Photoshop, continue to the next section. If not, skip to "Exploring on your own."

Exporting a layered file to Photoshop

Not only can you open layered Photoshop files in Illustrator, but you can also save layered Illustrator files and then open them in Photoshop. Moving layered files between Illustrator and Photoshop is helpful when creating and editing web or print graphics. You can preserve the hierarchical relationship of the layers by selecting the Write Layers option when saving your file. You can also open and edit type objects.

1 Choose File > Export.

2 Navigate to the folder where you'll save the file, and name the file **poster.psd**. Changing the file name preserves your original Illustrator file.

3 Choose Photoshop (PSD) from the Save As Type (Windows) or Format (Mac OS) menu, and click Save (Windows) or Export (Mac OS).

4 In the Photoshop Export Options dialog box, make sure that CMYK is the Color Model, select High (300 ppi) for the resolution, and make sure that Write Layers is selected. Leave the rest of the settings at their defaults. Preserve Text Editability is grayed out because all the text was already converted to outlines. Click OK.

● **Note:** After clicking OK, you may need to give it some time to save the file.

▶ **Tip:** In the Export dialog box, the Use Artboards option allows you to export the artboards as separate Photoshop PSD files.

● **Note:** After clicking OK, you may see a warning dialog box. Click OK.

The Anti-alias option removes jagged edges in the artwork. The Write Layers option lets you export each Illustrator top-level layer as a separate Photoshop layer.

▶ **Tip:** You can also copy and paste or drag and drop from Illustrator to Photoshop. When you copy and paste, a dialog box appears asking what type of object you'd like to place the content from Illustrator as: Smart Object, Pixels, Path, or Shape Layer. To learn more about bringing Illustrator content into Photoshop, search for "Duplicate selections using drag and drop" in Illustrator Help.

5 Start Adobe Photoshop CS5.

● **Note:** You can open Illustrator files in previous versions of Photoshop, but for this lesson, it's assumed that you are using Photoshop CS5.

6 Open the poster.psd file that you exported in step 4.

7 Click the Layers tab to view the Layers panel. Notice the layers. Choose File > Close, and don't save the changes.

● **Note:** Artwork that is too complex may be rasterized and flattened to one layer.

8 Close Photoshop CS5.

Illustrator and Adobe InDesign

You can place Illustrator (AI) files and PDF files in InDesign. You can also copy and paste content from Illustrator, and drag and drop from Illustrator into InDesign. To learn more about working with Illustrator and InDesign, see the PDF file, Adobeapps.pdf, on the Classroom in a Book CD.

Illustrator and Adobe Flash

Illustrator CS5 lets you use Illustrator content in Flash or export in the Flash file format (SWF). To learn more about working with Illustrator and Adobe Flash, see the PDF file, Adobeapps.pdf, on the Classroom in a Book CD.

Illustrator and Adobe Flash Catalyst

In Illustrator CS5, you can create and save an Illustrator file for use in Flash Catalyst. To learn more about working with Illustrator and Flash Catalyst, see the PDF file, Adobeapps.pdf, on the Classroom in a Book CD.

Illustrator and Adobe Flex

In Illustrator CS5, you can save an Illustrator file for use in Flex. To learn more about working with Illustrator and Flex, see the PDF file, Adobeapps.pdf, on the Classroom in a Book CD.

Exploring on your own

Now that you know how to place and mask an image in an Illustrator file, you can place other images and apply a variety of modifications to the images. You can also create masks for images from objects that you create in Illustrator. For more practice, try the following.

1   In addition to adjusting color in images, apply transformation effects (such as shearing or rotating), filters, or effects (such as one of the Artistic or Distort filters/effects) to create contrast between the two cars in the movieposter.ai file.

2   Use the basic shape tools or the drawing tools to draw objects to create a compound path to use as a mask. Then place the woman.psd image into the file with the compound path, and apply the compound path as a mask.

3   Create large type and use the type as a clipping mask to mask a placed object.

4   Choose File > Close without saving.

Review questions

1 Describe the difference between linking and embedding in Illustrator.

2 How do you create an opacity mask for a placed image?

3 What kinds of objects can be used as masks?

4 What color modifications can you apply to a selected object using effects?

5 Describe how to replace a placed image with another image in a document.

6 Name two ways that you can bring content from Illustrator into InDesign.

Review answers

1 A linked file is a separate, external file connected to the Illustrator file by an electronic link. A linked file does not add significantly to the size of the Illustrator file. The linked file must accompany the Illustrator file to preserve the link and ensure that the placed file appears when you open the Illustrator file. An embedded file is included in the Illustrator file. The Illustrator file size reflects the addition of the embedded file. Because the embedded file is part of the Illustrator file, no link can be broken. You can update linked and embedded files using the Replace Link button in the Links panel.

2 You create an opacity mask by placing the object to be used as a mask on top of the object to be masked. Then you select the mask and the objects to be masked, and choose Make Opacity Mask from the Transparency panel menu.

3 A mask can be a simple or compound path. You can use type as a mask. You can import opacity masks with placed Photoshop files. You can also create layer clipping masks with any shape that is the topmost object of a group or layer.

4 You can use effects to change the color mode (RGB, CMYK, or grayscale) or adjust individual colors in a selected object. You can also saturate or desaturate colors or invert colors in a selected object. You can apply color modifications to placed images, as well as to artwork created in Illustrator.

5 To replace a placed image, select the image in the Links panel. Then click the Replace Link button, and locate and select the replacement image. Click Place.

6 Choose File > Place in InDesign to place a graphic and create a link to the original, or choose Edit > Paste after copying content from Illustrator. Pasting content does not create a link.

INDEX

SYMBOLS

* (asterisk), 58
^ (carat), 154, 155
/ (forward slash), 148
[(Left Bracket key), 104
+ (plus sign)
    red, 220, 222
    seen in Windows, 58
    style override indicator, 233
    Windows dragged content indicator, 58

A

Adjust Colors dialog box, 436
Adobe. *See also* combining Adobe graphics
    training and certification programs, 6
    website and Help from, 61
Adobe Bridge, 426–428
Adobe CS Live, 7, 11
Adobe CS Review, 11
Adobe Flash
    exporting symbols to, 418–421
    integrating Illustrator graphics with, 448
    movie clip symbols, 407, 418, 420
    pasting Illustrator artwork in, 421, 422
Adobe Flash Catalyst, 10, 446
Adobe Flex, 447
Adobe Illustrator CS5
    available fonts, 227
    checking for updates, 62
    copying/pasting between Photoshop and, 446
    copying/pasting content into Flash, 421, 422
    deleting current preferences, 4
    exporting layered files to Photoshop, 445–446
    further resources for, 4–5
    new features of, 8–11
    placing Photoshop files in, 21, 430–431
    printing from, 375
    restoring default preferences, 3, 4
    saving current preferences, 3
    saving documents for InDesign, 36

    starting, 34–35
    swatch libraries for, 184
    symbol workflow in, 418
    type features in, 217
    using raster effects in, 366–368
    website and Help for, 61
    when to use Photoshop vs., 429
Adobe InDesign
    saving documents for, 36
    using AI files in, 446
    when to use, 429
Adobe Photoshop
    copying/pasting between Illustrator and, 446
    creating layer comps, 433–434
    placing files in Illustrator, 21, 430–431
    using bitmap graphics from, 428–429
    using effects in Illustrator, 357, 366–368
    using Illustrator layered files, 445–446
    using raster effects in Illustrator, 366–368
AI files, 418, 446
Align panel. *See also* aligning
    aligning and distributing objects, 72–74
    features of, 75
    opening from Control panel, 72, 112
aligning
    canceling distribution and, 75
    with key object, 72, 75
    objects to each other, 72
    objects with artboard, 74
    paragraphs, 232
    points, 73
    reviewing, 83
    strokes, 100
    warped text, 238
alignment guides, 67
anchor points. *See also* direction handles
    adjusting curves using, 165–166
    adjusting Pencil Tool's, 170–171
    aligning, 73
    changing curved to corner, 153–155
    changing display and size of, 69
    converting between smooth and corner, 168–169
    deleting and adding, 166–167

colorization
    about, 344
    Hue Shift, 346–347
    Tints, 344–346
combining Adobe graphics
    about, 428
    Adobe Flex with Illustrator files, 447
    applying clipping mask to image, 437
    Bridge for, 426–428
    duplicating/editing placed images, 431–432
    editing color of placed images, 435–436
    editing masks, 437–438
    embedding Photoshop images in layer comps, 433–434
    exercises exploring, 447
    exporting layered file to Photoshop, 445–446
    masking images, 437
    masking objects with multiple shapes, 438–439
    opacity masks, 440–442
    placing Photoshop files, 430–431
    releasing masks, 439
    replacing placed, linked images, 444–445
    reviewing, 448
    sampling colors in placed images, 443
    using AI files in InDesign, 446
    using Illustrator files in Flash Catalyst, 446
    using raster effects in Illustrator, 366–368
    vector vs. bitmap graphics, 428–429
    working content in Flash, 446
computer platforms, 1. See also Mac OS; Windows OS
constraining
    artboard dimensions, 125
    shape's proportions, 95, 130
context-sensitive menus, 47
Control panel
    adjusting type opacity in, 243
    changing fonts from, 226
    displaying Character panel from, 233, 234
    finding Transform options on, 138
    hiding menus in, 101
    illustrated, 37
    opening Align panel from, 72, 112

opening Tracing Options dialog box from, 117
Convert Anchor Point tool, 169
copying
    artboards, 123–124
    and editing symbol sets, 416
    graphic styles, 396
    object's attributes, 188
    objects in perspective, 294–295
    placed images, 431–432
    while reflecting objects, 132
copying and pasting
    between Illustrator and Photoshop, 446
    Illustrator content into Flash, 421, 422
    layers, 256–258
copyright symbols, 231
corner points
    converting curved to, 153–155
    converting smooth to, 168–169
    defined, 151
current layer indicator, 260
cursors
    indicating grid plane, 278
    positioning to sample formatting, 236
curved points, 153–155
curves. See also direction handles
    adding for curved shapes, 157–158
    adding to existing curved segments, 158–159
    changing direction of, 159–161
    controlling direction handles for, 151–153
    converting curved to corner points, 153–155
    drawing curved paths, 149–150
    editing, 165–166
    selecting, 157
customizing
    color swatches, 182–183
    document views, 51
    Magic Wand tool, 70
    your own patterns, 203

D

dashed lines, 164
Define Perspective Grid dialog box, 276
deleting
    artboards, 124, 125
    current Illustrator preferences, 4
    saved workspaces, 46

stroke edit points, 106
unnecessary points, 166–167
Device N rasters, 430
Direct Selection tool
    dragging direction handle with, 168
    marquee selections with, 70
    using, 68
direction handles
    adjusting curves using, 151–153, 165–166
    constraining angle of, 154
    dragging with Direct Selection, 168
    Pen tool, 150
direction lines
    anchor point, 68
    splitting, 154
distorting
    objects, 134–136
    selections within documents, 141–142
distributing objects, 73–74, 75
docking
    Control panel, 42
    panels, 46
    Tools panel, 40
document grids, 92
document profiles. See profiles
Document Raster Effects Settings dialog box, 368
Document Setup dialog box, 126, 232
Document window, 37
documents
    adding artboards to, 123–124
    arranging multiple, 56–59
    artboard presets for, 126
    changing ruler units for, 88
    creating, 14–15
    custom views for, 51
    distorting selections within, 141–142
    editing unit of measure for, 129
    groups of, 59–60
    importing Word, 221–222
    keyboard shortcuts between, 57
    loading swatches from other, 182
    multiple artboards in, 14–15, 52–53
    navigating within, 52–55
    rulers for, 128
    scrolling, 50
    selecting color mode for, 179
    setting up multiple artboards for, 86–88
    setup options for, 232

Don't Show Again checkbox, 34
double-headed pointer, 139
drawing. *See also* Pen tool; Pencil
    tool
    Blob Brush tool for, 348
    curved paths, 149–150
    curved shapes, 157–159
    editing with Eraser tool, 104,
        349–350
    enhancements to, 10
    first lines, 147
    objects in perspective, 272–273,
        277–279
    with Paintbrush tool, 330–331
    Pencil tool for, 170
    setting up Perspective Grid for,
        274–277
    smoothing paths while, 332
    straight paths, 161–162
    undoing steps in, 153
drawing modes
    choosing, 18, 90, 96
    Draw Behind mode, 89, 90
    Draw Inside mode, 89
    Draw Normal mode, 89
    types of, 89
    uses for, 18
Drop Shadow dialog box, 26, 349,
    357, 388
drop shadows
    adding to shape, 366
    applying, 357–358, 381
drop zone, 40

E

Edit Colors dialog box, 191–194, 195
editing
    appearance attributes, 381–383
    art and grid planes, 285–290
    Art brushes, 334
    artboards, 15, 124–127
    artwork color, 192, 194–195
    bleeds, 126–127
    blend options for objects, 317
    brushes, 328–329, 334
    clipping masks, 437–438
    color groups, 189, 191–194
    color of placed images, 435–436
    curves, 165–166
    document's unit of measure, 129
    drawings with Eraser tool,
        349–350
    effects, 359–360
    ellipses, 94–95
    Flash Catalyst's round-trip, 10

font attributes, 226–229
gradient fills, 27–28, 306–309
graphic styles, 394–396
grid extent, 281
isolated objects, 76
layers in isolation mode, 264–265
lines, 147
masks, 437–438
paths with Paintbrush tool,
    331–333
paths with Path Eraser, 331
paths with Pencil tool, 171–172
Pattern brush tiles, 344
pattern swatches, 204–205
Perspective Grid, 274–277
placed images, 431–432, 435–436
precision selections with Zoom,
    111, 115
shapes with Pathfinder effect,
    363–364
spine of path, 317–319
symbol sets, 413
symbols, 403–405, 407–409,
    414–415
text attributes, 229–231
warped text, 237
width points, 105–108
effects
    applying from Graphic Styles
        panel, 386
    drop shadow, 357–358
    editing, 359–360
    exercises exploring, 375–376
    Intersect, 363
    mapping symbol to 3D art, 372–
        374, 418
    offsetting paths, 364–366
    Pathfinder, 363–364
    Photoshop raster, 357, 366–368
    reviewing, 377
    saving as graphic style, 381
    scaling, 129–131
    Scribble, 362
    styling text with, 360–362
    3D Revolve, 369–370
    types of 3D, 369
    using for objects in perspective,
        288
    vector, 357
    warping text, 236–238, 360–362
ellipses, 94–95
envelope warps, 236–238
envelopes, 137–138
Eraser tool
    editing drawings with, 349–350
    resizing diameter of, 104

expanding panels, 43, 44–45
exporting
    layered file to Photoshop,
        445–446
    naming instances before, 419
    symbols to Flash, 418–421
Extrude & Bevel 3D effects, about,
    369
Eyedropper tool, 188, 235–236

F

Fidelity value for Pencil tool, 171
files. *See also* lesson files
    AI, 418, 446
    Classroom in a Book, 2
    compatible formats for
        Illustrator, 219
    copying layers to new, 256–258
    exporting layered, 445–446
    fonts for lesson, 2
    linked, 444–445
    locating preferences, 3
    PDF, 446
    SWF/SVG, 418
fills. *See also* gradient fills
    adding fill color with brush, 329
    adjusting from Appearance panel,
        381
    choosing from Tools panel, 15
    color for, 180
    content selection by color of, 71
    gradient, 299
    overridden by revolved object,
        369
    selecting for object, 174
    using additional, 384–385
filters, 135
Flash. *See* Adobe Flash
Flash Catalyst, 10, 446
flattening layers, 261, 265
Flex, 447
floating
    Control panel, 41
    document groups, 59–60
    Tools panel, 39, 40
fonts
    changing size of, 228
    choosing, 226–227
    lesson file, 2
    OpenType, 228
    using text outlines instead of, 242
foreshortening, 273
formatting type, 226–232
    adding on closed paths, 240–242
    changing font size, 228

choosing fonts, 226–227
keyboard shortcuts to adjust font size, 228
maintaining imported formatting, 222
modifying font color, 229
placing text on open paths, 239–240
positioning cursor to sample formatting, 236
using OpenType fonts, 228
wrapping text around objects, 239
forward slash (/), 148
Free Distort dialog box, 142
Free Transform tool, 138

G

Gap Options dialog box, 210–211
getting started, 1–5
global color
changing background swatch to, 183–184
color groups for, 188–189
creating tint from, 187–188
Glyphs panel, 230–231, 240
gradient annotator, 28
gradient fills
about, 299, 301
adding to multiple objects, 309–312
adding to outlined stroke, 109
adjusting gradient rotation, 305
applying linear, 301–303
creating and editing, 27–28
defining transparency in, 313–314
direction and angle of blend, 304–305
editing, 306–309
filling text outlines with, 244
gradient swatches, 201
radial, 305–306
Gradient panel
adjusting gradient rotation, 305
illustrated, 28, 301
gradient stops. *See also* gradient fills
about, 305
defined, 301
moving start and end of, 306–309
graphic styles
about, 385–386
adding properties to applied, 392–394
applying to object, 387
creating and saving, 386–387

editing, 394–396
layers with, 387–390
selecting from library, 390–392
using, 385–386
Graphic Styles panel, 385–386, 395
graphic tablets, 338
graphics. *See also* combining Adobe graphics; graphic styles
sharp web and mobile device, 11
vector vs. bitmap, 428–429
grid extent widget, 281
grid planes. *See also* perspective
adding text to, 290–291
cursor indicator for, 278
editing art and, 285–290
moving objects separate from, 286
positioning automatically, 289, 290
selecting and checking, 277
undoing edits to, 286
grid presets, 273–274, 276
ground level point, 275
groups
about, 75
aligning objects as, 74
document, 59–60
isolating, 76
Live Paint, 206–208, 211
nesting objects in, 76–77
panel, 43, 45–46
selecting objects for, 75
guides. *See also* smart guides
alignment, 67
snapping and locking, 129

H

Hand tool, 50
harmonizing colors
deselecting, 192
selecting, 181, 190–191
Harmony Rules menu, 181, 190
help
Adobe Community Help, 4–5
Adobe website and, 61
hidden tools, 39
hiding
bounding box, 97, 161
layers, 254–256
menus in Control panel, 101
objects, 79–80, 254–256
panels, 42–43, 44
Perspective Grid, 279
Plane Switching Widget, 288
template layers, 170
Hue Shift colorization, 346–347

I

icons
carat with Pen tool, 154, 155
collapsing panel to, 43
crosshair, 146
current layer indicator, 260
Layers panel target, 390
lock, 253
Pen tool, 146, 148
Pencil tool, 170
white triangle on swatch, 184
Illuminate Styles panel, 392
Illustrator. *See* Adobe Illustrator CS5
Illustrator Options dialog box, 444
images. *See also* artwork; placed images
copying and editing placed images, 431–432
finding with Bridge, 427
linked, 21
importing
plain text files, 219–220
swatches from saved documents, 182
Word documents, 221–222
installing
Classroom in a Book files, 2
lesson file fonts, 2
instances
about, 403
adding symbol, 407–409
breaking link to symbol, 409–410
naming before exporting, 419
original symbols vs., 404–405
replacing with modified symbol, 410
spraying symbol, 411–413
symbol sets and, 413, 416
unable to edit symbol, 404
Internet
accessing Kuler themes via, 196
checking for updates, 62
connecting from Illustrator Help, 61
Intersect effect, 363
intersect message, 94
isolation mode
editing layers in, 264–265
entering and exiting, 76, 113
working with groups in, 76

J

joining paths, 102–103

Contributors

Brian Wood   Brian Wood is an Adobe Certified Instructor in Dreamweaver CS4, Acrobat 9 Pro, Illustrator CS4, and the author of five training books (Illustrator, InDesign), all published by Peachpit Press, as well as numerous training videos and DVDs on Dreamweaver & CSS, InDesign, Illustrator, Acrobat, including Acrobat multimedia and forms, Expression Web and others.

In addition to training many clients large and small, Brian speaks regularly at national conferences, such as Getting Started with Dreamweaver and CSS tour, The InDesign Conference, The Web Design Conference, The Creative Suite Conference, as well as events hosted by AIGA, GAG, STC, CASE and other industry organizations. To learn more, visit www.askbrianwood.com

Wyndham Wood   Wyndham Wood is a professional writer with 10+ years of marketing and business experience, including eight years as President of an Adobe Authorized Training Center. In addition to helping write and edit training books, she has authored articles and white papers that have appeared in several industry publications.

Production Notes

The *Adobe Illustrator CS5 Classroom in a Book* was created electronically using Adobe InDesign CS4. Art was produced using Adobe InDesign, Adobe Illustrator, and Adobe Photoshop. The Myriad Pro and Warnock Pro OpenType families of typefaces were used throughout this book.

References to company names in the lessons are for demonstration purposes only and are not intended to refer to any actual organization or person.

Images

Photographic images and illustrations are intended for use with the tutorials.
Image provided by Clipart.com: Lesson 2 (French fries).

Typefaces used

Adobe Myriad Pro and Adobe Warnock Pro are used throughout the lessons. For more information about OpenType and Adobe fonts, visit www.adobe.com/type/opentype/.

Team credits

The following individuals contributed to the development of this edition of the *Adobe Illustrator CS5 Classroom in a Book*.

Project Manager: Wyndham Wood
Developmental Editor: Brian Wood
Design: Sibyl Perkins
Production Editor: Brian Wood
Technical Editors: Lara Mihata, Joan Vermeulen
Compositor: Brian Wood
Copyeditor: Resources Online
Proofreader: Resources Online
Indexer: Rebecca Plunkett
Cover design: Eddie Yuen
Interior design: Mimi Heft

AdobePress

Newly Expanded LEARN BY VIDEO Series

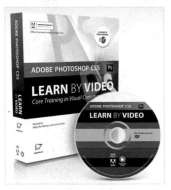

Learn Adobe Photoshop CS5 by Video:
Core Training in Visual Communication
(ISBN 9780321719805)

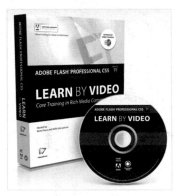

Learn Adobe Flash Professional CS5 by Video:
Core Training in Rich Media Communication
(ISBN 9780321719829)

Learn Adobe Dreamweaver CS5 by Video:
Core Training in Web Communication
(ISBN 9780321719812)

The **Learn by Video** series from video2brain and Adobe Press is the only Adobe-approved video courseware for the Adobe Certified Associate Level certification, and has quickly established itself as one of the most critically-acclaimed training products available on the fundamentals of Adobe software.

Learn by Video offers up to 19 hours of high-quality HD video training presented by experienced trainers, as well as lesson files, assessment quizzes and review materials. The DVD is bundled with a full-color printed book that provides supplemental information as well as a guide to the video topics.

Up to 19 hours of high-quality video training

Tutorials-to-Go! Transfer selected movies to your iPhone, iPod, or compatible cell phone

Table of Contents never more than a click away

Watch-and-Work mode shrinks the video into a small window while you work in the software

Video player remembers which movie you watched last

Lesson files are included on the DVD

Additional Titles

- **Learn Adobe Photoshop Elements 8 and Adobe Premiere Elements 8 by Video** (ISBN 9780321685773)
- **Learn Photography Techniques for Adobe Photoshop CS5 by Video** (ISBN 9780321734839)
- **Learn Adobe After Effects CS5 by Video** (ISBN 9780321734860)
- **Learn Adobe Flash Catalyst CS5 by Video** (ISBN 9780321734853)
- **Learn Adobe Illustrator CS5 by Video** (ISBN 9780321734815)
- **Learn Adobe InDesign CS5 by Video** (ISBN 9780321734808)
- **Learn Adobe Premiere Pro CS5 by Video** (ISBN 9780321734846)

For more information go to **www.adobepress.com/learnbyvideo**

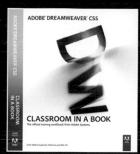
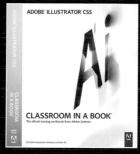
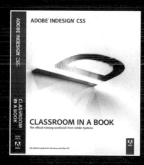